W9-ABS-860

3 3311 00199 679 4

TRANSIT COOPERATIVE RESEARCH PROGRAM

Report 39

The Costs of Sprawl—Revisited

ROBERT W. BURCHELL
NAVEED A. SHAD
DAVID LISTOKIN
HILARY PHILLIPS
Center for Urban Policy Research
Rutgers University

ANTHONY DOWNS
The Brookings Institution

SAMUEL SESKIN
JUDY S. DAVIS
Parsons Brinckerhoff Quade and Douglas, Inc.

TERRY MOORE
DAVID HELTON
MICHELLE GALL
ECONorthwest

Subject Areas

Public Transit

Research Sponsored by the Federal Transit Administration in
Cooperation with the Transit Development Corporation

TRANSPORTATION RESEARCH BOARD
NATIONAL RESEARCH COUNCIL

NATIONAL ACADEMY PRESS
Washington, D.C. 1998

TRANSIT COOPERATIVE RESEARCH PROGRAM

TCRP REPORT 39

The nation's growth and the need to meet mobility, environmental, and energy objectives place demands on public transit systems. Current systems, some of which are old and in need of upgrading, must expand service area, increase service frequency, and improve efficiency to serve these demands. Research is necessary to solve operating problems, to adapt appropriate new technologies from other industries, and to introduce innovations into the transit industry. The Transit Cooperative Research Program (TCRP) serves as one of the principal means by which the transit industry can develop innovative near-term solutions to meet demands placed on it.

The need for TCRP was originally identified in *TRB Special Report 213—Research for Public Transit: New Directions,* published in 1987 and based on a study sponsored by the Urban Mass Transportation Administration—now the Federal Transit Administration (FTA). A report by the American Public Transit Association (APTA), *Transportation 2000,* also recognized the need for local, problem-solving research. TCRP, modeled after the longstanding and successful National Cooperative Highway Research Program, undertakes research and other technical activities in response to the needs of transit service providers. The scope of TCRP includes a variety of transit research fields including planning, service configuration, equipment, facilities, operations, human resources, maintenance, policy, and administrative practices.

TCRP was established under FTA sponsorship in July 1992. Proposed by the U.S. Department of Transportation, TCRP was authorized as part of the Intermodal Surface Transportation Efficiency Act of 1991 (ISTEA). On May 13, 1992, a memorandum agreement outlining TCRP operating procedures was executed by the three cooperating organizations: FTA; the National Academy of Sciences, acting through the Transportation Research Board (TRB); and the Transit Development Corporation, Inc. (TDC), a nonprofit educational and research organization established by APTA. TDC is responsible for forming the independent governing board, designated as the TCRP Oversight and Project Selection (TOPS) Committee.

Research problem statements for TCRP are solicited periodically but may be submitted to TRB by anyone at any time It is the responsibility of the TOPS Committee to formulate the research program by identifying the highest priority projects. As part of the evaluation, the TOPS Committee defines funding levels and expected products.

Once selected, each project is assigned to an expert panel, appointed by the Transportation Research Board. The panels prepare project statements (requests for proposals), select contractors, and provide technical guidance and counsel throughout the life of the project. The process for developing research problem statements and selecting research agencies has been used by TRB in managing cooperative research programs since 1962. As in other TRB activities, TCRP project panels serve voluntarily without compensation.

Because research cannot have the desired impact if products fail to reach the intended audience, special emphasis is placed on disseminating TCRP results to the intended end users of the research: transit agencies, service providers, and suppliers. TRB provides a series of research reports, syntheses of transit practice, and other supporting material developed by TCRP research. APTA will arrange for workshops, training aids, field visits, and other activities to ensure that results are implemented by urban and rural transit industry practitioners.

The TCRP provides a forum where transit agencies can cooperatively address common operational problems. The TCRP results support and complement other ongoing transit research and training programs.

Project H-10 FY'95
ISSN 1073-4872
ISBN 0-309-06306-X
Library of Congress Catalog Card No. 98-61200

© 1998 Transportation Research Board

Price $62.00

FOREWORD

By Staff
Transportation Research
Board

TCRP Report 39 will be of interest to individuals involved in ongoing discussions and debates about urban sprawl and its effects. This report is a literature review that represents the culmination of the first phase of TCRP Project H-10, "The Costs of Sprawl—Revisited." The report was prepared by Rutgers University's Center for Urban Policy Research, in conjunction with The Brookings Institution, Parsons Brinckerhoff Quade and Douglas, Inc., and ECONorthwest. Urban sprawl is a topic that interests urban planners, economists, environmentalists, sociologists, transportation professionals, policymakers and public officials, academics in many fields, and the general public.

Regardless of the focus of any particular debate or discussion on urban sprawl, most such discussions attempt to define sprawl and address whether it is "good" or "bad." Consequently, Chapter 1 of Section I of *TCRP Report 39* provides a working definition of sprawl and its associated costs. The next chapter provides historical discussion, dating back to the early 1920s when zoning acts were initially developed, and to the 1950s when the term "sprawl" entered the planning literature. As indicated by the title of this research project, the seminal 1974 report *The Costs of Sprawl,* prepared by the Real Estate Research Corporation, serves as a springboard for this research effort.

Section II of the report contains the Literature Synthesis. This section systematically presents the literature on sprawl in chapters that focus on the following major areas of impact:

- Public/private capital and operating costs,
- Transportation and travel costs,
- Land/natural habitat preservation,
- Quality of life, and
- Social issues.

Throughout this section, the research team discusses the literature and identifies the extent to which there is agreement and disagreement about the premises and conclusions.

Section III of the report presents annotations of studies, organized in chapters that focus on the same five major impact areas as Section II.

While this report will not resolve the debate on the benefits and costs of urban sprawl, it provides an important repository of information for the debaters.

CONTENTS

PREFACE

In 1974, the Real Estate Research Corporation published a three-volume study entitled *The Costs of Sprawl*. The study consisted of an Executive Summary, Detailed Costs Analysis (Volume I), and Literature Review/ Bibliography (Volume II). It encompassed more than one thousand pages. From the time of its publication until today, it has been regarded by the social science community as one of the most significant critiques of sprawl and among the most influential studies ever undertaken. *The Costs of Sprawl* has been cited in countless environmental and planning reports and journals; it has been reviewed—both positively and negatively—by more than one hundred journals and magazines; and it has been presented as the seminal study on growth impacts to numerous Congressional committees and bodies. *The Costs of Sprawl* was funded jointly by the U.S. Council on Environmental Quality, the Department of Housing and Urban Development, and the Environmental Protection Agency.

The Costs of Sprawl, like no other study before, sought to isolate both density and location of development as significant contributors to the costs of development.

The study analyzed six hypothetical new communities of 10,000 dwelling units each, from high density (19-20 units per acre) to intermediate density (3-4 units per acre); from communities with high levels of planning and design to those lacking significant planning. The study analyzed impacts on infrastructure, housing, transportation, energy, environmental, and quality of life costs of sprawl (Real Estate Research Corporation [RERC] 1974).

Although *The Costs of Sprawl* was influential, it was also flawed. The analyses of community types allowed unit size and number of occupants to vary, and the savings attributed to different community types were actually a function of the differing size (and types) of units and numbers of people found there. The absence of sprawl was not the reason for the savings; smaller units and fewer people to service were the cause of the savings. Yet, even though these shortcomings were uncovered, the direction of the findings so paralleled past and current intuitive feelings that the study continues to be used twenty-five years later as one of the most cogent arguments against sprawled development patterns.

Why such interest in sprawl? Although Americans like their single-family residences, automobiles, and suburban lifestyles, there is a nagging feeling that both the aesthetics of how communities develop and the efficiency of movement within and between them could be improved. In addition, buried down deep is a recognition that Americans are wasteful in their consumption of man-made (infrastructure) and natural (land) resources, and that their development choices are selfish in terms of impacts on central cities and the populations within them. But first it must be shown to the citizenry at large that there is a problem, because life is good and "If it ain't broke, don't fix it." Is suburban sprawl different from an alternative form of development? Is it less efficient? Does it cause resources to be needlessly consumed? Is there an alternative? What do those who have studied this issue say? How substantively strong is the evidence they bring to bear?

The study that follows is a detailed examination of most of the information that can be assembled on both sprawl and its costs in an effort to answer the above questions. The monograph views the *costs of sprawl* (with lower-case letters) as investigated in a variety of types and forms of about 500 studies. These studies vary between those that: (1) focus specifically on sprawl, and those that deal with suburban or exurban development; (2) are highly quantitative, involving modeling or econometric analyses, and those that are qualitative and purely descriptive; (3) concern the "harder" or physical/engineering aspects of sprawl, and those that substantively involve "softer" or quality of life/social issues; (4) are primary analyses and break new ground, and those that are secondary analyses of the works of others that add very little; and (5) vilify sprawl and see no positive effects, and those that champion the development form as purely and

unequivocally "American" with few, if any, negative impacts.

With regard to the latter, this assemblage of material identifies and provides evidence for both negative and positive impacts of sprawl in each of five impact categories. These are: (1) *public and private capital and operating costs;* (2) *transportation and travel costs;* (3) *land/natural habitat preservation;* (4) *quality of life;* and (5) *social issues.*

The work contained in this monograph is divided into three sections and thirteen chapters. *Section I* contains two chapters that provide an introduction to, and an historical overview of, sprawl's "growth." Chapter One contains an introduction to the concept of sprawl, including its defining traits; Chapter Two highlights significant events in the evolution of the sprawl literature. *Section II* is a synthesis of the literature of sprawl's impacts: To what degree can the impact be recognized, and what is its relation to sprawl? It divides sprawl's impacts— more than 40 in total, two-thirds negative and one-third positive—into the above five impact categories. The first five chapters of this section discuss each of the above categories of impacts. The sixth chapter in this section presents in summary form information from the previous chapters both quantitatively and qualitatively. *Section III* individually annotates approximately one-quarter of the sprawl literature. Again, this section is broken down into five chapters according to the five sprawl impact categories.

The review of the sprawl literature is designed to be historical, substantive, comprehensive, and integrative. Presented in this way, the reader will be drawn into the argument about sprawl from its origins to the present.

SECTION

INTRODUCTION

The literature review that follows is an analysis of the writings and studies concerning a pattern of land development in the United States termed "sprawl." Sprawl is the spread-out, skipped-over development that characterizes the non-central city metropolitan areas and non-metropolitan areas of the United States. Sprawl is one- or two-story, single-family residential development on lots ranging in size from one-third to one acre (less acreage on the West Coast), accompanied by strip commercial centers and industrial parks, also two stories or less in height and with a similar amount of land takings (Ewing 1997).

Sprawl occurs on a micro basis in almost every county of the United States (although it occurs in significant amounts in only about one-fifth of the nation's 3,200 counties). Sprawl also occurs in Western and Eastern European, Latin American, and Asian countries in response to increased affluence and growing dependence on the automobile as the preferred method of intra- and inter-metropolitan travel. Most United States counties that contain sprawl have it in its residential form—i.e., low-density residential development in rural and undeveloped areas. Some counties are characterized by nonresidential sprawl, commercial and industrial development with floor-area ratios less than 0.2 located in the same types of areas (Burchell and Shad 1998).

> *Sprawl is the spread-out, skipped-over development that characterizes the non-central city metropolitan areas and non-metropolitan areas of the United States.* — Ewing 1997

Sprawl occurs, in part, because local governments in the United States encourage this form of development via zoning and subdivision ordinances which, in turn, reflect the desires of a large share of their citizenry. This type of development is favored by the general public because it (among other factors):

1) dilutes congestion while accommodating unlimited use of the automobile;

2) distances new development from the fiscal and social problems of older core areas;

3) provides a heterogeneous economic mix;

4) fosters neighborhoods in which housing will appreciate;

5) fosters neighborhoods in which schools provide both education and appropriate socialization for youth; and

6) requires lower property taxes to pay for local and school district operating expenses than locations closer in. (Burchell 1997a)

Sprawl is so well-accepted by the public that the AAA-rated locations for both residential and nonresidential development are increasingly farther out rather than closer in, and more rather than less segregated by type of land use (Gordon and Richardson 1997a). Gated communities, farmettes, research parks,

Large regional malls, initially located along undeveloped highway interchanges, stimulate rapid additional surrounding development.
Source: Constance Beaumont, NTHP.

law offices, medical groups, megahardware and home improvement stores, theatrical and comedy clubs, new and used car lots, and restaurants all now

seek peripheral locations in pursuit of their markets. The move to the far reaches of the metropolitan area began with single-family subdivisions; shopping centers and garden apartments sprang up next; then research and industrial parks; then restaurants and entertainment facilities; and finally, discounters of every form.

The unique aspect of all this development is that few entities have ever failed because their outward locational decisions were in the wrong direction. Occasionally, a retailer or a residential development has gone under because an exit on the interstate or beltway wasn't developed as planned, but rarely has an economic entity failed in the United States because it was developed too far out.

> *The move to the far reaches of the metropolitan area began with single-family subdivisions; shopping centers and garden apartments sprang up next; then research and industrial parks; then restaurants and entertainment facilities; and finally, discounters of every form.*

The newest and soon-to-be one of the most successful airports in the United States is 33 miles from the city of Denver; a taxi ride from the airport baggage claim to the downtown Hyatt costs $40. Is this an anomaly? No. Cincinnati's new airport is so far from the downtown that it is not even in the same state! Both airports have already drawn nonresidential development and are now drawing residential development to their edges. Both are tens of miles from the nearest existing development of these types. But neither can justify its location solely on flight pattern interference with residential environments. Instead, the locations were chosen for exactly the same reason other land use locations are chosen: an abundance of land was available, and it was both relatively inexpensive and easy to assemble.

If sprawl is so desirable, why should the citizens of the United States accept anything else? The answer is that they no longer can pay for the infrastructure necessary to develop farther and farther out in metropolitan areas. In the state of South Carolina, if sprawl continues unchecked, statewide infrastructure costs for the period 1995 to 2015 are projected to be more than $56 billion, or $750 per citizen per year for the next twenty years. In addition to a massive infrastructure conservation program and the adoption of numerous technological cost savers, funding infrastructure in this state could require an increase in the gasoline tax of 2¢/gallon; an increase in the state sales tax of 0.5%; an increase in property taxes of 12.5%; the tolling of all interstates at 30-mile intervals; impact fees on residential and nonresidential development of $2,000 per unit and per 1,000 square feet, respectively; and a mandatory 10 percent set-aside for infrastructure in all state, county, municipal, and school district general funds and intergovernmental transfer revenues (Burchell 1997b).

Despite massive road expenditures, I-395 in Arlington, Virginia, slows to a gridlock during rush-hour traffic.
Source: Virginia Department of Transportation.

The big-ticket item in all infrastructure projections is roads. In South Carolina, roads are expected to cost $25 billion, almost half of the total $56 billion infrastructure budget. In South Carolina,

roads will cost 2.5 times what will be spent on primary, secondary, and higher education infrastructure; three times what will be spent on health infrastructure, including all hospitals, institutions, and all water-sewer treatment systems; ten times what will be spent on public safety, administration, and justice infrastructure; fifteen times what will be spent on environmental protection infrastructure; and twenty-five times what will be spent on all cultural and recreational infrastructure.

Dually supporting and underutilizing two systems of infrastructure—one that is being abandoned in and around central cities and close-in suburbs, and one that is not yet fully used in rural areas just beginning to be developed—is causing governments to forgo the maintenance of much infrastructure and the provision of anything *other* than growth-related infrastructure. The United States, in other words, is funding road infrastructure by:

1) not funding all infrastructure;
2) not *fully* funding developmental infrastructure;
3) not repairing or replacing most types of infrastructure; and
4) not taking advantage of the technological improvements in rehabilitation, repair, and provision of infrastructure that could be passed on to taxpayers as savings.

Still, by no means is an alternative to the current pattern of land development the panacea. If South Carolina were to switch to compact development and managed growth measures to curtail spread development, the state would be able to save only about 10 percent of the projected $56 billion infrastructure costs, or approximately $5.6 billion. This is because about 40 percent of public infrastructure costs are not growth-related, and only about two-thirds of the remainder is *new* growth-related. When development pattern savings are applied to the appropriate portion of new growth-related infrastructure costs, therefore, the saving is only 12–15 percent.

On the other hand, increasing the gasoline tax by 2¢/gallon in South Carolina, would have raised only $56 million in new revenues statewide—one one-thousandth of the total required infrastructure costs—and one one-hundredth of the amount that potentially could be saved by altering land development patterns (Burchell 1997b).

In sum, most of the American public is not unhappy with the current pattern of development in metropolitan areas—it simply can no longer afford it. Thus, the primary concern about sprawl development, at a time when the average American is satisfied with its outcome, is *cost*. And costs need to be measured not just in terms of capital improvement but also in terms of resource depletion. Land in the United States is being consumed at triple the rate of household formation;

automobile use is growing twice as fast as the population; and prime agricultural land, forests, and fragile lands encompassing natural habitats are decreasing at comparable reciprocal rates (Landis 1995).

In sum, most of the American public is not unhappy with the current pattern of development in metropolitan areas—it simply can no longer afford it.

As a result, the professional transportation and city planning communities are beginning to look at sprawl to determine whether an alternative to this growth pattern can be conceived, and even more importantly, whether it makes sense to pursue an alternative pattern of growth. Does any alternative pose a viable option to current methods and forms of metropolitan development? A significant literature has developed in this area and is overviewed in this section.

CHAPTER

DEFINING SPRAWL

Sprawl, in its broadest sense, has long been an American zeitgeist. Alexis de Tocqueville, touring the United States in the early 1800s, observed "no urban growth boundaries," but rather marveled at "America ... where everything is in constant motion ... and where no boundaries were set to the efforts of man." Today's sprawl is the frontier of long ago; it is akin to the post-war suburb—both of which have been extolled as defining American influences.

John Delafons, Fellow at the Harvard/MIT Joint Center in 1961, chose as a research topic a comparison of British and American land-use controls. His work, *Land Use Controls in America*, provides an insightful look at the growth of the U.S. "system" of controls from 1920 to 1960 by an outsider who came from a country with a very formal system of land-use controls.

Delafons describes the U.S. system of master planning, zoning, and subdivision control as heavily influenced by a "prairie psychology." He explains that U.S. development patterns are characterized by:

a) a supply of land which is viewed as virtually unlimited;

b) land that is open to all and property ownership rights that are encouraged and protected by the U.S. Constitution;

c) economic forces that are barely understood and should not be tampered with;

d) development professionals who prepare land for development and do not question whether the land should be developed (i.e., they make sure utilities are in place and feeder roads have been planned for); and

e) a basic distrust of elected and appointed officials, so that all procedures are codified and development that qualifies under these procedures does so "as of right," with minimal public review. (Delafons 1962)

U.S. development controls, he claims, are "static" and thus lack the ability to control tempo (timing) and sequence (which location first) of development. Development is free to wander and to take place incrementally in jurisdictions in the United States because existing land use controls allow this to happen (Delafons 1962).

Many agree with Delafons' insight. Although some view contemporary development patterns as a reflection of the invisible but sure hand of the market (Gordon and Richardson 1997a), the unbridled movement outward of leapfrog, low-density development is increasingly being viewed as an American ill (Richmond 1995). Sprawl has taken on both a pejorative as well as a descriptive connotation, an intermixing that makes a balanced discussion, which attempts to disentangle the costs and benefits of sprawl, difficult.

> *U.S. development controls are "static" and thus lack the ability to control tempo (timing) and sequence (which location first) of development.*

The shift to the suburbs has, of course, been manifest for more than half a century. In 1940, only 15 percent of the United States population resided in the suburbs (defined as metropolitan areas outside of central cities). As the millennium approaches, about 60 percent of the population is counted as suburban. Even the most vehement critics of sprawl recognize that suburban and exurban growth patterns have been and will continue to be inescapable development forms in the United States. The recent population increase of some 20 million people per decade is likely to continue for at least the next quarter-century. As a result, there will continue to be skipped-over development in rural and undeveloped areas. It would be totally unrealistic to expect even a moderate share of growth to occur solely in already built-up neighborhoods in cities or in close-by inner suburbs. Even the suburbs are being bypassed now by development seeking locations at the fringe of

metropolitan areas (Nelson and Sanchez 1997).

A WORKING DEFINITION OF SPRAWL

Density, or more specifically, *low density*, is one of the cardinal defining characteristics of sprawl. But density has to be set in context; cross-cultural and place-oriented differences factor into the definition of sprawl. Densities in the United States overall are roughly one-tenth what they are in Western Europe; in turn, Western European density is much lower than that of Japan and only a fraction of what is found in such locations as Hong Kong and Indonesia (Jackson 1985). And in all of the above locations, suburban densities are lower than the densities of central cities. Sprawl is not simply development at less-than-maximum density; rather, it refers to development that, given a national and regional framework (i.e., suburbs in various locations of the United States), is at a low *relative* density, and one that may be too costly to maintain.

Sprawl refers to a particular type of suburban peripheral growth. It refers to development that expands in an *unlimited and noncontiguous (leapfrog) way outward* from the solidly built-up core of a metropolitan area. In terms of land-use type, sprawl includes both *residential and nonresidential development*. Residential development contains primarily single-family housing, including significant numbers of distant units scattered in outlying areas. Nonresidential development includes shopping centers, strip retail outlets along arterial roads, industrial and office parks, and free-standing industrial and office buildings, as well as schools and other public buildings.

These different types of land uses are, for the most part, *spatially segregated* from one another. The components of this development are individually located in small subdivisions in zoning districts. Within each district, usually only one type of use is permitted—e.g., single-family residential, shopping centers, strip commercial, industrial, or office parks.

Another of sprawl's distinguishing traits is its *consumption of exurban agricultural and other frail lands* in abundance; these are the types of land found at the periphery of development. The loss of agricultural acreage takes place in significant amounts because it often is the cheapest land available for development. Fragile environmental lands are swallowed up because they are part of the otherwise developable tracts. These tracts would not be developed if the environment was adequately protected.

Under sprawl conditions, there is almost total *reliance upon the automobile* as a means of accessing the individual land uses. Seventy years ago, the streetcar was the most popular form of transportation to the suburbs. Nowadays the automobile is the most efficient means of accessing sprawl's outward extension and skipped-over development. For seven-day-a-week business and recreational use, including both at-peak and off-peak use, nothing can match the automobile for cost, efficiency, and versatility—at least in the short term.

Some analysts also include *the small developer* and *a lack of integrated land-use planning as important aspects of suburban sprawl*, and point to the relatively small residential subdivisions and nonresidential site plans created by individual developers operating independently of each other within the zoning districts of the 10,000 local governments found throughout the

United States. The legal framework within which sprawl occurs is fragmented into numerous relatively small units, separately controlled by discrete local governments with unique rules and regulations. These localities have different fiscal resources per capita (assessed valuation of residential and nonresidential properties). Some are quite wealthy; others have limited ability to pay for local services. The poorer localities are at a severe disadvantage when competing for development.

The automobile has replaced the streetcar, stimulating sprawl development.
Source: Minnesota Historical Society.

Still, it must be stressed that sprawl is almost impossible to separate from all conventional development. Even though one may be able to comprehend what appears to be a better method of development, it is difficult to translate that method into practice.

Some components of sprawl are not easily measured. For example, although it is possible to track residential single-family and nonresidential commercial and retail development taking place at low densities in the United States, accessed by automobiles in rural and undeveloped areas, this is the point at which almost all tracking stops. Measures of leapfrog development or development that is spatially segregated are virtually impossible. Measures of how much development is being delivered by small developers in local jurisdictions is achievable but generally unproductive.

Finally, although a measure of gross residential density (number of dwelling units divided by area of jurisdiction) is available from several sources and can provide some indication of land taken per developed unit, the gross measure often masks the actual land takings of individual new developments.

On the other hand, there is little evidence to suggest that conventional development in a given location is anything other than leapfrog, segregated, and land-consuming. Thus, sprawl development can be characterized with some certainty as low-density residential and nonresidential intrusions into rural and undeveloped areas, and with less certainty as leapfrog, segregated, and land-consuming in its typical form.

A WORKING DEFINITION OF THE COSTS OF SPRAWL

The "costs" of sprawl have been talked about for decades, often without a full understanding of what these costs are and to what level they should be assigned. In the original RERC (1974) *Costs of Sprawl* study, costs were calculated in six different substantive areas and assigned to three different levels: infrastructure and transportation costs were assigned to the community, housing and quality-of-life costs to the individual, and energy and environmental costs to both the community and to society as a whole (RERC 1974). This is a characteristic of the sprawl literature which is only beginning to be addressed at the end of a twenty-five-year observation period. The work of Sam Seskin of Parsons Brinckerhoff and Terry Moore of ECONorthwest on full-cost accounting of transportation

costs is breaking new ground in viewing the totality of costs of public policy decisions (Parsons Brinckerhoff and ECONorthwest 1996). Their work is the exception. *Most cost-accounting efforts assign sprawl costs to either the easiest or the most common level of measurement.*

For definitional purposes, *the "costs" of sprawl are the resources expended relative to a type, density, and/or location of development.* These "costs" involve physical, monetary, temporal, and social/psychological resources. They involve costs to the individual, to the community, and to society. Most of the costs specified to date are physical or monetary, although occasionally social costs (e.g., the loss of upward mobility) or psychological costs (e.g., the loss of sense of community) are documented.

> *There is little evidence to suggest that conventional development in a given location is anything other than leapfrog, segregated, and land-consuming.*

The "benefits" of sprawl are mirror images of costs. They involve resource gains due to type of development pattern and include categories of gain similar to those of losses stated above. This might involve a temporal gain in suburb-to-suburb travel time because most residences and jobs are now both suburban, or monetary gains due to reduced housing costs also from building farther out, or social gains such as the ability to achieve homeownership, again due to location in more distant places.

Costs and benefits are reported in the form that the primary research provides. In almost all cases, these are *costs* at the *community* level as opposed to costs at the individual or societal levels, or benefits at any level.

CHAPTER

HISTORICAL OVERVIEW

Sensitivity to the consequences of sprawl-like settlement predates the coining of the term. The 1929 Regional Plan of the New York Metropolitan area, for instance, warned of a steady decrease in farms and open-space acreage in the region and underscored the need for settlement patterns that encouraged "the face to face association that characterized the old village community" (Regional Plan 1929, 23 and 216). At the same time, the Regional Plan spoke approvingly of "many carefully planned outer subdivisions with good features" (Regional Plan 1929, 1).

Concern about sprawl-like patterns of development was appropriate at this time. The Standard Zoning Enabling Act (1922), drafted under the aegis of Secretary of Commerce Herbert Hoover, the Standard City Planning Enabling Act (1928), and the legalization of zoning that resulted from the 1926 Supreme Court decision (Euclid v. Amber Realty) unleashed a barrage of "model" zoning and planning-enabling legislation across the United States. Euclidean zoning of segregated land uses and the emergence of the automobile began to establish the first distant "suburbs" throughout the United States.

It was not until roughly the late 1950s and early 1960s, however, that sprawl as a planning term entered the literature. The land development pattern it depicted was typically criticized. Herbert Gans in The Levittowners described Levittown development of the 1950s as "residents living in a sea of cell-like structures on a

Levittown, Pennsylvania: post-World War II suburbia.
Source: Carl Byoir and Associates (New York).
          Courtesy American Planning Association.

remote potato farm with cars spilling out of every street" (Gans 1967). In 1956, a Canadian planning study described urban sprawl as "scattered building development" that had led to "inconveniences in the placement of public and business facilities" (Lower Mainland Regional Planning Board 1956). A year later, William H. Whyte, describing urban sprawl as leapfrog, scattered development, spoke of it as "a problem that had reached national proportions" (Whyte 1957).

The political and social climate of the period, however, provided definite financial incentives for building homes in the suburbs in the form of federally insured low-cost mortgages. This period also witnessed the massive federally subsidized expansion of U.S. highways *(1956 Interstate Highway Act),* including the establishment of the interstate system. The new roadway system, together with the growth in accessible, low-cost mortgages, helped push development far beyond the nation's central cities (APA 1997). Relatively few people seriously challenged this new pattern of growth in the outlying areas or questioned the changes in central cities brought about by multi-lane freeways.

Others soon entered the discussion, however. Marion Clawson, in 1962, described sprawl as a "lack of continuity in expansion," and noted it was both fostered by, and contributed to, land speculation (Clawson 1962). Similar literature of the period, including Lessinger (1962), Harvey and Clark (1965), and Bahl (1968) viewed sprawl as characterized by such features as low-density, scattered, and leapfrog patterns. Harvey and Clark (1965) identified the three cardinal traits of sprawl as low-density, ribbon, and leapfrog development.

Even at this early stage, pundits acknowledged the difficulty in defining the term sprawl. Writing in 1972, David McKee and Gerald Smith observed that:

Urban sprawl is rather difficult to define. In some circles the term is thought to be synonymous with suburbia. Certainly the problem exists in suburbia but suburbia itself is not the problem. Some equate sprawl with expansion. But this type of definition is not too helpful. (McKee and Smith 1972, 181-182)

McKee and Smith went on to describe sprawl in four forms: 1) very low-density development (i.e., two- to five-acre zoning); 2) ribbon-variety development extending along access routes; 3) leapfrog development; and 4) a "haphazard intermingling of developed and vacant land" (McKee and Smith 1972). The authors claimed that sprawl aggravated suburban problems (e.g., automobile dependence and the high cost of services and infrastructure) and also deleteriously affected cities by depressing real estate values, among other things.

> **The political and social climate of the period provided definite financial incentives for building homes in the suburbs.**

Discussion of sprawl's effects transcended economics. Although the 1973 Rockefeller Brothers Task Force publication, *The Use of Land,* did not speak of sprawl per se, it concluded that the dominant pattern of "unrestrained, piecemeal urbanization" was leading citizens to ask how such growth affected their "quality of life" (Reilly 1973, 33). In a similar vein, *The Language of Cities* and the *Encyclopedia of Community Planning and Environmental Management* defined sprawl, respectively, as:

the awkward spreading out of the limbs of either a man or a community. The first is a product of bad manners, the second of bad planning. Sprawl is a by-product of the highway and automobile, which enabled the spread of development in all directions. As builders scramble for lots to build on, the journey to work is lengthened and green spaces are consumed by gas stations and clutter. (Abrams 1971, 293-294)

the uncontrolled growth of urban development into previously rural areas. Sprawl refers to a mixture of land uses occurring in an unplanned pattern. Urban sprawl has been strongly criticized as an unattractive and inefficient use of land and resources, causing excessive infrastructure costs related to extending utilities to remote areas. It has also been accused of eliminating environmentally important open space while leapfrogging developable parcels. (Schultz and Kasen 1984, 378-379)

THE FIRST STUDIES ON THE COSTS OF SPRAWL

In the 1960s, professional research began to be undertaken in numerous areas relevant to the study of sprawl. Examples of this early research include *Innovation Versus Tradition in Community Development* (ULI 1963), which looked at the effects of development patterns on road lengths; *Howard County Study* (Howard County 1967), which considered comparative, countywide costs of roads, utilities, schools, and open space under sprawl versus more planned scenarios; *Urban Form and the Cost of Public Services* (Kain 1967), which considered public service costs at varying densities; *Planned Residential Environments* (Lansing 1970), which looked at how different overall development patterns influence trip generation rates and distances; *Total Energy Demonstration* (HUD 1972), which measured likely savings in energy consumption in planned communities; and *The Relationship of Land Use and Transportation Planning to Air Quality*

Management (Hagevik 1972), which examined how development planning affects air pollution on a regional basis. Although not articulated, the substantive foci in analyzing sprawl versus alternatives—namely, the issues of transportation, infrastructure, public service costs, and land and environmental issues—were already being formulated.

Many of these early studies were referenced by the bellwether study, *The Costs of Sprawl,* authored by the Real Estate Research Corporation in 1974. As summarized by RERC:

This analysis presents a complete and internally consistent set of estimates for direct costs and adverse effects resulting from prototypical housing types and land development patterns at neighborhood and community levels. Six neighborhood prototypes— differing in housing type and density—are analyzed, along with six community prototypes which represent different degrees of community-wide planning. ... Stated in the most general form, the major conclusion of this study is that, for a fixed number of households, sprawl is the most expensive form of residential development in terms of economic costs, environmental costs, natural resource consumption, and many types of personal costs. (RERC 1974, 2-7)

The Costs of Sprawl did not explicitly define the term "sprawl." As a matter of fact, those close to the study indicate that the term appeared as an afterthought in the title and summary of findings and was not used explicitly elsewhere in the study. The analysis of six community-level growth patterns within the study implied that sprawl development had at least two major traits: low average residential density (3 units or less per net residential acre), and a lack of overall planning at either the regional or community level. RERC did not define sprawl's specific density characteristics, nor did it define its residential and nonresidential components.

RERC considered approximately 20 individual effects (see Table 1). As seen in Table 2, these costs can be grouped into four overall categories encompassing:

1) public-private capital and operating costs;
2) transportation and travel costs;
3) land and natural habitat preservation; and
4) quality of life.

Not considered in *The Costs of Sprawl*, and not part of its research charge, was any examination of sprawl's social effects, such as its impacts on cities.

The RERC study evoked a flood of commentary—much praise as well as some criticism. Two of the better known criticisms were articulated by Altshuler (1977) and Windsor (1979). Among other points, Altshuler argued that RERC underestimated the demand for services by higher-density development and commingled the effects resulting from high density and smaller-unit size. Windsor, in parallel, criticized RERC for not disentangling density from other factors, and among other shortfalls, argued that RERC ignored the benefits of sprawl, such as its "response to consumer preference" for single-family detached homes. These early points of opposition on the costs/benefits of sprawl are still present twenty years later and can be seen in the recent exchanges between Gordon/Richardson and Ewing on the subject (Gordon and Richardson 1997a; Ewing 1997).

Although the findings of *The Costs of Sprawl* dominated the literature for some time, new analyses continued to be published. Examples include David Popenoe's (1979) depiction of sprawl as

low-density, scattered strip development, which focused on its adverse sociological implications. In 1981, David Mills described sprawl as scattered, leapfrog development, and discussed how it both abetted and resulted from land speculation.

> *Not considered in* **The Costs of Sprawl***, and not part of its research charge, was any examination of sprawl's social effects, such as its impacts on cities.*

BURCHELL/LISTOKIN AND TISCHLER ON FISCAL IMPACTS

During the time period between the first and interim studies on the *capital* costs of growth, the national work of Robert W. Burchell/David Listokin of Rutgers University and Paul Tischler in fiscal impact analysis, or the examination of the *operating* costs of growth, came to the fore. From the early 1970s to the late 1980s, numerous studies were undertaken on the municipal and school district costs of growth. Burchell and Listokin were participating authors in *Housing Development and Municipal Costs* (Sternlieb 1975) and coauthored *The Fiscal Impact Handbook* (1978) and *The Practitioner's Guide to Fiscal Impact Analysis* series (1980, 1985). Paul Tischler, a private consultant, undertook studies throughout the country using the *MUNIES* and *FISCALS* models developed by him and others.

The fiscal impact studies sought to preview for a community, county, or school district the impact of projected development on future educational and noneducational public service demands. Burchell and Listokin offered an *average costing* approach built on regional and statewide demographic multipliers for the demand for public services, and average historical costs for the costs of public services. Burchell and Listokin balanced the calculation of costs with revenue calculations in three categories: property tax, non-tax, and intergovernmental transfers. This was termed the *Per Capita Multiplier* fiscal impact technique, which became the method used in creating their fiscal impact hierarchy and the basis of their *Development Impact Assessment Handbook* (Burchell, Listokin, and Dolphin 1994). Burchell and Listokin found that most conventional residential development negatively impacted the host service provider, whereas open space development and nonresidential development broke even or positively impacted the host service provider. These studies paid little attention to explicit capital costs except that ongoing debt service was a component of operating costs.

Paul Tischler used a *marginal costing* approach in most of his fiscal impact analyses. In *MUNIES* and *FISCALS*, a great deal of time was spent gathering both site-specific data and information on excess or deficient service capacity locally. Tischler actually termed a component of his overall fiscal impact analysis a "level of service analysis." The Tischler studies involved detailed calculations of how a specific community with a particular set of financial conditions would respond if growth were to take place immediately.

Paul Tischler headed the economic committee of the American Planning Association from 1980 to 1990. Tischler generally reached the same conclusions on the fiscal impacts of residential development, open space, and nonresidential development as did Burchell/Listokin. Conventional residential development was generally found to be fiscally negative, open space or undeveloped land to be break-even,

and nonresidential development to produce positive fiscal impacts. Tischler and Associates was involved in costs of growth studies in numerous locations nationally and has also been involved in alternative development and impact fee studies.

These two groups, with different approaches and different audiences, found generally the same conclusions on the fiscal attributes of various types of land uses. They established for the planning and land development fields a solidification of opinion on the future public costs of residential and nonresidential development.

THE INTERIM STUDIES: MANAGED GROWTH COSTS IN CALIFORNIA; THE COSTS OF SPRAWL IN FLORIDA (DUNCAN AND FRANK)

In the early 1980s, in response to the rampant development of the 1970s, growth control ordinances began springing up in California and Florida cities. These included Davis (CA), Petaluma (CA), and Boca Raton (FL). Before one or more of these ordinances were challenged and set aside, initial inquiry concerned their potential impact on local housing costs. If growth were curtailed through building permit or population caps or through adequate public facilities ordinances, would these factors contribute to increased housing costs? Almost everyone looking at these issues concluded that growth control ordinances did increase local housing costs (Katz and Rosen 1987; Schwartz et al. 1981, 1989). Further, excessive growth management through protracted permitting processes, including fiscal impact analysis, coastal zone management procedures, natural resource inventories, and other mechanisms, was also found to increase housing costs (Parsons 1992).

TABLE 1
REAL ESTATE RESEARCH CORPORATION (RERC 1974a)
THE COSTS OF SPRAWL: SUMMARY OF FINDINGS

Category	Community Prototypes (10,000 units)					Neighborhood Prototypes (1,000 units)				
	Low-density Sprawl	Low-density Planned	Sprawl Mix	Planned Mix	High-density Planned	Single-family Conventional	Single-family Clustered	Townhouse Clustered	Walk-up Apartment	High-rise Apartment
INFRASTRUCTURE										
Capital costs per unit										
Recreation	$ 268	$ 297	$ 268	$ 297	$ 297	$ 220	$ 274	$ 274	$ 252	$ 203
Schools	4,538	4,538	4,538	4,538	4,538	5,354	5,354	4,538	4,538	1,646
Public Facilities	1,662	1,626	1,645	1,622	1,630	3,080	2,661	2,111	1,464	801
Roads/streets	3,797	3,377	3,235	2,708	2,286	5,483	3,649	2,369	1,579	958
Utilities	6,197	4,744	3,868	3,323	2,243					
Infrastructure	16,462	14,582	13,556	12,487	10,995	14,137	11,938	9,292	7,833	3,628
Subtotal Construction/Other[a]	34,994	34,398	23,728	23,266	17,711	34,774	34,320	17,967	13,449	17,088
Total Unit Costs	$ 51,456	$ 48,981	$ 37,283	$ 35,753	$ 28,706	$ 48,911	$ 46,258	$ 27,259	$ 21,282	$ 20,696
Public Proportion	19%	12%	24%	16%	18%	15%	15%	20%	25%	13%
Public Costs	$ 9,777	$ 5,878	$ 8,948	$ 5,720	$ 5,167	$ 7,337	$ 6,939	$ 5,452	$ 5,321	$ 2,690
OPERATING										
Annual Nonresidential Operating and Maintenance Costs per Unit (in year 10)										
Operating Costs	$ 2,111	$ 2,067	$ 1,965	$ 1,937	$ 1,873	$ 1,721	$ 1,720	$ 1,388	$ 1,319	$ 548
Public Proportion	57%	51%	61%	55%	55%	67%	67%	72%	74%	57%
Public Costs	$ 1,203	$ 1,054	$ 1,199	$ 1,065	$ 1,030	$ 1,153	$ 1,152	$ 999	$ 976	$ 312
LAND										
Land Required (for 10,000 units)										
Total Acres	NA	NA	NA	NA	NA	5000	4000	3000	2000	1000
Developed Acres	4,590	4,113	2,780	3,040	2,173	NA	NA	NA	NA	NA
Vacant, Improved Acres	459	206	278	152	109	NA	NA	NA	NA	NA
Vacant, Semi-improved Acres	951	617	1,390	456	326	NA	NA	NA	NA	NA
Vacant, Unimproved Acres	—	1,064	1,552	2,352	3,392	NA	NA	NA	NA	NA
Total Vacant Acres	1,410	1,887	3,220	2,960	3,827	NA	NA	NA	NA	NA
ENVIRONMENT										
Principal Environmental Impacts (for 10,000 units)										
Non-auto Air Pollutants[b]	1,420	1,420	1,034	1,034	809	1,420	1,420	951	738	644
Sewage Effluent[c]	4.5	4.5	4.5	4.5	4.5	4.5	4.5	4.5	4.5	4.5
Water Use[d]	1,170	1,100	910	910	760	1,205	1,059	913	730	639
Non-auto Energy Use[e]	2,355	2,355	1,750	1,750	1,400	2,398	2,398	1,595	1,232	1,056

Notes: All dollar figures are per dwelling unit in 1973 dollars.
NA = Not applicable
[a] Includes construction cost of the unit and other expenses such as land dedication.
[b] Lbs. per day.
[c] Billion liters per year.
[d] Million gallons per year.
[e] Billion BTU's per year.

Source: RERC (1974), Vol. 1, *Executive Summary*.

TABLE 2
REAL ESTATE RESEARCH CORPORATION (RERC 1974)
THE COSTS OF SPRAWL: **SUBSTANTIVE AREAS OF INQUIRY**

Topics Considered By RERC (1974)	*Public-Private Capital and Operating Costs*	*Transportation and Travel Costs*	*Land and Natural Habitat Preservation*	*Quality of Life*
Capital and Operating Costs				
Capital				
• Recreation	X			
• Schools	X			
• Public Facilities	X			
• Utilities	X			
• Road/streets		X		
Operating	X			
Land Requirements				
• Total acres			X	
• Developed acres			X	
• Vacant, improved/semi-improved acres			X	
• Vacant unimproved acres			X	
Principal Environmental Impacts				
• Nonauto air pollutants				X
• Sewage effluent				X
• Nonauto energy use				X
• Water use				X

By the late 1980s, two important costs of sprawl studies were undertaken in Florida. James Duncan, a consultant working for the Florida Department of Community Affairs, studied the capital infrastructure requirements of sprawl (scattered) versus compact development forms. Duncan found that various forms of scattered development could be as much as 70 percent more costly than equivalent forms of compact development (Duncan et al. 1989).

A colleague, James Frank of Florida State University, in research conducted for the Urban Land Institute, updated several early (1950s and 1960s) isolated costs of

> *Various forms of scattered development could be as much as 70 percent more costly than equivalent forms of compact development.*

sprawl studies with 1987 data and prices, and assembled their results. His findings were similar to Duncan's: "contiguous" development was 45 percent less expensive for roads, water, and sewer than "leapfrog, far-out" development (Frank 1989). The Duncan and Frank studies are cited throughout the costs of sprawl literature.

CHARACTERIZING SPRAWL: CRABGRASS FRONTIERS AND EDGE CITIES

Kenneth Jackson's *Crabgrass Frontier: The Suburbanization of the United States*, published in 1985, received much acclaim. Although sprawl per se was not mentioned in this monograph, numerous traits attributed by Jackson to the "crabgrass frontier" were clearly sprawl-like in character. These attributes were:

> 1) low residential density and the absence of sharp divisions between town and country
> 2) the socioeconomic distinction between the center and the periphery
> 3) a lengthy journey to work in terms of distance and time.

Jackson attributed the permanence of the crabgrass frontier to physical as well as political factors (e.g., that America was land-rich and had fragmented local governments). He also noted its problems (e.g., high local public service costs and increased automobile dependence) as well as its benefits (high level of housing amenity and individual open space).

Approximately six years after the publication of *Crabgrass Frontier*, journalist Joel Garreau published *Edge City: Life on the New Frontier* (portions of the book were actually in print before this time). Unique to Garreau's work was the concentration on peripheral *nonresidential* clusters brought together at suburban junctures of major beltways and axial interstate roads. These "edge cities" formed a new kind of metropolis because nonresidential development was soon joined by high-density residential development to form relatively self-sustaining urban clusters at edges of built-up areas. These clusters were unique; no more than fifty existed in the United States, and they represented sprawl at an urban scale (Garreau 1991).

Tyson's Corner in Fairfax County, Virginia, the prototypical "edge city."
Source: County of Fairfax (Virginia), Office of Comprehensive Planning.

During the early part of the 1980s, in a country with a newly refound admiration for capitalism, and in the latter part of that decade, in a recession that paid the price for earlier deficit spending, the literature on sprawl was relatively quiescent. The trend has reversed itself in the 1990s; as will be seen, there has been an outpouring of studies. These studies are reviewed in Section II of this report by substantive area. To give a sense of the current literature—and the current definition of sprawl and its alleged costs and benefits—a sampling is discussed here.

These "edge cities" formed a new kind of metropolis.

SPRAWL AND CITIES: DOWNS, RUSK AND BARNETT

In his 1994 book, *New Visions for Metropolitan America*, Anthony Downs adopted a broader approach for defining sprawl that primarily referred to density but included some other characteristics as well. Downs, building on an earlier work, *Stuck in Traffic* (Downs 1992), defined sprawl as encompassing five major elements:

1) low-density, primarily single-family residential settlement (without any numerical density specified)
2) heavy dependence upon private automotive vehicles for all types of travel
3) scatteration of job locations widely across the landscape in mainly low-density establishments (also without any numerical density specified)
4) fragmentation of governance authority over land uses among many relatively small localities
5) widespread reliance on the filtering or "trickle down" process to provide housing for low-income households.

New Visions for Metropolitan America proposed a basic method for analyzing sprawl—i.e., comparing its results to the results that might arise from alternative forms of metropolitan growth. Downs described a way of formulating alternative outcomes through an analysis of the basic traits of different growth strategies. Downs's approach is incorporated and described in more detail later in Section II.

As is apparent, even the most current literature on sprawl tends to *describe* its attributes rather than *quantify* them. Very few quantified analyses of sprawl's impacts or relationships to other variables appear anywhere in the literature. As a result, few studies have mathematically or statistically linked sprawl to other conditions or metropolitan traits.

A limited attempt at quantification was put forth in the 1993 work by David Rusk in *Cities Without Suburbs.* He calculated an "index of elasticity" that measured the ability of cities to extend their boundaries to encompass surrounding urbanized development. "Elasticity" is essentially the same as annexation, i.e., movement outward from the city center (sprawl) without the creation of new political

jurisdictions. Rusk claims that cities with high indices of elasticity are superior to those with low indices of elasticity, in terms of income distribution, racial integration, population growth, and economic development. The best cities are "elastic" cities, he claims, and applies his index both to cities themselves as well as their metropolitan areas.

Rusk himself did not perform mathematical or statistical analyses relating the variables just described, but three reviewers of his book did. John P. Blair, Samuel R. Staley, and Zhongcai Zhang (1996) used multiple regression employing measures of growth and economic welfare over the period 1980–1990 as independent variables, against Rusk's index of elasticity as the dependent variable. These reviewers concluded that Rusk's index of elasticity had statistically significant effects of the expected types on *city* employment,

> *The most current literature tends to describe sprawl's attributes rather than quantify them.*

population, poverty, and per capita income growth and significant effects of the expected types on *metropolitan-area* population and employment growth—but not of the expected types on *metropolitan-area* per capita income or poverty growth. However, even where the regression equations identified statistically significant effects, they had low R^2s (low explanatory power), an outcome that indicated that other unspecified variables were possibly not included in the regression equation. An implication of this analysis was that either Rusk's index of elasticity is not a useful indicator of sprawl or the indicator itself, due to its construction, inherently produced low levels of explanation.

City-suburban relationships were also considered by Jonathan Barnett in his 1995 book, *The Fractured Metropolis.* This analysis of metropolitan area trends was strictly narrative and advanced the thesis that U.S. metropolitan areas were splitting into "old cities" and "new cities." Barnett proposed that future growth be redirected into the "old cities." Much of his work was skewed toward physical design and planning; it favored compact development over sprawl and encouraged commercial development within, and the creation of urban growth boundaries around, older metropolitan cities.

SECOND GENERATION STUDIES ON THE COSTS OF SPRAWL

Research into methods to address the costs of sprawl and a study of the underlying data have been undertaken at both the Center for Urban Policy Research at Rutgers University and at the University of California—Berkeley. Starting in the early 1990s, Rutgers University researchers, led by Robert W. Burchell, began to quantify the relative impacts of alternative patterns of development. One or two years later, under John D. Landis, similar efforts were undertaken at the Institute of Urban and Regional Development at Berkeley. Both research organizations have looked at the prospective impacts of alternative development patterns. Both research organizations developed comprehensive land-use models to carry out these analyses (Burchell 1992a, 1992b; Landis 1994, 1995).

Costs were defined primarily in terms of resource consumption at the community level. Sprawl was defined as skipped-over, low-density residential and nonresidential development.

The Rutgers effort involved an analysis of the differing effects of "trend development" (sprawl-like) and "planned development" (compact form with managed growth attributes) in New Jersey. The results obtained are shown in Table 3. This Rutgers study was preceded by similar work for the State of Maryland as part of its original attempt at a Growth Management Act. Significant efforts to confine sprawl to the Baltimore-Washington corridor have been undertaken in Maryland.

> **Sprawl is defined as skipped-over, low-density residential and nonresidential development.**
> **— Burchell 1992a; Landis 1994**

The New Jersey and Maryland analyses were followed by similar studies for Lexington, Kentucky (Burchell and Listokin 1994b), the Delaware Estuary (Burchell and Moskowitz 1995), and the States of Michigan (Burchell 1997a) and South Carolina (Burchell 1997b). Research is also currently underway, at Rutgers, for the State of Florida as part of its *Eastward Ho!* initiative, a development plan aimed at keeping a large share of future development east of Route I-95 in five southern counties. In all instances,

Florida's Future?

Florida's *Eastward Ho!* initiative hopes to avert this potential future.
Source: Tim Reilly, *Sunshine: The Magazine of South Florida.*

TABLE 3
BURCHELL (1992)—NEW JERSEY IMPACT ASSESSMENT:
SUMMARY OF IMPACTS OF TREND VERSUS PLANNED DEVELOPMENT

Growth/Development Impacts	Trend Development	Planned Development	Trend Versus Planned Development	
			Difference	%
I. POPULATION GROWTH (persons)	520,012	520,012	0	0
II. HOUSEHOLD GROWTH (households)	431,000	431,000	0	0
III. EMPLOYMENT GROWTH (employees)	653,600	653,600	0	0
IV. INFRASTRUCTURE				
A. ROADS ($ millions)				
Local	$2,197	$1,630	$567	25.8
State	727	595	132	18.2
Total Roads	$2,924	$2,225	$699	23.9
B. UTILITIES—Water ($ millions)	$ 634	$ 550	$ 84	13.2
C. UTILITIES—Sewer ($ millions)	$6,790	$6,313	$477	7.0
Total Utilities	$7,424	$6,863	$561	7.6
E. SCHOOLS ($ millions)	$5,296	$5,123	$173	3.3
F. ALL INFRASTRUCTURE (sum of A–E in $ millions)	$15,644	$14,211	$1,433	9.2
V. LAND CONSUMPTION				
A. Overall Land (acres)	292,079	117,607	174,472	59.7
B. Frail Lands (acres)	36,482	6,139	30,343	83.2
C. Agricultural Lands (acres)	108,000	66,000	42,000	38.9
VI. HOUSE PRICE				
A. Median Cost per Unit (1990 $)	$172,567	$162,162	$10,495	6.1
B. Housing Index	118	126	8	6.7
(higher is more affordable)				

Source: Robert W. Burchell 1992a, b

TABLE 4

BURCHELL (1992-1997) FINDINGS OF SAVINGS OF COMPACT GROWTH VERSUS CURRENT OR TREND DEVELOPMENT

Area of Impact	Lexington, KY and Delaware Estuary	Michigan	South Carolina	New Jersey
I. Public-Private Capital and Operating Costs				
1. Infrastructure Roads (local)	14.8-19.7%	12.4%	12%	26%
2. Utilities (water/sewer)	6.7-8.2%	13.7%	13%	8%
3. Housing Costs	2.5-8.4%	6.8%	7%	6%
4. Cost-Revenue Impacts	6.9%	3.5%	5%	2%
II. Land/Natural Habitat Preservation				
1. Developable Land	20.5-24.2%	15.5%	15%	6%
2. Agricultural Land	18-29%	17.4%	18%	39%
3. Frail Land	20-27%	20.9%	22%	17%

Source: Robert W. Burchell 1992-1997

polar development patterns are contrasted—i.e., "current" or "trend" growth is measured against "compact," or "planned" growth. The exact nomenclature in the studies is unimportant; what is important are the differing land-use configurations and their impacts, which are related below:

> *Current, or trend, development* is historical development in an area. The land-use literature describes this type of development as skipping over existing development; land-consumptive and inefficient use of available land at or near the core of the metropolitan area; and requiring significant accompanying infrastructure in the form of roads, water and sewer lines, public buildings, and the like. *Compact, or a more managed, type of development* attempts to direct growth to already existing locations of development while preserving yet-to-be developed areas. Nationally, the land-use literature portrays compact development as more efficient in its land-use patterns and thus less land-consumptive. Accordingly, it often requires somewhat less development infrastructure. Compact development is also viewed as not limiting or restricting population or employment growth at the county, regional, or state levels. (Burchell 1997a, A-1)

Burchell developed a series of quantitative models relating to land consumption, road, transit, water/sewer infrastructure, fiscal impacts, housing cost, and quality of life to examine the relative effects of alternative development patterns. Application of these models across the aforementioned jurisdictions indicated comparable order-of-magnitude findings. For instance, a shift away from sprawl to compact growth was projected by Burchell to reduce water/sewer utility *infrastructure* costs by 8 percent in New Jersey, 7 percent in Lexington, 8 percent

in the Delaware Estuary, 14 percent in Michigan, and 13 percent in South Carolina. Table 4 summarizes the array of findings from the various Burchell studies (1992-1997). Table 5 groups the effects of sprawl, some dozen in all, into five overall categories.

The Berkeley effort employed the California Urban Futures (CUF) model of the San Francisco Bay Area to tabulate land consumed under three scenarios: (a) "business as usual"; (b) "maximum environmental protection"; and (c) "compact cities." These scenarios were differentiated, respectively, by (a) not restricting development either within the city or within unincorporated areas; (b) applying a range of environmental restrictions to both locations, but not restricting growth per se; and (c) restricting growth to acknowledge some environmental limitations and countywide minimum population projections. The two latter alternatives showed considerable overall *land* savings, particularly sensitive environmental land savings relative to the business-as-usual scenario. Total land saved in scenarios b and c was 15,000 and 46,000 acres, respectively. Scenario b saved nearly 60,000 acres of prime agricultural land, 10,400 acres of wetlands, and 2,800 acres of steep-sloped land; Scenario c saved 28,000 acres of prime agricultural land, 10,400 acres of wetlands, and 8,000 acres of steep-sloped lands (Landis 1995).

In a series of relatively current articles in *Environment and Planning Behavior*, Landis discussed the development and use of the second generation of the California Urban Futures Model. These articles were less about sprawl and land savings and more about urban modeling; still they suggested a framework for understanding and predicting the land- and habitat-taking effects of sprawl.

STUDIED REACTIONS TO SPRAWL—LUTRAQ (OREGON) AND CONCURRENCY (FLORIDA)

In the late 1980s and early 1990s, sprawl growth on the northwestern and southeastern coasts of the United States resulted in two different reactions—both supported by so-called "friends" organizations. In the first case, the organization was the *1000 Friends of Oregon*, in the second case, the *1000 Friends of Florida*.

In the early 1990s, growth in the Portland region was believed to hinge on the construction of a Western Bypass around the city. An alternative plan was sought to try to accommodate growth without the need for more highways. Sam Seskin of Parsons Brinckerhoff, leading a team of researchers in the Land Use Transportation Air Quality simulation (LUTRAQ), compared the transportation impacts of a transit-oriented development (TOD) plan to the impacts of a preferred Bypass alternative. The LUTRAQ alternative shifted the location of 65% of new residential units and 78% of new jobs to locations within walking distance of light rail or bus transit lines by reconfiguring expected development into a series of mixed-use centers. The alternative showed a reduction in vehicle miles traveled and a reduction of the use of the automobile (Davis and Seskin 1997). Portland voters responded by approving a $1 billion rail line along which TOD will occur, and Seskin received an American Planning Association award for the research effort.

Subsequent analyses produced by Genevieve Giuliano, however, found only small gains associated with non-automobile mode shares and very small reductions in vehicular travel. Equally

TABLE 5

BURCHELL (1992-1997) ANALYSIS OF TREND VERSUS PLANNED DEVELOPMENT: SUBSTANTIVE AREAS OF INQUIRY

Topics Considered By Burchell (1992-1997)	Public-Private Capital and Operating Costs	Transportation and Travel Costs	Land and Natural Habitat Preservation	Quality of Life	Social Effects
• Water/sewer infrastructure	X				
• School capital facilities	X				
• Housing cost	X				
• Fiscal impacts	X				
• Roads		X			
• Transit		X			
• Land capacity			X		
• Agricultural lands			X		
• Frail lands			X		
• Quality of life				X	
• Intergovernmental coordination				X	
• Effects on urban and rural centers					X

Source: Robert W. Burchell 1992-1997

distressing, the magnitude of investment in transit services needed to be quite large to achieve the resulting changes in mode shares. The LUTRAQ study unintentionally demonstrated the limits of making large investments in transit to influence travel patterns (Giuliano 1995b).

In Florida, meanwhile, the reaction to sprawl was to limit development if it could not be shown that sufficient public facilities would be in place at the time that development occurred (Florida Growth Management Act 1985). This procedure, termed "concurrency," included both mandatory (transportation) and voluntary (schools) components. At first, those distant from the scene thought that the procedure was responsible for shutting down growth in the state. After the dust from the housing recession of the late 1980s settled, however, those originally opposed to concurrency reluctantly agreed that it had channeled growth effectively. In the meantime, those who originally favored concurrency vehemently opposed it because roads were being built and widened and new schools were being constructed (albeit at developer cost) too far from the locus of existing development. Growth was slowed, but it also was accommodated in locations where it should not have been (Mofson 1997).

AT WHAT SCALE IS MEASUREMENT TO TAKE PLACE? URBAN FORM AND TRANSPORTATION

At about the same time that Burchell and Landis were looking at development form and its effect on resource consumption, two other important considerations began to emerge. The first was the scale at which transportation impacts were being viewed; the second was the effect of transportation on urban form, and vice versa. In other words, while attempting

to define the indicators of sprawl and more compact forms of development and their resulting impacts, it became apparent that one needed to specify at what level impacts were being measured—individual, community, or societal. Almost all studies to date have been undertaken with impacts specific to the community level. But Sam Seskin from Parsons Brinckerhoff, and Terry Moore from ECONorthwest, began pursuing the issue of "full" costs of transportation, attempting to view the costs of transportation decisions at the individual and societal scales as well as at the community level. They determined, for instance, that although using an automobile was efficient at the individual and community scales, it was expensive at a societal scale (air pollution). Although transit was efficient at individual and societal scales, it was expensive at a community scale (the cost to deliver transit). And walking, although efficient at community and societal scales, was expensive at an individual scale (the cost of the individual's time) (Parsons Brinckerhoff 1996; Moore and Thorsnes 1994).

Seskin and Moore shifted the inquiry to issues of the impact of urban form on transportation, and vice versa. The urban form impacts on transportation were much as expected. Seskin and Moore determined that sprawl development could be served well only by the automobile; much more compact development led to transit solutions. Mixed-use development enabled walking and biking. Transportation impacts on urban form were not quite a mirror image of the first, however. Significant use of the automobile led to unlimited spread development. Transit presence brought users who also needed an automobile; mixed-use development promoted foot and bicycle use, but an automobile was still required. Land use can affect transportation mode and vice versa, but American society today remains heavily dependent upon the automobile (Parsons Brinckerhoff and ECONorthwest 1996).

CERVERO AND TRANSPORTATION ACCESSIBILITY MEASURES

One of the most widely published academics in the field of transportation planning is Robert Cervero, from the University of California at Berkeley. Ever since his first book, *Suburban Gridlock*, was published in 1986, Cervero has been solidly represented in the land-use/transportation literature. His latest book, *The Transit Metropolis* (1998), deals with transit-oriented cities. Cervero has done important sprawl work relating a jobs-housing "imbalance" to expanding commutes (Cervero 1996), and Bay Area growth trends of job decentralization to increased VMT per worker (Cervero and Wu 1996). Other aspects of his work involve (1) suburban congestion as well as measures for its relief (Cervero 1986, 1991a); (2) the role of suburban activity centers as alternatives to sprawl, and commuting patterns within these centers (Cervero 1989, 1991b, 1996); and (3) the feasibility of transit in suburban locations—i.e., the required density and implementation costs (Cervero 1994a, 1994b).

Cervero's latest contributions from a sprawl perspective are two papers he co-authored on suburban accessibility: (1) a 1997 paper co-authored by Timothy Rood and Bruce Appleyard, entitled "Job Accessibility as a Performance Indicator: An Analysis of Trends and their Social Policy Implications in the Bay Area"; and (2) a 1996 paper co-authored by Kara Kockelman, entitled "Travel Demand and the 3Ds: Density, Diversity, and Design." In these papers, Cervero and his colleagues show through factor and regression analyses the effect of current development patterns on employment accessibility. They try to document, in

other words, how well transportation serves employment markets. In the first article, Cervero finds that current sprawl development patterns have the largest impact on severely poor neighborhoods because they separate jobs from job seekers. Minorities are particularly disadvantaged, because even with equal education, vehicle availability, and accessibility, blacks still had disproportionately high unemployment rates.

> *Current sprawl development patterns have the largest impact on severely poor neighborhoods.*

In Cervero's second article, he looks at what can be done. He measures the effects of density, diversity, and design on accessibility, and finds that compact mixed-use, pedestrian-friendly designs can reduce vehicle trips, vehicle miles traveled, and the use of the automobile. Density, he concludes, affects business trips; diversity affects both work and non-work trips, but has less of an effect than density; and design affects primarily non-work trips. He upholds the views of the new urbanists—somewhat, because he shows that sensitive land design and building arrangements can reduce travel distances and alter modes of travel.

THE BANK OF AMERICA STUDY: BUSINESS EMBRACES THE ANTI-SPRAWL MOVEMENT

In 1995, four groups—Bank of America, California Resources Agency, Greenbelt Alliance, and Low-Income Housing Fund—published a study on sprawl that quickly came to be known as the *Bank of America Study*. Those who champion land development alternatives to sprawl point to this study, the work of one of the private sector's most influential members, as a landmark. If the banks finally realize that sprawl can no longer be tolerated, recognition of the impacts of differing land development patterns on society's resources has indeed hit the big time.

The Bank of America study summarized changes in population, demographics, and employment that had taken place over the two decades prior to 1990. It also referenced a land-use pattern that had taken place during this same period of time and termed it "sprawl." Sprawl was characterized by decentralized employment centers and residential tracts accessed almost exclusively by the automobile. These decentralized locations were safe and cheap places in which to locate and had plucked all fiscal and physical benefits from the central city. Further, the study noted that the trend toward sprawl was aided and abetted by the federal subsidies given to the automobile.

> **If the banks finally realize that sprawl can no longer be tolerated, recognition of the impacts of differing land development patterns on society's resources has indeed hit the big time.**

The Bank of America report was criticized for its inability to adequately interpret the long-standing criticisms of RERC's (1974) *The Costs of Sprawl* report. The Bank of America study seemed to buy into many of the arguments that favored the anti-sprawl position without an adequate look at contrary evidence. Nonetheless, those who championed the study as a summary of the ills of sprawl used the Bank of America imprimatur to promote the position that the business community, at long last, was calling for managed growth to conserve national resources.

IS SPRAWL LIKED OR DISLIKED BY THE GENERAL PUBLIC? FANNIE MAE VERSUS "VISION PREFERENCING" SURVEYS

A question discussed and debated in a number of circles is whether Americans like their current development patterns. Often, those responding have difficulty making the distinction between shelter and location, and between both of these and way of life.

There is a popular literature that rates places on such indices as cost of living, public safety, climate, job growth, transportation accessibility, and access to cultural and recreational amenities (Savageau and Boyer 1993). Clearly, suburbs in the Southeast and Southwest fare better on this rating scale than cities in the Northeast and North Central regions of the country, or, for that matter, rural areas in any location. An economics literature looks at the determinants of worker migration, identified as job availability, good climate, and lower housing costs (Duffy 1994; Greenwood et al. 1991; Roback 1988; Rosen 1979). Psychological reasons for moving often parallel the economic determinants: physical (safety), physiological (economic), belongingness (sense of place), and personal satisfaction (cultural and recreational amenities) (Zinam 1989). Again, suburban locations appear to do better than urban locations on both of the above sets of criteria.

Americans are asked about their environments through two basic devices: a national, annual, in-person, in-home *Fannie Mae* survey of owners and renters on their housing (Lang and Hornburg 1997) or an occasional, professionally administered "visual preferencing" survey on their environments (Nelessen 1994).

Eighty percent of Americans contacted in the first survey identified the traditional single-family home with a yard as the ideal place to live. To afford it, they would rather live farther out than take a second job, tie up savings, put children in day care, or incur heavier debt. Finally, they would rather occupy an average house in a good neighborhood than a good house in an average neighborhood (Fannie Mae 1994).

> *Respondents often have difficulty making the distinction between shelter and location, and between both of these and way of life.*

Visual preferencing surveys are typically employed by planners and architects to test sentiment for a redirection in current development patterns and forms (Nelessen 1994). These surveys contrast the current versus an alternative development pattern and architecture and ask those surveyed to pick between the two. Often it is hoped by those who administer these surveys that the alternative development pattern will be chosen and, accordingly, localities will develop residential and residential areas in a different way (Calthorpe 1993). Most of those who experience this exercise of choice opt for the alternative, which typically shows a denser, more traditional residential village center and less spread-out residential subdivisions and strip commercial developments (Nelessen 1994).

The results of most of the two surveys on consumer preference and sprawl indicate that people feel comfortable with their current housing and its suburban location but also think that sprawl has an ugly look and that suburbs are becoming increasingly congested. Whether people would change their housing type (single-family), form (single-lot subdivision), or location (suburbs) to achieve a different "look" or "feel," or to be free from congestion, remains a crucial question.

AN UNUSUAL FINDING: THE CITY IS IMPORTANT TO THE REGION; THE USUAL FINDING: PEOPLE DON'T CARE

The United States has had a love–hate relationship with its cities for at least fifty years. This has taken two forms. The first is inquiry into the continued importance of the central city; the second is whether or not people will choose to live and work there.

In the mid-1990s, two articles rekindled interest in, and attempted to quantify the importance of, the central city to its surrounding area. One was written by Elliot Sclar and Walter Hook in 1993, "The Importance of Cities to the National Economy"; the other was written by Keith Ihlanfeldt in 1995 and entitled "The Importance of the Central City to the Regional and National Economy." At a time when most scholars viewed the central city's role in the region and nation as not critical and one of declining value, Sclar/Hook and Ihlanfeldt breathed new life into the debate on the role and future of the central city with the following arguments:

- In most metro areas, the higher-paying jobs are found in the central city.

- In the metro areas of the 100 largest U.S. cities, half of suburban families had at least one worker employed in the central city.

- Sixty-seven percent of suburban residents surrounding the 100 largest U.S. cities depend on the city for major medical care; 43 percent have a family member attending an institution of higher learning there.

- Cities provide low-cost housing for low-wage workers employed in—and necessary for—the activities of suburbs.

- The overall appeal of a region is influenced by conditions prevailing within its central city.

Sclar and Hooks argued that the United States subsidizes suburbs through home-ownership income tax deductions and by federal/state cost-sharing of highway construction. Continued subsidization will cause increasing auto dependence, and a further channeling of most infrastructure expenditures to road building, at the expense of education operating costs. According to the authors, the United States ranked lowest among the seven most industrialized nations in percent of GNP that supported education.

Ihlanfeldt found that central cities possess certain "agglomeration economies" (the benefits of scale) that will sustain their primacy in a region. These include communications, labor, and producer concentrations. Moreover, financial services such as investment banking, commercial banking, legal auditing, and actuarial services were provided primarily by central city firms to suburban markets, and in many cases to world markets. According to Ihlanfeldt, these activities were not likely to be taken on by suburban firms, because few suburban firms have the appropriate scale to conduct them.

The United States subsidizes suburbs through homeownership income tax deductions and by federal/state cost-sharing of highway construction.

The second issue regarding urban areas was whether upwardly mobile households will continue to reside there. In the 1970s, the United States experienced significant movement of jobs and residents to exurban or rural areas. During this period of time, non-metropolitan areas were the locations of the fastest relative employment and household growth (Sternlieb and Hughes 1983). During the 1980s, there was stabilization, if not growth, of metro-politan areas. Buoyed by significant immigration and a slowing of metropolitan to non-metropolitan out-

migration, metropolitan areas were beginning to grow (Gordon, Richardson, and Yu 1997; Nelson et al. 1995, 1997). According to Peter Gordon, recent Bureau of Economic Analysis (BEA) Regional Economic Information System (REIS) data indicate that the trend is once again toward outer areas; indeed, over the last six years, outward metropolitan movement is almost as pronounced as it was during the 1970s. Gordon et al. finds that the one constant in all of this has been strong suburban growth, with parallel rural growth tilting the scale to outward movement, and even stronger suburban growth with reduced declines of urban areas tilting the scale toward inward movement. The consistency of the suburban component of this trend and renewed non-metropolitan growth (the outward movement) do not bode well for the future of the central city. Gordon and his colleagues conclude, citing additional data from the Economic Census CBD file, that:

The location decisions of households are influenced less by workplace accessibility than by availability of amenities, recreational opportunities, and public safety. In addition, the locations of firms are clearly becoming more footloose under the influence of the information revolution, just at a time when core *agglomeration diseconomies* (pollution, congestion, crime, fiscal instability, etc.) appear to be outweighing the original agglomeration economies that pulled people and economic activities together. In this view, the central cities are not coming back any time soon (Gordon, Richardson, and Yu 1997)

The suburban component and renewed non-metropolitan growth (the outward movement) do not bode well for the future of the central city.

THE VALUE OF OPEN SPACE AND FARMLAND: THE FARMER AND CONSERVATIONIST AS PLAYERS IN THE SPRAWL ARGUMENT

In the latter part of the 1980s and the early 1990s, the American Farmland Trust (AFT) began a series of studies to discourage the conversion of farm tracts to sprawled residential subdivisions. Not only was farmland ideal for developers because it was flat, it also was, for the most part, the cheapest land available. The percentage of farmland being lost in the United States was many times the percentage growth of household formation. The analyses of the AFT, called "Cost of Community Services," presented detailed case studies of the cost/revenue superiority of farmland to other types of land uses. Studies were undertaken in Massachusetts, Connecticut, Pennsylvania, Virginia, and the Midwest, and are heavily cited today. The conclusions drawn always demonstrate this group's advocacy and point to farmlands as a fiscal benefit to communities in which they are located. Regardless of methodology, the studies achieve their goal of representing farmland not merely as fiscally neutral but as fiscally positive. "Smart" communities should not want to lose this net revenue producer to other forms of development (especially residential), which would be more costly (AFT 1992b).

Growing out of this new attention to farmland was the recognition that farmers, as owners of this land, were often opposed to growth management (and thus pro-sprawl) and needed to be brought into the negotiation process. Otherwise, they would sell their land to developers before it could be acquired via public purchase or through some type of transfer of development rights. Farmers prevented passage of the original Maryland Growth Management Act and threatened to do the same to the New Jersey State Plan if their real estate interests could not be protected. In Maryland, it appeared that the farmers could not be assuaged, and the Growth Management Act[1] failed. In New Jersey, farmers were appeased at the eleventh hour with a promise from the New Jersey State Planning Commission that their development rights would be purchased at a price somewhere between crop and real estate value, and the planning statute passed.

Randall Arendt, influenced by living in both walkable and planned open space communities in New Jersey as a child, and seeing these concepts implemented in England as an adult, built upon Ian McHarg's *Design with Nature* (1969) in an attempt to make current development patterns greener. In three of his latest books, *Rural by Design* (1994b), *Conservation Design for Subdivisions* (1996), and *Growing Greener* (1997), he provides convincing evidence that open space adds to the value of surrounding real estate and to the quality of life of those who live within it. Arendt sees the combination of compact development and open space as leading to interconnected networks of green space (Arendt 1994b). An area-wide, interconnected greenway can extend open space and wildlife benefits to the larger region. Further, successful control of sprawl will retain the "traditional character" of communities (Arendt 1996).

The Sierra Club, among other conservationist groups, is actively campaigning against sprawl. Its 65 chapters and 450 groups are challenging sprawl at the grassroots level in communities across America (Sierra Club 1998).

---

[1] Maryland ultimately passed a diluted version of the original act and has adopted a variety of "smart growth" procedures.

THE MECHANICS OF PAYING FOR SPRAWL: IMPACT FEES, TAKINGS, AND PROPERTY RIGHTS

In order to pay for sprawl and not impact current residents, local governments have turned to economists and land-use attorneys to devise a system of assigning a share of new required public service infrastructure to new owners of developed property. These mechanisms are termed impact fees, developer exactions, or proffers and are based on the rationale of charging development costs to those who have caused them. Impact fees are calculated by determining the specific costs that one new unit of residential development or 1,000 square feet of nonresidential development will cause in roads, water/sewer, public buildings (schools and municipal), and other capital infrastructure. Impact fees, developer charges, or whatever moniker they are known by, are currently the fastest-growing source of municipal revenues. Principal players in this group are James Nicholas of the University of Florida and Christopher Nelson of the Georgia Institute of Technology (Nelson 1988; Nicholas et al. 1991). Nicholas has constructed impact fee schedules in numerous counties and municipal jurisdictions; both Nicholas and Nelson have significant academic and professional publications in this area.

> *In order to pay for sprawl and not impact current residents, local governments have turned to a system of assigning a share of new required public service infrastructure to new owners of developed property. These mechanisms are termed impact fees.*

The issue with impact fees specifically, and growth management strategies generally, is that these mechanisms presuppose government capacity to regulate land. This amounts to a taking and thereby affects individual property rights. Although most of these techniques have been upheld, when they become overly aggressive, they are subject to judicial review.

This gets to what land-use attorneys describe as the "black hole" of takings jurisprudence. Until recently, a severe test of a taking has been applied. A land-use regulation is a taking if it: (1) does not substantially advance a legitimate state interest; or (2) denies an owner all economically viable use of his or her property. Post-1990, there appears to be an easing of this test that favors property owners. Charles Siemon (Siemon 1997), Robert Freilich (Freilich and Peshoff 1997), and Jerold Kayden (Young 1995) are recurringly involved in litigation concerning these issues or in designing land-use regulations to avoid such litigation. Suburban development ordinances that require payment for costs or link "social" objectives to the development of real property will be tested by the courts. To pay for sprawl, local governments have become quite inventive at both deriving fee schedules and in locating property owners to whom the costs can be assigned. Much as other forms of payment for sprawl are drying up, if governments are not careful, so too will these mechanisms.

SPRAWL'S CRITICS AND THE NEW URBANISTS

In 1993, a study conducted for the Chesapeake Bay Program defined sprawl as "residential development at a density of less than three dwelling units per acre" (CH2M Hill 1993). This definition did not have a "locational component" and was a modification of a definition presented in an earlier draft—i.e., "developments having gross development densities of less than three or four dwelling units per acre or minimum lot sizes of at least one-quarter of an acre, and frequently of at least one acre." The latter definition had been criticized by Uri Avin (1993) for including properties with too high a density; it could be applied to many existing, close-in subdivisions in both Maryland and Virginia. On the other hand, in California, sprawl is currently taking place on 9,000-square-foot lots; obviously the upper-level density cutoff varies considerably by region.

Sprawl, and more generally, suburbanization, were condemned in a polemical book by James Kunstler (1993). The title of the book, *The Geography of Nowhere: The Rise and Decline of America's Man-Made Landscape*, conveys his message. The strident tone of the message is reflected by the following statement:

> We have become accustomed to living in places where nothing relates to anything else, where disorder, unconsciousness, and the absence of respect reign unchecked. (Kunstler 1993)

Peter Calthorpe's book *The Next American Metropolis*, published in 1993, offered a method for determining population densities in an idealized form of modern settlement. He presented a scheme for clustering housing and other improvements around transit stops at specified densities which could, in turn, be used to compute overall densities for ideal future metropolitan settlements. His scheme involved creating Transit Oriented Developments (TODs) around stations in a system of radial fixed-rail transit lines emanating from a region's major downtown. This approach quantified aspects of an alternative form of future growth. However, Calthorpe did not present any method of measuring the costs and benefits of sprawl, nor of the alternative form he suggested. Neither did

he present any database to use in carrying out such measurements.

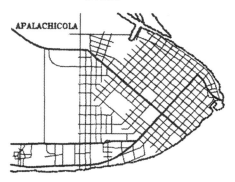

Traditional Urban Grids

Contemporary Suburban Networks

Street patterns of neo-traditional versus typical suburban neighborhoods.
Source: Florida Department of Community Affairs.

Calthorpe is a "new urbanist," part of an urban design movement called "neo-traditionalism." Neo-traditionalism calls for the development of neighborhoods that resemble those of the past—i.e., with grid street patterns, fronted by proximate single-family houses with porches, sidewalks, alleys, and other traditional features. The elements returned to neighborhood design include mixed uses, the grid-based street structure, higher densities, pedestrian circulation, and transit use. The elements removed include single uses, cul-de-sacs, low densities, and automobile-dominated neighborhood access.

The neo-traditionalists, led by Andres Duany, and joined by Elizabeth Plater-Zyberk (1995), Anton Nelessen (1994), Peter Calthorpe (1993), and others, view current development patterns (sprawl) as driven by engineering standards and, accordingly, devoid of the capacity for human interaction. Neo-traditionalism is often proposed as a design alternative to sprawl, even though developments incorporating this type of design can be found in sprawl locations. Nelessen's vision preferencing analyses are sometimes cited by those who oppose sprawl as evidence that the American public is ready for this type of design. The Duany-led new urbanists propose that the new urban-like grids replace the current sprawl-like suburban networks.

MORE SPRAWL CRITICS— "TRUSTS" AND "OLD FRIENDS"

A critique of strip commercial development, and sprawl in general, permeates the current literature of the National Trust for Historic Preservation (NTHP) and its leadership (NTHP 1993; Moe 1996). At a 1995 conference on "Alternatives to Sprawl," Richard Moe, president of the National Trust, defined sprawl as low-density development located on the outer fringes of cities and towns that is "poorly planned, land-consumptive, automobile-dependent development designed without regard to its surroundings." He described two types:

> "sellscape" retail development frequently spurred by major discount chains such as Wal-Mart and K-Mart,

occurring along major arteries and at highway interchanges; and "spread out" residential development, usually consisting primarily of single-family detached houses, located on the edges of existing communities or "leap-frogging" into previously unde-veloped areas. (Moe 1996, 3)

In a later work, *Changing Places: Rebuilding Community in the Age of Sprawl*, Moe and Carter Wilkie (1997) indicated that sprawl was causing communities to be dysfunctional and diminishing a sense of connections between people. The authors suggested that if sprawl were tested by a truly "free" market, far less sprawl would occur on private financing alone. They proffered that sprawl developers captured benefits for themselves while everyone else in the community bore the costs. Both authors called for better land-use planning and more creative reuse of older urban and suburban areas.

Commercial strip development is a manifestation of nonresidential sprawl.

A more comprehensive view of the components of sprawl was offered in Henry Richmond's 1995 book, *Regionalism: Chicago As An American Region*. Richmond's conceptualization of sprawl included eight components:

1) low residential density;
2) unlimited outward extension of new development;
3) leapfrog development;
4) spatial segregation of different land uses;
5) decentralized land ownership;
6) primacy of automobile transportation;
7) fragmentation of governmental land use authority; and
8) disparity in the fiscal capacity of local government.

Richmond, former director of 1000 Friends of Oregon and a participant in the LUTRAQ simulation study, offered a wide-ranging critique of sprawl and included numerous carefully culled statistics supporting his allegations. Many of his criticisms are drawn from the subject of his continued research—the Chicago metropolitan area. His criticisms form the basis for his definition of sprawl. In defining sprawl, however, Richmond does not present specific alternative forms of growth, either conceptually or in terms of quantified analysis. Instead, he continues to propose an agenda of specific policy actions that would encourage a regional approach to managing future growth. His analysis, therefore, does not provide either a method for measuring the costs of sprawl or a specific alternative development form that would provide a better outcome.

SPRAWL EVENTS: LINCOLN INSTITUTE/GEORGIA CONSERVANCY CONFERENCES

In the spring of 1995, the Lincoln Institute of Land Policy hosted two important conferences on sprawl. The first took place in Washington, DC, and was co-sponsored by the National Trust for Historic Preservation and The Brookings Institution. This conference brought all the national actors on sprawl together in a debate format. Sprawl's good and bad attributes were debated before a national audience. This was the first appearance of the defenders of sprawl. Peter Linneman from the University of Pennsylvania and Peter Gordon from USC proved to be strong supporters of the free-market merits of continued suburbanization.

So successful was the conference in drawing national attention to the sprawl issue, as well as in drawing attention to the institutions that sponsored the conference, that the Lincoln Institute held

derivative conferences in two locations— Florida and California. Even though no debate was scheduled, again the issue was raised: How bad is sprawl? Gordon, joined by colleague Genevieve Giuliano, provided a strong and cogent argument in favor of sprawl and presented findings contrary to the research of Seskin (LUTRAQ), Landis (California Futures Studies), Burchell (Rutgers Modeling Studies), and Downs (*New Visions for Metropolitan America*). The savings gleaned from LUTRAQ were described as minimal, and the land/infrastructure savings of the California Futures and Rutgers studies were trivialized. Downs was also criticized for assigning causes of central city decline to sprawl that could not be defended.

In 1996 and 1997, at the annual meetings of the Georgia Conservancy, sprawl was again the topic of consideration. Like the National Trust, the Georgia Conservancy shifted its focus slightly from historic preservation and was making a major substantive thrust at curbing urban sprawl. These conferences, which again attracted national spokespersons on the manifestations and costs of sprawl, were not a debate, but rather represented a summation on the ills of sprawl. The Atlanta region was growing at a rate of 55,000 jobs per year, and the economy was in such a boom period that growth was flooding the arterials in and around the city. Sprawl needed to be contained, and the conferences were the beginning steps in an attempt to create a mood for regional growth management. However, even though some sentiment for growth was apparent, the consensus was that political jurisdictions in Georgia were a long way from being able to implement, even on a regional scale, the most elemental of growth management techniques (a growth boundary).

THE SPRAWL DEBATE: EWING VERSUS GORDON— IN PRINT AND IN PERSON

The debate over sprawl was brought front and center in two "point" and "counterpoint" articles in the *Journal of the American Planning Association*. The point article by Peter Gordon and Harry W. Richardson (1997a) critiqued the arguments and evidence frequently presented in favor of compact development (i.e., energy, transportation, and infrastructure efficiencies) and argued that the decentralized suburban pattern of development, in fact, offered many advantages, including reduced travel times and lower housing costs, as well as higher consumer satisfaction. In counterpoint, Reid Ewing (1997) made a strong case for the adverse effects of sprawl (as opposed to the benefits of compactness). Ewing pointed to increased infrastructure costs, increasing travel distances, and significant amounts of developable and lost fragile lands as the adverse effects of sprawl.

For the purposes of this review, the authors' respective definitions of terms bear note. For Ewing, sprawl was defined both by a series of three *characteristics*—(1) leapfrog or scattered development; (2) commercial strip development; and (3) large expanses of low-density or single-use developments—as well as by such *indicators* as low accessibility and lack of functional open space (Ewing 1997). Gordon and Richardson did not specifically define sprawl (nor compactness, for that matter). Instead, they referenced sprawl's various traits. Sprawl was alternatively denoted by Gordon and Richardson as low-density, dispersed, or decentralized development, whereas compactness was associated with higher densities and a downtown or central-city spatial pattern versus a

polycentric (or dispersed) spatial pattern (Gordon and Richardson 1997a, 95).

> *Adverse effects of sprawl include increased infrastructure costs, increasing travel distances, and significant amounts of developable and lost fragile lands.*

Although the point-counterpoint authors addressed more than 15 different subjects in discussing sprawl and its alternatives, the subjects can be grouped into five broad areas, as shown in Table 6.

The debate moved from print to person in a forum held at the University of California—Berkeley in late November 1997. Both Ewing and Gordon had significantly increased the weaponry used to support their individual positions.

Ewing began the session with points of mutual agreement and spun out a longer list than most expected. These included that: (1) the market for transit was limited; (2) infrastructure costs were higher for sprawl development initially but could diminish over time with infill; and (3) automobile costs as a function of suburban residence were high, but few alternatives to this mode of travel and its costs existed. Ewing and Gordon continued to disagree about whether resource consumption (energy, land) differences under sprawl and compact development in light of national and global resources were sufficiently significant to cause concern, and whether the traffic consequences of sprawl (excessive travel and roadway congestion) could be argued away in terms of either current or future methods of resolution (higher travel speeds, congestion pricing). The session was narrowly focused on primarily transportation issues and never really dealt with social or quality of life issues of sprawl.

TABLE 6

EWING AND GORDON-RICHARDSON IN PRINT SUBSTANTIVE AREAS OF INQUIRY

Author	Topics Considered By Authors	Public-Private Capital and Operating Costs	Transportation and Travel Costs	Land and Natural Habitat Preservation	Quality of Life	Social Effects
Ewing (1997)	• Infrastructure costs	X				
	• Public service costs	X				
	• Transit		X			
	• Vehicle miles traveled		X			
	• Loss of resource lands			X		
	• Energy consumption				X	
	• Psychic and social costs				X	
	• Impact on central cities					X
	• Infrastructure and operating efficiency	X				
	• Transit		X			
Gordon and Richardson (1997a)	• Economical resource allocation	X				
	• Congestion		X			
	• Open space and agricultural land			X		
	• Energy glut				X	
	• Density preferences				X	
	• Downtown impacts					X
	• Equity					X

CONTINUATION OF SPRAWL PRINT— *HOUSING POLICY DEBATE* AND *THE URBAN LAWYER* SYMPOSIA

One of the leading housing journals, Fannie Mae's *Housing Policy and Debate*, and a respected legal journal, *The Urban Lawyer*, both published symposia on sprawl. Several of the individual articles bear mentioning, but an important first point is that both housing and urban legal journals have come to recognize that suburban sprawl is an important topic for inclusion in their journals. This is significant. Both of the journals have had special issues on homelessness, exclusionary zoning, affordable housing, the economies of cities, the spatial mismatch of the poor in cities and available jobs in suburbs, and so on. Neither journal strays far from housing and urban problems. Thus, implicit in the publication of the two special issues on sprawl is the notion that at least some component of sprawl impacts on housing issues and quality of life. Sprawl does not only potentially cause excess resources to be expended in providing public infrastructure or, similarly, contribute to the loss of special lands and habitats. Sprawl does not only chain users to a single source of transportation for access to residential and employment opportunities. Sprawl has significant social and quality-of-life effects as well.

> *Suburban sprawl is an important topic for inclusion in housing and urban legal journals.*

In *The Urban Lawyer* compilation of articles, Robert Freilich traced significant suburbanizing periods and methodically viewed their impact on central cities. Sprawl, he noted, is the force that distills the city's economic base, and it is orchestrated by suburban land-use controls that promote exclusion (Freilich

and Peshoff 1997). Charles Siemon pointed to the very limited number of techniques available to implement growth management and the difficulty of using them without encroaching upon property rights (Siemon 1997).

In the *Housing Policy Debate* articles, Robert Lang pointed to the voracity of sprawl and terms it suburbanization that was thriving and would not be shelved. Lang further commented that it was not productive to refer generically to nonresidential sprawl as "edge cities," a very limited phenomenon whose time may be past. To Lang, sprawl epitomizes current market preference, and its direction is clear—a continuing outward thrust from its urban core (Lang and Hornburg 1997). William Fischel of Dartmouth also proffered in the special issue of *Housing Policy Debate* that too much growth management could cause housing markets to diminish. According to Fischel, if you continue to castigate sprawl, you may turn around and not find any growth (Fischel 1997).

The upshot of this debate was that whereas at one time sprawl had only a solid line of inquiry detailing its costs; there was now a growing line of inquiry detailing its benefits.

> *If you continue to castigate sprawl, you may turn around and not find any growth.*

YET ANOTHER CONFERENCE: CONTROLLING SPRAWL IN THE LAND OF BARRY GOLDWATER

In the summer of 1998, in Phoenix, Arizona, the sprawl debate continued, this time in a conference sponsored by the Drachman Institute of the University of Arizona and the Fannie Mae Foundation.

By now, the agenda and faculty had predictable topics and representations: Chris Nelson (Georgia Institute of Technology), Gary Pivo (University of Arizona), and John Holtzclaw (Sierra Club) were there to plead the case against sprawl. Peter Gordon (University of Southern California), Genevieve Giuliano (University of Southern California), and Robert Lang (Fannie Mae) countered with the benefits and normalcy of market-driven development.

The polarized positions of forum speakers left little room for anything other than agreeing to disagree. Armed with data to bolster their cases, speakers clung steadfastly to their agendas. In the few instances where the data were similar, these data were interpreted as consistent with diametrically opposed positions. The sprawl-anti sprawl positions hardened.

While established players echoed now-familiar refrains, several new players entered the debate. The strongest of these favored the pro-sprawl position. Robert Bruegmann, an urban historian (University of Illinois), spent considerable time debunking the myth that sprawl development patterns are either uniquely American or associated with the growth of the automobile. According to Bruegmann, sprawl was spawned in the nineteenth century by the horse and buggy and later by streetcars. Suburban-type neighborhoods were actually found throughout Europe in the nineteenth century, having nothing to do with either American cultural norms or the appearance of its automobile. Bruegmann sees the new urbanists as adding little but design innovations to sprawled locations, while mouthing the platitudes of the new community advocates of the 1970s (Bruegmann 1998).

The negative side of the Portland, Oregon growth boundary was clearly articulated by Jerald Johnson, an economic consultant from that city. According to Johnson, the Portland urban growth boundary has succeeded in both increasing density and containing growth, but even more so, it has caused housing prices to rise. Johnson presented information indicating that housing prices in the city of Portland had increased at multiples of the level of density increases. Portland is becoming a victim of its own success. Housing demand and prices are high in a community noted for outward growth restraints and attention to quality of life (Johnson 1998).

Controlling free market development is a difficult sell in the Southwest, yet the importance of desert lands preservation was clearly articulated at this conference. In a state known for its creativity in siphoning off Colorado's water to reclaim the desert, there was recognition that development had to be contained and the more valuable parts of the desert inventoried and preserved.

RESPONDING TO THE CHARGE: REGIONAL COOPERATION AND REGIONAL/STATEWIDE PLANNING

A one-man crusade against factionalized government, because it creates sprawl, has been waged by Myron Orfield, state representative for the City of Minneapolis in the Minnesota House of Representatives. Orfield believes that the best way to control sprawl is to get local governments to cooperate in developing regional strategies, land-use policies, and regulatory mechanisms. In his book *Metropolitics*, Orfield composed an aggressive regional strategy that links tax base sharing to affordable housing provision, farmland protection, and urban/inner-suburb redevelopment

(Orfield 1997). Orfield is a realist, however, and acknowledges that regional governments are not growing nationally but regional cooperation is. Currently, there is increased willingness to share selected municipal service delivery systems; there is virtually no interest in forming new regional governments (Petersen 1996).

At another level, there is an ongoing effort to promote planning at state and regional levels and to coordinate planning with infrastructure provision. State plans and growth management initiatives have been successfully put in place for the entire states of Colorado, Florida, Georgia, Maine, Maryland, New Jersey, Oregon, Rhode Island, and Washington, and for specific areas (e.g., the Coastal Zone, etc.) in California and North Carolina (DeGrove 1990). The guru of statewide planning, who has followed it for most of his career and has testified as an expert witness in most state house hearings, is John DeGrove of Florida Atlantic University. DeGrove is also politically astute and realizes that even the most encompassing state plan or growth management act will either be voluntary for compliance by subunits of government, or non-punitive for non-compliance by these same subunits.

No discussion of growth management would be complete without discussing the work of Douglas Porter of the Growth Management Institute and Arthur C. Nelson of Georgia Tech. For a decade, Porter has been a focal point of the literature on growth management. Porter participated in Sam Seskin's "Transit and Urban Form" study (Parsons Brinckerhoff 1996d), Reid Ewing's *Best Development Practices* (Ewing 1995a), and the LUTRAQ study (Davis and Seskin 1997). From *State and Regional Initiatives for Managing Development* to

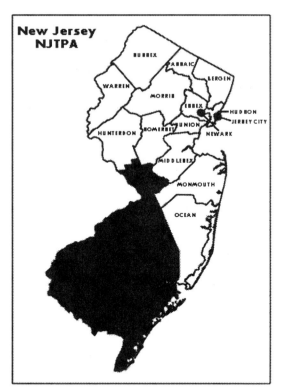

The New Jersey Transportation Planning Authority, Inc. (NJTPA) serves as a forum for cooperative decision-making in the 13-county, northern New Jersey regional area.
Source: New Jersey Institute of Technology and Rutgers University. *TELUS: Transportation Economic and Land Use System—State-of-the-Art Information System for the 21st Century* (April 1998).

Managing Growth in America's Communities (Porter 1992; Porter 1997), Porter has been involved in implementing managed growth alternatives. This includes model regulatory and programmatic techniques and pairing these specific techniques with a particular growth management issue or problem.

Nelson has similarly authored *The Regulated Landscape* (Knapp and Nelson 1992) and *Growth Management Principles and Practices* (Nelson and Duncan 1995) and has been a principal in multiple regional costs of growth studies. One of the most difficult tasks in land use is to effect meaningful regionwide growth management. Both Porter and Nelson have been involved with many regional growth management implementation efforts.

RESPONDING TO THE CHARGE: SUSTAINABLE DEVELOPMENT AND SMART GROWTH

As yet another response for a new direction in land use, the sustainable development and smart growth movements have emerged in the United States. The U.S. *sustainable development* movement is a direct outflow of the World Congress on Sustainable Development held in Rio de Janeiro in 1992. This philosophy of development reflects a desire to "develop today without compromising available resources for future generations." For the most part, overburdened U.S. communities in the South, Southwest, and West have justified growth management programs under the guise of compliance with this norm (Krizek and Power 1996).

Currently, twenty-one communities in the United States have adopted sustainable development ordinances that essentially limit growth to the degree that public facilities and services are in place to

> *This philosophy of development reflects a desire to "develop today without compromising available resources for future generations."*

accommodate this growth. Counties and regions are preparing development policies consistent with the goals of sustainability. In Florida, the Governor's Commission for a Sustainable South Florida in December 1997 enacted an energy conservation policy for the southern portion of the state. Among energy-conserving ideas, the Commission required utility companies to derive

measures other than expansion of the user base as appropriate indices of company performance. Further, this Commission is deciding how improved transportation, education, and employment opportunities either add to or possibly detract from the goals of sustainability.

Precursors to current sustainability regulations were the 1970s growth control efforts of California and Florida cities, and the concurrency requirement of the Florida Growth Management Act of 1985. In the United States, the President's Commission on Sustainable Development, the U.S. Department of Commerce, the U.S. Economic Development Administration (EDA), and the U.S. Environmental Protection Agency (EPA) have implemented sustainable development objectives that their funded projects must observe. For the most part, the emphasis on sustainable growth ensures that capital projects respect the environment of which they are a part and do not unnecessarily spur growth in locations where existing infrastructure cannot support the growth.

Smart growth was an initiative of the American Planning Association (APA), the U.S. Department of Housing and Urban Development (HUD), and the Henry M. Jackson Foundation on the one hand, and the National Resource Defense Council (NRDC) and the Surface Transportation Policy Project (STPP) on the other. The APA/HUD initiative called for an updating of land-use controls to make them more sensitive to the ongoing problems of lack of housing diversity, traffic congestion, and environmental degradation. The initiative also called for land-use controls that emphasized compact development to conserve resources; that limited development in undeveloped areas while encouraged investment in older central cities; that promoted social equity in the face of economic and spatial separation; and that were sensitive to the role of the private market and the need for simplicity and predictability in land use (APA 1997).

The NRDC/STPP Smart Growth effort consisted of a "Toolkit" for policymakers that attempts to promote growth that is "compact, walkable, and transit accessible" and will ultimately "compete better with sprawl in policy forums and in the marketplace." The Toolkit contains: (1) three policy reports on sprawl's environmental, economic, and social impacts; (2) research reports on sprawl-induced fiscal impacts and infrastructure requirements (including utilities and roads); and (3) a "Smart Growth Guidebook" (NRDC/STPP 1997).

Maryland adopted smart growth legislation at the state level in 1997. This legislation withholds, or at least sharply limits, any subsidies for new roads, sewers, or schools for political jurisdictions outside state-targeted smart growth areas (Maryland Office of Planning 1997). Rhode Island and Colorado have also adopted similar initiatives (ULI 1998).

The Smart Growth initiative calls for an updating of land-use controls to make them more sensitive to the ongoing problems of lack of housing diversity, traffic congestion, and environmental degradation.

Each of the above techniques has as its basis the better management of growth and more compact development for the purpose of resource conservation.

In a September 1998 speech in Chattanooga, Tennessee, Vice President Al Gore recommended a "renewed federal commitment to the policies of smart growth (Gore 1998).

A GROWING CONCERN— THE EQUITY ISSUE IN SUSTAINABLE DEVELOPMENT

One of the under-researched sides of the sustainable development movement is whether there is a dark side to the goal of not compromising the physical environment for future generations. At the regional level, this dark side might take the form of freezing the movement of minority and ethnic populations to the outer reaches of the metropolitan area by making inner cities and inner suburbs "more attractive" to all, and especially to these groups. Thus, exurban resources would be "sustained" by reduced access to these resources by those with the least economic wealth (Lake 1997). The central thesis of the equity issue is that better environments for some will mean worse environments for others. Even if there is a solution that improves conditions for some without hurting others, the benefits of better environments will still be unevenly distributed (Marcuse 1998).

New urbanists take a hit in this literature in that their new environments for the most part continue to promote new space consumption: suburban-bound, affluent housing seekers (few "new urban" environments accommodate the poor in urban areas). Resultantly, many of these new environments do little to improve the physical sustainability of urban areas.

In a four-day National Science Foundation (NSF) workshop at Rutgers University in the spring of 1998, Robert W. Lake of Rutgers and Susan O. Hanson of Clark University brought together environmental and first/third world researchers from the United States, Canada, and the United Kingdom to propose an integrated agenda for studying urban sustainability. This involved differentiating between such terms as *urban sustainability* (developed areas function to minimize the consumption of resources and manage equity) and *sustainable development* (an increment of land is developed to minimize the consumption of resources), and determining the effect of scale (local versus global) on both definitions and issues. The results of this workshop will be used by NSF to formulate a research program on urban sustainability.

The workshop focused on four issues, and a research agenda will be prepared regarding each. These are:
- economy–environment,
- local–global,
- urbanization as process,
- and governmental and institutional intervention.

SUMMARY

According to Robert G. Healy of the Nicholas School of the Environment at Duke University, the time may be right for an "alignment of the stars" on land use policy affecting sprawl. Healy points out the following signs: (1) the transit bike path and urban trail initiatives of the 1998 Transportation Equity Act for the 21st Century (TEA-21); (2) states moving to sustainable development, smart growth, or open space land acquisition initiatives; (3) citizens approving park and recreation bond issues of $1.37 billion in 1997; and (4) private industry initiatives such as the Silicon Valley Manufacturers Group's attempts to support public transportation, affordable housing, and environmental protection to ensure that sought-after workers will continue to be attracted to the San Francisco region (Healy 1998).

Healy notes that the situation is different from federal land use initiatives of the 1970s that failed to get out of Congress because:

1) There is agreement in the environment and development communities that growth is inevitable but must be carefully monitored;
2) Sprawl is understood as an outcome of current conditions, and positions—both positive and negative—have been taken about it; and
3) Federal, state, and local governments are moving in similar directions in land use, and their sprawl-abetting and sprawl-controlling roles are being carefully examined.

Sprawl is a type of growth in the United States that even the most unenlightened realize needs rethinking. Yet sprawl is so endemic to the culture of the United States that it is almost impossible to change. Americans like its outcome. It provides safe and economically hetero-geneous neighborhoods that are removed from the problems of the central city. In low-density, middle-class environments, life takes place with relative ease, and when residents wish to relocate, they typically leave in better financial condition—the result of almost certain housing appreciation in these locations.

The public services available to residents in sprawl locations are more than adequate—and their cost, until recently, has been relatively inexpensive. But costs are beginning to increase. Americans are looking, albeit halfheartedly, for an alternative to current development patterns. There is a general sentiment that communities and individuals specifically, and society as a whole, cannot continue to pay for the costs of sprawl. Costs have been held at a manageable level only because overall infrastructure is under-provided and developmental infrastruc-ture is not repaired adequately or replaced.

Over time, sprawl has garnered a long list of detractors, but increasingly observers are asking that the issues be discussed fairly. Most of the early literature criticized sprawl, but much of the recent literature asks for an analysis that deliberately isolates both the costs and benefits of sprawl. This is the emphasis of Section II of this study: to break down the phenomenon of sprawl into its basic alleged impacts, both positive and negative, and to detail deliberately the strengths and weaknesses of each impact statement with specific citations from the literature. Impacts are categorized in five groupings. These are:

1) public-private capital and operating costs;
2) transportation and travel costs;
3) land and natural habitat preservation;
4) quality of life; and
5) social issues.

The above categories obviously contain significant overlap. The objective is not to define mutually exclusive groups but to begin to point out and synthesize the major concerns of the literature.

SECTION

II

LITERATURE SYNTHESIS

The purpose of this section is to divide the literature on sprawl into major fields and subfields of impact in an effort to synthesize the most important studies in a systematic way.

This effort identifies what researchers on the subject have considered and debated; what data have been used and how the data have been analyzed; and where the gaps in the state of knowledge are.

The section is divided into two parts. The first is a synthesis of the literature as described above. The second is a summary of the literature, including: (1) topical coverage, databases, methodologies, and deficiencies; and (2) alleged negative and positive effects of sprawl. Thus, the synthesis of the literature in the first part of the section serves as a basis for statistical summaries of literature by type, database, methodology, and category of impact in the second part of the chapter. The statistical summary is one of the first of

its type. Although different literature citations could signal different emphases, it is believed that these citations and resulting emphases are correct in both direction and magnitude.

Analysis of the Literature

A search of the literature reveals that various commentators have attributed more than two dozen negative and more than one dozen positive impacts to sprawl. These impacts are set forth in Table 7. The list is not a scientific tax-onomy; it does not include all the alleged effects of sprawl. Rather, in the judgment of those reviewing the literature, it includes some of sprawl's most significant impacts. Further, not all of the allegations can be substantiated; nor are they of equal importance. However, this inventory presents a comprehensive set of allegations based on the literature assembled here.

TABLE 7

ALLEGED NEGATIVE AND POSITIVE IMPACTS OF SPRAWL

Substantive Concern	Alleged Negative Impacts	Alleged Positive Impacts
Public-Private Capital and Operating Costs	Higher infrastructure costs Higher public operating costs More expensive private residential and nonresidential development costs More adverse public fiscal impacts Higher aggregate land costs	Lower public operating costs Less expensive private residential and nonresidential development costs Fosters efficient development of "leapfrogged" areas
Transportation and Travel Costs	More vehicle miles traveled (VMT) Longer travel times More automobile trips Higher household transportation spending Less cost-efficient and effective transit Higher social costs of travel	Shorter commuting times Less congestion Lower governmental costs for transportation Automobiles most efficient mode of transportation
Land/Natural Habitat Preservation	Loss of agricultural land Reduced farmland productivity Reduced farmland viability (water constraints) Loss of fragile environmental lands Reduced regional open space	Enhanced personal and public open space
Quality of Life	Aesthetically displeasing Weakened sense of community Greater stress Higher energy consumption More air pollution Lessened historic preservation	Preference for low-density living Lower crime rates Enhanced value or reduced costs of public and private goods Fosters greater economic well-being
Social Issues	Fosters suburban exclusion Fosters spatial mismatch Fosters residential segregation Worsens city fiscal stress Worsens inner-city deterioration	Fosters localized land use decisions Enhances municipal diversity and choice

The allegations have been classified into five substantive categories:

1) public/private capital and operating costs;
2) transportation and travel costs;
3) land/natural habitat preservation;
4) quality of life; and
5) social issues.

Each of the alleged negative and positive impacts found in the literature search under these groupings uses a common presentation format as follows:

1) *Topic.* What is the specific subject matter of the alleged cost or benefit?
2) *Allegation/Basis.* Synopsis of the alleged cost or benefit and the basis or logic of the supposed effect.
3) *Literature Synthesis.* Pertinent studies on the allegation are cited, either supporting or rebutting it. The presentation of the literature synthesis is accomplished using both text and a matrix. The matrix distinguishes:
   a) Whether or not the alleged factual condition exists under conditions of sprawl (or more generally whether development pattern affects the item in question).
   b) Whether or not the alleged factual condition—if it exists—has been significantly linked to sprawl (i.e., to development pattern).

For example, one allegation is that "sprawl generates more vehicle miles of travel than higher-density forms of development." The literature synthesis first notes whether there is, in fact, agreement among observers who comment on this subject. (There appears to be general agreement in this regard.)

The next observation addresses the question of whether there is agreement in the literature that the presence of greater vehicle miles of travel in low-density settlements is significantly related to sprawl. (There is, again, general agreement on the second count.) For simplification, these judgments are shown in the form of a matrix:

	+2 General Agreement	+1 Some Agreement	0 No Clear Outcome	–2 Substantial Disagreement
Does this condition notably exist?	X			
Is it strongly linked to sprawl?	X			

An "x" is placed in the matrix cell that contains the appropriate answer to the question on that line.

The above matrix is not a rigorous measuring instrument. It could have been produced in a variety of ways. Even as currently structured, there are areas of disagreement among reviewers on how to "slot" an item—i.e., whether there is "general agreement" or "some agreement" in the literature that the situation as described indeed exists. For that matter, there are also areas of disagreement on how convincing the literature is in linking identified development impacts to sprawl.

CHAPTER

3

Literature Synthesis

PUBLIC/PRIVATE CAPITAL AND OPERATING COSTS

*P*ublic capital and operating costs of sprawl refers to the construction of roads, water and sewer infrastructure, and public buildings, as well as the annual expenditures necessary to maintain them. These costs are incurred both in small enclaves in remote locations of the metropolitan areas where population is growing and in central cities from which some of the population growth is drawn. *Private* capital and operating costs of sprawl refers to the construction and occupancy costs of private housing and commercial and industrial space. Most of the literature discusses how metropolitan location and density/form of development cause these costs to vary.

Engineering-per capita analyses examine the costs of different types of development by applying such factors as cost per linear foot of roadway, expense per gallon of treated sewage, and police expenditures per resident or per employee.

Alternative growth analyses are broader-scale analyses that employ a series of land use, transportation, and infrastructure models to examine the effects of two differing growth scenarios on development costs. These models begin with per capita averages but extend them to capture the effects of variables that affect costs. For instance, water consumption is related not only to population growth but also to housing type, density, and the demographics of occupation of structures; housing costs are related to population growth and influences such as density, housing type, and location of development.

Regression analyses apply multivariate statistical tools to further refine linkages between growth and public-private capital and operating costs.

A final group of studies includes a number of *retrospective case studies*. These view the effects of the overlay of regulations inherent in managed growth on the costs of local housing. Each of these types of research techniques is found in the literature that is discussed below.

Sprawl's Alleged Negative Impacts

Higher Infrastructure Costs
Higher Public Operating Costs
More Expensive Private Residential and
    Nonresidential Development Costs
More Adverse Public Fiscal Impacts
Higher Aggregate Land Costs

Sprawl's Alleged Positive Impacts

Lower Public Operating Costs
Less Expensive Private Residential and
    Nonresidential Development Costs
Fosters Efficient Development of
    "Leapfrogged Areas"

SPRAWL'S ALLEGED NEGATIVE IMPACTS

Higher Infrastructure Costs

Allegation/Basis

Infrastructure of a wide scope—e.g., local and regional roads, water and sewer systems, and schools—is more expensive under sprawl than under compact development. This allegation alludes to infrastructure that is primarily public (i.e., state, county, or local government roads; public utility systems; and public schools) and occasionally private (i.e., privately owned utility systems and subdivision-level roads that are not dedicated to the public sector).

The effect of sprawl on the cost of infrastructure allegedly occurs for several reasons. At sprawl's lower development densities, various components of infrastructure that are linearly related (i.e., sidewalks, curbs, subdivision-level roadways, and water and sewer mains) serve a lesser increment of development than these components of infrastructure would serve at higher levels of density.

The segregation of land uses associated with sprawl further increases infrastructure costs. Segregation of land uses by residential and nonresidential types often means that parallel infrastructure systems have to be provided to individual residential and nonresidential locations. Further, sprawl's leapfrog development, which locates growth away from existing development, does not capitalize on pockets of surplus infrastructure capacity that may already be present in and around existing development. Finally, fragmented governance, a seemingly natural accompaniment to sprawl, often leads to duplicative city halls, police stations, courts, fire houses, schools, water/sewer treatment facilities, and so on.

Literature Synthesis

As shown earlier in Table 1, *The Costs of Sprawl* (RERC 1974) found that capital costs per unit were higher in the "low-diversity sprawl" and "sprawl mix" neighborhood prototypes than they were in the "planned mix" or "high-density planned mix" prototypes. *The Costs of Sprawl* also found that capital expenses per unit were higher in detached housing (more pronounced under sprawl) than they were in attached housing (more pronounced under compact development). The first finding of *The Costs of Sprawl,* although criticized, has basically stood the test of time (Altshuler 1977); the second finding proved to be the undoing of the study (Windsor 1979).

Frank (1989) reanalyzed (using current cost numbers) several studies conducted between the 1950s and the 1980s that examined relationships between land use and infrastructure costs (including *The Costs of Sprawl).* Accounting for the limitations of *The Costs of Sprawl* study, he concluded that infrastructure costs were *highest* in situations of low density and for development located a considerable distance from centralized public services (conditions of sprawl). Infrastructure costs were *lowest* in situations of higher density and for development that was centrally and/or contiguously located (conditions of compact development). Duncan (1989) analyzed the infrastructure costs of multiple Florida residential and nonresidential developments with varying patterns of development. Costs were *higher* for those with *sprawl* characteristics than they were for those with compact development characteristics (see Table 8).

> *Infrastructure costs were highest in situations of low density and for development located a considerable distance from centralized public services.*

The longest-run modeling of infrastructure costs under different development scenarios was performed by Burchell (1992-1997) in New Jersey and in other locations. The infrastructure models applied by Burchell relate development density and housing type to the demand for local/state roads and water/sewer infrastructure. The studies found that the *amount of land consumed* for development was *directly* related to lane-miles of road required for two-lane (local) and four-lane (state) roads. Thus, *density* of development was found to be *inversely* related to lane-miles of local and state roads and their attendant infrastructure costs. Housing type and, to a lesser extent, density were related to the amount of water and sewer services consumed (measured in gallons) by development. Almost all of the difference in residential water usage related to whether or not occupants of residential and nonresidential facilities watered their lawns. Lawn watering takes place primarily in single-family detached residences and high-value research and

commercial headquarters uses. The difference in water usage among various commercial and industrial uses is also related to the service or product that is generated by the facility.

Larger and more significant than water/sewer usage are differences observed in water/sewer *infrastructure*, particularly as related to the number of feeder hookups from the trunk line that an individual land use requires. Higher density, the clustering of land uses, and attached housing and linked nonresidential uses all contribute to a reduced number of infrastructure feeder lines and reduced costs. A model sensitive to these differences, applied in New Jersey to alternative growth scenarios differentiated by sprawl-like versus more compact development patterns, showed the former's infrastructure costs to be considerably higher. The findings were basically similar in order of magnitude across most of the other locations analyzed by Burchell (Burchell and Listokin 1995a) (see earlier Tables 3 and 4). The findings were also comparable to those arrived at by Frank (1989) and Duncan (1989) in their studies (see Table 9).

Billions of dollars are spent annually on massive road infrastructure projects.
Source: U.S. Department of Housing and Urban Development.

TABLE 8

DUNCAN (1989)—FLORIDA GROWTH PATTERN STUDY: CAPITAL FACILITY COSTS UNDER SPRAWL VERSUS COMPACT DEVELOPMENT
(per dwelling unit; 1990 dollars)

Category of Capital Costs	Average of Case Studies under Sprawl Development[1]	Average of Case Studies under Compact Development[2]	Sprawl Versus Compact Development	
			Difference	*# / %*
Roads	$ 7,014	$ 2,784	(+) $4,230	60.3
Schools	6,079	5,625	(+) 454	7.4
Utilities	2,187	1,320	(+) 867	39.6
Other	661	672	(–) 11	1.7
TOTAL	$15,941	$10,401	(+) $5,540	36.7

Notes: 1.   Sprawl development as defined here include the following patterns of "urban form" analyzed by the Florida study: "scattered," "linear," and "satellite." The capital cost figures shown in this table are averages of the Florida case studies characterized by the scattered, linear, and satellite patterns (i.e., Kendall Drive, Tampa Palms, University Boulevard, and Cantonment).

   2.   Compact development as defined here includes the following patterns of "urban form" analyzed by the Florida study: "contiguous" and "compact." The capital cost figures shown in this table are averages of the Florida case studies characterized by the contiguous and compact patterns (i.e., Countryside, Downtown Orlando, and Southpoint.)

Source: Memorandum from James Duncan and Associates to Robert W. Burchell and David Listokin, May 8, 1990; and James Duncan et al., *The Search for Efficient Urban Growth Patterns.* Report prepared for the Governor's Task Force on Urban Growth Patterns and the Florida Department of Community Affairs (Tallahassee, July 1989).

Other relevant research indicating higher infrastructure costs under conditions of sprawl includes Archer (1973) and Duensing (1977). Base data on infrastructure and its costs not related to development pattern, such as average capital outlays per single-family house or costs per linear foot of roadway, are provided by FACIR (1986), Fodor (1995), Nelson (1988), Nichols et al. (1991), and California OP&R (1982).

Carson, in a study on the costs of growth in Oregon, uses these prior studies to estimate the costs of growth in that state. Again, these costs were not related to specific development patterns (Carson 1998).

The above body of research which reflects, in part, an approach dating back to *The Costs of Sprawl*, has been criticized on several counts by Altshuler (1977) and Altshuler and Gomez-Ibanez (1993) for the following reasons:

1) The higher infrastructure costs found in instances of lower versus higher density (i.e., sprawl versus compact development) are not meaningful because the housing units and their attendant scale found under the different development alternatives (i.e., more detached housing under sprawl and more attached housing under compact development) are not comparable.

2) The higher infrastructure costs attributed to sprawl due to its leapfrog patterns will essentially be neutralized as areas that were initially passed over are ultimately developed. The next wave of growth will capitalize on the infrastructure in place. Thus, the higher initial costs will be recouped. "The cost of sprawl is the cost of supplying some infrastructure in advance of its eventual need and will ultimately be lower the more rapidly that infill takes place" (Altshuler and Gomez-Ibanez 1993, 72-73).

3) The higher infrastructure costs (under sprawl) attributed to the distance of development from central facilities does not consider potential economies of scale that could be realized in regionalized, oversized trunk lines or similarly located water/sewer treatment plants (Altshuler and Gomez-Ibanez 1993, 73). In other words, the added "costs of distance" because feeder lines are longer under sprawl are not significant if the feeder lines are attached to regionally located (and oversized) trunk lines and water/sewer plants.

Holding aside the above criticisms, at least one researcher, Richard Peiser, found the cost difference in infrastructure between sprawl and compact development patterns to be quite slight.

Peiser (1984) examined infrastructure costs for new residential development in two Texas "prototype" communities— one planned, the other unplanned. The planned and unplanned developments were located on 7,500-acre sites in Houston. The planned community was designed to accommodate a population of about 80,000 residents in 26,500 dwelling units and a workforce of 72,000 in 24 million square feet of office and industrial space. The development was largely self-contained and near existing development in the form of a large center. The unplanned development was located in a primary growth corridor at the urban fringe, typical of Houston's sprawl pattern (100- to 500-acre subdivisions, strip malls, and shopping centers). The Houston development was designed to accommodate about the same number of residents (80,000) and workers (72,000) as the planned development. In Peiser's model, the difference in capital expenses for the planned and unplanned scenarios was about 5 percent in favor of the planned development. The finding in the Peiser study that contradicts other findings in the field was the inclusion in overall planned development infrastructure savings of higher road costs associated with planned as opposed to unplanned development (Table 10).

TABLE 9
RELATIVE INFRASTRUCTURE COSTS OF SPRAWL VERSUS
COMPACT DEVELOPMENT FROM THREE MAJOR STUDIES

Compact Development Costs as Percent of Sprawl Development Costs: Findings from Three Major Studies					
Infrastructure Cost Category	Sprawl Development	Duncan Study (1989)	Frank Study (1989)	Burchell Studies (1992-1997)	Compact Development Costs: Synthesis from Three Major Studies (in percent, relative to sprawl)
Roads (local)	100%	40%	73%	74-88%	≈75%
Schools	100%	93%	99%	97%	≈95%
Utilities	100%	60%	66%	86-93%	≈80%

TABLE 10
Infrastructure Costs for Planned and Unplanned Development
The Peiser Model

Infrastructure Costs Component	Planned Development (for 80,000 residents) ($ in millions)	Unplanned Development (for 80,000 residents) ($ in millions)
Roads	$10.0	$8.0
Sewer	4.3	4.7
Water	9.2	11.8
Drainage	16.3	17.4
TOTAL	$39.8	$41.9

Source: Richard B. Peiser 1984

In sum, although there is general agreement that development density is linked to infrastructure costs, there is less agreement about the interrelationship between sprawl (as a less carefully defined development form) and infrastructure costs.

Literature Synthesis Matrix

	+2 General Agreement	+1 Some Agreement	0 No Clear Outcome	−2 Substantial Disagreement
Does this condition notably exist?	X			
Is it strongly linked to sprawl?		X		

Higher Public Operating Costs

Allegation/Basis

Sprawl generates greater local/school district operating costs than higher density forms of development. This allegation relates to splintered public local and educational agencies that provide duplicative administrative and operating services.

Literature Synthesis

Operating costs are those costs that accrue on a day-to-day basis and form the annual expenses of local government. These costs include public workers' salaries and benefits; normal expenditures for supplies, repairs, and replacement items; and debt service for capital facilities purchased or contracted for at the local government level (municipal and county). The literature is rich with descriptions of variations in local (county and municipal) costs as a function of jurisdiction size, wealth, growth rate, and density of development.

Generally speaking, per capita *local* costs are "U" shaped as a function of population size—i.e., they are expensive for jurisdictions with populations under 2,500 and over 50,000, with points of most efficiency in those locations where the population is between 10,000 and 25,000. School district per pupil costs increase with school district size. Districts with more than 3,000 pupils spend 20 to 30 percent more per pupil than districts of fewer than 1,000 pupils; districts of 1,000-3,000 pupils spend 10 percent more than districts of fewer than 1,000 pupils (Sternlieb and Burchell 1977; Burchell and Listokin 1996).

Both local (municipal and county) public service costs per capita and school district public service costs per pupil also vary directly with the wealth of the jurisdiction. The citizens of wealthier jurisdictions demand greater qualities and quantities of local and educational public services and are willing to pay for them (Burchell and Listokin 1996).

Fiscal Impact Analysis—Overview

FISCAL IMPACT ANALYSIS
Comparison of the Public Service Costs and Revenues Related to Development

COSTS →
- Operating
- Statutory
- Capital

County
School District
Municipal

← **REVENUES**
- Property Tax
- Intergov. Transfers (State & Federal)
- Other Revenues (Permits, Fees, Fines)

NET DOLLARS
SURPLUS (+) or DEFICIT (-)

$$\frac{\text{DOLLARS SURPLUS OR DEFICIT}}{\text{EXISTING PROPERTY VALUATION}} = \text{CHANGE IN TAX RATE}$$

Fiscal impact analysis compares the public costs versus public revenues generated by growth.
Source: National Association of Home Builders.

Per capita local and school district costs also have been found to vary directly with density, and inversely with the growth rate of the jurisdiction. Generally speaking, the higher the density, the higher the per capita and per pupil costs; the faster the growth rate, the lower the per capita and per pupil costs (Ladd 1992). Two caveats are noteworthy, however. First, comparisons almost always are made between suburban- and urban-level densities and rarely between densities that reflect more- versus less-intense suburban development. Second, none of the analyses performed to date standardize the quality or quantity of public services delivered (Altshuler and Gomez-Ibanez 1993).

Thus, buried in the above findings is the fact that public services that are delivered in very large and dense local (municipal and county) jurisdictions are more complex and more individualized than those delivered in smaller, more sparsely populated jurisdictions. Foot patrol or

two-person automobile police patrol takes the place of one-person automobile police patrol; full-time paid fire department employees take the place of volunteers; and significant numbers of special education teachers must be hired instead of contracting out special education services. All these examples point to the service differences that complicate comparison of costs in more intensely populated versus less intensely populated jurisdictions.

Local government costs nationally average about $700 per capita; school district costs average about $7,000 per pupil (*Census of Governments* 1997). Of the former, about 60 percent goes toward salaries and benefits, 35 percent toward other expenses, and 5 percent toward capital purposes. Of the latter, 70 percent goes toward salary and benefits, 20 percent toward other expenses, and 10 percent toward capital purposes.

Compact or managed growth, the opposite of sprawl development, may encourage more regionalism in school systems and more sharing of non-police, local public resources. It also reduces the amount of local roads and water/sewer utility lines and hookups that are *constructed* and paid for by local debt service and *maintained* and paid for out of annual operating budgets.

Burchell, in his analysis of the growth alternatives in the *Impact Assessment of the New Jersey State Development and Redevelopment Plan*, found that combined municipal and school district operational costs could be reduced by 2 percent annually under planned (compact) growth as opposed to trend (sprawl) growth (Burchell 1992a). Although the percentage seems small, the savings occur annually; they are not a one-time windfall, and the savings could potentially be applied nationally to local budgets that sum to $175 billion per year, and to school district budgets that sum nationally to $500 billion annually.

Service differences complicate the comparison of costs in more intensely populated versus less intensely populated jurisdictions.

In similar type studies in the Delaware Estuary, and in the state of Michigan, municipal costs were found to be 5-6 percent less annually under compact growth scenarios than they were under sprawl development.

Basically equivalent findings were arrived at earlier by James Duncan in Florida (Duncan 1989). Conflicting findings have been suggested, but not empirically tested, by Altshuler and Gomez-Ibanez (1993) and Gordon and Richardson (1997a). Altshuler and Gomez-Ibanez indicate that the inability to control for the quality and quantity of services under comparison renders most of these studies at best "time and location bound" by who is providing the services, the types of public services, and when they are provided. At worst, most of the studies cannot be used to draw appropriate conclusions, given their inability to differentiate between levels of service provided (Altshuler and Gomez-Ibanez 1993).

Gordon and Richardson indicate that Burchell's prospective alternative development scenarios allow no flexibility for the trend (sprawl) scenario to improve over time and no flexibility for the plan (compact growth) scenario to be worse than envisioned due to the lack of full compliance with this alternative (Gordon and Richardson 1997a).

Literature Synthesis Matrix

	+2 General Agreement	+1 Some Agreement	0 No Clear Outcome	−2 Substantial Disagreement
Does this condition notably exist?		X		
Is it strongly linked to sprawl?			X	

More Expensive Private Residential and Nonresidential Development Costs

Allegation/Basis

Sprawl causes residential and nonresidential building and occupancy costs to rise due to the larger lot and structure sizes in locations where land is less expensive.

Literature Synthesis

Development costs include land and improvement costs, and are impacted by the scale of each. Spacious single-family dwellings on large lots are usually the most expensive types of housing; similarly, spread-out, low-rise non-residential development on large parcels of land are the most expensive type of commercial and/or industrial development. Both are low-density examples of their respective development forms.

To the degree that density increases in residential development and floor-area-ratios increase in nonresidential development, holding all other structure/environmental amenities constant, residential and nonresidential development costs should decrease. Similarly, to the degree that structures are smaller, holding all other structure/ environmental amenities constant, residential and nonresidential development costs will also be less.

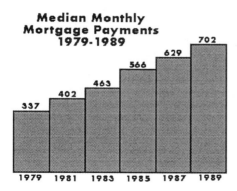

Median Monthly Mortgage Payments 1979-1989

Housing costs have been rising consistently during the past decade.
Source: U.S. Bureau of the Census.

Other factors that affect the costs of residential and nonresidential development include: 1) the amount of zoned land available for development, as determined by the local zoning ordinance; and 2) the time it takes development to engage and clear the permitting process (which is also largely determined by local land-use regulations). If land is limited or inappropriately zoned, residential and nonresidential development costs will rise. If government regulations are excessive, permitting time will increase, and the costs of development will also rise.

In the *Impact Assessment of the New Jersey State Development and Redevelopment Plan*, Burchell (1992a) found that if new development is contained around existing development and is also increased somewhat in terms of density and floor-area ratio, even with significant decreases in density to preserve lands at the periphery, overall residential and nonresidential development costs will be approximately 10 percent less per unit or per 1,000 square feet. Somewhat lesser savings (6-8%) emerged from studies conducted in Lexington, Kentucky (Burchell and Listokin 1994b), the Delaware Estuary (Burchell and Moskowitz 1995), and the state of Michigan (Burchell 1997a).

Other studies of residential development have produced essentially parallel findings on the effects of increased lot and structure size on housing costs. Downs (1973), Schafer (1975), Seidel (1978), and others have found that large-lot zoning and minimum building size increase the costs of new housing. This same type of analysis applied to nonresidential development—although not often looked at by researchers in the field—has produced similar findings (Burchell 1992-1997).

Some researchers have found that large-lot single-family zoning and minimum building sizes are associated with sprawl development. Smaller lot sizes (zero lot line) and different types and intensities of development (single-family attached and multifamily) are associated with compact development (Avin 1993; CH2M Hill 1993). Linking the above two sets of findings, the savings noted by housing type should then extend to these two polar development forms.

> *Large-lot single-family zoning and minimum building sizes are associated with sprawl development.*

One cannot assume, however, that housing preference changes will accompany development pattern shifts. In other words, if compact development is opted for, and denser forms of housing comprise this type of development, it cannot be assumed that market preferences will correspondingly shift and families previously occupying less dense types of housing under sprawl will opt for the more intense development forms under compact development. Further, if there is a crossover between housing types, one must carry the occupancy profile of the former to the new type of housing unit. Otherwise, false conclusions could be drawn with regard to development cost savings associated with the often smaller and less intensely occupied housing of compact development, and with the annual fiscal impact savings resulting from this development form. A critical error was discovered by Windsor in his review of *The Costs of Sprawl* (Windsor 1979). According to Windsor, *The Costs of Sprawl* study failed to account for the fact that the characteristics of new townhouse occupants who switched from detached single-family occupancy (if they could be assumed to do so) would be closer to the characteristics of occupants of the units that they had left than to the characteristics of the occupants of units similar to their new housing. This lack of realization led to the erroneous conclusion that compact development (containing a larger percentage of townhouses) was less expensive to service than sprawl development (containing a larger percentage of single-family homes), when the same households that occupied the former would likely be the ones moving to the latter.

Literature Synthesis Matrix

	+2 General Agreement	+1 Some Agreement	0 No Clear Outcome	−2 Substantial Disagreement
Does this condition notably exist?		X		
Is it strongly linked to sprawl?			X	

More Adverse Public Fiscal Impacts

Allegation/Basis

Sprawl generates more adverse fiscal impacts than compact development because public operating costs are significantly higher and residential uses and attendant revenues do not compensate for these costs. Further, fragmented governments compete for land uses according to these land uses' fiscal superiority. Most "good" (from a local fiscal impact perspective) economic uses have been withdrawn from central cities and transplanted to suburban jurisdictions. Since there are not enough "good" land uses to go around, only the wealthiest jurisdictions truly benefit fiscally from these land uses.

Literature Synthesis

In analyzing the impacts of land uses, the notion that some types of land uses are better fiscally than others has become widely accepted. Nonresidential land uses, for the most part, have been shown to be more profitable than residential uses, and most standard forms of residential land uses less profitable (see Table 11). Further, within the nonresidential and residential sectors, varying degrees of advantage and disadvantage exist. Some land uses produce more revenues than costs; if service levels are maintained at the same level after development, taxes could be decreased. The reverse is also true. In some cases, costs exceed revenues and, all things being equal, taxes might have to be increased (Burchell and Listokin 1994a).

Position on the fiscal impact hierarchy depends on the type of unit (the size or intensity of use) within both residential and nonresidential classifications. Fiscal position also depends on the service district in which impact is being viewed. Often, for instance, a small condominium or age-restricted housing unit may be break-even or have a slightly positive or negative impact on the municipal service jurisdiction, yet both may be very positive fiscal ratables in the school district. On the other hand, larger townhouses may be just below break-even in the school district yet significantly negative in the municipal jurisdiction.

Fiscal impacts and observed differences under sprawl versus compact growth are dependent upon two different influences from development patterns. The first is the ability of the development pattern to influence *type* of development. To the degree that dwelling type can be changed by compact development in sub-state settings, the demographics and, consequently, the public service costs of development will change. The second is the ability of the development pattern to influence the intensity of development and geographic spread of new neighborhoods. If compact development can provide tighter development patterns, infrastructure provision will be less. So too will the annual debt service on capital costs for roads, water/sewer lines, and so on, as well as the annual costs of maintenance associated with these new facilities. The location where development takes place is also an important factor. If located near existing development, excess service capacity may be drawn upon. If development is skipped over, public service infrastructure will almost always have to be provided at costs greater than if existing facilities were extended.

> **If development is located near existing development, excess service capacity may be drawn upon.**

Burchell's *Impact Assessment of the New Jersey State Development and Redevelopment Plan* (Burchell 1992a) employed a fiscal model to view the effects of trend versus planned development. The Rutgers fiscal impact model estimated the number of people, employees, and students that were generated under each of the development scenarios and projected their future costs and revenues to host public service jurisdictions. Although at the regional and state levels population and employment

projections did not vary between alternatives, at the municipal level the

The Fiscal Impacts of Growth

Unplanned Growth   Planned Growth

Unplanned growth is believed to result in greater costs to municipalities.
Source: Michigan Department of Natural Resources.

differences were significant. In the compact development case, urban communities with slack service capacity received more growth than rural areas with lesser amounts of public service infrastructure. The reduced infrastructure provision and potentially reduced annual maintenance on this infrastructure led to diminished fiscal impacts for this alternative.

Burchell's study in New Jersey found that by containing population and jobs in already developed areas and by creating or expanding centers in newly developing areas, the State Plan offers an annual $112 million [or 2 percent] fiscal advantage to municipalities. This advantage reflects the ability under plan to draw on usable excess operating capacity in already developed areas as well as efficiencies of service delivery. For instance, fewer lane-miles of local roads

TABLE 11

THE HIERARCHY OF LAND USES AND FISCAL IMPACTS

	RESEARCH OFFICE PARKS	
	OFFICE PARKS	
	INDUSTRIAL DEVELOPMENT	
	HIGH-RISE/GARDEN APARTMENTS *(STUDIO/1 BEDROOM)*	
	AGE-RESTRICTED HOUSING	
(+)	GARDEN CONDOMINIUMS *(1-2 BEDROOMS)*	
MUNICIPAL BREAK-EVEN	OPEN SPACE	
	RETAIL FACILITIES	
	TOWNHOUSES *(2-3 BEDROOMS)*	
	EXPENSIVE SINGLE-FAMILY HOMES *(3-4 BEDROOMS)*	(+) **SCHOOL DISTRICT BREAK-EVEN**
	TOWNHOUSES *(3-4 BEDROOMS)*	(–)
	INEXPENSIVE SINGLE-FAMILY HOMES *(3-4 BEDROOMS)*	
	GARDEN APARTMENTS *(3+ BEDROOMS)*	
	MOBILE HOMES *(UNRESTRICTED AS TO OCCUPANCY LOCALLY)*	

Note: The above list contains too many disclaimers to include here. Suffice it to say that specific fiscal impacts of a land use must always be viewed in the context of other land uses' impacts and within the fiscal parameters of the jurisdiction in which the land use is being developed.

Source: Burchell, Robert W., "Fiscal Impact Analysis: State of the Art and State of the Practice."

will have to be built under plan, thus saving municipal public works maintenance and debt service costs.

Public school districts will realize a $286 million [or 2 percent] annual financial advantage under the State Plan, again a reflection of drawing on usable excess public school operating capacity and other service and fiscal efficiencies realized due to the redirection of population under the plan alternative. Thus, municipal and school district providers of public services could be ahead fiscally by close to $400 million annually under plan compared to trend, while meeting similar population demands for public services.

Under trend, the state's school districts will have to provide 288,000 net pupil spaces to the year 2010 (365,000 gross need less 77,000 usable excess spaces); for plan, the net need is lower at 278,000 pupil spaces based on excess space available in central cities. Overall, if new space had to be built to accommodate net new students, costs of new school facilities would be approximately $5.3 billion under trend and $5.1 billion under plan. Thus, $200 million (or approximately 3 percent) is potentially saved due to more excess capacity in closer-in areas being drawn upon by plan as opposed to lesser amounts of excess capacity available to trend in suburban and rural areas (Burchell 1992a).

Literature Synthesis Matrix

	+2 General Agreement	+1 Some Agreement	0 No Clear Outcome	−2 Substantial Disagreement
Does this condition notably exist?		X		
Is it strongly linked to sprawl?		X		

Higher Aggregate Land Costs

Allegation/Basis

Total land costs of urban settlements are higher under sprawl. This occurs even though the average price of land per acre may be lower, because a given total population occupies more suburban land than under higher density urban forms of growth.

Literature Synthesis

Most of the modeling efforts to date that involve prospective development futures have found that alternatives to "status quo" development patterns (i.e., sprawl), consume less overall land than the sprawl development pattern does. In New Jersey, Lexington (Kentucky), the Delaware Estuary, and Michigan, alternatives to sprawl consumed 20-40 percent less overall land (Burchell 1992-1997). In the San Francisco Bay area, alternatives to sprawl consumed 10-25 percent less overall land than did sprawl (Landis 1995). Thus, land consumed under sprawl has almost always been shown to be more than land consumed under compact growth patterns.

Further, in the Burchell (1992-1997) studies, because densities were increased to design levels under compact growth, housing costs decreased as a result of the reduction in land costs associated with this alternative. In other words, in situations where there were no growth restrictions, housing costs were higher

> *Land consumed under sprawl has almost always been shown to be more than land consumed under compact growth patterns.*

under sprawl because land costs were higher. In the above four Burchell study locations, for example, housing costs under sprawl development were more due to the land component of these costs. This was true because under compact development, the majority of development taking place closer-in was subject to density increases of 10 to 30 percent. Total land costs of urban settlements have been found to be generally higher under the sprawl alternative.

(See also Land/Natural Habitat Preservation—Negative Impacts).

Literature Synthesis Matrix

	+2 General Agreement	+1 Some Agreement	0 No Clear Outcome	−2 Substantial Disagreement
Does this condition notably exist?		X		
Is it strongly linked to sprawl?		X		

SPRAWL'S ALLEGED POSITIVE IMPACTS

Lower Public Operating Costs

Allegation/Basis

Local and school district operating costs are lower under sprawl development because service demands and the costs of meeting these demands increase with higher densities (compact development).

Literature Synthesis

Gordon and Richardson express this argument, citing the research of Ladd:

> Ladd (1992) argued that except within a range of very low densities, per capita public service costs for traffic management, waste collection and disposal, and crime control, increase with higher densities. (Gordon and Richardson 1997a, 99)

Again, this is the type of research that has not standardized for the quality and quantity of public services delivered in jurisdictions of varying densities. Nonetheless, the above research indicates that without taking into account what services are delivered or who delivers them in a service district—operating costs, whatever they are comprised of, appear to be less in jurisdictions of low density than in jurisdictions of high density.

> *Operating costs appear to be less in jurisdictions of low density than in jurisdictions of high density.*

However, comparisons of operating costs are usually made between locations of rural-suburban (1 to 3 units per acre) density and those of urban density (16 to 30 or more units per acre). These studies may well be measuring the differences in range and complexity of public services delivered in densely populated urban areas versus rural-suburban areas, where the public services delivered are very limited and much simpler.

Literature Synthesis Matrix

	+2 General Agreement	+1 Some Agreement	0 No Clear Outcome	−2 Substantial Disagreement
Does this condition notably exist?		X		
Is it strongly linked to sprawl?			X	

Less Expensive Private Residential and Nonresidential Development Costs

Allegation/Basis

Sprawl has lower housing costs because it does not limit the amount of development. Many managed approaches to growth seek also to control growth. Various forms of growth control limit housing production and drive up the costs of housing.

Literature Synthesis

Does the overlay of regulations inherent in managed growth drive up the cost of housing? A number of studies reveal that in the immediate area where growth restrictions exist, housing prices increase (Fischel 1990). Schwartz, Hansen, and Green (1981) followed the effects over time of the Petaluma (California) Plan which severely limited building permits, favoring dwellings with costly design features and developer-provided amenities and services to the community. Using a statistical (i.e., hedonic) pricing technique, the authors compared the price of a standard bundle of housing characteristics to the corresponding price in nearby Santa Rosa, which had not adopted growth controls during the period. The authors found that after several years, Petaluma's housing prices had risen 8 percent above those of Santa Rosa.

Schwartz, Zorn, and Hansen (1989) did a similar study of the growth controls in Davis, California, comparing house prices in Davis to those in a sample of other Sacramento suburbs. They found that growth controls caused house prices in Davis to be nine percent higher in 1980 than they would have been without them.

In Petaluma (Schwartz, Hansen, and Green 1981) and in Davis (Schwartz, Zorn, and Hansen 1989), the effects on the housing stock affordable to low- and moderate-income households relative to control areas were also monitored. In Petaluma, the authors found that the percentage of the housing stock that was affordable to low- and moderate-income households dropped significantly below that of a control group (Fischel 1990).

In Davis, on the other hand, growth controls required those who received building permits to construct some units earmarked for low-income occupants. Thus, the limited growth that did occur in Davis contained both low-income and high-income housing. According to Fischel (1990), however, an unanticipated offset to this apparent success occurred: the existing housing in Davis increased not only in price but in quality. Fischel's interpretation of this outcome was that older housing was filtering up rather than down.

Katz and Rosen (1987) analyzed 1,600 sales transactions of single-family houses during 1979 in 64 communities in the San Francisco Bay Area. Of these transactions, 179 involved houses located in communities where a building permit moratorium or binding rationing system had been recently, or was currently, in effect. According to Fischel (1990), this study is particularly valuable since, unlike the other California studies, it did not focus on just a single community. The authors found that the price of houses sold in the growth-controlled communities was *higher* than the price of houses sold in other communities. Where growth is *controlled* as opposed to *managed*, housing costs are higher.

Literature Synthesis Matrix

	+2 General Agreement	+1 Some Agreement	0 No Clear Outcome	−2 Substantial Disagreement
Does this condition notably exist?		X		
Is it strongly linked to sprawl?		X		

Fosters Efficient Development of "Leapfrogged" Areas

Allegation/Basis

Sprawl fosters efficient infill development. Sprawl permits appropriate, relatively high-density development of still vacant close-in sites late in the development period of a metropolitan area, without having either to demolish existing improvements on those sites at great cost, or to expend public funds buying such sites in advance and reserving them for later development. The "leapfrogging" aspect of sprawl leaves sizable tracts of land vacant and undeveloped. Parcels remain vacant long after the wave of current growth has passed them by. These parcels can be developed later as "infill" sites at relatively high densities, which are more appropriate to their more central locations. This process of deferred development is more efficient than first developing all peripheral land at low densities, and then tearing down the existing structures when the development market, reflecting the preferences of structure occupants, shifts to higher densities.

Literature Synthesis

This allegation is considered by Peiser (1984) and is also discussed by Altshuler and Gomez-Ibanez (1993). But it is often a highly neglected component of the analysis of infrastructure costs related to sprawl. Just as there are those who call for full costing methods to expand and

account for the costs of sprawl to the private sector and to society as a whole, there are also those who believe that the secondary benefits of sprawl (i.e., its lagged infill economies) must be adequately tabulated in any accounting scheme related to development alternatives.

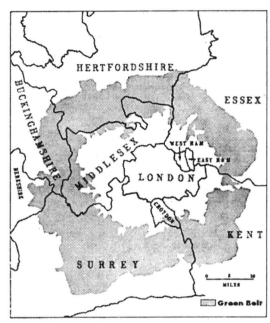

Greenbelts provide open space for recreational uses and for future infill development.
Source: Cartographic Laboratory of the University of Wisconsin.

In an accounting system, the land areas that are skipped over and initially not used become relatively inexpensive to access and service secondarily. Further, the potential for using these skipped-over lands as inner-ring open space also becomes apparent. Only Altshuler and Gomez-Ibanez (1993) have begun to address these issues.

Literature Synthesis Matrix

	+2 General Agreement	+1 Some Agreement	0 No Clear Outcome	−2 Substantial Disagreement
Does this condition notably exist?			X	
Is it strongly linked to sprawl?			X	

CHAPTER

4

Literature Synthesis

TRANSPORTATION AND TRAVEL COSTS

Transportation is a discipline unto itself with a vast number of monographs, journals, and other publications devoted to it. The body of literature considered here includes key transportation studies relevant to the current investigation of the costs and benefits of sprawl. Many of these studies are not about sprawl per se but contain information on changes in travel over time, which are then associated with coterminous development (e.g., decentralized suburbanization) or characteristics linked to coterminous development (e.g., low density and segregation of land uses), which in turn are related to travel criteria. Costs of travel are considered as well.

The changes in travel studies report on such characteristics as the number of total trips, the number of trips by type (e.g., work versus nonwork), and commutation distances and time.

In addition to the study and deciphering of gross travel statistics, the transportation literature looks at characteristics that both define development type and affect travel behavior. Here again, the characteristic most studied is density, particularly how density affects trip length, mode choice, and other transportation decisions.

To a much lesser extent, land-use characteristics other than density are examined with respect to their travel influences. Some studies consider the effect of leapfrog development on commuting times; other studies view the effect of integration of land uses on walking for internal trips and enhanced transit use for external trips.

A final component of the transportation literature establishes baseline figures on the costs of travel. Numerous site-specific investigations concentrate on user, governmental, and societal costs of travel and how they vary by travel mode (e.g., auto, transit, walking); type of trip (e.g., work versus shopping); time (off-peak versus at-peak hours); the physical environment (higher- versus lower-density); and other factors (e.g., single-occupancy vehicle [SOV] versus high-occupancy vehicle [HOV] trips).

Sprawl's Alleged Negative Impacts

More Vehicle Miles Traveled (VMT)
Longer Travel Times
More Automobile Trips
Higher Household Transportation
*   Spending*
Less Cost-Efficient and Effective Transit
Higher Social Costs of Travel

Sprawl's Alleged Positive Impacts

Shorter Commuting Times
Less Congestion
Lower Governmental Costs for
*   Transportation*
Automobiles Most Efficient Mode of
*   Transportation*

SPRAWL'S ALLEGED NEGATIVE IMPACTS

More Vehicle Miles Traveled (VMT)

Allegation/Basis

Sprawl generates more total miles of vehicle travel than more compact forms of development. Sprawl generates more travel because the places where people live, work, shop, and play are spread over a larger total area. Vehicle miles of travel also increase because sprawl developments are designed so that virtually the only way to make most trips is by automobile.

Literature Synthesis

There is no question that vehicle miles of travel are increasing. Vincent et al. (1994) found that on an annual basis, person miles of travel increased by 19 percent between 1983 and 1990, and vehicle miles of travel (VMT) increased at the even faster rate of 37 percent. Ray et al.

(1994) found that the number and length of vehicle trips were increasing at an accelerating rate between 1977 and 1990.

> *Sprawl, which creates the longer travel distances and increases dependence on the automobile, is a major source of increased vehicle use.*

The question is what proportion of the growth in VMT is due to sprawl versus other factors, such as a higher rate of women participating in the workforce, the baby boom generation being at the peak driving years, or rising incomes that allow every licensed driver in a household to own a car. Three factors have contributed about equally to the growth in VMT—changing demographics, growing dependence on the automobile, and longer travel distances (Dunphy et al. 1997). Thus, sprawl, which creates the longer travel distances and increases dependence on the automobile, is a major source of increased vehicle use.

Numerous studies have linked lower vehicle miles of travel with more compact mixed-use developments. In a 1990 analysis of the San Francisco Bay area and a 1994 study of 28 California communities, Holtzclaw found that residents of the denser neighborhoods drove fewer miles per year. In a second study, where Holtzclaw (1994) controlled for the levels of transit service and vehicle ownership, a doubling of residential densities was associated with 16 percent fewer vehicle miles of travel. Other research by Harvey (1990), 1000 Friends of Oregon (1996), and the Urban Land Institute (Dunphy et al. 1997) confirm that as densities increase, per capita vehicle miles of travel decline.

The interspersing of residents, employment, shopping, and other functions can also reduce VMT, by allowing shorter trips and the use of non-vehicle modes. An empirical analysis by Frank and Pivo (1994) in the Puget Sound region and a simulation of the Trenton region undertaken in central New Jersey by the Middlesex, Somerset, Mercer Regional Council (1990) show that greater land-use mixes (with a higher jobs-housing balance) decrease trip distances and automobile mode shares.

Commute Profile				
	1983	1990	1995	'83 - '95 % Change
Average Work Trip Length (Miles)	8.5	10.6	11.6	36.5
Average Work Travel Time (Minutes)	18.2	19.7	20.7	13.7
Average Work Trip Speed (MPH)	28	32.3	33.6	20

The daily commute length increased 36.5 percent from 1983 to 1995; the trend is continuing.
Source: Federal Highway Administration.

The segregation of uses and a leapfrog development pattern were both linked to increased travel in a recent Cervero (Cervero and Wu 1996) study of dispersed subcenters in the San Francisco Bay area. Between 1980 and 1990, the workers at these subcenters experienced a 23 percent increase in average commuting VMT. Cervero attributes 80 percent of the increase to longer distances between home and work.

Simulations of alternate growth patterns have also shown that sprawl development produces more VMT than more compact development. A simulation by Metro (1994) of growth in the Portland, Oregon metropolitan area compared a "Growing Out" scenario with new development continuing at current types and densities with a "Growing Up" scenario that kept all growth within the existing urban growth boundary by reducing lot sizes

and introducing more multifamily housing. Average daily VMT was estimated to be 15 percent higher in the "Growing Out" scenario than in "Growing Up."

Gordon and Richardson (1997a), however, do not agree that VMT would be reduced by more compact development. They contend that market forces embodied in sprawl may ultimately result in *less* VMT as households and businesses locate near one another. They further argue, based on Crane's (1996) theoretical analysis of travel on the grid street networks of neo-traditional development, that this neo-traditional, or compact, type of development may produce more VMT due to the ease of automobile travel. But Ewing (1997) points out that the demand for activities is relatively inelastic and residents of more compact, neo-traditional developments are unlikely to drive more simply because of better street design. A preponderance of evidence contradicts Gordon and Richardson's claim that sprawl is not a factor contributing to increased VMT.

Market forces embodied in sprawl may ultimately result in less VMT as households and businesses locate near one another.

Literature Synthesis Matrix

	+2 General Agreement	+1 Some Agreement	0 No Clear Outcome	−2 Substantial Disagreement
Does this condition notably exist?	X			
Is it strongly linked to sprawl?	X			

Longer Travel Times

Allegation/Basis

Sprawl requires that more time be spent traveling than do more compact forms of development. The greater dispersion of activities in sprawl makes it necessary to spend more time traveling between activities than in more compact, mixed-use areas where trips are shorter and can serve multiple purposes. Workers in mixed-use settings can eat lunch or run errands at noon without using significant amounts of time for travel. Residents of compact neighborhoods can meet many of their needs at community shopping centers.

Literature Synthesis

The evidence is mixed on the effects of sprawl on total travel times. Ewing (1995c) has shown that total travel time varies with regional accessibility. His Florida study found that residents of areas with high levels of access to a mix of uses including jobs, schools, shopping, and other services spent up to 40 minutes less per day in vehicular travel than residents in less accessible neighborhoods. Time was saved by linking trips into tours and by making shorter trips. Dunphy et al. (1997), on the other hand, also report that according to surveys, people are willing to accept longer travel times to work and shopping in order to have the quality of housing they desire. Thus, the segregation of land uses and less expensive land at the periphery—two characteristics of sprawl—can increase travel times, whereas mixed-use developments, wherever they are located, appear to decrease travel times.

Others contend that travel times do not increase with sprawl because more trips are made by the automobile, the fastest mode of travel, and people and activities adjust over time to keep travel times relatively constant (Gordon and Richardson 1997a). A study by the European Conference of Ministers of Transport (1994) found that people in four cities with very different urban structures (Wismar, West Germany; Delft, The Netherlands; Zurich, Switzerland; and Perth, Australia) made about the same number of trips and spent about the same amount of time traveling even though modal shares differed significantly. The average time spent traveling ranged only from 62 to 69 minutes.

Purvis (1994) reported that travel time budgets remained fairly constant in the San Francisco Bay Area between 1960 and 1990. In the latest survey, the number of trips per person declined, but travel times remained constant because of the longer duration of trips. Purvis says the results are comparable to those in other metropolitan areas and consistent with the travel time budget studies of the 1970s and 1980s.

> *Residents of areas with high levels of access to a mix of uses including jobs, schools, shopping, and other services spent 40 minutes less per day in vehicular travel than residents of the least accessible neighborhoods.*

Overall, the evidence is not clear about the relationship between sprawl and households' total travel times. On the one hand, some metropolitan-wide data suggest that people have fairly constant travel time budgets. On the other hand, a finer level of analysis indicates that the outward expansion of urban areas and the segregation of uses has boosted the amount of time some households spend traveling to their daily activities.

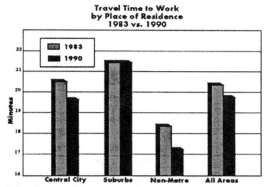

Travel Time to Work by Place of Residence 1983 vs. 1990

Suburban residents spend more time commuting to work than central city residents.
Source: Federal Highway Administration.

(See also Positive Impacts—Shorter Commuting Times, for a discussion of the mixed evidence on work trip duration under sprawl.)

Literature Synthesis Matrix

	+2 General Agreement	+1 Some Agreement	0 No Clear Outcome	-2 Substantial Disagreement
Does this condition notably exist?			X	
Is it strongly linked to sprawl?			X	

More Automobile Trips

Allegation/Basis

A greater share of trips are made by car and a lesser share by transit, walking, and bicycling in sprawled development than in more compact development. This assertion is almost true by definition since one of the defining characteristics of sprawl is that motor vehicles are the dominant mode of transportation. Sprawl, with its low densities and spatial segregation of uses, requires that virtually all trips be made by automobile, whereas residents of areas with higher densities and a greater mix of uses have the option of riding transit, biking, or walking.

Literature Synthesis

An extensive literature shows that when development is more compact and land uses are mixed, transit and walking mode shares rise and vehicle mode shares decline. Research for TCRP H-1 (Parsons Brinckerhoff 1996c) shows that residents of denser, more mixed-use neighborhoods were more likely to go by transit or to walk for all types of trips. Another part of this project showed that higher residential densities in rail corridors and higher employment densities in the CBDs increase rail use (Parsons Brinckerhoff 1996b).

Empirical research by Cervero (1986, 1989), Cervero and Gorham (1995), Dunphy and Fisher (1994), Frank and Pivo (1994), Handy (1992, 1995), Kenworthy and Newman (1993), and Kitamura et al. (1994) confirm that higher density, more pedestrian-friendly neighborhoods and employment centers support travel by non-automotive modes. Kenworthy and Newman compared the rates of growth in central, inner, and outer neighborhoods in the United States (where those with higher incomes move to the edge) and Australia (where those with lower incomes move to the edge) and found that automobile travel was growing rapidly in the outer areas of cities in both counties. Their conclusion:

> It is clear that the level of automobile use is not simply a matter of how wealthy people are, but is also heavily dependent on the structure of the city and whether transport options are available other than the automobile. Thus as cities become more dispersed and lower in density towards the edges, the level of compulsory automobile use rises markedly, regardless of income level.
> (Kenworthy and Newman 1993, 12)

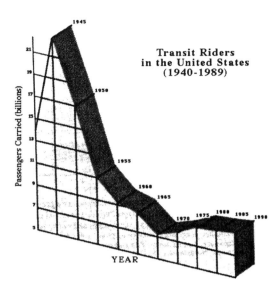

Transit riders
in the United States
(1940-1989)

Transit ridership fell dramatically after World War II. The automobile accounts for the decline.
Source: American Public Transit Association, *Transit Fact Book 1990.*

Even Gordon and Richardson (1997a, 99) agree that "...the spreading out of cities reduces markets for conventional public transit (especially fixed rail, which is spatially inflexible and usually oriented to downtown)..."

> **Residents of denser, mixed-use neighborhoods were more likely to use transit or to walk for all types of trips.**

Literature Synthesis Matrix

	+2 General Agreement	+1 Some Agreement	0 No Clear Outcome	−2 Substantial Disagreement
Does this condition notably exist?	X			
Is it strongly linked to sprawl?	X			

Higher Household Transportation Spending

Allegation/Basis

Households living in sprawl developments must spend higher fractions of their incomes for transportation. Households under sprawl spend more for transportation than those in higher density forms of development because the residents of sprawl areas travel greater distances and make more of their trips in automobiles.

Literature Synthesis

That household spending on transportation is higher under sprawl would appear to be a logical consequence of the greater miles of travel and more travel by the automobile. However, only a few studies directly address the issue of household costs for transportation under different development scenarios.

Holtzclaw (1994) concludes that residents of denser, more transit-friendly neighborhoods are able to spend a smaller share of their budgets on travel due to greater use of transit and walking. The impact is especially great if households can reduce their automobile ownership levels because of the viability of other modes of travel. However, it is unclear whether the lower transportation costs are a direct or indirect result of sprawl, due to the types of people who choose to live in the denser, more transit-friendly neighborhoods.

> **Residents of denser, more transit-friendly neighborhoods are able to spend a smaller share of their budgets on travel due to greater use of transit and walking.**

The current literature suggests that sprawl has higher transportation costs, but more studies are needed to substantiate this conclusion.

Literature Synthesis Matrix

	+2 General Agreement	+1 Some Agreement	0 No Clear Outcome	−2 Substantial Disagreement
Does this condition notably exist?			X	
Is it strongly linked to sprawl?			X	

Less Cost-Efficient and Effective Transit

Allegation/Basis

Sprawl reduces the cost-efficiency and effectiveness of transit service compared to more compact development. Transit service is not as efficient or effective in sprawl development because of the dispersion of origins and destinations. The higher ridership generated by denser developments improves the cost-efficiency (cost per vehicle mile) and effectiveness (passenger-miles per line-mile) of transit.

Literature Synthesis

Research for TCRP H-1 has shown that the use of light rail and commuter rail increases when more people live in the rail corridor and work in the central business district. Because density boosts ridership, the cost per vehicle mile declines and the passenger-miles per line-mile of transit increase. For example, consider a ten-mile light rail line serving a corridor with a medium residential density gradient and 100,000 employees in the CBD. If the residential density gradient were to increase by 1 to 4 persons per acre throughout the length of the line, the cost per vehicle mile would decline by about 5 percent and the effectiveness would increase by about 26 percent. Adding 50,000 jobs to the CBD and increasing employment densities would lower costs per vehicle mile by about 9 percent and increase effectiveness

by 44 percent (Parsons Brinckerhoff 1996b, 1996d).

> *Transit service is not as efficient or effective in sprawl development because of the dispersion of origins and destinations.*

As the section in this report on More Automobile Trips also shows, higher densities support higher bus use. Pushkarev and Zupan (1977) and a number of other authors have identified thresholds at which transit use substantially increases. Frank and Pivo (1994), using data from the Puget Sound region, identify thresholds of 50 to 70 employees and 9 to 13 persons per gross acre for work trips and 75 employees and 18 persons per gross acre for shopping trips. Due to the increase in ridership at these densities, the cost-efficiency and effectiveness of transit service increases.

Most suburbs do not have the densities necessary to make effective use of mass transit.
Source: Courtesy CUPR Press.

Of course, development patterns are not the only factor affecting the efficiency and effectiveness of transit. The level of transit use is also related to the quality of the transit service and the ease of access (i.e., walking environment, park-and-ride facilities). Costs are also related to wages and other aspects of transit operations.

Literature Synthesis Matrix

	+2 General Agreement	+1 Some Agreement	0 No Clear Outcome	−2 Substantial Disagreement
Does this condition notably exist?	X			
Is it strongly linked to sprawl?		X		

Higher Social Costs of Travel

Allegation/Basis

Travel in sprawl development generates higher social costs than in more compact development. Social costs include air and water pollution, waste, barrier effects, noise, and the costs of parking and accidents that are not paid by the transportation user. Because more travel is by automobile in sprawled development, these cost rise.

Literature Synthesis

Various studies of the full costs of travel have found that social costs are highest per passenger mile for single-occupant vehicles, the dominant mode of travel under sprawl conditions. Studies using similar methods and location-specific data for Boulder, Colorado; Boston, Massachusetts; and Portland, Maine report that 16 to 17 percent of the costs per passenger mile for single-occupant vehicles (SOV) are social costs, whereas only 1 to 7 percent of the total costs for transit use and a negligible share of the costs for walking and bicycling are social costs (Apogee Research 1994; Parsons Brinckerhoff 1996a). Todd Litman's (1995) study estimating the national costs of travel reports that social costs represent a higher share of total costs due to different assumptions. He finds that 43 percent of the cost per passenger mile by SOV is a societal cost compared to 6 percent of the cost per passenger mile by transit.

Previous studies examined the social costs of travel from both a trip and a national perspective. The issue of whether the total costs of travel vary with the type of development, however, has not been studied systematically.

> *Various studies of the full cost of travel have found that social costs are highest per passenger mile for the single-occupant vehicle, the dominant mode of travel under sprawl conditions.*

Literature Synthesis Matrix

	+2 General Agreement	+1 Some Agreement	0 No Clear Outcome	−2 Substantial Disagreement
Does this condition notably exist?		X		
Is it strongly linked to sprawl?		X		

SPRAWL'S ALLEGED POSITIVE IMPACTS

Shorter Commuting Times

Allegation/Basis

Commuting times are reduced in sprawl development, compared to those in more dense settings. The suburban-to-suburban commute, which characterizes sprawl, is shorter in time, if not in distance, than commuter trips between suburbs and central cities, due to higher speeds of travel. In addition, more trips are made by automobile, especially the single-occupant vehicle, the fastest and most direct mode of travel.

Literature Synthesis

Gordon and Richardson (1997a) argue that businesses follow people to the suburbs, thereby making trips to work shorter as measured in time, not in distance. The correction is not instantaneous, but over time, businesses move to suburban locations near workers, creating a new equilibrium with shorter work times. Although some people have longer trips, especially during the adjustment period, on average, commuting times have not increased due to sprawl.

Pisarski (1992a) found that average work trip times in the U.S. increased by only 40 seconds in the 1980s. Gordon, Richardson, and Jun (1991) and Levinson and Kumar (1994) found that work travel times remained stable over time in the core counties of the 20 largest metropolitan areas and in the Washington, D.C., metropolitan area, respectively. Dueker et al. (1983), Zimmer (1985), Gordon, Kumar, and Richardson (1989), and Dubin (1991) all found that the suburbanization of jobs has shortened commuting times, although not necessarily distances.

> **The suburbanization of jobs has shortened commuting times, although not necessarily distances.**

But, there is contrary evidence. Vincent et al. (1994) analyzed the National Personal Transportation Survey Data for 1990 and found that commute times for residents of urbanized areas outside of central cities were longer than those for central city residents. The average peak period commute length for suburbanites was 21.6 minutes, compared to 18.9 minutes for central city residents. Likewise, the average length of off-peak commutes for suburbanites was 19.7 minutes compared to 17.2 minutes for central city residents. Pisarski (1992a) further reports that suburbanites had much greater increases in commute times between 1980 and 1990 than central city residents. The average travel time for suburban residents who commuted either to suburban or

central city locations increased by 14 percent over the period, while the average commute time for a central city resident increased by only 5 to 7 percent.

The extreme outward extension of urban areas may have also increased travel times. Davis (1993) found that the average commute of exurbanites in the Portland metropolitan area was seven minutes longer than that of suburbanites, holding constant occupations, household structure, and other factors affecting commuting times.

> **Commute times for residents of urbanized areas outside of central cities were longer than those of central city residents.**

Thus, researchers have drawn substantially different conclusions, sometimes utilizing the same data sets. Most of their studies addressed issues other than the effects of sprawl versus compact development on commuting time, however, leaving the results unclear.

Literature Synthesis Matrix

	+2 General Agreement	+1 Some Agreement	0 No Clear Outcome	-2 Substantial Disagreement
Does this condition notably exist?			X	
Is it strongly linked to sprawl?			X	

Less Congestion

Allegation/Basis

Sprawl reduces congestion by spreading trips out over more routes. Sprawl has improved travel by spreading out origins and destinations and utilizing the capacity of suburban roads and highways. The shift to suburban destinations has relieved traffic on the routes to the city center.

Literature Synthesis

Gordon and Richardson (1994c) claim that suburbanization has reduced congestion, citing the lack of growth in travel times. Specifically, they say:

> [S]uburbanization has been the dominant and successful mechanism for reducing congestion. It has shifted road and highway demand to less congested routes and away from core areas. All of the available recent data from national surveys on self-reported trip lengths and/or durations corroborate this view. (Gordon and Richardson 1994c, 1)

They argue that, over time, people and firms make adjustments in their locations to keep travel times from growing. The spreading out of urban areas has kept congestion from overwhelming urban areas, as some have predicted.

Cervero (1986, 1989), however, found that congestion has followed jobs to the suburbs. Since jobs have moved to areas where there is little, if any, transit service, people have no choice but to drive to these jobs. This increase in traffic has used up all the available highway capacity near suburban activity centers, creating congestion in these areas. An index developed by the Texas Transportation Institute indicates that congestion (defined as the ratio of freeway and arterial VMT to capacity) worsened in 47 out of 50 major U.S. cities between 1982 and 1991. Two of the cities where congestion decreased, Houston and Phoenix, made sizable investments in highway capacity during the time period. This research points to a factor other than development pattern which contributes to congestion, namely, investment in transportation. In most areas, highway capacity additions have not kept pace with the growth in traffic, due to lack of funds, opposition to road

building, environmental regulations, and other factors (Dunphy et al. 1997).

Suburban office parks usually front wider, less congested roadways than their central city counterparts.
Source: Courtesy CUPR Press.

Congestion worsened in 47 out of 50 major cities between 1982 and 1991.

Simulations also show that in addition to the pattern of development, roadway networks and capacity, congestion levels depend upon opportunities to use alternative transportation modes. The LUTRAQ analysis of alternate development patterns for a suburban county in the Portland, Oregon metropolitan area, for example, forecast the least congestion for a pattern of sprawled development with substantial investments in additional highway capacity and transportation demand reduction measures, such as pricing. Compact transit-oriented development focused on an expanded transit system, using the same transportation demand measures, had the second lowest levels of congestion. Building highways in sprawl development without controlling travel demand had higher levels of congestion than either of these two alternatives (1000 Friends of Oregon 1996).

Because researchers disagree about how to measure congestion, they also disagree about whether congestion is getting better or worse. Regardless, both sides agree that suburbanization is one of the major factors affecting congestion levels.

Literature Synthesis Matrix

	+2 General Agreement	+1 Some Agreement	0 No Clear Outcome	–2 Substantial Disagreement
Does this condition notably exist?			X	
Is it strongly linked to sprawl?	X			

Lower Governmental Costs for Transportation

Allegation/Basis

Much of the cost of building and operating highways and streets, the dominant mode of travel under sprawl, is paid for by users, through gas taxes and licensing fees. In contrast, transit users pay a lower share of the costs of building and operating transit systems, especially rail systems. Thus sprawl, with its emphasis on highway investment, requires less subsidization of transportation systems even when governmental costs, such as highway patrols and publicly provided parking, are considered.

Literature Synthesis

Considerable disagreement exists about whether transit or automobile governmental subsidies are higher, as evidenced by the debate between Gordon and Richardson (1997a) and Ewing (1997). Although government subsidies are a visible part of transit budgets, there is much dissension about what constitutes a subsidy for highways. As Deluchi notes:

> There is a good deal of argument about whether motor vehicle users "pay" fully for government-provided infrastructure and services (i.e., Lee 1994: Green 1995). This

disagreement, of course, results from different opinions about what should count as a public-sector cost of motor vehicle use, and what should count as a payment by motor vehicle users for motor vehicle use. (Deluchi 1996, 43)

> *There is a good deal of argument about whether motor vehicle users "pay" fully for government-provided infrastructure and services.*

Most federal and state funding of highways derives from the gas taxes and registration fees that are dedicated to highways. However, as Hanson (1992) Litman (1995), and Dunphy (1997) point out, local governments finance a considerable share of road costs with property and sales taxes.

None of the costs of travel studies have analyzed whether governmental costs vary depending upon the type of development.

Literature Synthesis Matrix

	+2 General Agreement	+1 Some Agreement	0 No Clear Outcome	–2 Substantial Disagreement
Does this condition notably exist?			X	
Is it strongly linked to sprawl?			X	

Automobiles Most Efficient Mode of Transportation

Allegation/Basis

Automobiles are the most efficient mode of transportation in sprawl. The low-density, dispersed patterns of sprawl development were designed for automobile access and make the automobile the most efficient means of travel for many trips.

Literature Synthesis

An analysis of the total cost of travel for ten diverse, prototypical trips in Boulder, Colorado showed that the automobile is clearly the *least* costly means of travel for trips between dispersed, low-density destinations even when estimates of user, governmental, and social costs are totaled. Although the cost per passenger mile of the single-occupant automobile is higher than the cost of any other mode during peak times, automobiles are more efficient for many off-peak trips because they can take direct routes, are faster, and allow drivers to avoid waiting times. Getting to destinations that require bus transfers, taking trips that link many destinations, or taking trips involving more than one person are often most efficiently done in the automobile.

Only the automobile can offer the convenience of door-to-door transportation.
Source: Thomas Johnston, AIA. Courtesy American Planning Association.

Literature Synthesis Matrix

	+2 General Agreement	+1 Some Agreement	0 No Clear Outcome	−2 Substantial Disagreement
Does this condition notably exist?		X		
Is it strongly linked to sprawl?	X			

CHAPTER

Literature Synthesis

LAND/NATURAL
HABITAT PRESERVATION

This subset of the literature includes, as a starting point, investigations about overall land consumption trends and the threats to such fragile lands as wetlands and prime agricultural acreage. Numerous studies deal specifically with how different development patterns affect land and natural habitat preservation.

Following this overview, the chapter examines the evidence on reduced farmland productivity and viability resulting from proximate suburban development. Do invading suburban land uses threaten cropland harvests, and does this phenomenon reduce the value of land for farming?

Finally, do skipped-over lands destroy the possibility of garnering meaningful regional open space, or does this pattern leave for future development land interstices that can be used for small-scale, community, or personal open space at a later period?

Because there is a view that Americans are wasteful in their use of land for development and that land savings are an "obvious" outcome of some forms of managed growth, there is less empirical

research that focuses on the topic of preservation and sprawl.

Sprawl's Alleged Negative Impacts

Loss of Agricultural Land
Reduced Farmland Productivity
Reduced Farmland Viability
Loss of Fragile Environmental Lands
Reduced Regional Open Space

Sprawl's Alleged Positive Impacts

Enhanced Personal and Public Open
*   Space*

SPRAWL'S ALLEGED NEGATIVE IMPACTS

Loss of Agricultural Land

Allegation/Basis

Sprawl removes more prime agricultural land from farming use than other more compact forms of development. Three reasons are usually cited. First, the low-density uses inherent in sprawl's residential development patterns require more space for the direct placement of dwelling units than the higher-density uses under compact development. Second, the scatteration of dwelling units across the landscape far from the edges of built-up settlements renders the agricultural use of much of the land adjacent to the scattered dwellings inefficient and under intense development pressures. Third, the prospect of obtaining high prices for land motivates farmers and land speculators to assemble large parcels of farmland because these lands are contiguous and can be bought in bulk.

Literature Synthesis

Multiple studies have documented the significant loss of agricultural lands to the current development process. These studies range from national reviews of the loss of farmlands and farms over time, such as the National Agricultural Lands study (1981) and the American Farmland

Farms near metropolitan areas are increasingly facing intense development pressures.
Source: Peter Dunning. Courtesy American Farmland Trust.

Trust's *Farming on the Edge* (1994), to regional/state investigations of a similar type (i.e., Nelson [1992b] in Oregon and Adelaja et al. [1989] in New Jersey). There is substantial disagreement, however, about whether this loss of agricultural land has created significant social costs. To some observers, it

appears that there is no shortage of prime agricultural land in the United States, since the nation has often produced crop surpluses (Gordon and Richardson 1997a), and 2,000 of the 3,000 counties in the United States can still be counted as rural and undeveloped (Burchell and Shad 1997). Yet, demands for food are rising sharply as living standards increase in once-poor locations throughout the world. Prices of major agricultural crops have increased substantially in just the last few years. Hence, the argument is made that in the long run, the world will need all the food production capacity it can muster (Ewing 1997).

On the domestic front, there are widespread policy initiatives that seek to preserve farmland as much with the goal of maintaining a diverse economy as any other reason. Many states (e.g., Maryland, New Jersey, and Vermont) and other levels of government (e.g., Lancaster County, Pennsylvania) have adopted programs in recent years, ranging from the purchase of development rights to the enactment of "right to farm" laws, in order to foster land, particularly farmland, preservation (Nelson 1992b).

Numerous growth management plans— attempting to reverse sprawl—include farmland preservation as an objective (Maine 1988; Vermont 1988; New Jersey 1991). They address preservation as a goal of planned development, not merely an attempt to curtail sprawl. The limited empirical investigations of sprawl's impact on "consuming" farmland—and in opposition, the impact of alternatives to sprawl on farmland—that have been done were performed by Burchell (1992-1997) in New Jersey, Lexington (Kentucky), the Delaware Estuary, Michigan, and South Carolina, and by Landis (1995) in the San Francisco Bay area. These analyses employed land consumption models at the minor civil subdivision level to view differences between trend development or "business as usual" scenarios and more environmentally conscious land development approaches. The business-as-usual scenarios embodied sprawl-like characteristics; the latter, more compact, planned development characteristics. These models allowed future projections of households and jobs to be converted to the demand for residential and nonresidential structures, and ultimately to demand for residential and nonresidential land, with allowances for spillover to adjacent municipalities and to unincorporated areas.

In both the Burchell and Landis studies, historical rates of farmland takings were applied to land consumed under existing development patterns, and the goal of farmland retention was applied under the alternative development patterns. (A similar procedure was used for environmental land consumption comparisons.) In the Burchell studies, agricultural lands included such categories as cropland that is harvested, lands in permanent pasture, and woodlands that could be used for agricultural purposes. Fragile environmental lands encompassed floodplains and wetlands, acreage with steep slopes or with critical habitat designation, aquifer recharge areas, critical sensitive watersheds, and stream buffers (Burchell 1992-1997).

> *Numerous growth management plans include farmland preservation as an objective.*

The models, employing different densities, development locations, and occasionally different housing types under the alternatives for future growth, calculated the total agricultural (and fragile environmental lands) that would be consumed. Burchell's results showed

savings in the consumption of agricultural acreage of roughly 20 percent in South Carolina, Michigan, and Lexington under plan versus trend development; savings of about 30 percent in the Delaware Estuary; and savings of 40 percent in New Jersey (Burchell 1992-1997). (See Tables 3 and 4 for details.) Landis's results in the San Francisco Bay Area were even more pronounced. His "scenario C" (compact growth) saved nearly 50% of farmland acreage and steep-sloped areas, and close to 100% of wetland areas (Landis 1995, 449).

Literature Synthesis Matrix

	+2 General Agreement	+1 Some Agreement	0 No Clear Outcome	–2 Substantial Disagreement
Does this condition notably exist?	X			
Is it strongly linked to sprawl?	X			

Reduced Farmland Productivity

Allegation/Basis

The productivity of land being farmed near scattered sprawl settlements is reduced by the difficulty of conducting efficient farming operations near residential subdivisions. Subdividing land into small lots for residential purposes inhibits farmers' ability to operate on large contiguous land parcels and thereby reduces the efficiency of mechanized agricultural operations. Furthermore, under sprawl development, subdivisions and farms may be interspersed, and residents often object to the odors, noise, truck traffic, and other local conditions associated with active agricultural uses. When this contiguous development occurs, local governments sometimes opt to impose restrictions on farming. These conditions bring about an "impermanence syndrome" that is antithetical to sustained farmland productivity.

Literature Synthesis

There is an extensive literature on constraints to farming in urbanizing locations (Lisansky 1986; Lopez et al. 1988; Nelson 1992b). In rural areas that can be readily developed, high land values often shift farmers' "objective function" from agricultural operations to capital gains from real estate sales. Real estate sales, in turn, reduce the average farm size, thus limiting the realization of economies of scale—a characteristic of U.S. agriculture. A variety of other restraints on farmland productivity have also been imposed, ranging from restrictive regulations to recurring vandalism. All of these factors generate an "impermanence syndrome"—a

Increasing numbers of farms have been sold and converted into sprawl development.
Source: Peter Dunning. Courtesy American Farmland Trust.

reluctance by the farmer to invest in new technology and farm infrastructure. Land remains idle, awaiting conversion to other uses. Studies involving sprawl development allege that this

impermanence syndrome is deleterious to farmland productivity (AFT 1997).

The direct relationship of sprawl development patterns to farmland consumption was examined by Burchell (1992a) in the state of New Jersey. In addition to projecting the total farmland that would be lost under sprawl versus planned development, the New Jersey analysis identified the quality of farmland that would likely be consumed—"prime," "marginal," or "poor." The New Jersey

> *No analysis to date has examined how development pattern (i.e., sprawl versus compact) would affect the productivity of farmland that remains in agricultural use.*

analysis showed that not only would continued sprawl development draw down more farmland, but since better quality farmland is the most amenable for development (in that it is flatter, drains better, and so on), the loss of farmland to sprawl would be concentrated in the "prime" and "marginal" categories. Farmland consumption under planned development would be less overall and wholly contained in the subprime or "poor" farmland category.

The Burchell (1992a) New Jersey study thus considered the association of farmland quality and development patterns—but only from a farmland consumption perspective. No analysis to date has examined how development pattern (i.e., sprawl versus compact) would affect the productivity of farmland that remains in agricultural use.

Literature Synthesis Matrix

	+2 General Agreement	+1 Some Agreement	0 No Clear Outcome	−2 Substantial Disagreement
Does this condition notably exist?		X		
Is it strongly linked to sprawl?			X	

Reduced Farmland Viability (Water Constraints)

Allegation/Basis

Growth through sprawl causes great expansion in the demand for water for urban uses, and thereby reduces the amount of water available for agriculture. The reduction in available water is especially significant in the southwestern regions where sustained shortages of water exist. However, agriculture currently uses much more water than urban settlements in many states where farming depends upon irrigation, such as Arizona, California, Colorado, Oklahoma, and Texas. As urban settlements expand in these areas, more water will have to be diverted from agriculture to supply the basic human needs of the resident population. This diversion will restrict the operation of farming in such areas. Furthermore, single-family property owners and corporate commercial facilities often use vast amounts of water for lawn sprinkling, an excessive use of this natural resource that is needed for food production.

Literature Synthesis

Multiple studies have examined how development in more arid locations, especially in the West and Southwest United States, is drawing down the water supply, potentially in conflict with the irrigation needs of agriculture. The literature has not examined the specific association of sprawl and farmland viability with respect to water supply. This would involve a multi-linked analysis of:

1) how development affects water demand;
2) whether development's consumption of water would differ under sprawl versus other forms of development in these areas; and

3) the relationship of steps (1) and (2) to the amount of water supply for agricultural and residential settlements in given locations, compared to the total supply available there.

Although a fully linked analysis such as the one described above has not been undertaken, some research has been undertaken on water demand relevant to steps (1) and (2). For instance, the Army Corps of Engineers incorporates in its water demand forecasting model, among other factors, the magnitude of lawn sprinkling, which is likely to be higher under sprawl versus compact development (Consultants 1980). The Hittman water demand model includes housing density as one factor—a variable clearly different under sprawl versus more compact development. In a similar vein, the multivariable IWR-Main water forecasting model (Baumann and Dziegielewski 1990) incorporates in its multiple coefficients development density and the number of housing units by type (detached versus attached)—variables that differ under sprawl versus compact development.

Development, both residential and nonresidential, demands more water than its agricultural predecessors and neighbors.
Source: Courtesy CUPR Press.

The Burchell (1992a, 1992b) analysis of trend versus plan development in New Jersey considered how water demand influenced water consumption under these two scenarios and incorporated some of the variables (i.e., housing type) noted above. Burchell found only small differences in water demand by development scenario; from 1990 to 2010, the increase in statewide water demand was projected to be 60.1 million gallons per day (MGPD) for trend, versus 58.0 MGPD for plan. This analysis did not, however, relate the 2-MGPD variation finding to the demands on water supply for residential development versus agricultural uses in New Jersey. Water supply is not a development-constraining issue in New Jersey—as it is in more arid regions of the United States.

Literature Synthesis Matrix

	+2 General Agreement	+1 Some Agreement	0 No Clear Outcome	-2 Substantial Disagreement
Does this condition notably exist?			X	
Is it strongly linked to sprawl?			X	

Loss of Fragile Environmental Lands

Allegation/Basis

More frail lands are destroyed by sprawl than by more compact settlement patterns. Because sprawl spreads urban development over a much larger area than more compact settlement patterns, it inherently consumes more land. Because land development under sprawl is not centrally planned or supervised, there is a greater probability that fragile environmental lands will be converted to residential and other uses. Local governments are likely to misjudge the consequences of environmental degradation because they are not concerned with the overall balance between environmentally sensitive lands and developing land uses in the region as a whole.

Literature Synthesis

Several studies document losses of, and threats to, fragile lands. Dahl (1990) estimates that since colonial times the United States (48 lower states) has lost about 110 million acres of wetlands— about 55 percent of the starting wetlands inventory. The Michigan Society of Planning Officials (MSPO) estimates that 20 percent of Michigan's forested, wetland, and steeply sloped areas was lost to development between 1970 and 1990 (MSPO 1995).

Numerous growth management plans— attempting to reverse sprawl—have evaluated how managed versus traditional development patterns would affect fragile lands. These plans include the Orlando, Florida, *Urban Area Growth Management Program* (Orlando, FL 1981), the *Evaluation of City of San Diego Growth Management Program* (1978), and *the Report of the Year 2020 Panel of Experts* (Chesapeake Bay Executive Council 1988). The Orlando study examined how managed growth versus a "continuation of past trends" would affect the preservation of wetlands and flood plains. It projected a saving under managed growth of almost 20 percent in the inventory of these fragile environmental lands (i.e., 20 percent less acreage lost).

> *The Michigan Society of Planning Officials (MSPO) estimates that 20 percent of Michigan's forested, wetland, and steeply sloped areas were lost to development between 1970 and 1990.*

Analyses of sprawl's impact on fragile lands have been conducted by Burchell (1992–1997) in New Jersey, Lexington (Kentucky), Delaware Estuary, and Michigan. Similar studies were also done by Landis in the San Francisco Bay area. Burchell found that plan (compact) versus trend (sprawl-like) development would reduce consumption of fragile environmental lands by almost one-fifth.

Homes are being built on unsuitable and unsafe, but available and less-expensive lands.
Source: U.S. Department of Agriculture, Soil Conservation Service.

The range of the saving was from 12 to 27 percent, depending on the starting level and location (see Tables 3 and 4). Landis found even larger land savings under his compact growth scenario. His findings were calculated separately for steep slopes and wetland areas (Landis 1995).

Literature Synthesis Matrix

	+2 General Agreement	+1 Some Agreement	0 No Clear Outcome	−2 Substantial Disagreement
Does this condition notably exist?	X			
Is it strongly linked to sprawl?	X			

Reduced Regional Open Space

Allegation/Basis

The setting aside of open space for public use by residents of an entire region may be "underfinanced" in sprawl-dominated areas, compared to those with more regionally oriented governance structures. Municipal governments, motivated by

fiscal pressures to provide benefits only for their own residents, may be unwilling to devote resources to creating facilities for use by persons throughout a region.

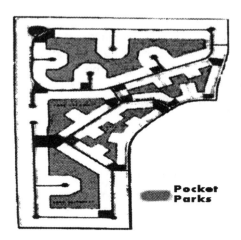

Many neighborhoods incorporate pocket parks, accessible only to their residents, instead of relying on regional open space.
Source: Florida Department of Community Affairs

Literature Synthesis

There is scant literature dealing with this issue explicitly; it is difficult to determine whether a substantial consensus exists. The only literature that does exist finds that very large-scale developments and conservation developments, both generally "nonsprawl" in nature, frequently have significant set-asides for contiguous open space. Most of the local ordinances of the 1970s and the new countywide community general development plans of the 1980s called for mandatory provisions of continuous open space as an alternative to traditional subdivision development (Burchell, Listokin, and Dolphin 1994).

Very large-scale developments and conservation developments, both often of a nonsprawl nature, frequently have significant set-asides for contiguous open space.

Arendt (1994a) points to a movement away from golf course communities to open space communities that give the private and public sectors a greater chance to share in the land resources. The Sterling Forest Corporation, potential developers of a 17,500-acre site in Tuxedo, New York, pledged 75% of the land would remain as some form of private/public open space (Sterling Forest Corporation 1995). Much of the site was later bought by federal and state governments.

Literature Synthesis Matrix

	+2 General Agreement	+1 Some Agreement	0 No Clear Outcome	−2 Substantial Disagreement
Does this condition notably exist?			X	
Is it strongly linked to sprawl?			X	

SPRAWL'S ALLEGED POSITIVE IMPACTS

Enhanced Personal and Public Open Space

Allegation/Basis

(a) *Sprawl provides more open space directly accessible to individual households in the form of larger private yards attached to their dwellings than is possible via more compact forms of settlement.* The average lot size in sprawl settlement patterns is much larger than in more compact forms of settlement, and a higher fraction of dwellings have individual yards. Therefore, more households have direct access to their own private open space, and the space is larger, on average, than the equivalent in more compact settlements.

(b) *Sprawl's leapfrog development provides both larger amounts of, and more accessible, open space without significant*

public expenditures, by leaving large unsettled sites "inboard" of the farthest-out urban subdivisions. This provides aesthetic and recreational benefits to the public without requiring use of taxpayers' funds.

Literature Synthesis

Personal open space continues to be high on the list of the desires of most Americans (Fannie Mae 1995). In surveys conducted by the Federal National Mortgage Agency, prospective home buyers want not only yards, but yards on all sides. In the mid-1990s, according to the most current surveys of buying preference, single-family detached housing was more popular than it was a decade ago. Much of the appeal is related to occupants' dislike of the instability or fee structure of condominium associations. But at least some of the appeal is related to the desire for more, rather than less, personal open space (Fannie Mae 1994).

Large yards on all sides of the house appeal to suburban home buyers.
Source: Copyright 1997. The Georgia Conservancy. All rights reserved.

> *Although a potential for inner-city/suburban open space appears to be the result of skipped-over lands, rarely does this happen in either developed or redeveloping neighborhoods.*

A very limited literature indicates that the skipped-over development patterns of sprawl create parcels of land that can be used for inner-suburban or urban open space as this becomes a local priority. Except in the wealthiest and most resilient of inner suburbs, open space is almost never a choice or option of local government. Most governments in these localities are pressed for fiscal resources and dispose of these land parcels to the highest bidder. Thus, the opposite to what is popularly assumed to be a trend often takes place. Through the local variance process, the lands frequently are given a higher intensity residential or nonresidential use designation. The abutting properties, rather than receiving permanently improved open space, are subject to more intensive and occasionally disruptive land uses, which can pay more in taxes than either existing neighboring uses or the previously undeveloped vacant land. Thus, although a potential for inner-city/suburban open space appears to be the result of skipped-over lands, rarely does new open space materialize in either developed or redeveloping neighborhoods (Downs 1994).

Literature Synthesis Matrix

	+2 General Agreement	+1 Some Agreement	0 No Clear Outcome	−2 Substantial Disagreement
Does this condition notably exist?		X		
Is it strongly linked to sprawl?			X	

CHAPTER

6

Literature Synthesis

QUALITY OF LIFE

This subset of the literature, like the preceding subject areas, consists first of general investigations on the concept of "Quality of Life" (QOL) and how it can be measured, as well as specific studies that attribute both positive and negative QOL attributes to sprawl and its alternatives. As one would expect, there is no consensus on what QOL entails, so the review of the literature begins with numerous studies that grapple with defining the concept and monitoring its attributes.

While the vast majority of the literature on QOL deals generally with the overriding issue of what QOL is, a smaller number of studies focus specifically on the QOL–sprawl nexus. Some current studies add as a QOL critique that contemporary, single-use residential subdivisions, accessible primarily by the automobile, have lost their sense of "place." Others indicate that traveling through the congestion and aesthetics of sprawl is stressful.

Yet another group of studies points to the fact that sprawl development consumes unnatural amounts of energy, contributes to regional air pollution, and lessens the

regional and national resources that might be devoted to historic preservation, cultural infrastructure provision, and the like.

The chapter concludes with a discussion of the premise that low-density living is preferred by most of the population: Outer-metropolitan locations separate them from the problems of the poor, reduce the costs of housing and public services, and are the locus of the greatest appreciation of housing values.

Sprawl's Alleged Negative Impacts

Aesthetically Displeasing
Weakened Sense of Community
Greater Stress
Higher Energy Consumption
More Air Pollution
Lessened Historic Preservation

Sprawl's Alleged Positive Impacts

Preference for Low-Density Living
Lower Crime Rates
Enhanced Value or Reduced Costs of
  Public and Private Goods
Fosters Greater Economic Well-Being

SPRAWL'S ALLEGED NEGATIVE IMPACTS

Aesthetically Displeasing

Allegation/Basis

Low-density patterns are less pleasing aesthetically and provide fewer cultural opportunities than high-density patterns. An important element of the quality of life of any community is the aesthetic and cultural satisfaction of its residents in daily life. If the environment they normally encounter is dominated by the homogeneous architecture of subdivisions and strip malls, the absence of quality civic spaces and landmark buildings, and a lack of pedestrian-scale amenities, the aesthetic satisfaction people derive from their surroundings is reduced. Moreover, sprawl does not easily lend itself to the formation of communities that have a feeling of cohesiveness and can organize to support the arts or other cultural institutions.

Literature Synthesis

The aesthetically less-pleasing aspects of sprawl, such as visual uniformity, are often cited as a cost of this form of development (Nelessen 1994). Critics of sprawl often decry its ugliness. For example, Shore (1995) maintains that "spread city" is inherently ugly because the settlement pattern has no clear form; retail businesses located along highways must use "raucous" signs to attract passing motorists; and a significant portion of the land is given over to the automobile. Diamond and Noonan (1996) find a growing portion of suburbanites faced with "real burdens on the texture, continuity, and depth of social life, as well as on the diversity, beauty, and health of the surrounding landscape."

Strip commercial development along heavily traveled routes is both unappealing and unsafe.
Source: George Hull and W. C. King. The Chattanooga Times, Chattanooga, TN.

Low-density developments, however, are not necessarily less-pleasing aesthetically than more compact forms of development. The aesthetics vary from development to development. Some low-density residential developments, particularly high-income ones, have much more open space and elaborate landscape designs than high-density residential areas. In fact, defenders of sprawl often contend that the individually owned, discrete open spaces of sprawl make it more attractive than compact forms of development.

> *Sprawl does not easily lend itself to the formation of communities that have a feeling of cohesiveness and can organize to support the arts or other cultural institutions.*

The literature reflects these two conflicting opinions. There is little evidence within the literature, however, to suggest that Americans find sprawl less attractive than more compact forms of development or that low-density living provides them with fewer cultural opportunities. Visual preference surveys have been used to gauge the reaction of Americans to sprawl, although such studies are often criticized for failing to make a distinction between sprawl and factors not typically associated with that form of development (e.g., architectural design). Moreover, survey research does not consistently indicate that Americans overwhelmingly find sprawl to be aesthetically less pleasing than compact forms of development. When shown images of both sprawl and traditional communities, some surveys have revealed that individuals favor the latter by a wide margin (Neuman 1991). But some aspects of sprawl appear to appeal to Americans. Individuals were found to favor homogeneous neighborhoods over mixed neighborhoods by a margin of two to one (Bookout 1992). Survey research in Florida has suggested that individuals there have a strong preference for low-density or exurban living (Audirac and Zifou 1989).

> *There is little evidence within the literature, however, to suggest that Americans find sprawl less attractive than more compact forms of development.*

On the subject of cultural activities, Shore (1995) contends that sprawl does not allow for the formation of communities that easily organize to support activities such as the arts. As a result, low-density residential communities may have fewer and lower-quality cultural activities than urban areas. Shore argues that a movement away from "spread city" and toward the restoration of downtown areas would result in more cultural activities and other services that are typically supported by large communities.

In general, few argue with the belief that an attractive and aesthetically pleasing community increases the overall quality of life. Within the economics and migration literature, it has been well documented that a community viewed as having a high quality of life will attract and retain individuals. Studies of migration patterns find that a community's scenery, natural environment, and outdoor recreational opportunities are

important factors in attracting and retaining individuals. A survey study of migrants to and residents of 15 wilderness counties found that scenery and environmental quality were *more important factors* in attracting settlers than employment opportunities or cost of living (von Reichert and Rudzitis 1992). Two of the most important conditions that "lone eagles" (individuals who are able to live anywhere and telecommute to work) cited as influences on their decision to move to the state of Washington were the quality of the natural environment and the outdoor recreational opportunities found there (Salant et al. 1996). Cushing (1987) demonstrated that proximity to mountains and coastlines influenced population migration because of these natural resources' aesthetic qualities and the recreational opportunities that they provided. Empirical results indicated that interstate migrants were attracted to hilly terrain and major coastlines.

As noted, however, there is only some agreement about whether low-density developments are aesthetically less-pleasing than more compact development patterns. In particular, the literature fails to indicate a significant causal relationship between sprawl and aesthetically less-pleasing low-density development; there are numerous examples of unattractive higher-density inner suburbs in the Northeast and Midwest. What the literature does indicate, however, is that the aesthetics of low-density areas vary from place to place, and that the preferences of individuals vary from person to person.

Literature Synthesis Matrix

	+2 General Agreement	+1 Some Agreement	0 No Clear Outcome	−2 Substantial Disagreement
Does this condition notably exist?		X		
Is it strongly linked to sprawl?			X	

Weakened Sense of Community

Allegation/Basis

Low-density development weakens households' connections to both their immediate neighbors and to the larger metropolitan community, and encourages unsociable values. Sprawl weakens the linkages of residents—both among nearby neighbors, and among all other residents of their metropolitan area. Linkages with neighbors are reduced because low residential density, the heavy orientation toward car travel rather than foot travel, and the lack of neighborhood retail outlets and other meeting places diminish interpersonal contacts. Linkages with other residents throughout the metropolitan area are also diminished by the fragmentation of governance and fiscal resources that prevent commonality of purpose, and by the extreme diffusion of households and jobs throughout an area. The resultant loss of sense of community makes it difficult to generate support for region-wide attacks on social and other problems that cannot be solved by purely local policies and actions. Finally, because sprawl in its most pejorative manifestations is believed by most to be wasteful, unaesthetic, and antisocial, it does not nurture the important social values of ecology, sustainability, and community.

Literature Synthesis

Critics of sprawl often claim that a loss of "sense of community" is one of its greatest social costs (Ewing 1997). Defenders of low-density settlements, however, deny that residents experience any less "sense of community" than residents in big cities or more compact settlements (Gordon and Richardson 1997a). In fact, the evidence from as far back as 1954 (Herbert Gans as cited in Jacobs 1961) indicates that some dense

areas lack community while some suburban areas have it. Much of the controversy arises because "sense of community" is difficult to define and even more difficult to measure.

In his review of the literature on "sense of community," Cochrun (1994) finds that the term has been used to describe a number of disparate elements, but the most comprehensive definition was developed by McMillan and Chavis (1986). McMillan and Chavis identified four factors that contribute to a sense of community:
   1) membership;
   2) influence;
   3) integration and fulfillment of needs; and
   4) shared emotional connection.

> *"Sense of community" is difficult to define and even more difficult to measure.*

Cochrun offers a definition of "sense of community" that incorporates the four factors identified by McMillan and Chavis:

> People who have a strong sense of community feel like they belong in their neighborhoods, they believe they exert some control over what happens in their neighborhoods while also feeling influenced by what happens in them, and they believe that their needs can be met through the collective capabilities of their neighborhoods. (Cochrun 1994, 93)

In *Edge City: Life on the New Frontier*, Garreau (1991) searches for a definition of community, particularly within edge cities, and reaches the conclusion that community and neighborhood no longer mean the same thing. Instead, Garreau maintains that "mobility" and "voluntary" are two important terms that help to define community—individuals want to be able to both join and leave communities at their choosing. Moreover, Garreau contends that a community should be a "social grouping" that is readily available to individuals and does not interfere with individual freedoms.

In partial contradiction, Lemann (1989), in an article examining changes in sub-urban Illinois, found that community-building efforts in Naperville, a fast-growing suburb of Chicago, were hindered by the high rate of turnover of its residents.

Curved streets and mixed uses help to create a sense of community.
Source: Courtesy American Planning Association.

Critics of sprawl argue that residents in mixed-use neighborhoods have more sense of community and social interaction than do residents living in low-density developments because they are more likely to walk from place to place and, consequently, they are more likely to have contact and interaction with others. Residents in low-density areas, on the other hand, rely more on their cars for shopping and recreation trips and, hence, are less likely to develop contacts and friendships with neighbors (Nasar and Julian 1995). Drawing on the work of Glynn (1981), Nasar and Julian assessed the psychological sense of community across different neighborhoods and housing conditions in northwestern Columbus, Ohio. They found that residents of mixed-use areas had

significantly more sense of community than residents of single-use neighborhoods.

Opponents of sprawl also maintain that low-density development weakens a "sense of community" by segregating residents (Duany and Plater-Zyberk 1995; Kelbaugh 1993). According to Kelbaugh, suburban insularity breeds "ignorance, misunderstanding, and ultimately builds tension" among residents. Kelbaugh prefers high-density, mixed socio-economic, racial, and ethnic neighbor-hoods because they allow individuals to "rub shoulders" with fellow residents on a daily basis and work out differences. Similarly, Duany and Plater-Zyberk contend that suburban housing fosters a breakdown of the larger community because it segregates residents by income into enclaves.

Kunstler (1996a) attacks suburban sprawl and the zoning laws that have created it. The allegation that low-density residential living lowers "sense of community" may be inferred from his remark that "The model of human habitat dictated by zoning is a formless, soulless, centerless, demoralizing mess. ... It corrupts and deadens our spirit." Like Duany and Plater-Zyberk (1995), Kunstler argues for development patterns that are mixed-use and provide housing for people with different incomes.

Sprawl may weaken not only neigh-borhood connections but also connections between family members who occupy the same residence. Some contend, for example, that sprawl reduces the amount of time parents spend with their children because more households must have two people working outside the home in order to pay for the multiple automobiles required by daily life.[1] This need to

---

[1] Some have argued that even if only one person working outside the home could support a one-car

support the household's transportation facilities may, in fact, even reduce the quality of child care provided by parents. Some contend that mothers working outside the home provide lower quality child care than those who stay at home. The subject is fraught with controversy (Joseph 1992). Meanwhile, Kelbaugh (1993) examines another potential noneconomic social cost associated with sprawl—the tensions that result from parents spending long hours commuting instead of with their children or each other.

> *Sprawl may weaken not only households' connections to neighbors and the larger community, but it may also weaken connections between family members who occupy the same residence.*

The literature does not readily provide support for the opposite allegation—i.e., that low-density development strengthens households' connections to both their neighbors and larger community. Ewing suggests, however, that low-density development does not provide residents with any less "sense of community" than higher-density development. After reviewing extensive literature on sprawl, he concludes that there is not enough evidence to determine whether a lack of an identifiable community is associated with sprawl (Ewing 1994).

One further issue related to a lack of "sense of community" is the emergence of a "throw-away" mentality or, more elegantly, the lack of value for ecology and sustainable lifestyles. Some argue that sprawl encourages a "throw-away" mentality among households.

family, most residents of sprawl settlements need two cars for conducting daily family life. The low-density pattern of both housing and jobs makes use of public transit impractical for commuting and daily errand-running.

> *Sprawl development may be seen as a continuation of the "prairie psychology" of early American settlers who believed they could change their current situation by leaving existing homes and problems behind and moving west onto vacant land.*

In a sense, sprawl development may be seen as a continuation of the "prairie psychology" of early American settlers who believed they could change their situation by leaving existing homes and problems behind and moving west onto vacant land (Delafons 1962). More recently, millions of American households have moved out of central cities and older inner-ring suburbs for the same reason—to escape the problems of those areas. They have left the problems behind for others to solve. Few, if any, studies of sprawl have dealt with this issue, and none have proposed any way to measure the "throw-away" mind-set.

Literature Synthesis Matrix

	+2 General Agreement	+1 Some Agreement	0 No Clear Outcome	−2 Substantial Disagreement
Does this condition notably exist?		X		
Is it strongly linked to sprawl?			X	

Greater Stress

Allegation/Basis

Because people spend more time driving, they have less free time and more stress. This allegation has two components: first, that sprawl increases the time people spend in cars relative to higher-density forms of development and, second, that increased travel time leads to stress and other impacts. It has also been alleged that commuting through the aesthetically unattractive environments of commercial strip development that are typical of sprawl produces more psychological stress on commuters than would commuting through environments dominated by trees and open space.

Literature Synthesis

Here, as with many of the topics evaluated in this report, there is substantial overlap with other topics and their alleged effects. In this case, the overlap is with transportation effects, which include allegations about traffic congestion and travel times.

Much of the debate about commute time has been based on data that compare travel times for residents of suburbs and central cities. There is little data on travel times associated with density of development. Ewing (1997), in his analysis of household travel patterns in a sprawling Florida county, purports to show that households living in the most accessible areas spend about 40 minutes less per day traveling by vehicle than do households living in the least accessible locations (Ewing 1995c; Ewing et al. 1994). Ewing states that this savings in travel time is due almost entirely to shorter auto trips, and that the significant land-use variable affecting travel times is regional accessibility, not local density (Ewing 1997).

There is also evidence that greater commuting time increases the stress of commuters. Novaco et al. (1990) found that increased travel impedance, as measured by commuting distance and time, is associated with increased measures of stress. Travel impedance was also found to have statistically significant effects on job satisfaction, work absences due to illness, and overall incidence of colds or flu. Subjective or perceived conditions of travel impedance were found to have statistically significant

effects on mood at home in the evening and chest pain. Consequently, the study found that job change, in its sample, was primarily related to commuting satisfaction. The study validated results from the author's previous work, which had found that impedance characteristics of commuting raise stress levels, as measured by effects on blood pressure, tolerance for frustration, negative mood, and overall life satisfaction. This earlier work also found that the desire to change residence because of transportation conditions was related strongly to high impedance (Novaco et al. 1979; Stokols and Novaco 1981; Stokols et al. 1978). The physical stress effects of impedance have also been corroborated by a study of the effects of average commuting speed on blood pressure and frustration levels (Schaeffer et al. 1988).

> *Increased travel impedance, as measured by commuting distance and time, is associated with increased measures of stress.*

Koslowsky and Krausz (1994) directly addressed the links among commuting time, stress, and workers' attitudes toward their jobs, in a statistical analysis of survey responses from more than 600 nurses. The researchers found that commuting is a possible source of recurrent stress, which can lead to undesirable organizational consequences. This study also found that the correlation between commuting time and stress was stronger for those who drove to work than for those who used public transit. But the authors do not rigorously explore the reasons for this difference. Koslowsky and Krausz do cite prior literature that found a relationship between the commuting experience and such organizational outcomes as absenteeism (Taylor and Pocock 1972), lateness (Gaffuri and Costa 1986), and turnover (Seyfarth and Bost 1986).

Although the link between commuting and stress is well established, the literature on the stress effects of commuting does not rigorously address the link between commuting stress and the density of development or urban form. Novaco et al. (1990) begin to address this link with their finding that stress effects are strongly associated with freeway travel and with road exchanges; they also assert that freeway travel in southern California has become increasingly congested because roadway capacity has not kept pace with continued growth.

> *Literature on the stress effects of commuting does not rigorously address the link between commuting stress and the density of development.*

Although it has been alleged, as noted earlier, that commuting through the aesthetically unattractive commercial strip development typical of sprawl produces more psychological stress on commuters than does commuting through environments dominated by trees and open space, very little literature pertaining to this allegation exists. One study, however, claims to have tested commuters psychologically and arrived at a finding that supports this claim (Ulrich et al. 1991).

Other sections of this report comment in more detail on the evidence regarding sprawl and travel time. No conclusion is made here. The professional literature suggests, however, that commuting can be shown statistically to contribute to stress—a happy coincidence of science and common sense.

Literature Synthesis Matrix

	+2 General Agreement	+1 Some Agreement	0 No Clear Outcome	−2 Substantial Disagreement
Does this condition notably exist?		X		
Is it strongly linked to sprawl?		X		

Higher Energy Consumption

Allegation/Basis

Under sprawl, society consumes more scarce energy, especially imported oil. Sprawl requires more travel overall and more of this travel is by energy-inefficient automobiles instead of more efficient modes of transit.

Literature Synthesis

Ewing (1997) and many other researchers contend that the evidence consistently demonstrates that automobile use, and hence energy use, is higher with sprawl. Yet, Gordon and Richardson (1997a) are not convinced that the link between vehicle miles of travel, energy use, and density is firmly established.

Americans are among the heaviest consumers of energy in the world. Although oil is primarily imported, the government subsidizes and reduces the cost of gasoline.
Source: Anton Nelessen, Rutgers University, Urban Design Studio.

Coloring this argument are the differing perspectives on energy availability.

Gordon and Richardson (1997a) speak of an energy glut and an OPEC cartel that has lost its clout, while Ewing (1997) cautions that energy sources are not unlimited, and reliance on foreign energy supplies is a continuing concern for United States foreign policy.

Literature Synthesis Matrix

	+2 General Agreement	+1 Some Agreement	0 No Clear Outcome	−2 Substantial Disagreement
Does this condition notably exist?		X		
Is it strongly linked to sprawl?		X		

More Air Pollution

Allegation/Basis

Sprawl worsens the overall air pollution in a metropolitan area. Sprawl is alleged to generate more vehicle miles of travel than other forms of development and to produce more total vehicle emissions as a result. Under many local climatic conditions, this can generate a greater total amount of air pollution, even though it may result in less intense local pollution than would occur in some very high-density portions of more compact regions.

> *Sprawl can generate a greater total amount of air pollution, even though it may result in less intense local pollution.*

Literature Synthesis

Most, but far from all, observers agree that low-density settlements generate more total automotive travel than more compact settlements, other things being equal (see prior discussion). Therefore, low-density settlements are presumed to generate more auto-oriented emissions per 100,000 residents. However, the

intensity of air pollution in each metropolitan area is affected by many factors, including the locations of major urban centers, prevailing winds, mountain barriers, temperature inversions, and general climate. Hence, there is substantive disagreement whether sprawl is a key factor in determining the degree of air pollution in each metropolitan area.

> *There is substantive disagreement whether sprawl is a key factor in determining the degree of air pollution in each metropolitan area.*

Burchell, in the *Impact Assessment of the New Jersey State Development and Redevelopment Plan*, found that air pollution would be very similarly reduced in the future under either sprawl or compact development scenarios (Burchell 1992a). Most of the reduction would be due to more stringent emission controls that would affect the entire motor vehicle fleet of New Jersey, as opposed to the region where this fleet would be replaced. In other words, development pattern, at least in this instance, did not significantly influence air pollution levels. (The New Jersey *Impact Assessment* also considered effects on water pollution under trend [sprawl] and plan [compact] conditions. Plan conditions were found to generate about one-third less water pollution than trend, although heavy metals in urban stormwater runoff were increased under the plan development scenario.)

Literature Synthesis Matrix

	+2 General Agreement	+1 Some Agreement	0 No Clear Outcome	−2 Substantial Disagreement
Does this condition notably exist?		X		
Is it strongly linked to sprawl?				X

Lessened Historic Preservation

Allegation/Basis

Sprawl makes it difficult to preserve historically significant older structures. Sprawl encourages businesses and households to leave older cities and inner-ring suburbs by permitting them to move to the exurban areas without paying the full marginal costs of their doing so. Through publicly financed roads, water and sewer line extensions, and special tax benefits, taxpayers are often forced to subsidize sprawl-type development. Simultaneously, regulatory and policy barriers make it more difficult for developers to rehabilitate and revitalize existing communities. Therefore, the economic base supporting older structures of historical significance located in inner-city neighborhoods is weakened. Neighborhood conditions in the vicinity of such structures also worsen because of the increased concentration of poverty; historic structures located there are eventually consumed by these forces.

> *Sprawl encourages businesses and households to leave older cities and inner-ring suburbs by permitting them to move to the exurban areas.*

Literature Synthesis

This allegation has been put forward mainly by the National Trust for Historic Preservation in its various publications attacking sprawl.

The following argument (Beaumont 1996a) summarizes the reasoning behind the professed association between sprawl and preservation. Beaumont is one of the few observers of sprawl who has commented on whether or not this association is valid.

As residents and businesses leave the urban areas, older buildings are often abandoned and begin to decay.
Source: Courtesy CUPR Press and HUD Photo Library.

According to Beaumont, sprawl affects historic preservation in five major ways:

1) Sprawl adversely affects older downtown areas and neighborhoods, where historic buildings are concentrated. When the economic vitality of a historic area suffers, the buildings in it often become underused or empty. Over time, many of them are "demolished by neglect" or torn down to make way for surface parking lots.

2) Sprawl destroys community character and the countryside. Cohesive main streets, old stone fences, historic trees, country roads—these and other features of the American landscape are rapidly being destroyed by sprawl development and the vast expanses of asphalt required to accommodate it.

3) Sprawl reduces opportunities for face-to-face interaction among people, thereby making it more difficult to create, or retain, a sense of community. By scattering the elements of a community across the landscape in a haphazard way, sprawl provides no town centers and reduces the sense of ownership—and therefore also the commitment—that people have toward their community.

4) Sprawl forecloses alternatives to the automobile as a means of transport, thereby adding to pressures to create or widen roads that often result in the demolition of historic resources or the degradation of their settings.

5) Sprawl leaves older cities and towns with excessively high concentrations of poor people with social problems, making these places a very difficult environment in which to revitalize communities. (Beaumont 1996a, 264)

Literature Synthesis Matrix

	+2 General Agreement	+1 Some Agreement	0 No Clear Outcome	−2 Substantial Disagreement
Does this condition notably exist?		X		
Is it strongly linked to sprawl?			X	

SPRAWL'S ALLEGED POSITIVE IMPACTS

Preference for Low-Density Living

Allegation/Basis

Many households prefer low-density residential living. Many consumer preference surveys reveal that a key part of the "American dream" is ownership of a detached, single-family home with attached private open space in the form of a backyard. More important than the stated preference, however, is the revealed preference: for the last 50 years, suburban development has been the primary form of metropolitan residential growth, and single-family housing units have been the dominant residential form. Consumers clearly choose low-density suburban living given existing alternatives and prices. Most housing developers consistently build low-density subdivisions because they are easier to market than higher-density developments. In order to make this low-density single-

family, detached housing affordable to most people, it is generally built at the urban fringe where land prices are lower (Downs 1994).

Literature Synthesis

The suburbanization of population and jobs in the United States has been well documented. In 1950, almost 70 percent of the population of 168 metropolitan areas lived in central cities; by 1990 over 60 percent of the population of 320 metropolitan areas lived in the suburbs, and a majority of jobs in metropolitan areas were in the suburbs as well (Rusk 1993). The process of suburbanization has lowered average population densities in urban areas. Between 1950 and 1990, the number of residents in urbanized areas, with populations over one million in 1990, increased 92 percent, while average population density decreased 44 percent (Wendell Cox Consultancy 1996). The fact that so many Americans choose to live in low-density areas has been cited as strong evidence that Americans prefer that lifestyle.

> **The fact that so many Americans choose to live in low-density areas has been cited as strong evidence that Americans prefer that lifestyle.**

People appear to be willing to pay for different land use and community forms. The most recent annual survey by Fannie Mae (1996) shows that homeownership is a top priority for 69 percent of Americans, and 73 percent desire a single-family detached house with a yard on all sides.

Another study that generated quality-of-life rankings for the fifty U.S. states over the period 1981–1990 found that sparsely populated, mountainous Western states such as Montana and Wyoming had a higher quality-of-life ranking than the more densely populated states in the East and Midwest (Gabriel et al. 1996). Urban congestion has been cited by "lone eagles" (individuals who are able to live anywhere and telecommute to work) as a factor influencing their decision to move (Salant et al. 1996).

A 1997 issue of the *Journal of the American Planning Association* (Winter 1997) has two articles dealing with sprawl that summarize many of these arguments. Gordon and Richardson (1997a) revisit several issues relevant to the compact cities discussion, including residential density preferences. They maintain that consumers, given the choice between low-density suburban living and high-density urban living, overwhelmingly choose the former: "But that suburbanization itself should be an object of attack is amazing, given the expressed preferences of the majority of Americans for suburban lifestyles and the supposed sanctity of consumer sovereignty." Drawing on the literature, they attempt to dispel the belief that the choice of low-density residential living is a constrained choice, strongly influenced by government policies that promote suburbanization, including subsidized automobile use and zoning laws that restrict high-density development. Gordon and Richardson argue that more subsidies per user are given to public transit than to auto travel; hence, government policies do not necessarily promote low-density living over high-density living. In response to the argument that developers are prevented by zoning and land-use regulations from building at higher densities, Gordon and Richardson maintain that developers just offer what the market demands: "The risks of building an unacceptable product are very high, and builders are well aware of the strong consumer preference for the single-family detached home."

The single-family detached home, with garage, in the suburbs is the preferred housing type in America.
Source: Florida DCA.

Though Ewing (1997) agrees with Gordon and Richardson (1997a) that the recent choice of U.S. households has been for low-density suburban living over high-density urban living, he contends that given a larger set of single family residential environments, consumers do not necessarily favor the former: "There is strong consumer preference for new single-family detached housing—a housing type concentrated in the suburbs. But most people could do without the rest of the suburban package" (Ewing 1997). Ewing maintains that compact development is capable of holding its own in the marketplace and cites evidence from the literature on consumer preferences. According to Ewing, the literature reveals several interesting facts:

1) The suburbs often rank below small towns, villages, and rural settings as a desirable place to live.

2) Home buyers, given a choice, are evenly divided on whether they prefer low- or medium-density residential settings.

3) Home buyers in high-priced housing markets often prefer small-lot houses.

4) The public, given a choice, is almost evenly divided on whether it prefers mixed- or single-use areas.

In his earlier study, "Characteristics, Causes, and Effects of Sprawl: A Literature Review," Ewing (1994) offered additional evidence to bolster his contention that consumer preference surveys do not clearly support low-density living over more compact forms of settlement. Surveys where people are shown images of both sprawl and traditional communities reveal that, for the most part, the latter are favored by wide margins (Neuman 1991). Some surveys, however, have found that people favor homogeneous neighborhoods over mixed-use neighborhoods by a margin of about two to one (Bookout 1992), and that people prefer low-density suburban or exurban living (Audirac and Zifou 1989).

> *Recent choice of U.S. households has been for low-density suburban living over high-density urban living.*

Other surveys of consumer preferences have also shown mixed results. A September 1995 survey of people who shopped and ultimately bought units in planned communities indicated that 57 percent of the respondents agreed with the statement "I'm tired of living in the sterile uniformity of most suburbs." Yet, more than three-fourths of the respondents believed in the American dream of a big yard and a house set back from the street (Bradford 1996).

There may be something approaching universal agreement that U.S. residential patterns in metropolitan areas have become increasingly suburbanized (i.e., have lower density or sprawl). There is probably close to general agreement that many, if not a majority, of U.S. households prefer single-family detached housing given current options and prices—albeit observers raise the issue whether households would move in

significant numbers if other options were available.

> *Fifty-seven percent of the respondents agreed with the statement "I'm tired of living in the sterile uniformity of most suburbs." Yet, more than three-fourths of the respondents believed in the American dream of a big yard and a house set back from the street.*

The question about whether sprawl is strongly linked to these residential choices is a matter of interpretation. At one extreme, the choice of low-density housing is, in essence, the definition of sprawl, so the question of whether it is caused by sprawl is a circular one. Another interpretation is that the mere existence of the pattern (sprawl) and its accompanying low-density housing influences people's preferences, like the advertising of any product.

Literature Synthesis Matrix

	+2 General Agreement	+1 Some Agreement	0 No Clear Outcome	−2 Substantial Disagreement
Does this condition notably exist?	X			
Is it strongly linked to sprawl?		X		

Lower Crime Rates

Allegation/Basis

Low-density development patterns have lower crime rates. Households move out of central cities to escape the high rates of crime encountered there. Relatively high crime rates are statistically associated with very low-income areas, especially within large cities. Such areas also often have much higher population densities than the neighborhoods typical of sprawl development.

Literature Synthesis

Statistics appear to indicate that urban residents experience higher rates of crime than their suburban or rural counterparts. In 1994, the estimated rate (per 1,000 persons aged 12 and older) of personal victimization, which includes robbery, assault, rape, and personal theft, was highest for inhabitants of urban areas (67.6). Suburban areas experienced a rate of personal victimization of 51.8; rural areas had a rate of 39.8 (Pastore and Maguire 1996). Crime statistics released by the Federal Bureau of Investigation (FBI) for 1995 indicate that the Crime Index (comprised of selected violent and property offenses) was higher in Metropolitan Statistical Areas (MSAs) (5,761 per 100,000 inhabitants) than cities outside MSAs (5,315 per 100,000). Rural counties had the lowest index number—2,083 per 100,000 inhabitants (Federal Bureau of Investigation 1996).

> **Research does not strongly indicate that the higher-density living commonly found in urban areas is associated with higher crime rates.**

Other research, however, does not strongly indicate that the higher-density living commonly found in urban areas is associated with higher crime rates. Using 1974 census data, Newman and Kenworthy (1989a) correlate density with crime statistics for 26 major U.S. cities. Simple linear correlations suggest that there is no significant relationship between crime and density. Similarly, correlational studies within the environmental psychology literature find no consistent relationship between population density and social pathologies (Sherrod and Cohen 1979).

Several studies indicate that communities with high quality-of-life rankings exhibit low crime rates (Roback 1982, 1988). The amount of crime in a community may also affect migration patterns for both workers and firms. Salant et al. (1996) and von Reichert and Rudzitis (1992) found that the amount of crime was a factor that influenced individuals' decisions to migrate to a community that they perceived would provide a better quality of life.

Results from the Salant et al. study also indicated that individuals were attracted to locations that provided a safe place to live. A study using data from the *1983 Annual Housing Survey*, however, found that few individuals moved to a particular neighborhood for greater safety (Spain 1988). The main reasons for moving that survey respondents reported were to find a less expensive place to live and to reduce their commuting times.

A study by Gottlieb (1995) concludes that firms in the high-tech sector are less willing to locate in areas characterized by high levels of violent crime.

Inner-city, high-density areas are believed by some to foster crime and decay.
Source: Courtesy CUPR Press and HUD Photo Library.

Other studies have found that perceptions of personal safety differ between residents of high-density urban areas and low-density suburban areas. A 1995 nationwide telephone survey of more than 1,400 adults attempted to discern how safe individuals felt in their communities. When asked, "In the past year do you feel safer, not as safe, or about the same on the streets in your neighborhood?" 14 percent of suburban residents, compared to 22 percent of urban residents, felt less safe. On the other hand, 12 percent of urban residents, compared to 9 percent of suburban residents, felt their safety had increased over the past year (Pastore and Maguire 1996). Through interviews, Hummon (1990) determined that rural residents view danger as both an integral part of city life and an indicator of social problems. Urban residents, however, consider crime and danger to be more a factor of socioeconomic conditions and location than an integral part of city life. Using surveys of low-income, single mothers, Cook (1988) found that urban women were two times more likely than suburban women to indicate they felt unsafe in their apartments and neighborhoods.

> *A low crime rate is one of the top 10 quality-of-life characteristics desired by* **Money** *magazine subscribers.*

Researchers within the criminal justice field conclude that perceptions of crime and security vary with site characteristics and socioeconomic conditions; thus, fear of crime does not always accurately reflect actual crime rates. Instead, fear of crime is often derived from incomplete knowledge of crime rates, observable evidence of disorder, and prejudices arising from neighborhood change (Skogan 1986). Other studies conclude that the direct effects of the physical environment on crime rates range from small to moderate (Taylor and Gottfredson 1986).

Within the popular literature, there appears to be agreement that crime reduces a community's overall quality of

life. Studies from popular literature commonly use crime as one measure of a community's desirability. Quality-of-life rankings of cities in the *Places Rated Almanac* (Savageau and Boyer 1993), *Money* magazine's "Best Places to Live in America" (Fried et al. 1996), and *Fortune* magazine's "Best Cities: Where the Living is Easy" (Precourt and Faircloth 1996), all include some measure of crime as a component of a community's overall quality of life. In particular, Fried et al. found that a low crime rate is one of the top 10 quality-of-life characteristics desired by *Money* magazine subscribers.

In short, selected crime statistics obtained from the Federal Bureau of Investigation indicate that lower-density developments, such as suburban and rural areas, have lower crime rates than high-density urban areas. Empirical studies that have examined the relationship between crime and density, however, have found mixed results—increased density does not necessarily result in higher crime rates. The mixed results may be a factor of how individual studies define and measure crime and crime rates. There appears to be agreement that suburban residents perceive themselves to be safer than their urban counterparts.

Although the literature appears to demonstrate, at best, correlation between density and crime, it does not demonstrate causality between sprawl and low crime rates. Studies have found that the effect of physical environment on crime rates ranges from minimal to moderate and that crime is more a factor of socioeconomic conditions than density. An argument might be made that sprawl reduces crime rates in a round-about way—sprawl is correlated with higher incomes which, in turn, are often correlated with greater spending on home protection and public safety. This argument, however, does not demonstrate that sprawl causes lower crime rates.

Literature Synthesis Matrix

	+2 General Agreement	+1 Some Agreement	0 No Clear Outcome	−2 Substantial Disagreement
Does this condition notably exist?		X		
Is it strongly linked to sprawl?			X	

Enhanced Value or Reduced Costs of Public and Private Goods

Allegation/Basis

Many households find the cost of public services and some private services in suburban locations a better value. For the public sector, suburban locations often provide better services (especially schools) for an equivalent or lower tax burden. For private-sector goods and services, particularly retail sales, the lower land values in suburban areas allow land-intensive development formats, which include expansive ("big box") floor space and parking. These development formats, in turn, attract high-volume, low-cost retailers.

Literature Synthesis

The alleged benefit for *public* services substantially overlaps the alleged benefits reviewed under the heading Social Issues in this literature review. Two of the alleged benefits discussed there are germane here:

1) The ability of jurisdictions to define a relatively homogeneous population with relatively similar service needs (which also provides opportunities for both economies of scale and concentration), and the ability to drop services not needed by the homogeneous population (i.e., social services for low-income households).

2) The ability to have different tax levels and service qualities.

There is an ongoing professional debate about the institutional structures by which public services are most efficiently and fairly provided, and a large body of literature on the subject. Not surprisingly, the poles of the debate are occupied by those who believe in the efficiency of markets and those who believe markets operate imperfectly without government intervention. In the 1950s, Tiebout (1956) laid out the basic arguments for market choice (which, when applied to government, is sometimes referred to as "public choice"). He argued in favor of multiple small governments that allow households to "vote with their feet," choosing to live where the combination of public services, quality, and cost best meet their preferences.

> *Multiple small governments allow households to "vote with their feet," choosing to live where the combination of public services, quality, and cost best meets their preferences.*

In contrast are those who argue (see, for example, Foster [1996]) that typical market failures in the provision of public goods require larger units of government so that external costs can be internalized, increasing the odds that sufficient public goods will be provided. Arguments are made for the improvement of both efficiency and equity.

Because this topic is considered elsewhere in this report, it is merely alluded to here. There is certainly no agreement on this subject. Nor is any likely, since to come to a conclusion would require, among other things, agreement on two issues on which people's opinions derive as much from underlying philosophies as from the results of social science: 1) the proper scope of government intervention, and 2) the trade-offs between efficiency and equity.

For *private* goods, there is ample anecdotal evidence that big box retailers make their money by high volumes on low margins, which for consumers means low cost. The growth of these retailers (e.g., Wal-Mart, Home Depot, Costco) is evidence of demand and suggests that they are giving consumers more of what they want (Linneman 1995). Additional anecdotal evidence suggests that many people who would oppose such retailers in their neighborhoods are some of the same ones who drive, often substantial distances, to shop at these stores in other parts of a region.

The next question, however, is: To what extent are low-density development patterns essential for these cost savings? Recent work done to help evaluate the impacts of managed growth plans for metropolitan Portland, Oregon (ECONorthwest 1996) sheds some light on this issue. After quantifying vacant land supply, researchers conducted focus groups and work sessions with retail developers and brokers. Their opinion was that to satisfy today's consumers most retail development had to accommodate the automobile, and as a result, vacant, low-priced land in sizable parcels was critical to retail development, especially big box retail. High density areas are likely to have higher land values, less vacant land, smaller parcels, and more existing residents to oppose the new retail development.

A few central cities have seen new discount retailing. In most cases, however, the development has occurred on underutilized industrial parcels whose zoning either defines the retail uses as

compatible or makes variances easy to receive. In these cases, low-value land is still the primary factor allowing the development to proceed.

> **Market failures in the provision of public goods require larger units of government so that external costs can be internalized.**

There is reasonable evidence to conclude that people want goods at lower prices in lower-density parts of metropolitan areas. As with other effects, whether sprawl *causes* this effect is a matter of interpretation. On one hand, sprawl *is* the effect; the low-density retail pattern is what enables retailers to reduce prices. On the other hand, a pattern of sprawl may be causal if it implies more retail of the same type is desirable and allowable, and if it creates a pattern that allows more low-cost land to be developed more easily. Sprawl probably does both.

Literature Synthesis Matrix

	+2 General Agreement	+1 Some Agreement	0 No Clear Outcome	-2 Substantial Disagreement
Does this condition notably exist?		X		
Is it strongly linked to sprawl?			X	

Fosters Greater Economic Well-Being

Allegation/Basis

As an outcome of a free market, sprawl benefits from the market decisions made by individual households and firms to maximize their welfare (as measured by utility or profit). By restricting these individual choices, efforts to limit sprawl will reduce the overall standard of living.

A central tenet of free-market economics is that individual households and firms act in ways to maximize their welfare, and the result of these individual decisions is to maximize welfare for society as a whole. In this context, sprawl is considered to maximize welfare for society because it represents the outcome of individual choices by households and firms about where to locate and how to build homes and businesses.

Critics of free-market economics point out that decisions are based solely on the costs and benefits faced by the individual household or firm, and so do not consider the costs or benefits to others that may result from their decision (the costs and benefits to others are referred to as *externalities*). Critics of sprawl point out the negative externalities—traffic congestion, increased public infrastructure costs, and accelerated development of farmland and open space, for example—and argue that these externalities reduce social welfare. Critics of sprawl often suggest policies to address the negative externalities of sprawl. It is the debate over these policies that the alleged impact on economic well-being is most often discussed.

There is also extensive debate about the level of negative externalities; whether these externalities are caused by sprawl, and the effectiveness of policies to address these externalities. This debate occasionally touches on whether the policies will affect the costs and benefits faced by individual households and firms.

A primary concern is whether policies to limit sprawl will increase the cost of housing—this impact is addressed elsewhere in this literature review. An argument that is also occasionally raised is whether policies to limit sprawl will in turn limit job growth in an area, thereby reducing income for area residents and limiting economic development opportunities. These are the impacts that are focused upon in this section.

Literature Synthesis

In the New Jersey impact assessment, Burchell (1992a) found that New Jersey could accommodate similar magnitudes of population and employment growth under both trend and plan development patterns. Distributional patterns would differ, however. Plan development would direct more jobs to urban and rural centers and fewer to suburban areas than trend.

Sheppard (1988) relates sprawl to the economic well-being of residents. Sheppard found that an increase in space available to a particular class of residents results in lower rents at all locations, increased "suburbanization" for all classes, and increased utility for all classes. Sheppard cautions the reader, however, that the results consider neither externalities nor the public good associated with the exercise of development controls.

Most authors argue simply that sprawl must maximize societal welfare because it results from free-market decisions (Gordon and Richardson 1997a). This obviously ignores the public contributions of both highway and arterial capacity. The benefits of sprawl that affect economic well-being are most often addressed in arguments against policies to limit sprawl. These arguments are based on the considerable literature that shows that increased density increases the cost of land. It is argued that an increase in density will reduce job growth and economic development opportunity by increasing the cost or limiting the number of sites available for commercial development, and by increasing the cost of housing, which in turn will limit the supply of labor (ECONorthwest 1994).

Growth controls raise housing prices in communities where they are established.

There is considerable evidence that measures to control growth cause the price of land to increase. Shilling et al. (1991) found that state land-use controls both restrict the supply and increase the demand for residential land, driving up its price. Brueckner (1990) cites a large empirical literature documenting the effects of growth controls on housing and land markets. His evidence points to the fact that growth controls raise housing prices in communities where they are established (Dowall and Landis 1982; Katz and Rosen 1987; Schwartz et al. 1981, 1989).

Most of the literature that addresses the impact of growth controls on land prices focuses on the residential land market. There appear to be very few articles that address the impact of sprawl, or measures to control sprawl, on commercial land markets, the level of employment growth, or wage income. While there are logical reasons to suspect that uninhibited growth fosters more employment and wage growth than limited growth, the literature does not document this at all.

Literature Synthesis Matrix

	+2 General Agreement	+1 Some Agreement	0 No Clear Outcome	−2 Substantial Disagreement
Does this condition notably exist?		X		
Is it strongly linked to sprawl?		X		

CHAPTER

7

Literature Synthesis

SOCIAL ISSUES

There are many social issues related to sprawl. Assembled for this review is literature focusing on how sprawl affects the places and the people that are not part of this phenomenon. This includes, as a starting point, studies on the "condition" or "health" of cities, especially relative to proximate suburban communities.

Examined next is a group of studies considering the historical development of suburbs with the recurring leitmotif of separation of, and exclusion from, the older urban center. Also considered are numerous recent studies that link the welfare of cities to the economic and social health of the overall metropolitan area and propose, in turn, that urban revitalization is futile without a closer integration of cities and their suburbs.

Conditions of cities and the interconnections between cities and suburbs are viewed in depth in this literature. Cities are considered not only as being important in their own right for retaining higher-order central place functions but are linked to suburbs as a necessary stabilizer of the overall metropolitan economy. In much of this literature,

sprawl, which encourages outward movement of population and functions from cities, is cast as a detriment both to cities and ultimately to suburbs as well.

But there is an alternative view. Cities are viewed in this literature as relics that have lost much of their purpose as population and employment have suburbanized. Yet, for the urban poor and minorities, there was hope in the form of zones of emergence (Sternlieb and Beaton 1972). These were the better areas of cities and inner-ring suburbs which, as their more mobile populations left for the more vigorous outer-ring suburbs, offered themselves as places for the disenfranchised to emerge.

This view is analogous to the concept of filtering in housing. Filtering provides housing to the poor in the form of modest units that are vacated over time as former occupants seek housing with more amenities. Similarly, more affordable inner-ring suburbs filter down to become, over time, the suburban zone of emergence for urbanites and minorities. In this view, an unrestrained ability to move to the suburban outer ring—one of the characteristics of sprawl—is essential to allow inner-ring neighborhoods and communities to filter down, much as the ability to consume better housing is the linchpin on which housing filtering rests.

Sprawl's Alleged Negative Impacts

Fosters Suburban Exclusion
Fosters Spatial Mismatch
Foster Residential Segregation
Worsens City Fiscal Stress
Worsens Inner-City Deterioration

Sprawl's Alleged Positive Impacts

Fosters Localized Land Use Decisions
Enhanced Municipal Diversity and Choice

SPRAWL'S ALLEGED NEGATIVE EFFECTS

Fosters Suburban Exclusion

Allegation/Basis

Suburban exclusionary zoning increases the concentration of low-income households in certain neighborhoods. Most low- and moderate-income households cannot afford to live in suburbs where exclusionary zoning raises housing costs; thus, such households become disproportionately concentrated within central cities and older inner-ring suburbs. Housing in many parts of these communities is generally older, smaller, more functionally obsolete, less well-maintained, and much less costly to occupy than housing in newer suburbs. Moreover, subsidized housing units—especially those in public housing projects—are heavily concentrated within older neighborhoods in central cities and inner-ring suburbs, because residents of other areas—including most suburbs—refuse to permit them within their boundaries. This further concentrates very low-income households both within central cities and older suburbs, and within particular inner-city neighborhoods. The concentration of high proportions of very poor residents within older, deteriorated neighborhoods fosters conditions that are adverse to the welfare of residents. These include high rates of crime, drug abuse, delinquency, births out of wedlock, welfare dependency, unemployment, alcoholism, and mental illness. In addition, the quality of education received in public schools in these areas, or where children from such areas dominate, is very low.

Literature Synthesis

There is some disagreement about the degree to which suburban exclusionary zoning is responsible for poverty concentrations in core-area neighborhoods. Some observers believe other factors are as important in producing such neighborhoods (Downs 1994). These other factors include negative behavior patterns among the residents that make them unwelcome elsewhere; the concentration of deteriorated, very low-cost housing in such neighborhoods which attracts people who cannot afford better accommodations; the concentration of public housing units in such neighborhoods; the lack of public transportation in suburban areas that makes it difficult for poor persons without cars to live there; and the desire of poor households to live together in neighborhoods where public services aiding the poor are more easily accessible.

In contradiction, recent findings in New Jersey from the New Jersey Council on Affordable Housing (COAH) and similar findings from the Gautreaux (Chicago) and Special Mobility Program (SMP)

(Cincinnati) studies indicate that those who occupy affordable housing in more suburban locations take on the employment characteristics, ambition levels, and success rates of the population of those jurisdictions (Davis 1993; Fischer 1991; Wish and Eisdorfer 1996). In New Jersey, close to 15,000 affordable housing units have been built and occupied as a result of legislation emanating from the series of *Mt. Laurel* cases challenging exclusionary zoning practices in that state. Occupants of these housing units are employed, doing well at local schools, and integrated without incident in neighborhoods they would not have had access to without the court decisions.

The Gautreaux and Special Mobility Program studies show that residents moving from the central city to the suburbs using housing vouchers have higher rates of employment and higher salaries, and their children have better school attendance and higher grades, than families who choose not to move. While the confounding issue of self-selection is clearly present here—i.e., the successful and ambitious families are the ones that opted to participate in the moves—a growing body of literature indicates that "place" matters. There is a "rub-off" effect of place wherein success patterns can be communicated by residents to newcomers who specifically wish to improve their current economic and social positions (Poisman and Botein 1993).

Literature Synthesis Matrix

	+2 General Agreement	+1 Some Agreement	0 No Clear Outcome	−2 Substantial Disagreement
Does this condition notably exist?		X		
Is it strongly linked to sprawl?				X

Fosters Spatial Mismatch

Allegation/Basis

The resulting "spatial mismatch" between where most new jobs are being created (far-out suburbs) and where many low-skilled workers must live (inner-city neighborhoods) aggravates high rates of unemployment in inner-city neighborhoods. The unlimited extension of urbanized uses on the periphery of the metropolitan areas permits many employers to move to locations that are very far from inner-city neighborhoods. Consequently, unemployed workers living in those neighborhoods can neither readily learn about job opportunities in far-out locations nor afford to commute to such jobs even if they learn about and qualify for them. This mismatch aggravates both high rates of unemployment in inner-city neighborhoods and suburban shortages of unskilled labor.

Literature Synthesis

Kain (1992) was one of the first to examine whether a mismatch exists between the increase in lower-skilled and otherwise attainable jobs in the suburbs and the high levels of unemployment of residents in central cities who should be able to access these jobs.

Spatial mismatch has also been examined by sociologists Kasarda (1990) and Wilson (1987) and by economists Ihlanfeldt and Sjoquist (1990). Although the original literature related the mismatch to black workers of all ages, later studies focused on the spatial mismatch as it affected young black workers. Race as the causative agent is the main focus of inquiry throughout most of the studies mentioned above. In other studies by Harrison (1974) and Kasarda (1990), causes of the mismatch (which according to them may not be spatial) are extended to the inadequate skills and education of young black workers, and limited transportation or access to transportation. Findings on spatial mismatch, although not always consistent in unearthing a spatial component (see Harrison [1974], Ellwood [1986], and Leonard [1987]), are persistent in their specification of a mismatch of some type (Pugh 1998).

Poor inner-city residents often cannot reach jobs located in the suburbs.
Source: Bob Deammrich Photography.

The reality of this mismatch is a population desiring to be employed in one location and available jobs going unfilled in another. Often, the unfilled jobs are lower-order jobs that are not worth accessing by public transit if the prospective worker must also pay for child day care services to retain the job.

Other jobs similarly located in the suburbs may require skills that applicants, even after training, cannot meet. Or they may be jobs that casual workers available during the summer or during college breaks can easily meet without training.

The confluence of elements that create spatial mismatch is so complex that sprawl versus more compact development patterns probably play only a minor role. Spatial mismatch will grow to be a major issue with significant consequences as workfare replaces welfare. Moreover, the relationship between sprawl and central

city unemployment rates, the bottom-line issue of the above discussion, is even more complex than relationships between sprawl and spatial mismatch.

> *The confluence of elements that creates spatial mismatch is so complex that sprawl versus more compact development patterns probably play only a minor role.*

Literature Synthesis Matrix

	+2 General Agreement	+1 Some Agreement	0 No Clear Outcome	−2 Substantial Disagreement
Does this condition notably exist?	X			
Is it strongly linked to sprawl?		X		

Fosters Residential Segregation

Allegation/Basis

Residential segregation by race and income is greater under sprawl than where less fragmented governance over land uses exists. While socially segregated neighborhoods certainly exist in cities, exclusionary zoning by many outlying suburban communities inhibits the construction of relatively low-cost housing for low- and moderate-income households, most of whom are minorities. This occurs because residents of each community control land-use decisions therein. They usually take into account only their own interests in making such decisions—not the interests of the region as a whole or of citizens in other parts of it (Freilich and Peshoff, 1997). They have compelling economic motives for trying to minimize the number of low-cost housing units within their own communities. These include maintaining housing prices as high as possible and excluding households

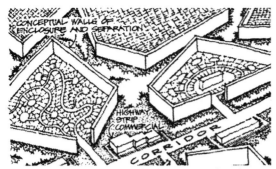

Euclidean zoning by district can be used to foster homogenous neighborhoods with residents of similar incomes, profiles, and backgrounds.
Source: Illustration by Roger Lewis in *Growth Management Handbook* published by MSM Regional Council.

whose need for public services—especially schools—will cost the community more than the taxes these households will contribute to the community (Fischel 1985). Because Blacks and Hispanics tend to have much lower incomes, on average, than other major groups in American society, such income segregation is also an effective means of achieving ethnic segregation in many areas.

Literature Synthesis

There is only partial agreement about this allegation. Such a small number of metropolitan areas without fragmented governance over land uses exist in the United States that statistical testing of conditions in them versus conditions elsewhere probably are not valid.

Yet coming at this issue from another direction, those states and regions that have made overt efforts to provide affordable housing in locations where it has not before existed are achieving integration in those locations. In New Jersey, where a municipality must provide its fair share of affordable housing or lose its right to zone, racial and ethnic integration is taking place in what were once predominantly white outer-ring neighborhoods. New Jersey's

affordable housing program requires that those who fill municipal quotas come from outside the municipality's boundaries but inside its commuting region. There are strict advertising and queuing requirements that ensure that minority households in central cities have an equal chance to occupy affordable housing in the suburbs. With these kinds of mandates, integration of neighborhoods moves quickly and directly (Wish and Eisdorfer 1996).

> *Those states and regions that have made overt efforts to provide affordable housing in locations where it has not before existed are achieving integration in those locations.*

Literature Synthesis Matrix

	+2 General Agreement	+1 Some Agreement	0 No Clear Outcome	–2 Substantial Disagreement
Does this condition notably exist?		X		
Is it strongly linked to sprawl?			X	

Worsens City Fiscal Stress

Allegation/Basis

Under sprawl, central city governments become fiscally strapped or "squeezed," because they must provide costly services to large numbers of very poor households, while the properties owned, occupied, or patronized by such households produce relatively low per capita tax revenues. Low-income neighborhoods in particular have higher costs of crime and fire prevention, street cleaning, and public health and welfare services than middle- and upper-income neighborhoods. Yet the former produce lower property and sales tax revenues per capita than the latter. This situation forces city governments serving such communities to either raise taxes above those in surrounding communities or to provide lower quality and quantities of key public services to their residents, or both.

Literature Synthesis

Only limited agreement exists on the extent to which sprawl is regarded as a major cause of fiscal stress. The concentration of very poor households within inner-city neighborhoods is surely not caused solely by suburban sprawl; many other causal factors largely unrelated to the specific form of growth within a metropolitan area also contribute to this result. Unfortunately, it is probably impossible to decide scientifically how to allocate "responsibility" for this outcome among these causal factors—a fact which presents an obstacle to "proving" that sprawl contributes significantly to this outcome.

As stores and offices move out, central cities must shift fiscal burdens onto those remaining, usually in the form of higher property taxes. *Source:* Teri Leigh.

The ability of households and employment to shift locations in a metropolitan area is virtually unrestrained. To the degree that households and employers seek safer and more aesthetically pleasing locations, even when these are found distant from the core, the households and employers will move there. If taxes are lower or tax incentives to relocate are offered, core-to-

peripheral relocation will also take place. If high-income residential and nonresidential properties are either "footloose" locationally or are being bid out of central locations to more distant locations, only those households and employers who are not footloose or are not bid out will remain. These are often the poorer households and businesses, which demand higher services and provide less revenues. The end result is a strain on public service districts in the form of higher service costs and reduced revenue receipts. When this happens, property taxes rise—sparking another wave of residential and nonresidential exodus (Sternlieb and Burchell 1977).

Most of the central city fiscal deterioration forces described above, although largely independent of development patterns, certainly need the defining characteristics of sprawl to operate. Fragmented governments in competition with each other for the "better" land uses create fiscal stress for those governments that cannot compete (Downs 1994).

> *Most of the central city fiscal deterioration forces described above, while largely independent of development patterns, certainly need the defining characteristics of sprawl to operate.*

(See also Public/Private Capital and Operating Costs—Negative Impacts—More Adverse Public Fiscal Impacts.)

Literature Synthesis Matrix

	+2 General Agreement	+1 Some Agreement	0 No Clear Outcome	−2 Substantial Disagreement
Does this condition notably exist?		X		
Is it strongly linked to sprawl?		X		

Worsens Inner-City Deterioration

Allegation/Basis

A self-aggravating downward spiral of negative conditions and the consequent withdrawal of viable resources occurs in inner-city neighborhoods, making them continually worse off. The presence of areas with deteriorating conditions in central cities tends to motivate many economically viable families and business firms to move elsewhere. The same conditions also discourage viable households and firms from moving into those cities in general, and into high-poverty neighborhoods in particular. As a result, the economic and social viability of the households and firms left residing in such communities deteriorates.

Literature Synthesis

There is only some agreement on the extent to which sprawl is a major cause of this downward spiral. The concentration of very poor households within inner-city neighborhoods is obviously caused by other factors largely unrelated to the specific form of growth within a metropolitan area.

A study of residential abandonment in cities nationally (Sternlieb and Burchell 1977) investigated numerous causal relationships including:

1) other abandoned structures on the block
2) race of tenant and owner
3) commercial use of part of the property
4) racial and economic characteristics of neighborhood and city.

The study found that the most significant causal relationship to central city abandonment was the amount of housing built outside the central city yet inside the

city's metropolitan area (Sternlieb and Burchell 1977).

Row houses in Washington, D.C., lie decaying and empty as residents moved into surrounding suburbs.
Source: Ellis Herwig/Stock, Boston.

To the degree that significant amounts of housing are built farther out in the metropolitan area and the occupancy costs of this housing are comparable to, or cheaper than, existing housing, this new housing will be sought in preference to closer-in housing (Schafer 1975).

The most significant causal relationship to central city abandonment was the amount of housing built outside the central city.

Unfortunately, however, as with fiscal stress, it is probably impossible to decide scientifically how to allocate "responsibility" for this outcome among multiple causal factors.

(See also Quality of Life—Positive Impacts—Reduced Costs of Public and Private Goods).

Literature Synthesis Matrix

	+2 General Agreement	+1 Some Agreement	0 No Clear Outcome	−2 Substantial Disagreement
Does this condition notably exist?		X		
Is it strongly linked to sprawl?		X		

SPRAWL'S ALLEGED POSITIVE IMPACTS

Fosters Localized Land Use Decisions

Allegation/Basis

Sprawl keeps government decisions about land use at the local level, where individual citizens have much more chance of influencing the results than they do where regional decision making predominates. Because sprawl involves fragmentation of government powers among many relatively small localities, it keeps land-use decision making closer to the people most directly affected by it. This satisfies the strong American desire for local sovereignty. Like-minded citizens can pass zoning and other regulations that exclude types of development from their communities they do not like. This in turn allows them to prevent "socially undesirable" influences in their neighborhoods and schools. Such negative influences include potentially dangerous households with characteristics markedly different from their own, as well as region-serving land uses with negative local spillovers, like airports or incinerators.

Literature Synthesis

The literature dealing with the merit of local government praises its democratic responsiveness, as is illustrated in the following quotations:

> Others came to suburbs for better schools. This has been due, at least in part, to the responsiveness of these schools to parental expectations, rooted in turn in the smaller size of many suburban school districts. Indeed, in an age primarily given over to state centralization, the suburbs have encouraged a countervailing decentralization governance, forcing a

healthy kind of competitiveness onto local governments. (Carlson 1996)

The trend in many places has been for cities to incorporate their surrounding suburbs, creating mega-jurisdictions without local identity and administrative nimbleness. This is a bad idea. Instead, cities ought to be breaking themselves into smaller political units that enjoy a degree of social consensus where governing can be done flexibly and with less impersonality. (Kotkin 1996)

The State of New Jersey alone has more than 500 independent municipal governments.
Source: New Jersey (State of), *Statement of Financial Condition of Counties and Municipalities.*

Obviously, the literature is divided on this point. One statistic beyond refute is that there is little growth in regional governments on a national basis, and although municipalities or counties may be willing to join together to distribute one or another carefully selected public services, they appear unwilling to join together for common governance. Further, on a national basis, the number of regional school districts currently desiring to split apart is greater than the number of school districts currently desiring to join together (Petersen 1996).

Literature Synthesis Matrix

	+2 General Agreement	+1 Some Agreement	0 No Clear Outcome	-2 Substantial Disagreement
Does this condition notably exist?	X			
Is it strongly linked to sprawl?		X		

Enhanced Municipal Diversity and Choice

Allegation/Basis

Sprawl provides citizens with a great variety of localities with differing tax levels, public service qualities, and housing costs, thereby increasing the range of choice available. The many individual localities in a metropolitan area function like suppliers of "bundles" of tax levels, public services, and local amenities in a market. Competition among them provides households with many more choices of living environments than would exist if all key fiscal and land-use decisions were made centrally and applied similarly throughout the metropolitan area. This process, first conceptualized by Tiebout, (1956) is widely praised by economists for bringing many of the virtues of a free market to the public sector, thereby benefiting potential residents of suburban communities.

Literature Synthesis

There is reasonable agreement that housing costs, public services (primarily education), tax levels, and housing stock aesthetics of a community form the bundle of goods that is bid for in community selection. Within a metropolitan area, citizens have significant choices of communities, and within a fragmented metropolitan area, they have even more choices.

> *Sprawl's contribution to diversity in choice is the massive amount of reasonable alternatives (not best or worst) that it offers the locational consumer.*

Those who "shop" for communities take all of the elements listed above into account before making a locational decision. Sprawl's contribution to diversity in choice is the massive amount of reasonable alternatives (not best or worst) that it offers the locational consumer. Some minor argument is found from those who contend that sprawl creates many similar communities, thus stifling diversity.

Fragmented governments, primarily supporting residential housing, offer infinite variations of the bundles of housing, public services, and tax structure described above. Most of the variations found at the periphery of metropolitan areas are superior in housing value, school systems, property tax levels, and housing amenities to locations found closer in. As such, these are the locations most often sought; the closer-in communities are the locations most often left behind. The most significant variables appear to be housing cost and housing appreciation, which in combination appear to be maximized in locations more distant from, as opposed to closer to, the urban core (Downs 1994).

Literature Synthesis Matrix

	+2 General Agreement	+1 Some Agreement	0 No Clear Outcome	-2 Substantial Disagreement
Does this condition notably exist?	X			
Is it strongly linked to sprawl?		X		

CHAPTER

8

Literature Synthesis

OVERALL SUMMARY OF THE LITERATURE

This chapter is divided into two parts. The first part aggregates the information presented in chapters 3, 4, 5, 6, and 7. It attempts to detail how much of the sprawl literature is represented by a topic such as *public and private capital and operating costs* versus other topics like *transportation and travel costs, land/natural habitat preservation, quality of life, social issues*, and so on. The first portion of the chapter further details the share of the sprawl literature that employs a certain methodology or type of empirical analysis as well as how much of the literature relies on particular databases. Finally, it discusses inherent weaknesses in the sprawl literature.

The second part of the chapter links, in summary fashion, sprawl's defining characteristics to its potential impacts. This is done to determine which of sprawl's characteristics are most associated with positive and negative impacts. The upshot of this analysis is that the three most defining characteristics of sprawl—*leapfrog development, low-density,* and *unlimited outward extension*—are associated with *both* sprawl's negative and positive impacts.

TOPICAL COVERAGE, DATABASES, METHODOLOGIES, DEFICIENCIES

Necessary Disclaimers

One logical starting point for summarizing the literature and analysis of this chapter is to review the distribution of the studies by topic and determine where there is more or less topical coverage. This can be done quantitatively, that is, by examining bibliographies on the topic—such as the one assembled here (see References), or by Ewing (1997), Gordon and Richardson (1997a), or the Growth Management and Research Clearinghouse (1993).

An overview of the literature could also be made by tabulating the numerical distribution of studies by subject type. This procedure raises its own issues, however, such as bias in the respective bibliographies (i.e., those emphasizing studies critical versus supportive of sprawl) and differences that reflect the varying professional orientations of the bibliography compilers (i.e., traffic engineer or historic preservationist).

In doing a quantitative census of the literature and topical coverage of sprawl, there is also a question of how to count multiple studies by the same author of a similar type. Should the Altshuler criticism of *The Costs of Sprawl* methodology, originally enunciated in 1977 and then essentially repeated in a jointly authored monograph by Altshuler and Gomez-Ibanez (1993), count as one or two entries in this census? Should Downs's prolific publications involving the issue of suburban exclusion of minorities which in some cases cover similar materials be individually counted (Downs 1970, 1973, 1981, 1985, and 1994)? The same problem of counting arises with the parallel series of publications by Gordon and Richardson (1989a, 1994a, 1996, 1997a, 1997b), Ewing (1994, 1995a, 1997), and Burchell (1992a, 1992b, 1994, 1995, 1996, 1997a, 1997b).

Another issue in undertaking a numerical tally of the literature is whether all entries should be weighted similarly. Do *The Costs of Sprawl* (RERC 1974) and the New Jersey *Impact Assessment* (Burchell 1992a, 1992b)—both influential analyses of hundreds of pages each—"weigh" the same as briefer and less substantive discussions?

Over and above these questions, an attempt to quantify the topical coverage of the literature on sprawl is frustrated by such fundamental issues as what is meant by sprawl and what counts as literature on this subject. Often sprawl is not defined in the literature, and its full elemental characteristics are not universally agreed upon. Should the literature that is to be tabulated consist only of materials on sprawl per se (i.e., examinations of sprawl's effects on infrastructure costs), or should it include broader topics relevant to a discussion of sprawl? The quality of life (QOL) subset

in this report is illustrative; there is very little literature directly dealing with QOL and sprawl. But there are many more studies on QOL that show impacts on quality of life by forces analogous to sprawl.

Even though there are persistent problems, some general census of the approximately 500 citations in the references is required. Since more than a year has been spent assembling, categorizing, and analyzing the literature, clearly some statements can and should be made concerning its topical concentration and, as well, methods and databases relied upon.

In the following analysis, except for related materials such as dictionaries and encyclopedias; economics, land use, housing, and zoning texts; and so on, all of the remaining 475 citations are included and counted equally. Citations are made part of the analysis whether or not they repeat information of another study or deal directly or indirectly with sprawl.

Topical Coverage— Sprawl Literature

Given equal weighting, the following approximate distribution of the sprawl literature appears as follows:

Impact Category	Percent of the Literature
I. Public and Private Capital and Operating Costs	≈ 20%
II. Transportation and Travel Costs	≈ 25%
III. Land/Natural Habitat Preservation	≈ 10%
IV. Quality of Life	≈ 20%
V. Social Issues	≈ 25%

Without providing a detailed statistical count but clearly paralleling concentrations found in the references, the literature is almost evenly distributed between the "harder," more quantifiable categories: *transportation/travel* and *public and private capital and operating costs*; and the "softer," less quantifiable impact categories: *quality of life* and *social issues*. These two combined categories represent about 90 percent of the literature. Comprising the remaining 10 percent of literature is material dealing with either the *loss of land or natural habitats* related to sprawl, or growth management as an alternative to sprawl.

Clearly, then, both social and quality-of-life considerations are significantly part of the sprawl literature and are represented far more than these categories are usually given credit for.

Methodologies— Sprawl Literature

There are differences in the analytic quality of the literature, as is indicated in the table at the bottom of this page.

In terms of analytic methods employed, *transportation and travel costs* have the most quantitative analyses (columns 2 and 3), followed by *public and private capital and operating costs*. In reverse fashion, *land/natural habitat preservation* and *quality of life* have the least quantitative and the most descriptive analyses (column 1).

The more rigorous quantitative simulations are found in *public and private capital and operating cost* studies, whereas *transportation and travel costs* studies rely most on the U.S. Census, the Nationwide Personal Transportation Survey and other empirical data. The *social issues* studies also rely heavily on national census-type empirical data.

Beyond this gross categorization, little can be said except that studies in the "harder" impact categories appear to address *sprawl* directly and by that term, whereas studies in the "softer" impact categories typically address sprawl indirectly as a form of low-density exurban or fringe-suburban development.

Examples of Data Employed by Impact Category

The five impact literature categories into which this report is divided apply both common and subject-distinctive data sources. Across all categories, socio-economic information from the decennial census (population and housing), the triennial *American Housing Survey* (AHS), and similarly broad databases are frequently tapped. Both published (e.g., printed census reports) and computerized (e.g., *Public Use Microdata Sample* of the decennial census) sources are accessed. Land-use information of

Impact Category	Levels of Analysis		
	(1)	(2)	(3)
	Descriptive: Little or No Analysis	*Empirical: Census or Case Study*	*Simulation: Econometric or Modeling*
I. Public and Private Capital and Operating Costs	≈ 15%	≈ 50%	≈ 35%
II. Transportation and Travel Costs	≈ 10%	≈ 80%	≈ 10%
III. Land/Natural Habitat Preservation	≈ 45%	≈ 35%	≈ 20%
IV. Quality of Life	≈ 40%	≈ 50%	≈ 10%
V. Social Issues	≈ 30%	≈ 60%	≈ 10%

various types is also employed across all literature categories. These include both descriptors of a gross or aggregate nature, such as population density derived from the *County and City Data Book,* and finer-grained land-use information, such as the neighborhood mix of land uses and urban design features that are found as part of local records (e.g., zoning maps) and individualized study surveys.

> *Across categories, socioeconomic information from the decennial census (population and housing), the triennial American Housing Survey (AHS), and similar bases are frequently tapped.*

Supplementing this common socio-economic and land-use information are data specific to the five literature categories. For the *public-private capital and operating costs* category, an array of engineering-infrastructure as well as financial information is utilized. Examples include the Institute of Transportation Engineers' *Recommended Guidelines for Subdivision Streets* (1984); DeChiara and Koppelman's *Manual of Housing Planning and Design Criteria* (1975); the Urban Land Institute, National Association of Home Builders, and American Society of Civil Engineers' *Residential Streets* (1976); the quinquennial *Census of Governments* (1992); and individual operating budgets from municipalities, counties, and school districts.

The other literature categories draw, in parallel, on sources pertaining to their respective disciplines and interests. Examples include the *Nationwide Personal Transportation Survey* for *transportation and travel costs*; the *Census of Agriculture* for *land/natural habitat preservation*; such guides as the *Places Rated Almanac* (Savageau and Boyer 1993) for *quality of life*; and the

County and City Data Book and specific city distress measures from Bradbury et al. (1982) and Rusk (1993) for *social issues* that pertain to cities.

This overview cannot convey the variety and richness of the data sources that are tapped by the subsets of the literature. To provide some example of the depth and complexity of the data, the information accessed by just one of the categories— transportation and travel costs—is described in detail here. This body of literature draws upon databases relating to travel as well as information on household and land-use characteristics. Travel sources typically relied on include, as noted, the *Nationwide Personal Transportation Survey* (Pisarski 1992a; Richardson and Gordon 1989, as examples); travel and commuting information from the decennial census and *American Housing Survey* (Gordon and Richardson 1993; Parsons Brinckerhoff 1996b); and a variety of other sources such as *Highway Statistics* (Dunphy and Fisher 1994), travel diaries kept by households being surveyed (Kitamura et al. 1994), and automobile odometer readings from California smog inspections (Holtzclaw 1994).

Household information such as that related to age, income, and occupation of residents is derived from the decennial census and the *American Housing Survey* (Gordon and Richardson 1989a; Parsons Brinckerhoff and ECONorthwest 1996; Pisarski 1992b). Household surveys may supplement/update the national and regional databases.

Land-use information comes from local planning and zoning records as well as from other sources. Gordon and Richardson (1989b), for instance, measured density from the U.S. Geological Survey LANDSAT files.

The costs of travel studies incorporate a broad array of data sources on topics ranging from accident-related medical expenses, to armed forces spending (e.g., providing security for overseas petroleum sources), to global warming.

One final note: Much of the data in the sprawl literature is of a secondary nature—that is, collected by one party and reanalyzed or cited by another. *The Costs of Sprawl* neighborhood prototype data originally assembled by RERC in the early- to mid-1970s (see Table 1), for example, is still being relied upon some two decades later by commentators on the subject of sprawl (Altshuler and Gomez-Ibanez 1993; Ewing 1997; Gordon and Richardson 1997a).

Examples of Methods Employed by Impact Category

Multiple choices are available to the analyst when considering specific methods. As mentioned previously, one choice is *empirical*—that is, one that observes something tangible; another method is a *simulation*, wherein events are modeled rather than observed. Both types are found in the literature on sprawl, with the incidence varying by subject. In the *public and private capital and operating costs* literature, because development's effect on infrastructure is projected into the future, many studies are *simulations*. Among these simulation studies are *The Costs of Sprawl* (RERC 1974); Downing's (1977) capital extension supplement to RERC's original work; Peiser's (1984) analysis of infrastructure costs in a hypothetical large subdivision; and Burchell's (1992–1997) and Landis's (1995) analyses in New Jersey, the Delaware Estuary, Kentucky, and Michigan (Burchell) and California (Landis). Operating costs, including operating expenses per capita, are also simulated in these types of studies (al-

though not necessarily linked to development pattern); other financial parameters, such as tax rates and levels of intergovernmental revenues, receive similar treatment. Ladd's (1991) regression analyses relating density to per capita government operational spending, and the DuPage County (1991) regression of observed nonresidential development to observed tax rates, are good examples.

As noted earlier, because travel information is routinely studied and counted, much of the literature on *transportation and travel costs* is empirical. Examples include Pushkarev and Zupan's study (1977) linking density and transit use in 100 urbanized areas; Cervero's (1989) study examining density and modal choice in 57 "suburban employment centers"; and Parsons and ECONorthwest's (1996) study examining the effects of density, urban design, and mixed use on the demand for transit in various locations, ranging from 11 metropolitan areas to individual cities (Chicago and San Francisco). At the same time, the *transportation and travel costs* literature, reflecting the underlying discipline of transportation engineering with its modeling prowess, also incorporates some large-scale *simulations*, such as the 50-year simulation by Metro (1994), and Downs's (1992) *Stuck in Traffic* modeling.

The remaining literature categories (*Land/Natural Habitat Preservation, Quality of Life, and Social Issues*), though they apply some simulations, such as *The Costs of Sprawl* modeling of land consumption in alternative neighborhood prototypes, are largely a combination of empirical and descriptive analyses. The *Green Index* of locations (Hall and Kerr 1991) incorporates more than 250 quality-of-life indicators related to environmental quality (e.g., air and water pollution, and community and workplace health statistics). The literature on urban decline focuses mainly on such observed characteristics as unemployment, housing loss, and tax base decline (Bradbury, Downs, and Small 1982).

Some of the empirical work tends to be microanalysis. The case study and per capita engineering studies are commonly used to describe what occurred at one or more locations. Examples of this format include Duncan's (1989) analysis of infrastructure costs in a number of Florida developments; Ewing's (1995b) analysis of household travel patterns in a Florida county; and Ewing, Haliyur and Page (1994) and Cambridge Systematics (1994) examinations of travel in Palm Beach County, Florida, and Los Angeles, California, respectively. Not coincidentally, most of the case analyses and per capita engineering studies are focused on locations experiencing rapid growth— often Sunbelt locations. In fact, so many of the investigations of travel profile as it relates to urban design have taken place in California, especially around San Francisco and Los Angeles, that questions about the replicability of the results observed to the rest of the country are beginning to be raised by the research community.

Descriptive analyses are found in significant numbers in the impact categories of *land/natural habitat preservation, quality of life,* and *social issues.* These analyses include Arendt's various (1994a, 1996, 1997) guides to developing with open space; Kunstler's (1993) description of urban and suburban neighborhoods; and Moe and Wilkie's (1997) prescription for improved metropolitan areas.

Various quantitative skills are incorporated in the literature. The per capita infrastructure studies, for instance, are essentially arithmetic compilations;

but higher-order applications are also found, especially within the transportation and travel costs analyses. These studies apply such statistical tests as analysis of variance—e.g., comparing travel behavior in auto-oriented versus transit-oriented neighborhoods (Handy 1995) and multivariate regression—e.g., using regression to show that much of the variation in transit use can be explained by density (Pushkarev and Zupan 1977). Even the most "statistical" of studies, however, are still cross-sectional. In the travel literature, for example, they show the correlation between current urban form (i.e., low to high densities, and segregated or mixed uses) and current travel behavior (i.e., mode choice or VMT). But they do not show how changes in urban form have influenced changes in travel choices. This is one of numerous deficiencies in the literature noted below.

Limitations of the Literature on Sprawl

1. *Almost no analyses of sprawl adequately define it.* Surprisingly, the landmark study, *The Costs of Sprawl* (RERC 1974), did not define sprawl explicitly, and the omission of a definition has continued throughout the literature. Where sprawl is defined, or at least characterized, reference is often made to a limited number of traits such as low-density or leapfrog scattered development (Ewing 1997). Many studies, however, omit several other defining traits that cause many of the alleged negative impacts of sprawl, such as dependence on the automobile and fragmentation of governmental land-use authority. These are admittedly difficult to quantify.

2. *Most analyses of sprawl focus too narrowly on only a few of its key*

aspects. An adequate definition of sprawl must include the causal elements that underlie sprawl's many alleged negative impacts in order for subsequent analysis to respond to those impacts effectively. Therefore, a key part of this literature search is to specifically relate the negative and positive impacts of sprawl to their defining characteristics.

Almost no analyses of sprawl adequately define it.

3. *Other definitional cum measurement questions remain.* Take, for instance, "density." Several studies focus on the density of a region and relate certain characteristics, such as travel behavior or infrastructure costs, to the region's density. However, densities vary widely within regions and the real question is: How does the density of the specific places where people live and work affect, say, their travel choices? The densities of these places may be substantially different from region-wide averages. For instance, Gordon and Richardson (1989b) use SMSAs as the unit of measurement in their analysis of densities and commuting times in 82 SMSAs. But is this meaningful, given that no SMSA has uniform density throughout? And at the SMSA level, perhaps density is a proxy for age of development, city size, or some other factor that affects travel behavior (i.e., transit use), as opposed to the variable density per se.

In parallel are problems with the definition and measurement of "segregation of uses." What is the definition of "uses"? At which geographical scale is separation or integration measured? Cervero (1996) found that the job-housing (JH) balance at the city level was not

significantly associated with the variation in external (to the community) commuting. Does this mean that land-use integration as reflected in the JH ratio does not affect travel behavior? Or does it mean that land-use integration really does affect travel behavior—but that the measure of land-use integration is lost when the JH is scaled at the community-wide, as opposed to a neighborhood, level?

Quality-of-life measures also pose a definitional conundrum, as do other seemingly easier-to-ascertain effects. Take, for instance, land consumption. Although it is a tautology that development consumes land, does a single-family home built on a 50-acre farm "consume" all of those 50 acres? If it consumes only a fraction, on what basis is that fraction apportioned?

4. *Most critics of sprawl do not recognize that it provides substantial benefits to many households; hence, they do not take account of those benefits in their analyses.* Several critics of sprawl, such as Kunstler (1993), engage in rhetorical exaggeration to emphasize their negative views of sprawl. They present only one side of the issue instead of a balanced descriptions. This polemical rhetoric cannot be classified as a scientific—or accurate—observation about the reality of American suburbs. Significant exaggeration is also employed by some defenders of sprawl, such as Gordon and Richardson (1997a).

5. *Only a limited number of comprehensive empirical analyses have been undertaken.* There is much discussion on sprawl but far fewer

"facts" in the form of empirical, quantitative studies. The paucity of data is illustrated by the frequency of studies using "secondhand" or once-removed information. A good example, as noted earlier, is the reanalysis of *The Costs of Sprawl* (RERC 1974) neighborhood and community prototypes some 20 to 30 years after the fact by Altshuler and Gomez-Ibanez (1993). Frank's 1989 review and reorganization of prior studies conducted over three decades in his *Costs of Alternative Development* is yet another example. It is not that reanalysis or categorization per se is unimportant—on the contrary, it can be quite valuable. Rather, these studies point to the dearth of new empirical research on sprawl. In a parallel vein is the tendency of the empirical research to be of a case study nature. Case studies provide valuable insight, but they are place-specific. The ability to generalize from them is quite limited.

6. *Even when a quantitative analysis is attempted, the topical coverage is uneven, with much more attention paid to the "physical side" of infrastructure—transportation and land—and less attention paid to the service and social sides.* The reason is simple; far more complete and reliable data are available for physical costs (e.g., development-generated costs for roads, water systems, and sewer systems) than for service costs. An engineering manual, for instance, can provide guidance to the cost per linear mile of road, but there is scant literature on how road mileage affects police patrolling costs. And there is an even larger gap in our knowledge of social costs. Discussions of sprawl's effects on quality of life are often superficial if not polemical;

large gaps abound concerning sprawl's effects on cities. What is the true social cost of higher unemployment rates in inner-city areas? What is the cost of the exclusion of low-income households from outlying suburbs—assuming such unemployment or exclusion is sprawl-related? Measuring these costs is extremely difficult. Nevertheless, some attempt must be made in order to include such costs in an overall analysis of sprawl.

7. *Most discussions of sprawl focus almost entirely on new growth areas.* This focus may result from the fact that sprawl itself occurs almost entirely in new-growth areas around the metropolitan periphery. True, recent discussions of sprawl, such as those described earlier by Downs (1994) and Rusk (1993), have begun to recognize that draining valuable resources away from close-in areas has serious negative impacts upon these areas and, therefore, upon society generally. No quantitative analyses of sprawl, however, have attempted to estimate the size of these social costs; most analyses simply ignore them conceptually.

> **Most discussions of sprawl focus almost entirely on new growth areas.**

8. *The extant literature also has a limited scope in its time frame of analysis—looking only at effects over a few years rather than a longer span.* The concatenation of limited geographic scale (i.e., focusing only on newly developing areas) and limited time span may very well lead to an overestimation by the literature of the costs of leapfrog development, as noted below:

Estimates probably overstate the added costs of leapfrog development in communities that expect continued growth and eventual infill development on the vacant land. Compared with the planned communities, the sprawl communities contain substantially more vacant land that is improved or semi-improved by some road and utility access. Developing improved vacant land in the future presumably would cost less than developing unimproved land. If infill development is expected, then a portion of the added costs of leapfrogging eventually will be recouped—the costs of sprawl would be the costs of supplying some infrastructure in advance of its eventual need and would be lower the more rapidly infill was expected. (Altshuler and Gomez-Ibanez 1993, 72)

9. *Most commentators do not recognize that two types of fragmented governance—those over land uses and over fiscal resources—are fundamental causes of many of the most widely attacked results of sprawl.* The main reason for this failing is that the analyses are not comprehensive enough. They focus on a few of the most obvious elements of sprawl and their consequences, rather than look at the entire relevant spectrum of elements and consequences. In addition, many observers hesitate to recommend changes in such fundamental American precepts as local control over land uses and separation of communities' fiscal resources. Several recent opponents of sprawl have recognized these connections quite explicitly, however, including Downs (1994), Richmond (1995), and Rusk (1993).

10. *Most opponents of sprawl fail to describe feasible alternative forms of metropolitan settlement to remedy sprawl's alleged negative conditions.* Like most social critics, they concentrate on describing what they dislike, not how to remove those faults in a realistic manner. Furthermore, the aspects of society they want to change are inextricably bound up with other fundamental elements—such as a lack of regional governments. The changes they call for might have many more widespread repercussions than their analyses recognize. Indeed, every critic's call to radically change social condition "X" implies the following conditions:

a) X is socially undesirable because it imposes unacceptable costs on some people.

b) Therefore, society should greatly alter or eliminate X in the future.

c) X resulted from forces that could have been channeled differently; it was not an inevitable outcome of irreversible or uncontrollable forces.

d) We know what those changeable forces are, and how to handle them differently to avoid X in the future.

e) It is politically feasible to adopt other methods of handling those forces.

f) We know what the disadvantages of using those other methods are, and how large the costs are, even if the disadvantages and costs are wholly unrelated to X.

g) The future benefits of eliminating, or substantially altering, X are significantly larger than the costs and disadvantages of using those other methods.

All critics of sprawl postulate conditions (a) and (b), but many stop there. Some proceed through conditions (c) and (d) as part of their prescriptions for change. But few deal with condition (e), and almost none address conditions (f) and (g)—which require the ability to measure both the costs and benefits of X and its elimination. Yet, realistic social analysis requires meeting all observable conditions.

Even the most detailed quantitative analyses of sprawl's costs tend to define only one alternative to it, and compare the costs of future development under just those two scenarios. That limitation is present, for example, in the series of analyses directed by Robert W. Burchell (1992–1997). Sprawl is a complex phenomenon containing multiple future development scenarios, not just two. Therefore, an adequate analysis of sprawl's costs compared to the costs of alternative forms of settlement must allow for more than two alternatives. Conversely, no analysis can be useful if it presents dozens or hundreds of alternatives as equally plausible. The best approach is to define three or more (but less than ten) major alternative settlement patterns and to conduct multiple sensitivity analyses concerning key elements in each of those patterns—a very comprehensive and expensive process.

11. *The modeling of the analysis is often overly simplistic.* The per capita engineering studies, for instance, relate capital/operating costs linearly to lane-miles of roads and related factors. But they have been criticized (rightly) for not incorporating any information on how costs can increase as thresholds of density increase, due to congestion, public safety needs, and the like. Incorporating this dimension would increase the cost of compactness (Altshuler and Gomez-Ibanez 1993).

Comparisons of sprawl and its alternatives are also criticized for not sufficiently addressing the qualitative differences in housing amenity. Most analyses oversimplify the differences, alleging that the amenities are uniformly superior for the detached units that characterize sprawl (Gordon and Richardson 1997a; Windsor 1979).

The modeling of the analysis is often overly simplistic.

The limited depth of many analyses also renders the associations that are drawn open to question. Inadequately specified models or controls are part of the problem. For instance, Newman and Kenworthy (1989a) applied only a single variable—urban density—to explain automobile use, whereas other factors are clearly involved. These two authors, in analyzing per capita automobile dependence, used gasoline consumption per capita as a proxy for automobile dependence. That equivalence is questionable, given the fact that many other factors, such as gas prices and fuel efficiency characteristics, affect per capita gasoline consumption. Holtzclaw (1990) related density to VMT without controlling for income levels or other household characteristics that influence VMT. Cervero's (1989) analysis of 57 suburban employment centers did not control for the centers' transit availability or the quality of the pedestrian environment. Similarly, the Cambridge Systematics (1994) study of suburban work sites did not control for these sites' level of transit service.

The difficulty in extrapolating the factors that influence these dynamics, and the difficulty in incorporating controls, are illustrated by the scholarly analyses of the effect of urban design. Many researchers are interested in whether neo-traditional design features (combined with a greater mix of uses) will result in travel behavior different from the pattern observed in typical suburban development. There has been too little experience with these new types of suburban development to answer the question. Therefore, studies look at older neighborhoods that have a more pedestrian-friendly environment and a finer-grain mix of uses. But it is not clear whether behavior of long-standing residents of older neighborhoods accurately predicts the behavior of residents of new neighborhoods, who in all likelihood are more accustomed to using cars.

Furthermore, the matched pairing of existing neighborhoods into "transit versus auto-oriented" or "traditional versus suburban" to test the effects of alternate design patterns on travel runs headlong into the practical difficulty of coming up with these pairings. Neighborhoods often don't slot neatly into those two polar categories. Even if this demarcation can be realized, variables other than overall design can affect the travel behavior equation—e.g., resident income, occupation, and age. Matched pairing is a difficult exercise to accomplish, since design preferences and household profiles often interrelate.

The cross-sectional nature of many studies compound all these problems.

Infrastructure costs rise as development is effected in a sprawl pattern; thus, sprawl gets tagged with the heightened capital expenses. Clearly, however, many other factors, from rising income levels to changing amenity levels, are also at work (Altshuler and Gomez-Ibanez 1993). Gordon, Richardson, and Jun (1991) link decreasing commuting times to the suburban deconcentration of job and residences that has occurred at the same time. But does the former *cause* the latter, or is it merely coterminous? Similarly, Richardson and Gordon (1989) hypothesize that increases in nonwork trips are due to suburban decentralization. Again, this hypothesis could be true, or it could be unrelated to the spatial pattern and instead fostered by such influences as rising incomes, greater participation of women in the work force, and societal changes in leisure activities. In short, there is much peril attached to drawing conclusions from cross-sectional research—precisely the kind of research that characterizes many sprawl studies.

The obverse of these deficiencies must be employed to guide future research. As detailed elsewhere, sprawl and its alternatives must be explicitly and formally defined. This effort can build from the literature. As noted in Section II, some of the more recent studies on sprawl have differentiated it from other types of development. In *New Visions for Metropolitan America* (1994), Anthony Downs defined sprawl as characterized by low-density, primarily single-family, development, with widespread reliance on filtering to provide low-income housing. Henry Richmond's *Regionalism: Chicago as An American Region* (1995), brought forth eight components of sprawl (listed earlier). To Richmond's sound base, this literature review adds two more—(1) the commercial strip development described by Richard Moe (1995), and (2) a dependence on the filtering process to provide housing for low-income households as indicated by Downs (1994). Altogether, then, sprawl must be viewed as a form of urban development that contains most of the following ten elements:

1. Low residential density

2. Unlimited outward extension of new development

3. Spatial segregation of different types of land uses through zoning regulations

4. Leapfrog development

5. No centralized ownership of land or planning of development

6. All transportation dominated by privately owned motor vehicles

7. Fragmentation of governance authority over land uses between many local governments

8. Great variances in the fiscal capacity of local governments because the revenue-raising capabilities of each are strongly tied to the property values and economic activities occurring within their own borders

9. Widespread commercial strip development along major roadways

10. Major reliance upon the filtering or "trickle-down" process to provide housing for low-income households.

The above definition both builds from the literature on sprawl and stands in marked contrast to the studies that either do not define sprawl or else characterize it too simply and/or pejoratively—e.g., as a "lack of continuity in expansion" (Clawson 1962); a "low-density ribbon

or leapfrog development" (Harvey and Clark 1965); or an "awkward spreading out of a community" (Abrams 1971).

This literature review underscores the need for a comprehensive look at the effects of sprawl. To this end, a full menu of benefits as well as costs of the different development scenarios must be considered. These benefits and costs must span the range of physical as well as social consequences. Furthermore, the benefits and costs analysis must be territorially complete—encompassing urban, suburban, and exurban locations as well as developing and developed areas. The span of analysis must also be long enough to encompass the dynamic of shifts over time, to show what happens, for example, to areas initially leapfrogged under sprawl that are subsequently "filled in" by development. The analysis of costs and benefits must further incorporate the complexity of influences e.g., the varying threshold influences of density on capital-operating costs, and the recognition that varying density thresholds, as well as other factors, affect travel. Moreover, caution must be exercised so as to not ascribe causality when the underlying evidence is merely cross-sectional.

> *This literature review underscores the need for a comprehensive look at the effects of sprawl.*

ALLEGED NEGATIVE AND POSITIVE EFFECTS

Linking Sprawl's Defining Traits to Its Alleged Impacts

With a detailed analysis of both the def-inition of sprawl (Section I) and its impacts (Section II), it now becomes possible to link the two. Tables 12 and 13 evaluate the linkages between sprawl's ten defining traits and its alleged 27 negative and 14 positive impacts. In each matrix, sprawl's defining traits are set forth from left to right as vertical columns. The impacts are set forth from top to bottom as horizontal rows, grouped into the five impact categories defined earlier.

Each cell in the matrix indicates a "score" that represents literature-influenced judgments concerning the degree of linkage of the defined trait (at the top of the column) to the specified impact (at the left of the row). The "scores" are reflected by the following symbols:

+ 2   Indicates that the trait has a major linkage to the alleged impact.

+ 1   Indicates that the trait has a moderate or minor linkage to the alleged impact.

  0   Indicates that the trait has no linkage to the alleged impact.

– 2   Indicates that the trait has a negative linkage to the alleged impact; that is, the trait tends to reduce the incidence of the impact.

The Importance of Sprawl's Defining Traits

Determining, in a rough manner, the relative linkage of a trait to its impacts can be achieved by examining the total scores of the trait in the matrix. For example, the column labeled "leapfrog development" in the negative impact matrix (see Table 12) contains sixteen "major linkage ratings," five "moderate or minor linkage ratings," and six "no linkage ratings." These sum to a total of 37 for this trait and rank it the most significant of all sprawl's traits. Similar observations, summations, and

rankings have been carried out for the other nine defining traits.

Based on these calculations, three of sprawl's defining traits appear especially linked to *negative* impacts. These are *leapfrog development, low density, and unlimited outward extension*, each of which score in the thirties in terms of linkages. Two other traits—the spatial segregation of land uses and variance in local fiscal capacity—both scoring 10, seem to exhibit relatively weak linkages. Among the remaining traits, widespread commercial strip development, highly fragmented land use governance, and no central ownership or planning (scoring in the low twenties or high teens), seem somewhat more strongly linked than transport dominance by motor vehicles or reliance on filtering for low-income housing (both scoring 15).

Negative Impacts of Sprawl

Some individual sprawl traits, more so than others, *negatively* affect the five potential impact areas (public and private capital and operating costs, transportation and travel costs, land/natural habitat preservation, quality of life, and social issues). For instance, *leapfrog development, low density, and unlimited outward extension* negatively affect *public and private capital and operating costs* (because residential development and nonresidential development are distant from the core and from each other, and thus are difficult to service).

Following the above, *transportation and travel costs* are negatively impacted by the same three traits plus transport dominance by motor vehicles, and widespread strip development (again, because development is distant, spread out, and expensive to access).

TABLE 12

LINKAGES BETWEEN CHARACTERISTICS OF SPRAWL AND ITS NEGATIVE EFFECTS

NEGATIVE IMPACTS (27)	DEFINING CHARACTERISTICS OF SPRAWL									
	LOW DENSITY	UNLIMITED OUTWARD EXTENSION	LAND USES SPATIALLY SEGREGATED	LEAPFROG DEVELOPMENT	NO CENTRAL OWNERSHIP OR PLANNING	TRANSPORT DOMINANCE BY MOTOR VEHICLES	HIGHLY FRAGMENTED LAND-USE GOVERNANCE	GREAT VARIANCE IN LOCAL FISCAL CAPACITY	WIDESPREAD COMMERCIAL STRIP DEVELOPMENT	RELIANCE ON FILTERING FOR LOW-INCOME HOUSING
PUBLIC-PRIVATE CAPITAL AND OPERATING COSTS										
Higher infrastructure costs	2	2	1	2	1	0	1	0	0	0
Higher public operating costs	2	2	1	2	1	0	1	0	0	0
More expensive private residential and nonresidential development costs	2	1	0	2	1	0	2	1	1	0
More adverse public fiscal impacts	2	1	1	2	1	0	1	1	0	0
Higher aggregate land costs	2	1	0	2	1	0	1	0	0	0
TRANSPORTATION AND TRAVEL COSTS										
More vehicle miles traveled (VMT)	2	1	2	2	1	2	0	0	2	1
Longer travel times	2	2	1	2	0	-2	0	0	0	1
More automobile trips	2	1	1	2	1	2	1	0	2	1
Higher household transportation spending	2	2	1	2	0	2	0	0	2	1
Less cost-efficient and effective transit	2	2	1	2	0	2	1	0	0	0
Higher social costs of travel	2	2	1	2	1	2	1	0	0	0
LAND/NATURAL HABITAT PRESERVATION										
Loss of agricultural land	1	2	0	2	1	0	0	0	1	0
Reduced farmland productivity	1	2	0	2	0	0	0	0	0	0
Reduced farmland viability	0	0	0	1	0	0	0	0	0	0
Loss of fragile environmental lands	2	2	0	2	1	0	0	0	1	0
Reduced regional open space	1	0	0	0	1	0	1	0	0	0
QUALITY OF LIFE										
Aesthetically displeasing	0	0	0	0	0	0	0	0	2	0
Weakened sense of community	1	1	0	2	0	1	1	1	1	1
Greater stress	0	0	0	0	0	0	0	0	2	0
Higher energy consumption	2	2	0	2	0	1	0	0	1	1
More air pollution	1	0	0	1	0	2	0	0	1	0
Lessened historic preservation	0	1	0	0	0	0	0	0	1	1
SOCIAL ISSUES										
Fosters suburban exclusion	1	1	0	0	2	1	2	2	0	2
Fosters spatial mismatch	1	1	0	1	1	1	1	0	1	1
Fosters residential segregation	0	1	0	1	1	1	2	1	0	2
Worsens city fiscal stress	0	0	0	0	1	0	1	2	2	2
Worsens inner-city deterioration	0	1	0	1	1	0	0	2	1	1
LINKAGES										
SUM	33	31	10	37	17	15	18	10	21	15
IMPORTANCE	2	3	10	1	6	7	5	9	4	8

Key: 2 = Major linkage   1 = Moderate or minor linkage   0 = No linkage   -2 = Negative linkage

TABLE 13

LINKAGES BETWEEN CHARACTERISTICS OF SPRAWL AND ITS POSITIVE EFFECTS

POSITIVE IMPACTS (14)	DEFINING CHARACTERISTICS OF SPRAWL									
	LOW DENSITY	UNLIMITED OUTWARD EXTENSION	LAND USES SPATIALLY SEGREGATED	LEAPFROG DEVELOPMENT	NO CENTRAL OWNERSHIP OR PLANNING	TRANSPORT DOMINANCE BY MOTOR VEHICLES	HIGHLY FRAGMENTED LAND-USE GOVERNANCE	GREAT VARIANCE IN LOCAL FISCAL CAPACITY	WIDESPREAD COMMERCIAL STRIP DEVELOPMENT	RELIANCE ON FILTERING FOR LOW-INCOME HOUSING
PUBLIC-PRIVATE CAPITAL AND OPERATING COSTS										
Lower public operating costs	2	1	0	2	1	0	0	0	0	0
Less-expensive private residential and nonresidential development costs	2	2	0	2	0	0	0	0	0	0
Fosters efficient development of "leapfrogged" areas	1	1	0	2	1	0	1	0	0	0
TRANSPORTATION AND TRAVEL COSTS										
Shorter commuting times	2	2	0	2	0	2	0	0	0	0
Less congestion	2	2	1	2	0	1	0	0	1	0
Lower governmental costs for transportation	2	2	0	2	1	2	0	0	0	0
Automobiles most efficient mode of transportation	2	2	2	2	0	2	0	0	2	0
LAND/NATURAL HABITAT PRESERVATION										
Enhanced personal and public open space	2	2	0	2	0	1	0	0	0	0
QUALITY OF LIFE										
Preference for low-density living	2	1	0	1	0	2	1	0	0	0
Lower crime rates	2	1	0	1	0	1	0	0	0	0
Reduced costs of public and private goods	2	1	0	1	0	1	0	0	2	0
Fosters greater economic well-being	0	1	1	1	2	0	2	2	0	0
SOCIAL ISSUES										
Fosters localized land use decisions	0	1	0	1	2	0	2	0	0	0
Enhances municipal diversity and choice	0	1	0	1	1	1	2	2	0	1
LINKAGES										
SUM	21	20	4	22	8	13	8	4	5	1
IMPORTANCE	2	3	9	1	6	4	5	8	7	10

Key: 2 = Major linkage   1 = Moderate or minor linkage   0 = No linkage   -2 = Negative linkage

Basically similar to the above, *land and natural habitat preservation* seems to be negatively impacted by leapfrog development, unlimited outward extension, and low-density traits of sprawl (which consume significant amounts of land) yet by few others. *Quality of life* is worse (poor aesthetics of development and lack of sense of community) due to widespread commercial strip development and leapfrog development. *Social conditions* are worse (less affordable housing, smaller tax base per capita, and an absence of regionally provided services) due to sprawl's reliance on filtering for housing, great variance in local fiscal capacity, and highly fragmented land-use governance.

Obviously, the above are primarily inferences—but intuitively, these inferences appear to stand up.

Positive Impacts of Sprawl

The analysis further suggests (see Table 13) that the same three defining traits—*leapfrog development, low density*, and *unlimited outward extension*—appear to be the most important in causing *positive* impacts as well. The above three traits each score in the twenties and rank 1, 2, and 3 respectively. Next in relative importance is transportation dominance by private motor vehicles, followed by highly fragmented land-use governance, and no central ownership and planning. These range in score from a high of 13 to a low of 8. Least significant are the use of filtering for low-income housing, spatially segregated land uses, great variance in fiscal capacity, and widespread commercial strip development. These range from a low of 1 to a high of 5.

In terms of the positive effects of sprawl, *public and private capital and operating costs* are lower (because they are not as complex and there is less demand on

them) due to leapfrog and low-density development, and unlimited outward extension. *Transportation and travel costs* are lower (due to suburban-to-suburban commutes, reduced inner-suburban congestion, and use of the automobile) as a result of the above three traits plus transport dominance by motor vehicles, spatially segregated land uses, and widespread commercial strip development. *Quality of life* is better (residents like where they live; communities have lower crime rates) again due to the above three traits (leapfrog development, low density, unlimited outward extension) as well as to transport dominance by motor vehicles. *Social conditions* are better (more municipal diversity and choice) due to highly fragmented land-use governance and no central ownership or planning.

Clearly, there is a great deal of similarity between the positive and negative matrices of sprawl (Tables 12 and 13) as shown in Table 14. Paradoxically, the traits that seem key causes of many of sprawl's negative impacts also appear to be key causes of many of its positive impacts. This is true for such impact categories as public-private capital and operating costs, transportation and travel costs, land and natural habitat preservation, and quality of life. The fact that sprawl can be simultaneously associated with both costs and benefits in relatively narrowly defined fields shows how complex the phenomenon of sprawl is. The literature synthesis is summarized in Table 15. Evident from Table 15 is that the field tends to be much more prolific on criticisms (27) leveled at sprawl rather than its defense (14). There are about twice as many allegations of sprawl's negative impacts as there are of its positive impacts.

With regard to recognition that *"costs" of development* exist, there is more agree-

TABLE 14

Categories of Alleged Negative Impacts	Key Defining Traits Underlying Those Impacts
I. Public-Private Capital and Operating Costs	Leapfrog Development Low Density Unlimited Outward Extension
II. Transportation and Travel Costs	Leapfrog Development Low Density Unlimited Outward Extension Transport Dominance by Motor Vehicles Widespread Commercial Strip Development
III. Land/Natural Habitat Preservation	Leapfrog Development Unlimited Outward Extension Low Density
IV. Quality of Life	Widespread Commercial Strip Development Leapfrog Development
V. Social Issues	Reliance on Filtering for Low-Income Housing Great Variances in Local Fiscal Capacity Highly Fragmented Land-Use Governance
Categories of Alleged Positive Impacts	Key Defining Traits Underlying Those Impacts
I. Public-Private Capital and Operating Costs	Leapfrog Development Low Density Unlimited Outward Extension
II. Transportation and Travel Costs	Leapfrog Development Low Density Unlimited Outward Extension Transport Dominance by Motor Vehicles Spatially Segregated Land Uses Widespread Commercial Strip Development
III. Land/Natural Habitat Preservation	Leapfrog Development Low Density Unlimited Outward Extension
IV. Quality of Life	Leapfrog Development Low Density Unlimited Outward Extension Transport Dominance by Motor Vehicles
V. Social	Highly Fragmented Land-Use Governance No Central Ownership or Planning

TABLE 15

MATRIX SYNTHESIS OF THE LITERATURE ON SPRAWL ORGANIZED BY SUBSTANTIVE AREAS

Substantive Concern	Does Condition Notably Exist?				Is It Strongly Linked To Sprawl?			
	+2 General Agreement	+1 Some Agreement	0 No Clear Outcome	-2 Substantial Disagreement	+2 General Agreement	+1 Some Agreement	0 No Clear Outcome	-2 Substantial Disagreement
Public-Private Capital and Operating Costs								
Alleged Negative Impacts								
Higher infrastructure costs	X							
Higher public operating costs		X				X	X	
More expensive private residential/nonresidential development costs		X					X	
More adverse public fiscal impacts		X				X		
Higher aggregate land costs		X				X		
Alleged Positive Impacts								
Lower public operating costs		X					X	
Less-expensive private residential/nonresidential development costs		X				X		
Fosters efficient development of "leapfrogged" areas			X				X	
Transportation and Travel Costs								
Alleged Negative Impacts								
More vehicle miles traveled (VMT)	X				X			
Longer travel times			X				X	
More automobile trips	X				X			
Higher household transportation spending		X				X		
Less cost-efficient and effective transit	X					X		
Higher social costs of travel		X				X		
Alleged Positive Impacts								
Shorter commuting times			X				X	
Less congestion			X					X	
Lower governmental costs for transportation			X				X	
Automobiles most efficient mode of transportation		X			X			

TABLE 15 (continued)

MATRIX SYNTHESIS OF THE LITERATURE ON SPRAWL ORGANIZED BY SUBSTANTIVE AREAS

Substantive Concern	Does Condition Notably Exist?				Is It Strongly Linked To Sprawl?			
	+2 General Agreement	+1 Some Agreement	0 No Clear Outcome	-2 Substantial Disagreement	+2 General Agreement	+1 Some Agreement	0 No Clear Outcome	-2 Substantial Disagreement
Land/Natural Habitat Preservation								
Alleged Negative Impacts								
Loss of agricultural land	X				X			
Reduced farmland productivity		X					X	
Reduced farmland viability			X				X	
Loss of fragile environmental lands	X				X			
Reduced regional open space			X				X	
Alleged Positive Impacts								
Enhanced personal and public open space		X					X	
Quality of Life								
Alleged Negative Impacts								
Aesthetically displeasing		X					X	
Lessened sense of community		X					X	
Greater stress		X				X		
Higher energy consumption			X				X	
More air pollution		X						X
Lessened historic preservation		X					X	
Alleged Positive Impacts								
Preference for low-density living	X					X		
Lower crime rates		X					X	
Reduced costs of public and private goods		X					X	
Fosters greater economic well-being		X				X		
Social Issues								
Alleged Negative Impacts								
Fosters suburban exclusion		X				X		X
Fosters spatial mismatch	X					X		
Fosters residential segregation		X					X	
Worsens city fiscal stress		X				X		
Worsens inner-city deterioration		X				X		
Alleged Positive Impacts								
Fosters localized land use decisions	X					X		
Enhances municipal diversity and choice	X					X		

ment (general agreement and some agreement categories combined) in the areas of public and private capital and operating costs, quality of life, and social issues than there is in travel and transportation costs, and land/natural habitat preservation. That these "costs" are *linked specifically to sprawl* (holding aside the issue of causality), there is more agreement on public and private capital and operating costs, transportation and travel costs, and social issues than there is on land/natural habitat preservation and quality of life. Thus, more impact categories identify themselves as being affected by development; fewer categories identify themselves as being impacted by a type of development that is akin to "sprawl."

Areas of Future Research

The literature clearly signals areas of future research thrusts. On the "harder," more quantifiable, physical/engineering side—that is, the issues of infrastructure, transportation, and land consumption—the studies, to date, point to multiple

appropriate measures to be considered (e.g., vehicle miles traveled [VMT] and congestion), as well as important relationships to be examined (e.g., density's effect on modal choice and travel time). However, these analyses must be brought together more definitively, and areas of outstanding disagreement from prior work (e.g., are commuting times shorter or longer under sprawl) must be examined empirically so that answers can be had. The field must attempt to fill in the lingering gaps in knowledge concerning the effect of development patterns on operating costs, impact on productivity of farmland, and so on.

As to sprawl's effect on the "softer," less quantifiable, quality of life and social issues, the challenge to current research is even more formidable. Here, interrelationships are more complicated, measurement is more elusive, and the association with development pattern—whether sprawl or otherwise—much more obtuse.

SECTION

ANNOTATIONS OF STUDIES

This section contains detailed information on specific source materials of the literature on sprawl. The information is presented according to five basic categories (and their subcategories) of sprawl's impacts. A listing of works included here by author follows the references section of this monograph.

I. *Public and Private Capital and Operating Costs*
　1. Alternative Development Analyses
　2. Fiscal Impacts, Exactions, and Impact Fees
　3. The Effects of Growth Controls on Housing Costs
　4. Urban Form and Sprawl

II. *Transportation and Travel Costs*
　1. Changes in Automobile Travel
　2. The Effects of Density on Travel Choice
　3. Unlimited Outward Extension

　4. Spatial Segregation of Uses (Land Use Mix and Urban Design)
　5. Dispersed Employment
　6. The Costs of Travel

III. *Land/Natural Habitat Preservation*
　1. Land Preservation and Community Cohesion
　2. Land/Habitat Preservation: Empirical Studies

IV. *Quality of Life*
　1. Popular Literature
　2. Indicators, Report Cards, and Benchmarks
　3. Economics Literature
　4. Sociology Literature
　5. Psychology Literature

V. *Social Issues*
　1. The Growth of Cities and Metropolitan Areas
　2. Urban Decline
　3. Urban Renewal

The citations that have been annotated here are far from an exhaustive coverage of the individual topic. Yet, within the five basic categories of sprawl's impacts, there is a representation of some of the field's most important current and historical literature. Approximately 25 percent of the references have been annotated. Each of the annotated works is reviewed in a similar manner. The first portion of the analysis places the work in an overall context. A second component involves a discussion of why the work is important to the sprawl literature. A third component discusses methodology and data sources employed, if appropriate. A final component discusses results and conclusions of the work.

The annotations have been chosen to include both positive and negative positions on sprawl as well as a balance between descriptive and empirical works.

The annotations included here contribute to the judgments on strengths and weaknesses of the literature contained in the previous chapter. Sprawl has a rich and diverse literature, as will be seen in this compilation of annotations.

CHAPTER

Annotations of Studies

PUBLIC/PRIVATE CAPITAL AND OPERATING COSTS

This chapter annotates studies that relate to sprawl and the alleged *public/private capital and operating costs* that it imposes. *Public* capital and operating costs are costs associated with residential and nonresidential development: roads, utilities, public buildings and the costs of providing day-to-day police, fire, general government, recreational, and educational services. *Private* capital and operating costs are the expenses incurred in occupying residential and nonresidential properties—in other words, the costs imposed on housing and commercial development related to type, location, and density of development. The chapter is divided into four parts:

Alternative Development Analyses
Fiscal Impacts, Exactions, and Impact Fees
The Effects of Growth Controls on Housing Costs
Urban Form and Sprawl

The *Alternative Development Analyses* section includes the works of Robert W. Burchell (1997b, 1992a, and others), James Frank (1989), James Duncan (1989), RERC (1974), and Paul Tischler

(1994), among others. *Fiscal Impacts, Exactions, and Impact Fees* includes, in addition to the above, the works of the American Farmland Trust (1986, 1992) and DuPage County, Illinois (1989, 1991). The *Effects of Growth on Housing Costs* literature includes the works of Katz and Rosen (1987), George Parsons (1992), and Seymour Schwartz et al. (1981 and 1989). Finally, the section on *Urban Form and Sprawl* includes the articles of Helen Ladd (1991) and Richard Peiser (1989).

ALTERNATIVE DEVELOPMENT ANALYSES

Burchell, Robert W. 1997b. *South Carolina Infrastructure Study: Projection of Statewide Infrastructure Costs, 1995-2015*. New Brunswick, NJ: Center for Urban Policy Research, Rutgers University.

This study involves a 20-year projection of infrastructure need in the State of South Carolina. It encompasses all public and quasi-public infrastructure required in the state including developmental (roads, bridges, water/sewer), educational, commercial, public safety, public health, recreational/cultural, and environmental. Twenty-eight individual categories of infrastructure are contained in the above seven groupings listed above. Findings for the state are as follows:

- $56.7 billion in required infrastructure costs from 1995-2015
- $16.7 billion in potential infrastructure savings due to technology, differing means of provision, and costs of sprawl savings. Much of the above savings to come from technology and differing means of provision, as opposed to costs of sprawl savings
- Three-quarters of the remaining $40 billion ($2 billion per year for 20 years), or an average of $1.5 billion annually, could be raised via 10 percent infrastructure set-asides in all state, county, municipal, and school district general fund budgets and intergovernmental transfer revenues
- The remaining $500 million annually must be raised from a variety of revenue sources, including property tax, sales tax, the tolling of roads, development impact fees, water/sewer charges and the like. A 2¢/gallon gasoline tax increase would raise only $56 million in revenues annually for infrastructure purposes.

Burchell, Robert W. 1992a. *Impact Assessment of the New Jersey Interim State Development and Redevelopment Plan. Report II: Research Findings.* Trenton: New Jersey Office of State Planning.

This study is an analysis of the effects of implementing a managed growth strategy in the state of New Jersey in the form of a State Plan. Two alternative futures are modeled—one with development as usual (TREND), and one with development according to the proposed State

Development and Redevelopment Plan (PLAN).

The study showed that the state could save $1.4 billion in infrastructure funding over 20 years for roads, utilities, and schools, if it followed the PLAN versus the TREND scheme. This savings occurred mainly through more intensive use of existing infrastructure, as opposed to building additional infrastructure. The PLAN approach directed new growth to where excess capacity existed, rather than to virgin territories. The PLAN scheme was also more compact than the TREND scheme, therefore requiring less distance to be covered when linking developments by local and county roads. In addition, concentrating larger numbers of people in more compact areas provides for economies of scale, such as larger water and sewer treatment facilities, with lower costs per individual user. The Rutgers study, using the same increases in population (520,000 persons in 20 years), jobs, and households, for both TREND and PLAN, found that PLAN would save:

- $699 million in roads—a 24 percent savings
- $561 million in water and sewer costs—a 7.6 percent savings
- $173 million in school capital costs— a 3.3 percent savings
- $1.4 billion, overall, or just under 10 percent of all development-related (roads, water/sewer, public buildings) infrastructure expenditures.

Burchell, Robert W. et al.

1. *The Economic Impacts of Trend versus Vision Growth in the Lexington Metropolitan Area.* Report Prepared for Bluegrass Tomorrow, Lexington, KY. 1995b (November).
2. *Impact Assessment of DELEP CCMP versus STATUS QUO on Twelve Municipalities in the DELEP Region.* Report Prepared for by the Government Committee of the Delaware Estuary Program. Philadelphia, PA. August 15, 1995.
3. *Fiscal Impacts of Alternative Land Development Patterns in Michigan: The Costs of Current Development Versus Compact Growth.* Southeast Michigan Regional Council of Governments. 1997a.

COMPACT GROWTH VERSUS SPRAWL DEVELOPMENT: FINDINGS OF MULTIPLE STUDIES		
Area of Impact	Savings: Compact Growth Over Sprawl Development (Lexington, KY and Delaware Estuary Studies)	Savings: Compact Growth Over Sprawl Development (State of Michigan)
Developable Land	20.5–24.2%	15.5%
Agricultural Land	18-29%	17.4%
Fragile Land	20-27%	13.1%
Infrastructure		
Roads	14.8%-19.7%	12.4%
Utilities		
(Water/sewer)	6.7-8.2%	13.7%
Housing Costs	2.5-8.2%	13.7%
Fiscal Impacts	6.9%	3.5%

These three studies extend and broaden the application of Burchell's New Jersey modeling of development alternatives (sprawl versus compact growth) to different geographic settings. A broader base enables refinement and testing of the models under different taxing structures, differing means of providing and funding infrastructure, and differing geographic levels of investigation.

Each of the studies—Lexington, Kentucky, the Delaware Estuary, and the State of Michigan—looked at the land, infrastructure, housing, and fiscal costs of sprawl versus compact development. Compact development was differently defined in each study; sprawl which was equated with historical development, varied only marginally from place to place. There was much more consistency in the definition of trend development or sprawl across these studies than there was in the specific alternatives to sprawl. Findings from the studies are included in the following table:

Duncan, James E. et al. 1989. *The Search for Efficient Urban Growth Patterns.* Tallahassee: Department of Community Affairs.

This analysis encompasses detailed case studies of the actual costs (and revenues) incurred by several completed residential and nonresidential projects throughout Florida. The projects chosen are representative of five different development patterns ranging from "scattered" to "compact." Although the Florida study did not intend such an analysis, it is possible to group the five development patterns into two aggregate development profiles, "trend" and "managed/planned" growth. The term "trend" includes the Florida development patterns labeled "scattered," "linear," and "satellite"; the term "managed/planned" refers to the Florida patterns of "contiguous" and "compact" growth. With this grouping, the relative capital costs for trend versus managed or planned growth can be determined from the base Florida case study information. The data show that the total public capital costs for a detached unit built under trend conditions in Florida approached

$16,000; under planned development the capital cost was about $11,000 per unit, or roughly 70 percent of the cost of "trend" (see table below).

CAPITAL FACILITY COSTS UNDER TREND VERSUS PLANNED DEVELOPMENT (PER DWELLING UNIT; 1990 DOLLARS)				
Category of Capital Costs	Average of Case Studies Under Trend Development	Average of Case Studies Under Planned Development	Trend Versus Planned Development Difference #/	%
Roads	$7,014	$2,784	(+) $4,230	60.3
Schools	6,079	5,625	(+) 545	7.4
Utilities	2,187	1,320	(+) 867	39.6
Other	661	672	(-) 11	1.7
Total	15,941	$10,401	(+) 5,4540	36.7

ECONorthwest. 1994. *Evaluation of No Growth and Slow Growth Policies for the Portland Region.* **Portland, OR: Metropolitan Portland Government.**

As part of its *Region 2040* planning program, Metro (Portland, Oregon's metropolitan area's regional government) evaluated alternative futures for the region and the policies available to achieve those futures. This report examined whether the region could or should adopt policies to reduce and slow the anticipated growth in the region.

The study identifies both reactive and proactive policies which would slow growth. Reactive policies would discourage growth through a municipality's economic development activities, its investment in infrastructure and public facilities, and its programs for environmental amenities and social services. Proactive government policies would discourage growth by limiting the supply and use of buildable land (via zoning and planning regulations), charging more for public facilities, and imposing increased environmental and design standards on existing and new developments.

The authors concluded that while municipally initiated reactive or proactive policies would slow growth in the short run at the local level, a viable strategy for the Portland metropolitan area must be implemented at a regional scale, so that aggregate growth is decreased and not simply redistributed within the metropolitan area.

Finally, the study pointed out that although not always considered, slow growth policies could have negative effects on the local economy. These include decreased economic opportunities and income growth, and increased housing costs.

Fodor, Eben V. 1997. "The Real Cost of Growth in Oregon" *Population and Environment* **18-4.**

Oregon municipalities levy *system development charges* to offset development costs. Within Oregon, for a typical three-bedroom home, these development charges can range from $1,000 to $6,500 per unit. Fodor, however, conservatively estimates that the actual public cost is closer to $24,500 per unit. He provides a breakdown as shown in the table below.

Fodor concludes that Oregon (like other states) is only recovering a fraction of the public infrastructure costs through *system development charges* and other development fees. Rather, he postulates that communities are subsidizing growth by keeping housing prices artificially low. Implementing growth management strategies, while providing these subsidies, works at cross purposes. Fodor suggests that communities should pursue alternatives, such as the public acquisition of land to prevent development, as a viable, cost-saving policy for growth management.

DEVELOPMENT COSTS	
(PER DWELLING UNIT)	
Public Service	Amount
School Facilities	$ 11,377
Sanitary Sewage Facilities	5,089
Transportation Facilities	4,193
Water System	2,066
Parks and Recreation	797
Stormwater Drainage	510
Fire / EMS facilities	470
Total	24,502

Frank, James E. 1989. *The Costs of Alternative Development Patterns: A Review of the Literature.* **Washington, DC: Urban Land Institute.**

This study reviews the national literature conducted over roughly four decades concerning development costs. Frank orders the findings of the various reports and expresses them in equivalent dollar terms (1987 dollars). He concludes from the national literature that multiple factors affect development costs including density, contiguity of development, distance to central public facilities (e.g., sewage and water plants), as well as other characteristics, such as municipal improvement standards. In brief, capital costs are highest in situations of low-density sprawl, and for development located a considerable distance from central facilities. By contrast, costs can be dramatically reduced in higher-density development that is centrally and contiguously located. As described by Frank:

> When all capital costs are totaled ... the total cost for low-density ... sprawl ... is slightly more than $35,000 per dwelling unit. Further, if that development is located 10 miles from the sewage treatment plant, the central water source, the receiving body of water, and the major concentration of employment, almost $15,000 per dwelling unit is

added to the cost, for a total of $48,000 per dwelling unit ...

> The cost can be reduced to less than $18,000 ... by choosing a central location, using a mix of housing types in which single-family units constitute 30 percent of the total and apartments 70 percent, and by planning contiguous development instead of leapfrogging. (Frank 1989, 39)

To the extent that planned or managed growth fosters the more efficient patterns described above—centrally located, contiguous development that includes units at somewhat higher density—it can achieve infrastructure savings relative to traditional development.

Peiser, Richard B. 1984. "Does It Pay to Plan Suburban Growth?" *Journal of the American Planning Association* **50: 419-433.**

The aim of this study is to provide a comprehensive method for comparing one development pattern to another. To achieve this aim, Peiser conducts a quasi-controlled experiment comparing the planned development of a 7500-acre tract in southwest Houston with the hypothetical "unplanned" development of the same tract. Peiser patterns unplanned development after development that occurred to the north of Houston in an area called Champions. The author evaluates the capital costs associated with land development and transportation for each of the two development alternatives. Other social costs are also examined in a qualitative analysis. Unlike previous studies, Peiser includes non-residential land uses in his analysis.

Peiser makes four assumptions in his comparison. First, total density and total acreage of each case is assumed to be equal. Second, he assumes that each community derives the same level of total benefits. The relative advantage of one community over the other is determined by the differences in costs associated with each type of development. Third, the study focuses upon the differences in costs of the overall community design, not the costs associated with differences in housing, building types, interior streets or utilities for residential subdivisions. Finally, travel costs are accounted for to and from the edge of the development site.

Peiser finds that planned development produces higher net benefits than unplanned development for the three cost components investigated: land development, transportation, and social issues. Overall, transportation costs provide the greatest net benefit. However, the magnitude of the difference is small, only accounting for one to three percent of total costs. Further, Peiser acknowledges the obstacles to planning large-scale developments. He highlights several constraints associated with such development including the cost and availability of financing, the labyrinthine permitting process, and the difficulties of managing large-scale projects.

Real Estate Research Corporation (RERC). 1974. *The Costs of Sprawl: Environmental and Economic Costs of Alternative Residential Development Patterns at the Urban Fringe: (Volume I: Detailed Cost Analysis; Volume II: Literature Review and Bibliography).* **Washington, DC: U.S. Government Printing Office.**

Among the most often cited studies in the history of planning literature, this three-volume series is the final report of an

early effort to isolate the variable of density from those of structural age, obsolescent layout, and low-income population, in order to measure some of the most important and costly consequences of urban form. Sponsored jointly by the U.S. Council on Environmental Quality, the Department of Housing and Urban Development, and the Environmental Protection Agency, the project was carried out by the Real Estate Research Corporation. Its central conclusion, that low density development is extremely costly on energy, environment, and fiscal grounds, has been generally accepted as both intuitively correct and accurately determined.

The basic study method was to make detailed estimates of the costs associated with six hypothetical new communities—each containing 10,000 dwelling units, each housing an "average" urban fringe population mix, and each constructed in a "typical" environmental setting.

The report's basic conclusions are:

1) The high-density planned community would be optimal with reference to all four key indicators examined: energy cost, environmental impact, capital cost, and operating cost. The low-density sprawl community would be least desirable with reference to all four.

2) The high-density planned community would require 44 percent less energy than the low-density sprawl community.

3) The high-density planned community would generate 45 percent less air pollution.

4) The high-density planned community would require a capital investment 44

percent less than the low-density sprawl community; the largest proportionate savings would be in road and utility construction, but the largest absolute saving would be in the cost of residential construction itself.

5)   The operating cost of community services would be about 11 percent lower in the high-density planned community than in the low-density sprawl community

A classic in its field, *The Costs of Sprawl* has not failed to attract criticism. Perhaps the most glaring limitation is that its energy, pollution, and capital cost comparisons all require correction. The authors assumed different space standards for the different types of dwelling units. The savings in capital and operating costs calculated in the report are mainly a function of the difference in size, not where these units are located or the density of their development. Furthermore, the energy savings attributed in the report to high-density development appear significantly overstated; and since the estimates of air pollution reduction was made a direct function of energy savings, these estimates must be deflated to a similar degree.

Despite these qualifications, *The Costs of Sprawl* merits the close attention of those interested in an analysis of urban form. Although it is important to recognize the fragility of the main conclusions of *The Costs of Sprawl,* it is equally appropriate to recognize this report as a landmark from which most research on the consequences of urban form has branched.

Souza, Paul. 1995. *New Capital Costs of Sprawl, Martin County, Florida.* **Gainesville, Fl: University of Florida.**

This is a study of the capital requirements of growth in a developing county in South Florida. Souza assumes that Martin County's population will grow at a similar rate as the rest of South Florida. He then calculates the density- and distance-related costs of providing certain public infrastructure. Costs associated with providing roads, a potable water supply, and sanitary sewers within three different housing densities (3, 5, and 10 units per acre) are assessed using Martin County-specific unit costs and development assumptions. Souza then computes costs associated with connecting three sites at varying distances from the urban service area.

Souza finds that the provision of infrastructure within the *lowest density* development is over 100 percent more costly than the provision of infrastructure within the *highest density* development. He also finds that distance costs can not be separated from density costs. As distance from the center increases, density decreases.

The provision of infrastructure to the *lowest density* housing pattern situated on the site *farthest* from the urban service area is 181 percent more costly than the provision of infrastructure to the *highest density* housing pattern situated on a site *within* the urban service area. Low-density sprawl is significantly more costly than high-density non-sprawl. Roads comprise the largest proportion of both density- and distance- related costs.

Tischler & Associates. 1994. *Marginal Cost Analysis of Growth Alternatives— King County, Washington.* **Bethesda, MD: Tischler & Associates, Inc.**

This paper was prepared for the King County, Washington Growth Management Planning Council (GMPC) to evaluate options for future development. The analysis consists of three basic land-use scenarios, with and without high capacity transit between planned urban centers, yielding five alternatives for study.

The study identifies the costs of new development for each alternative over a twenty-year projection period, estimating costs and revenues associated with growth for roads, transit, water and sewer utilities, and government administration.

The study draws the following conclusions:

- The alternatives with more development in the urban centers and cities are more fiscally beneficial when roads, utilities, and general fund activities are considered.

- The scenarios using eight centers generate higher net revenues for the general fund and utility districts than those with fourteen centers, because the eight-center scenarios assume fewer new households in the unincorporated counties inside the urban growth area (UGA) than do the fourteen-center scenarios.

- The fourteen-center scenarios indicate net road costs which are 11 percent below those of the eight-center scenarios. Road costs (especially rights-of-ways) are higher for the eight-center scenarios because these alternatives include major increases in

new households and jobs, which entail both the construction of new roads and purchases of rights-of-ways in the maturing urban centers.

Windsor, Duane. 1979. "*A Critique of The Costs of Sprawl.***"** *Journal of the American Planning Association* **45, 2: (July) 279-292.**

This article is a critical review of the RERC study, *The Costs of Sprawl*. The first part summarizes the findings from the RERC study. The author then criticizes RERC for not disentangling density from other factors. Windsor criticizes RERC for using different size units for different densities, i.e., smaller units for higher densities. Because smaller units have lower floor areas, they are less costly to build. This is a major reason why larger low-density, single-family units are considered more costly to build and to publicly service than higher-density units. Total floor area is 44 percent lower in high-rise developments than single-family neighborhoods. Differences in housing costs and public capital costs largely parallel these floor area differences.

Windsor recomputes the RERC analysis assuming all housing units are 1,200 square feet. This computation greatly reduces the housing and capital cost advantages of high density, though the advantages still exist. However, this approach is equally unrealistic. In reality, higher-density units are indeed smaller, on average, so RERC is not entirely wrong. Windsor concludes that the only way to avoid the problem is to calculate results for both methods on a per square foot basis and compare them.

Another criticism Windsor levels at the RERC study is that it assumes structure costs are highest for single-family homes, lower for high-rise construction, and lowest for walk-up units. Windsor, in contrast, believes that high-rise units should have the highest costs per square foot. He also takes issue with RERC's assumption that developers have to contribute more land to the public sector under single-family development than under high-rise development.

RERC assumes that clustering in higher-density patterns results in savings of vacant land. But, Windsor argues that if the model assumed that a given amount of land is developed at different densities, the total population accommodated on the land could vary. Some ability to account for saved land when residents have more land immediately around them than permitted by existing zoning should have been developed.

The author also criticizes RERC for: "the underlying assumption that cost minimization is an appropriate principle for planning and development ... Cost minimization is not a planning principle unless benefits are constant." Since RERC ignores the benefit side, its conclusions of reduced costs ignore the reduced benefits. However, the author thinks it is not necessary to measure benefits. He claims the prevalence of low-density settlements reflects the benefits to consumers: "Consumers choose to live at high densities only where land costs are very high, as in central cities." Where land costs are lower, as in suburbs, they prefer low density environments.

The author claims that suburbs resist high density on several grounds, not just costs. "Voters are opposed to rapid population growth, the possible characteristics of new residents, the fiscal implications, and the loss of suburban amenities like open space, semi-rural ambiance, etc. Exclusionary land-use

controls are intended, in part, to force low-density development; they function as a form of growth management." (291)

By ignoring these nuances, says Windsor, RERC "does not properly evaluate the relative economic efficiency of alternative development patterns." (291)

York, Marie L. 1989. *Encouraging Compact Development in Florida.* Fort Lauderdale, FL: Florida Atlantic University–Florida International University Joint Center for Environmental and Urban Problems.

York analyzes three areas: growth management programs from around the country (Maine, Massachusetts, New Jersey, Oregon, Vermont); innovative development strategies by region; and problems with redevelopment. The analysis of the statewide programs consists of descriptive summaries of state policies designed to address increasing growth management problems, as well as summaries of the situations that prompted the development of these policies. Each state's section concludes with a discussion of how well the policies and legislation have worked in achieving the state's goals. Some of the difficulties, noted by York, revolve around definitions of rural versus urban uses; areas that are exempted from the legislation for one reason or another; property taxes as a disincentive to compact growth; opposition from developers and municipalities; and the methods of determining urban growth boundaries.

The innovative development strategies section of this document examines the use of urban growth boundaries (UGBs)—a proactive growth management tool to contain, control, direct, or phase growth close to existing urban development. Basic to this strategy is the delineation of perimeters around urban development areas, within which urban densities are normally encouraged, and outside which urban uses and densities are discouraged. Also discussed are transfers of development rights, point systems, and revenue sharing as means of growth management. All four of the subsections conclude with the experiences of communities in several states that have implemented these strategies.

The section on problems of in-fill and development provides overviews of issues and approaches, followed by discussions of programs and projects in Florida and other states.

A secondary analysis of several state studies is undertaken to quantify the impact of UGBs on land prices. However, York admits that the data are neither complete nor consistent enough to draw firm conclusions concerning the land price impacts of urban growth boundaries.

The report concludes with separate sets of recommendations for encouraging compact development, redevelopment, and in-fill development. The recommendations address land use, fiscal, and infrastructure issues.

FISCAL IMPACTS, EXACTIONS, AND IMPACT FEES

Altshuler, Alan. 1977. "Review of The Costs of Sprawl," *Journal of the American Planning Association* **43, 2: 207-209.**

This short article reviews the RERC report and was published about two years after the report. The review is so clear and so well done that it changed forever

the way the *Costs of Sprawl* report was viewed. For purposes of simplicity, Altshuler focuses on the two extreme cases analyzed by RERC—high-density multifamily housing and low-density single-family housing. He begins by summarizing the major findings of the RERC study. He then asks three questions: (1) Have the results of the theoretical analysis been calibrated against actual community experiences? (2) Does the report itself fully support the conclusions stated in its summary? and (3) Are the reported advantages of high-density over low-density development clearly differentiated as to reason? His answer to all three questions is "No"!

One key issue Altshuler raises is whether density per se affects the demand for community services. RERC explicitly assumes that it does not, but Altshuler challenges that assumption. Low-density areas often have no sidewalks; they have above-ground utility lines, and infrequent street lights, when measured against high-density areas. The demand for public safety services is also likely to be lower in low-density development. Further, RERC does not include any estimates of mass transit spending in its study, though such spending would surely be higher in high-density communities that rely more on mass transit. Therefore, Altshuler maintains high-density settlements are likely to have higher community service costs than low-density ones, which would offset many of the savings projected for the latter types of settlements.

According to RERC, the savings for high-density living versus low-density living are only $238 per year in operating costs, for a density rise from 3.5 to 19.0 units per acre plus more intensive planning. Four-fifths of the savings are attributed to density alone. Altshuler believes, given the omissions mentioned above, that this small amount would vanish if the analysis were done correctly.

He also makes the point, which Windsor later picks up on, that dwelling units in the high-density settlement are 34 percent smaller than those in the low-density settlement, and this accounts for a large part of their differences in capital and energy costs. Five-sixths of the heating and air conditioning savings in high-density development is attributable to smaller housing unit sizes.

RERC further assumes that average annual travel per household in high-density developments is about 9,891 miles versus 19,673 miles per household in low-density developments. Generally, only local trips vary by density, but RERC fallaciously attributes cost savings to the entire travel mileage. According to Altshuler, correcting this error eliminates four-fifths of the claimed savings in auto energy consumption. With proper analysis, the total energy savings of high-density versus low-density development is about 3 percent, of which only 1 percent is attributable to density alone.

Another issue Altshuler addresses is whether higher residential density leads to higher density in other types of land uses. He thinks not: "The case that low-density living is a highly expensive luxury remains to be made" (209).

Nonetheless, the author commends RERC for having putting forth a systematic analysis that can serve as a starting point for other studies.

Altshuler, Alan A., and Jose A. Gomez-Ibanez. 1993. *Regulation for Revenue: The Political Economy of Land Use Exactions*. Washington, DC: Brookings Institution.

The central issues and themes of this text relate to government-mandated exactions paid by real estate developers. Exactions may be in-kind or involve monetary outlays. The legal theory underlying development exactions is that governments, having reasonably determined that certain public needs are "attributable" to new development, may require that their costs be "internalized" as part of the development process. A key premise of the argument for exactions is that land development is a major cause of escalating local infrastructure demands and costs.

This study looks at the costs of growth in built-up communities. Alternative estimates of revenues and expenditures for the city of San Francisco are discussed, as are approaches for allocating public expenditures for growth among county businesses and residents in Montgomery County, Maryland.

This text also critiques the Real Estate Research Corporation's *The Costs of Sprawl* study. As Altshuler found in his 1977 study, the principal problem with the RERC study is the meaning associated with the cost differences. Altshuler and Gomez-Ibanez argue that the degree of variation between the quality of housing units from one community to another does not allow costs to be fairly compared. If conditions can not be replicated in future studies, community cost impacts will continue to be difficult to compare.

Overall, the chapter on fiscal impact analysis reflects at least one of the authors' inexperience with this technique.

The authors rely too heavily on secondary analyses and critiques. Furthermore, the book does not give enough recognition to the role (both constructive and destructive) of fiscal impact analysis to either counter or abet development (sprawl) during subdivision or site plan review.

American Farmland Trust. 1986.
Density-Related Public Costs.
Washington, DC: AFT.

This study tests the hypothesis that, in rural areas, public costs for new residential development exceed the public revenues associated with this type of development. Using Loudoun County, Virginia data, the study attempts to develop a methodology to estimate: (1) the net public costs (public costs minus public revenues) of new residential development; and (2) how these costs vary with different development densities.

The study's methodology entails a four-step process. First, major categories of public expenditures (education, health and welfare, and safety) and public revenues (property taxes, state funds, and other local taxes) are identified, based on the county's annual budget. Second, the demographic profile of a 1,000-household new development is determined, based on surrounding demographics, to consist of 3,260 residents (including 940 school-age children). Third, four development scenarios are projected at different density levels, varying from 0.2 dwelling units (d.u.) per acre (rural, low-density) to 4.5 d.u. per acre (suburban, high-density), while retaining the demographic profile of the development. Finally, fiscal impact analysis models are run to determine public costs and revenues associated with each density scenario.

The results reveal a public revenue shortfall for residential development at all densities. However, the lowest-density development results in a shortfall three times larger than the highest density development ($2,200 per d.u. versus $700 per d.u.). To cover the shortfall, the county would have to apply some combination of reduced public services, higher taxes, or increased commercial zoning. In addition to imposing higher public costs, the lower-density developments also remove larger amounts of agricultural land—a result counter to Loudoun County's goal to preserve its agricultural economy.

American Farmland Trust. 1992a. *Does Farmland Protection Pay? The Cost of Community Services in Three Massachusetts Towns.* **Washington, DC: AFT.**

This report summarizes the American Farmland Trust's findings from studies of three Pioneer Valley, Connecticut towns (Agawan, Deerfield, and Gill). The report addresses the five basic steps undertaken by the studies: 1) discussions with local sponsors to define land-use categories (residential, industrial, commercial, and farm/forest/open land); 2) the collection of data for each town; 3) the review of public revenues, allocated by land use; 4) the review of public expenditures, allocated by land use; 5) data analysis and calculation of revenue-to-cost ratios.

This study is part of a series of studies on the costs and benefits of unimproved land as it relates to a community's fiscal well-being. The bulk of support for these analyses comes mostly from groups desiring to preserve agricultural lands in perpetuity as opposed to general academic inquiry into this area.

It is important to summarize the results of these studies before talking about methodologies. In general, they conclude that:

- Residential development does not pay its own way.
- Nonresidential development does pay its own way but is a magnet for residential development.
- Open space or agricultural lands have higher revenue-to-cost ratios than both residential and non-residential development.

Several aspects of the American Farmland Trust studies cause concern. For instance, these studies are not termed "fiscal impact" but rather *Cost of Community Service* (COCS) studies. They are not approached in a standard cost/revenue framework, yet they proffer standard fiscal impact conclusions.

Further, no one is viewed as being at home "tending" the farm. The farm contains no residents or workers. The costs/revenues for residents are deflected to other land uses—predominantly residential. No costs are assigned to agricultural workers, and no highway costs, garbage costs, traffic costs, or health/social service costs are assigned to the farm. Nor are municipal legal or election costs factored in.

- If a reasonable cost-assignment method could not be found, a "default" procedure was used, which assigned costs by the distribution of revenues or by the value of property. Given the low agricultural assessments, predictably large shares of local costs were assigned to residential and nonresidential uses; very small amounts were assigned to agricultural uses. The study's conclusions were blunt: The results of the study show that the residential category is being supported by the

agricultural and commercial/industrial categories. The residential sector is demanding more in services than it is contributing in revenues.

- This study provides a fiscal argument for the protection of farmland and open space.

Despite the lopsided findings of the study, the fact remains that fiscal impact relationships between agricultural and other land uses are not well-documented. Most of the cost and revenue calculation procedures developed since *The Fiscal Impact Handbook* (Burchell and Listokin 1978), ignore open space and agriculture as either a significant cost or revenue. All costs are assigned to the residential and nonresidential sectors, and all forthcoming revenues come exclusively from developed properties whether or not they have inclusive open space. Most studies assume that open space or unimproved lands have neither a significant negative nor positive cost/revenue impact, which is probably an accurate assumption. Neither agricultural nor open space lands cost very much or provide much in local revenue.

Buchanan, Shepard C. and Bruce A. Weber. 1982. "Growth and Residential Property Taxes: A Model for Estimating Direct and Indirect Population Impacts." *Land Economics* 58, 3 (August): 325-337.

Buchanan and Weber's analysis is an attempt to determine the extent to which population growth affects single-family residential property taxes, and how these effects are transmitted. To answer these questions, the authors examine both tax rates and assessed values of properties in Oregon, and the possible influence of increased population on each of these variables. Among other procedures, they study intermediate variables, such as age of housing stock, personal income, and population density.

The authors find that up until 1979, increases in new single-family homes apparently both directly increased average homeowner assessments and indirectly increased tax rates on *all* properties. In 1979, however, the Oregon legislature enacted a tax relief program under which the average rates of increase in assessed valuation of both residential property and all other property on a statewide basis were limited to a maximum 5 percent per year. After this change was enacted, assessments and tax rates slowed in their rate of increase. The costs of servicing new properties could no longer be "exported" to old properties beyond a fixed percentage per year.

The authors suggest that similar legislation be enacted in other states where there is a quest for homeowner property tax relief. They assert that the model they developed for local governments in Oregon is generalizable to other states with similar tax systems. In addition, they believe that the model could be adapted for use in analyzing the impact of population growth on the tax bills of owners of all types of property.

Dougharty, Laurence, Sandra Tapella, and Gerald Sumner. 1975. *Municipal Service Pricing Impacts on Fiscal Position.* **Santa Monica, CA.: RAND.**

This report analyzes the impact of alternative municipal service pricing policies on urban structure and on a community's financial position. A pricing policy is a method of allocating the cost of a service to one sector or another of the community (e.g., new residents, existing residents, the entire community). In this report, primary attention is paid to pricing

policies for the capital infrastructure required to service new development.

The pricing structures estimated in the report are developed using actual data from San Jose and Gilroy, California. San Jose is a fairly large city that has already experienced fairly rapid growth; Gilroy is a city that could potentially undergo explosive growth. Both are believed by the authors to be prototypical of a number of American cities.

This analysis finds that pricing policies allocated to the largest base of payees has the least overall negative effect on the economy of the community.

Downing, Paul, ed. 1977. *Local Services Pricing and Their Effects on Urban Spatial Structure.* **Vancouver: University of British Columbia Press.**

The central claim of this book is that local governments are increasingly turning to alternative sources to raise revenues. Many now impose user charges.

A user charge is an explicit price on the consumption of a public service. In addition to being a source of revenue, user charges are also a direct measure of taxpayers' willingness to pay for the services provided by local government. A user charge makes the payment explicit and directly associated with the public service that is being delivered. It gives the taxpayer a better understanding of what the choices are, enabling a more intelligent decision regarding the array of goods provided by local government. In addition, the user charge performs the function of price. It rations demand, according to who values the service most highly.

The first section of this book presents the rationale for developing new sources of revenue for local government. It identifies the possible scope of user charges as a means of filling this demand, and presents a detailed examination of how a user charge is designed and calculated. The second section presents an analysis of spatial variation in the costs of providing public services. The third section is concerned with institutional systems and their effects on the financing and supply of services. The fourth section argues that while location may not affect costs, political bodies are willing to account for cost differences in the way they assign user charges. The final section presents the author's conclusions about the findings and relates their implications for future policy.

DuPage County Development Department. 1989, 1991. *Impacts of Development on DuPage County Property Taxes.* **DuPage County, IL: DuPage County Regional Planning Commission.**

Five years ago, a brouhaha emerged in the Chicago area involving the cost of nonresidential uses. Debate in DuPage County centered on whether or not commercial uses paid for themselves. A number of experts subsequently gathered to evaluate the findings of the DuPage County Planning Commission's study, *Impacts of Development on DuPage County Property Taxes.*

A regression analysis by DuPage County inferred *a strong relationship between nonresidential development and property tax increases.* Although preservationists leaped to defend these findings, others pointed to the weaknesses of the study. The most convincing of the critiques took a position in the middle—pointing out that some evidence backed up the findings of DuPage County, but the evidence was not nearly as strong as had been presented in the report.

The DuPage County report is not a classic fiscal impact analysis, but rather a regression equation in logarithmic form. The dependent variable is total property taxes levied; independent variables include change in nonresidential firms, change in ratio of nonresidential-to-residential equalized valuation, median residential property tax levy, and the ratio of taxes to the total municipal equalized assessed valuation.

Some critics of the analysis believed both sides of the regression equation formed an identity, whose intercorrelation prevented solution. Some thought the research design should undergo significant alteration; others thought both dependent and independent variables should be recast. DuPage County, however, continued to defend both the analysis and its results.

In reality, the analysis must be put into a fiscal impact frame wherein *all* costs can be compared to *all* revenues. In addition, the quality and quantity of services, the relative levels of tax and nontax revenue, the presence of deficient or excess service capacities, and the effects of other land uses in similar situations should be viewed. A number of studies with similar conclusions about nonresidential growth's impact on property taxes have been documented. Most results can be traced to the nonaccountability of elected/appointed officials, which in turn led to significant service increases for primarily nonresidential properties.

The DuPage study points out that nonresidential development and its associated surplus fiscal revenues could improve service quality and quantity in a community. However, it may also increase local expenditures. Without knowing the type and quantity of public services produced before and after the nonresidential development is put in place, no judgment can be made about nonresidential development and future tax rates.

Logan, John, and Mark Schneider. 1981. "Suburban Municipal Expenditures: The Effects of Business Activity, Functional Responsibility, and Regional Context." *Policy Studies Journal* **9: 1039-50.**

The authors set out to explain the variations in the level of suburban government spending. They first summarize existing explanatory models, which stress either local stratification and discrimination, the structure of local decision making, ecological position, or public choice. These models suggest varying hypotheses about which suburbs spend more and which less. Logan and Schneider then evaluate each of the alternative models and propose major directions for further research.

The authors conclude that each model has its strengths and certain hypotheses from each is supported by the data. Certain variables stand out, however, as having particularly strong explanatory power in all models. The strongest, in terms of determining suburban expenditures, is economic function. Regardless of any other differences among communities, suburbs with strong employment bases spend more than those with weak employment bases.

Of nearly equal importance is the set of service responsibilities that a suburban municipality assumes. This finding may take historical inquiry to fully explain.

Finally, differences in SMSA structure are shown to explain part of the expenditure variation, although no simple reason is given for this influence. Instead, the authors call for additional research to be directed towards explaining

what kinds of economic, historical, political, or social situations cause the differences in suburban expenditures detected in this study.

THE EFFECTS OF GROWTH CONTROLS ON HOUSING COSTS

Katz, Lawrence, and Kenneth Rosen. 1987. "Interjurisdictional Effects of Growth Controls on Housing Prices." *Journal of Law and Economics 30* **(April): 149-160.**

In this article, Katz and Rosen argue that the widespread proliferation of land use and environmental regulations, primarily imposed by local governments, forces the home-building industry to work within a much more complex and often more costly regulatory framework.

Local governments have used a wide variety of procedures to control residential development, and these controls have become increasingly complex and innovative over time. In many municipalities, traditional land-use controls have been augmented by environmental and fiscal impact procedures, urban growth management systems, utility connection moratoria, multiple permit systems, overall growth limitations, or a combination of these measures.

Katz and Rosen examine the effects of local land use regulations on house prices in the San Francisco Bay Area. They find that land use regulations appear to have had a substantial effect on housing prices. The authors conclude that the widespread use of controls in communities limits available housing supply. The spread of these regulatory techniques to metropolitan areas outside California could have substantial negative effects on the affordability of housing in these locations.

Parsons, George. 1992. "The Effects of Coastal Land Use Restrictions on Housing Prices." *Journal of Environmental Economics and Management* **(February): 25-27.**

In this paper, the author estimates the effect on housing prices of land-use restrictions for property abutting the Chesapeake Bay. He examines the change in housing prices before and after the introduction of restrictions in Anne Arundel County, the most populated of the 16 counties that were affected. The price changes are compared to the change in housing prices in several inland locations, not affected by the restrictions, over the same monitoring period.

Parsons finds that the coastal land-use restrictions appear to have caused a considerable increase in housing prices. To make this assertion, he assumes that, absent the controls, the change in housing prices in coastal areas would have been the same as it was for inland locations. Except for land use restrictions, the author believes, both locations share the same general market conditions. This is a significant assumption, considering the effect of "water frontage" on housing price.

Parsons also believes that the land use restrictions create winners and losers in the local housing market. The winners are the current owners of housing in the community. The losers include current owners of undeveloped and restricted land, renters, and future purchasers of housing in the coastal community.

Parsons closes with an admonition that the large transfer of wealth from future residents to current residents through

housing price increases, and the absence of future residents in the political process in which the restrictions were established raise suspicion about the fairness and efficacy of these regulations.

Propst, Luther, and Mary Schmid. 1993. *The Fiscal and Economic Impacts of Local Conservation and Community Development Measures: A Review of Literature.* **Tucson, AZ: Sonoran Institute.**

The authors undertook an effort to review about 200 articles and other publications, with a special emphasis on those dealing with actual experiences in real communities. This literature review includes economic studies of the impacts of zoning and other land use regulation, and the economic impacts of a community's appearance, architecture, and natural environment.

Both a subject-related analysis and annotations of the more important studies appear in this review.

The author's general conclusion is that environmentally sensitive land use planning need not have a detrimental effect on real estate values, economic vitality, or the local tax base. Rather, the opposite is often true.

The authors close on the optimistic note that the lessons contained in the studies may help Greater Yellowstone (near Bozeman, Montana) communities successfully manage rapid growth and change as they choose their own futures.

Schwartz, Seymour I., David E. Hansen, and Richard Green. 1981. "Suburban Growth Controls and the Price of New Housing." *Journal of Environmental Economics and Management* 8 (December): 303-320.

In this paper, the authors study the effects of suburban growth control programs upon the price of new housing. The programs that limit growth employ a variety of devices, including phased zoning, reduced development densities, and increased development charges. Some programs take an even more direct approach, by setting restrictions on the number of housing units permitted, or by imposing population or housing unit caps. The authors then analyze the effects of perhaps the most direct form of control: the housing quota of Petaluma, California.

To estimate price effects, the authors compare price changes of new single-family housing in Petaluma between 1969 and 1977 (after the quota was enacted) to the price changes in two nearby communities. The authors limit the analysis to new housing because it provides a relatively consistent basis for evaluation.

The study's results suggest that Petaluma's growth control program was responsible for an increase in housing prices. Because of the complexity of the issue, however, a totally unambiguous finding is not possible.

The authors are more confident when describing the effect of growth controls on the quality of construction. Here, they find evidence that higher construction quality and prices are attributable to growth controls. The authors close by calling for additional research to analyze the effects of growth controls on housing price.

Schwartz, Seymour I., Peter M. Zorn, and David E. Hansen. 1989. "Research Design Issues and Pitfalls in Growth Control Studies." *Land Economics,* 62, (August): 223-233.

In this article, the authors analyze the experiences of Davis, California, a community that attempted to mitigate the effects of growth controls on the price of housing. The authors seek to determine whether Davis was successful in reducing the expected increase in the per-unit price of housing services due to growth control, and also to determine the extent to which Davis was successful in limiting the exclusionary impact of growth controls on lower income households.

The authors discover that growth controls increased per-unit housing prices due to the reduction in supply, but that price-mitigating programs are also effective. Furthermore, the incentives created by price-mitigation lead developers to build smaller, lower quality units.

Surprisingly, the study's results also show that growth controls increase the sales price of older housing, but the per-unit price declines, implying an increase in the quality of old houses sold. This is explained by the fact that the decrease in the quality of new housing may have encouraged households desiring higher quality (larger) housing to turn to the older housing market, resulting in an increase in the demand for higher quality older homes.

The authors conclude that price-mitigating measures are only partially successful in reducing the price effects of growth controls, since they mostly shift the impacts of growth controls from the new to the old housing market.

URBAN FORM AND SPRAWL

Black, Thomas J. 1996. "The Economics of Sprawl," *Urban Land* **55, 3.**

For most businesses, the decentralization of activity and improvements in communications and transportation create a choice of location options. In addition, globalization trends (particularly in the production of some goods) are placing many U.S. businesses under increasing competitive pressure. According to Black, low-density, dispersed urban settlement patterns result from these powerful economic forces that continue to be driven primarily by changing transportation costs and production requirements.

The major benefit to businesses and residents in metropolitan areas of the dispersed settlements is reduced land rents, writes Black. Increased location options and lower transportation costs mean highly competitive land markets and, consequently, lower land prices, giving U.S. firms a significant advantage over their foreign competition. This translates into more competitive pricing by U.S. firms, a lower cost of living for workers, and higher returns on financial capital and labor.

It is obvious that high-density urban areas make sense only for economic activities that can justify hefty rents. As an alternative, extended transportation systems and lower-cost truck transportation also have enabled industrial and warehouse facilities to spread out to less dense locations to save money on building and land costs.

Black points out that another major issue surrounding current development patterns is the extent to which general taxpayers, especially those in built-out communities, subsidize new incremental, low-density development. Examples include subsidies in the form of income tax mortgage, interest, and property tax deductions; federal highway expenditures in excess of user taxes and fees; and state and local government subsidies for infrastructure expansion to support new development.

Views on these issues differ, and Black ends this article by calling for a realistic analysis of the forces at work to avoid faulty conclusions about the economics of sprawl.

Ladd, Helen, and William Wheaton. 1991. "Causes and Consequences of the Changing Urban Form." *Regional Science and Urban Economics* **(21): 157-162.**

The papers compiled in this work were initially presented at a conference on the *Causes and Consequences of the Changing Urban Form*, October 1990, run under the auspices of the Lincoln Institute of Land Policy. The goal of the conference was to bring together empirical, theoretical, and policy-oriented economists to improve the understanding of the nature, causes, and implications of polycentrism in metropolitan areas.

Recently, older, traditionally monocentric cities, such as Boston and Chicago, have developed significant suburban subcenters. Other newer cities, such as Phoenix, Dallas, and Los Angeles are perceived as lacking in any sense of "centrality."

Two of the papers in this collection provide insights on the nature and function of employment subcenters and decentralization; two develop and test empirical models that specifically include elements of polycentrism. One paper provides a new theory of subcenter formation in the context of a dynamic model; and two more examine various implications of changing urban form for labor markets.

McKee, David L. and Gerald H. Smith. 1972. "Environmental Diseconomies in Suburban Expansion." *The American Journal of Economics and Sociology* **31, 2: 181-88.**

In this paper, the authors set out to isolate and analyze the components of suburban sprawl. Causes of sprawl are discussed, and an attempt is made to specify the economic effects sprawl has on urban areas, people, and the economy. The authors intention is to develop suitable policy recommendations for dealing with sprawl.

The authors conclude that sprawl appears to be the result of strong market forces, and that solutions to the problem may be beyond the abilities of public policy makers to solve. They call for more government intervention, especially at the local level, and for action on the part of regional planning agencies. To date, these institutions have not been able to deal adequately with the problem, because of overlapping jurisdictions and other political considerations. The authors further call for greater cooperation and sharing of resources at all levels of government to find solutions to suburban sprawl.

Mills, David E. 1981. "Growth Speculation and Sprawl in a Monocentric City." *Journal of Urban Economics* **10: 201-226.**

Mills presents an economic theory of sprawl in a growing, monocentric city. He posits that where decision makers have perfect knowledge, leapfrog development and discontinuous land-rent

functions may occur and be efficient in both an ex-post and ex-ante sense. Where the extent of future growth is uncertain, decision makers become speculators, and the spatial pattern of development is more complicated. Ex-post inefficiency generally occurs.

In the context of Mill's formal monocentric-city model, three land-use patterns qualify as examples of sprawl. *Leapfrog development* occurs when a von Thunen ring of undeveloped land separates rings of developed land. This form of sprawl involves radical discontinuity. *Scattered development,* the second form of sprawl, occurs when there are annuli with both developed (homogeneously) and undeveloped land in them. *Mixed development* occurs when there are annuli with more than one developed use. Scattered development and mixed development forms of sprawl involve circumferential discontinuity.

Mills provides theoretical explanations for each form of sprawl. Leapfrog development can be explained by inter-temporal planning on the part of decision makers who anticipate future growth with certainty. The essential idea here is similar to the notion put forth by Ohls and Pines (1975), that is, that land inside of the urban fringe is sometimes withheld from early development and preserved for more remunerative future options. Theoretical explanations for scattered and mixed development forms indicate that decision makers are uncertain about future growth and make speculative decisions.

Several criticisms of sprawl are cited and addressed with evidence generated from the monocentric city model constructed for this analysis.

Ohls, James C., and David Pines. 1975. "Discontinuous Urban Development and Economic Efficiency." *Land Economics* **3 (August): 224-234.**

Many observers argue that discontinuous development (wherein land that is closer to urban centers is skipped over in favor of land further away) is inefficient for several reasons. First, this development pattern fails to make use of the most accessible land. Second, the expense of providing public services, such as roads and sewage systems, to new development is high. In contradiction, Ohls and Pines argue that discontinuous development may be desirable and efficient in certain cases. For instance, the development of retail and commercial services near the urban fringe must often wait for the maturation of critical scale. In rapidly expanding urban areas, contexts arise in which it may be efficient to skip over land for a period of time in order to reserve it for commercial uses after market scale increases.

This strategy has been implemented in some planned communities. In Columbia, Maryland, for example, the planners of this "new town" explicitly reserved vacant land in residential areas for the development of shopping clusters in the future—after increased residential densities make such shopping enterprises economically feasible.

Peiser, Richard B. 1989. "Density and Urban Sprawl." *Land Economics* **65, 3 (August): 193-204.**

In this article, Peiser argues that, contrary to accepted thinking, if a free urban land market were allowed to function it would inherently promote higher-density development. He offers theoretical arguments and empirical evidence to support this thesis.

Peiser argues that *uniformly* low-density urban development is inefficient, because it increases transportation costs, consumes excessive amounts of land, and adds to the cost of providing and operating public utilities and public services. Furthermore, he claims that the data show that over time discontinuous development patterns actually promote *higher* density. So public policies aimed at preventing discontinuous development may be misguided. They may lead to development patterns in which densities might be lower than they ordinarily would be without such a policy.

Three case studies (Dallas, TX; Montgomery County, MD; and Fairfax County, VA) are presented in which lot sizes are examined over time along major arterial roadways. Higher densities (i.e. smaller lot sizes) are found in later in-fill development.

Peiser concludes that polices that encourage sequential development should be avoided. Instead, he argues that a competitive land market will achieve higher density through discontinuous development followed by later in-fill development.

CHAPTER

Annotations of Studies

TRANSPORTATION AND TRAVEL COSTS

Transportation and travel costs as they relate to sprawl involve mode of travel, pattern of residential development and development access, density of residential development, and location/type of non-residential development. The specific topics that group the annotations of this section reflect the above topical concerns. They are:

Changes in Automobile Travel
The Effects of Density on Travel Choices
Unlimited Outward Extension
Spatial Segregation of Uses
Dispersed Employment
The Costs of Travel

Changes in Automobile Travel includes the works of Gordon and Richardson (1989, 1991) and Alan Pisarski (1992). *The Effects of Density on Travel Choices* includes the works of Anthony Downs (1992), Robert Cervero (1991b, 1996), Frank and Pivo (1994), John Holtzclaw (1990, 1994), and Newman and Kenworthy (1989). *Unlimited Outward Extension* includes the works of Judy Davis (1993) and Parsons Brinckerhoff (1997). *Spatial Segregation of Uses* includes the works of Robert Cervero

(1989, 1995, 1996), Reid Ewing (1994), S. Handy (1992, 1995), Robert Kitamura et al. (1994), and Parsons Brinckerhoff (1996c). *Dispersed Employment* includes the works of Robert Cervero et al. (1996, 1997). *The Costs of Travel* includes the works of Apogee Research (1994), M. E. Hanson (1992), J. J. MacKenzie et al. (1992), Parsons Brinckerhoff (1996a), and Michael Voorhees (1992).

CHANGES IN AUTOMOBILE TRAVEL

Gordon, Peter, Harry W. Richardson, and Myung-Jin Jun. 1991. "The Commuting Paradox: Evidence from the Top Twenty." *Journal of the American Planning Association* 57, 4: 416-20.

This comparison of mean commuting times of residents of core counties in the 20 largest U.S. metropolitan areas shows that average trips times declined or remained the same between 1980 and 1985, even as population increased in most areas. The authors hypothesize that constant or declining trip times were the result of commuters changing residences or jobs so that their origins and destinations were closer to each other or so they could travel faster on less congested routes. However, the *American Housing Survey* database they use does not contain the information needed to confirm or disprove this hypothesis.

Levinson, D. M., and A. Kumar. 1994. "The Rational Locator: Why Travel Times Have Remained Stable." *Journal of the American Planning Association* **60: 319-332.**

The authors compare travel diary data from the Washington, DC metropolitan area for the years 1968 through 1988. They conclude that greater dispersion of activities has helped keep travel times constant. During this 20-year period, the metropolitan area became more dispersed; population grew by 30 percent, employment grew by 85 percent, and the number of daily motorized trips per person increased from 2.3 to 2.8. Yet, differences of means test show that for most modes and purposes, average times for home-to-work and work-to-home were the same at the beginning and end of the period. The authors conclude that the "locators"—households and firms—acted rationally and relocated to keep travel times constant.

Pisarski, Alan E. 1992. *New Perspectives in Commuting.* **Washington, DC: U.S. Department of Transportation. July.**

Pisarski identifies trends in commuting using data from the *1990 Census* and the *1990 Nationwide Personal Transportation Study.* He shows that the proportion of all trips that were for work purposes declined slightly, from 20.4 percent in 1983 to 20.1 percent in 1990. Although the miles of travel for work increased, average travel times for work trips

increased by only 40 seconds. This result is partly due to a 35 percent increase in the number of work trips made in single-occupant vehicles, usually the fastest mode of travel. The additional 22 million people who drove alone exceeded the number of workers added to the labor force. Meanwhile, the absolute number of people using transit remained at about 6 million, but the share of users declined due to population growth.

Richardson, Harry W., and Peter Gordon. 1989. "Counting Nonwork Trips: The Missing Link in Transportation, Land Use, and Urban Policy." *Urban Land* **(September): 6-12.**

One recent transportation phenomenon in the United States has been the growth in non-work travel, both during peak and off-peak hours. Using data from the *Nationwide Personal Transportation Studies for 1977 and 1983,* the authors find that the number of non-work trips increased three to four times faster than work trips during that time frame in all sizes of SMSAs. Non-work travel even increased faster than work travel during the peak periods. Richardson and Gordon contend that suburbanization, especially in the largest metropolitan areas, was a principal cause of the increase in non-work travel, although they acknowledge that demographic and workforce changes were probably also involved. Suburbanization of businesses means that suburbanites have more close-by shopping and recreational opportunities and, therefore, may make more trips to satisfy immediate needs rather than wait until they have a list of needs. The study, however, does not demonstrate either that shopping and recreational opportunities have increased in suburbia or that households take more trips because of such an increase. Nor does the study rule out the effects of other factors such as rising incomes, greater participation of women in the workforce, and changes in leisure activities on non-work travel choices.

Rossetti, M. A., and B. S. Eversole. 1993. *Journey to Work Trends in the United States and Its Major Metropolitan Areas, 1960-1990.* **Washington, DC: U.S. Department of Transportation.**

The authors compare mean commuting times in 1980 and 1990 for the 39 metropolitan areas with populations in excess of one million in 1990. They find that commuting times increased in 35 of the metropolitan areas, and that the increases ranged from 0.47 percent in Philadelphia to 13.69 percent in San Diego. All four of the metropolitan areas with commuting time increases of more than 10 percent are Sunbelt cities: Los Angeles, San Diego, Sacramento, and Orlando. The only cities where commuting time declined are New York (-7.70 percent), Pittsburgh (-1.05 percent), New Orleans (-0.57 percent), and Salt Lake City (-1.92 percent).

THE EFFECTS OF DENSITY ON TRAVEL CHOICES

Simulations

Downs, Anthony. 1992. *Stuck in Traffic: Coping with Peak Hour Congestion.* **Washington, DC: Brookings Institution; and Cambridge, MA: Lincoln Institute of Land Policy.**

Downs develops a hypothetical urban area model to test the extent to which changes in the location and density of development would change average commuting distances. The basic model uses values for the proportion of jobs in the CBD, central city, suburbs, and exurbs, and commuting distances similar

to the averages for large metropolitan areas. Different densities are created by varying the size of the suburbs and exurbs (and adjusting the proportion of population and jobs in each area as needed to match the size). The study shows that the density of growth at the urban fringe has a significant impact on commuting distances; a move from very low to medium densities has the greatest impact. Increasing exurban densities from 886 persons per square mile to 2,800 reduces commuting distances by 8 percent. An increase from 886 persons to 4,363 persons per square mile decreases commuting trip lengths by 14 percent. Beyond that, large increases in density shorten trips by only a small amount.

Ewing, Reid. 1997b. *Transportation and Land Use Innovations.* **Chicago, IL: Planners Press, American Planning Association.**

The author's goal in this book is to provide suggestions for improving mobility by reducing congestion and automobile dependence. He defines mobility as "the ability [of individuals] to engage in desired activities at moderate costs to themselves and to society."

Ewing cites two key implementation strategies for solving mobility problems. First, according to the author, the length, mode, and frequency of trips of household travel is affected by residential accessibility—the accessibility from a person's home to their destination; and by destination accessibility—the accessibility from one destination location to another. Better accessibility can be achieved, according to Ewing, through better land-use planning at the regional and community levels.

The second strategy espoused by the author is travel demand management

(TDM). TDM attempts to reduce the number of automobiles on the roads at peak travel times. This strategy promotes such techniques as carpooling, staggered work hours, compressed work weeks, and telecommuting. The success of TDM programs hinges on employers' willingness to implement them and to provide incentives to their employees to utilize them.

The author also examines how cities can create conditions favorable to transit, pedestrian, and bicycle use. He notes that to accomplish this goal, these modes must become more flexible and feasible. Again, Ewing concludes that land use development patterns must become more supportive of transit and alternative modes of travel.

In conclusion, Ewing calls for a paradigm shift in land use and transportation planning. He believes there "should be less emphasis on how fast vehicles move and more emphasis on how well people's travel needs are met."

Metro. 1994. *Region 2040 Recommended Alternative Decision Kit*. Portland, OR.

This analysis of alternative urban forms of growth for the Portland, Oregon metropolitan area shows that more concentrated development, in conjunction with expansion of transit service, reduces vehicle miles of travel and use of the automobile. This study uses one of the most advanced travel demand models in the United States to simulate transportation outcomes. It determines that under continued current development patterns, the urban area would have to expand by more than half of its current size over the next 50 years.

The study also tests three different scenarios that concentrate various amounts of growth in transit corridors, centers, and in neighboring cities. In the "Growing Out" scenario, a larger share of single-family housing is built than the region has at present, with more than one-fourth of future growth placed outside the current urban growth boundary. The "Growing Up" scenario keeps all future growth inside the urban growth boundary by increasing densities and building a larger share of multifamily housing. The "Neighboring Cities" scenario moves about one-third of the expected growth to other cities within commuting distance of the urban area. Not surprisingly, the highly concentrated development of the "Growing Up" scenario produces the highest transit use (6 percent of all trips) and the greatest reduction in VMT over base case levels (16.7 percent). The more dispersed patterns, while consuming more land, have lower levels of congestion.

Despite the results of this study, the ability to change travel behavior is limited, because much of the capital infrastructure that will serve the built environment for the next 50 years is already in place. Some of the study's other proposed changes in the way the regions develop may also not be feasible to undertake for political and economic reasons.

Mobility for the 21st Century Task Force. 1996b. *Strategic Goals for the 21st Century*. Washington, DC: American Public Transit Association.

In 1995, the American Public Transit Association formed the Task Force on Mobility for the 21st Century (M21). The M21 Task Force believes that the problems caused by urban sprawl are rapidly worsening. The Task Force concluded that over the next fifty years, with continued existing development patterns, the nation will "slip into a downward spiral of economic, environmental, and social decline."

In response, the M21 Task Force engaged in a year-long strategic planning process to develop a plan for an alternative future. As a result, the Task Force devised four plausible scenarios for the future, developed a preferred vision for the year 2050, and adopted six goals and recommendations to make the vision a reality.

The four scenarios of how the Task Force believes urban development patterns may evolve over the next fifty years follow.

Boundless Sprawl—Continued growth and unchecked urban sprawl; U.S. maintains economic growth, but central cities decline and urban problems worsen.

Dying Cities—Continued growth and unchecked urban sprawl feed economic and social decline, causing a downward spiral. Central cities are faced with increased poverty, crime, and other problems.

Community-oriented Growth—Growth continues, but in the form of infill and mixed-use, pedestrian-scale communities centered around transit stations.

Reinventing the City—A new urban pattern emerges following the tenets of sustainable development. All development occurs within an urban growth boundary (surrounded by greenbelts), and every location can be reached easily by transit.

Based on the analysis of these plausible scenarios, the M21 Task Force developed a vision of their preferred future. This future, based on sustainable community development, benefits the economy, environment, social equity, community life, and individual quality of life.

In this vision, both central cities and suburbs thrive. Although people continue to live in suburbs, transit-oriented developments (TODs) have replaced low-density suburbs as the preferred neighborhood design. In addition, these neighborhoods allow easy pedestrian and bicycle movement. Also, TODs offer a wide choice of housing type, densities, and costs.

TODs offer numerous additional benefits. They require less new infrastructure and utilize existing infrastructure and maximum capacity, ease traffic congestion, save commuting time, and reduce pollution.

The Task Force acknowledges that the vision is a long stretch but believes that it is achievable if the following six strategic goals and recommendations are adopted.

1. Build on the principles of ISTEA.
2. Invest in innovative sustainable technologies.
3. Create desirable land-use and development patterns.
4. Strengthen regional and metropolitan planning and decision making.
5. Shift toward true cost pricing.
6. Provide creative leadership initiatives.

Empirical Studies

Cervero, Robert. 1991b. "Land Use and Travel at Suburban Activity Centers." *Transportation Quarterly* 45, 4: 479-491.

This article analyzes the effects of density, land-use mix, and parking characteristics on commuting behavior in suburban activity centers. The study uses data from

83 randomly selected buildings in six suburban activity centers, collected as part of a project called *Travel Characteristics of Large-Scale Suburban Activity Centers*, for the National Cooperative Highway Research Program.

The strongest relationship evidenced in the study was between density (measured as the height of each building) and transit use. Having retail operations in the building had only modest effects on mode choice; primarily it increased transit and walking mode shares. Parking supply had less effect on mode choice, probably because most of the office buildings had generous supplies of parking spaces.

Using buildings as the unit of analysis in this study poses some problems. For example, the study fails to consider other center characteristics that may play important roles in determining commuting behavior, such as distances between buildings and opportunities to shop and conduct personal business at other locations within the center.

Cervero, Robert, and Kara Kockelman. 1996. "Travel Demand and the 3Ds: Density, Diversity, and Design." *Transportation Research Digest* **2, 3:199-219.**

The authors claim that a host of urban design philosophies—new urbanism, transit-oriented development, traditional town planning—have gained popularity in recent years as ways of shaping travel demand. All share three common transportation objectives: (1) reduce the number of motorized trips; (2) of trips that are produced, increase the share that are non-motorized; and (3) of the motorized trips that are produced, reduce travel distances and increase vehicle occupancy levels. An expected outcome of weaning people from their cars,

proponents hope, will be a lessening of the negative consequences of an automobile-oriented society—namely, air pollution, fossil fuel consumption, and class and social segregation.

Cervero and Kockelman describe how new urbanists, neo-traditionalists, and other reform-minded designers argue for changing three dimensions, or the 3Ds, of the built environment—*density, diversity, and design*—to achieve these objectives. While the effects of density on travel demand have been acknowledged, the effects of diversity and design have just as long been ignored. This paper examines the connection between the 3Ds of the built environment and travel demand. It tries to sort through the relative influences of these three dimensions after controlling for other variables, such as travelers' demographic characteristics. It does this by applying the technique of factor analysis to gauge the relative influence of each dimension as well as their collective impacts.

The research findings of this paper lend some degree of credibility to the claims of new urbanists and others that compact, mixed-use, pedestrian-friendly designs can reduce vehicle trips, vehicle miles traveled (VMT) per capita, and motorized travel. The research suggests that the effects of the Bay Area's built environment on travel demand were modest to moderate at best. Densities exerted the strongest influence on personal business trips. Additionally, residential neighborhoods that were spatially accessible to commercial activities, reflected by an accessibility index variable, tended to average appreciably less VMT per household. Diversity also had a modest impact on travel demand, although where it was significant, its influences was somewhat stronger than that of density. Having retail activities within neighborhoods was most closely associated with mode choice for work trips. Further, the dimension of walking quality was generally moderately associated with travel demand. Finally, several specific design elements of the built environment seemed to be particularly relevant to non-work trip-making. Notably, neighborhoods with high shares of four-way intersections, as a proxy for grid-iron street patterns, and limited on-street parking abutting commercial establishments, tended to average less single-occupant vehicular travel for non-work purposes.

The researchers believe that higher densities, diverse land uses, and pedestrian-friendly designs must co-exist to a certain degree if meaningful transportation benefits are to accrue. Having nice sidewalks, attractive landscaping, and other pedestrian amenities in a low-density, residential-only neighborhood is unlikely to prompt many residents to walk to shops and stores. However, the synergy of the 3Ds in combination is likely to yield more appreciable impacts.

Dunphy, R. T., and K. M. Fisher. 1994. *Transportation, Congestion and Density: New Insights.* **Paper presented at the 73rd Annual Meeting of the Transportation Research Board, Washington, DC: January.**

Using data on urbanized areas from *Highway Statistics, 1990*, the authors investigate the relationships (using graphs) between density and vehicle miles of travel and travel use. They find some correlation between urbanized area population density and transit use (26 percent), but little correlation between vehicle miles of travel and density (8 percent). However, using data from the *1990 Nationwide Personal Transportation Survey*, the authors find that people in

denser areas make nearly the same number of daily trips as people at lower densities, but they drive less. At most densities the average number of person trips per day is just below 4.0; only at 30,000 persons/square mile or more do trip numbers dip to 3.4 trips per day. However, the average number of trips by car drops from about 3.5 at densities below 30,000 persons/square mile to 1.9 at 30,000 persons/square mile. People living at higher densities drive less because both transit and walking/biking are more viable options. The authors, however, find a strong correlation between density and life cycle stage. They contend that demographics may be more of a contributing factor to differences in travel behavior than density.

This study is descriptive, suggesting relationships that need further analysis with multivariate techniques to sort out the relative effects of household characteristics versus land-use density. The data analyzed in this study are also aggregate, comparing whole regions rather than specific places within regions where people live and work.

Dzurik, Andrew. 1993. "Transportation Costs of Urban Sprawl: A Review of the Literature." *State Transportation Policy Initiative.* **Center for Urban Transportation Research. November.**

This article cites nine studies that deal with transportation costs and sprawl, including the classic RERC *The Costs of Sprawl* study (1974a), reviews by Altshuler (1977) and Windsor (1979), and several others. The first part of the article cites a 1965 study—"The Nature and Economics of Urban Sprawl" by Harvey and Clark—that defined three characteristics of sprawl, low-density, ribbon, and leapfrog development.

Automobile use was also viewed as the catalyst for urban sprawl. John Kain (1967) argued, however, that any savings from developing high-density areas may be offset by higher construction costs per unit.

RERC's report is cited extensively. It estimated that a low-density sprawl community would require more than six times the amount of minor streets than a planned high-density community. Only road length costs were considered as direct costs in the analysis of transportation variations among these communities. However, two indirect costs were also considered: travel time and air pollution. The RERC report assumed twice as much VMT in a low-density community, which accounted for a large difference in such costs.

Dzurik's article then cites Altshuler's criticisms of the RERC report. Altshuler's book *The Urban Transportation System* (1979) argues that the American public has strong preferences for auto transportation and low-density settlements. Therefore, Americans will refuse to live in densities high enough to bring about any changes in the problems associated with sprawl, which he believes have been exaggerated anyway. Bowler completed a study in 1977 that showed that "user-operated transportation" accounted for about one-seventh of consumer spending, a proportion that stayed roughly constant from 1950 through 1973. He argues that suburban living results in higher use of energy and land resources for transportation than higher-density living.

When the urban environment is modeled as polycentric, however, the percentage of suburban dwellers who increase their travel distances for journeys to work no longer continues to rise, since work places also become decentralized. Yet many models assume that rising commuting costs are a major transportation cost of suburbanization.

Gordon also argues that because work trips are declining as a percentage of all trips, the relative importance of accessibility to workplaces as a motive for choosing places to work and places to live is falling. Gordon and Richardson argue that decentralization is an antidote to traffic congestion because it scatters both origin and destination points and makes suburb-to-suburb trips shorter than any other types.

BART failed to replace the auto as the preferred means of commuting in the Bay Area, in spite of its enormous cost. Where light rail systems have been created, cities have experienced small gains in public transit ridership over pure bus systems, but they have also incurred major cost increases. Light rail tends to replace bus travel more than auto travel.

Dzurik reviews the argument over compact development. One advantage compact development is supposed to have over sprawl is that it uses the excess capacity in existing infrastructures, rather than create a need to build new infrastructures. This was a major source of the economies found in the New Jersey sprawl studies. But such savings do not always materialize.

Dzurik discusses how much subsidy from local governments goes into highways and mass transit. In Milwaukee, Wisconsin, for example, he points out, the local burden of highway costs equals 59 percent of the local property tax levy. Because user fees do not pay the entire cost of auto travel, more sprawl occurs than would otherwise take place.

Dzurik's study claims that the transportation costs associated with urban sprawl have not been studied in the appropriate quantitative terms. Therefore, most questions about this issue are still unanswered. His article cites unfavorable views of sprawl's transportation costs in 12 articles and studies, with one-sentence summaries of their major complaints.

Dzurik's article contains almost no original quantitative analysis. Numerous cited studies offer contradictory evidence, and the author does not critically analyze why these differences exist. Further, he offers few better approaches to research the areas of transportation and urban sprawl.

Frank, L. D., and Gary Pivo. 1994. *The Relationship Between Land Use and Travel Behavior in the Puget Sound Region.* **WA-RD 351.1. Olympia, WA: Washington State Department of Transportation.**

The authors use data from the *1989 Transportation Panel Survey* for the central Puget Sound region, along with household characteristics from the *1990 Census*, employment data from the state employment agency, and land-use data from the county assessor to identify the factors that affect travel behavior. They find that density, mix, and jobs/housing balance are all related to travel behavior, with employment density and jobs/housing balance having the strongest relationships. At higher densities, trips are shorter but take more time. More trips are made using alternatives to the single-occupant vehicle. As land-use mix increases, trip distances, times, and auto-mode shares decrease. As jobs and housing become more balanced, trip distances and travel times go down. The relationships between density and mode split are not linear. The authors identify thresholds at which there is a substantial

increase in transit use. These thresholds are 50-75 employees and 9-13 persons per gross acre for work trips, and 75 employees and 18 persons per gross acre for shopping trips. The use of carpooling, however, seems unrelated to urban densities or other land-use attributes. The study controls for household characteristics, such as income and vehicle availability.

Gordon, Peter, A. Kumar, and Harry W. Richardson. 1989. "The Influence of Metropolitan Spatial Structure on Commuting Time." *Journal of Urban Economics*, **26: 138-151.**

The authors combine data on residential and employment densities (residents or workers per acre of land zoned for that purpose) for 82 SMSAs from twelve states (from the U.S. Geological Survey LANDSAT file) with census data to identify factors that influence commuting times by auto and transit. Their research finds that lower residential densities are associated with shorter commuting times both by car and by transit. For auto trips, concentration of industrial employment leads to shorter travel times, whereas concentration of commercial employment increases trip times. The clustering of manufacturing produces economies in driving, but the clustering of commercial activities (such as in the CBD) produces congestion that reduces times. Other variables (land area, income, economic structure) have the expected positive or negative influences, and the equations are fairly robust, explaining 61 to 87 percent of the variability in mean travel times. As a result, the authors conclude that polycentric or dispersed spatial structures reduce commuting times.

The authors' use of SMSAs as the unit of analysis, however, raises questions about what density means. No SMSA has uniform density throughout. Perhaps lower regional density is a proxy for age of development, city size, or some other factor that influences transit use.

Holtzclaw, J. 1990. *Explaining Urban Density and Transit Impacts on Auto Use.* Paper presented to the State of California Energy Resources Conservation and Development Commission by Natural Resources Defense Council and the Sierra Club. April 19.

Holtzclaw compares the annual vehicle miles of travel in five communities with various densities in the San Francisco Bay Area to test whether higher residential densities combined with better transit service and neighborhood shopping result in less driving. The study finds that doubling residential density reduces annual vehicle miles by 20 to 30 percent. Better transit access also reduces vehicle travel.

Holtzclaw's study, however, is a cross-sectional one, that only demonstrates correlation between density and vehicle miles of travel. It does not show, for example, that increasing density in a particular neighborhood would reduce vehicle miles of travel. Neither does the study control for income levels or other characteristics of households that influence vehicle miles of travel.

Holtzclaw, J. 1994. *Using Residential Patterns and Transit to Decrease Auto Dependence and Costs.* San Francisco, CA: Natural Resources Defense Council.

Holtzclaw uses smog check odometer readings for 28 communities in San Francisco, Los Angeles, San Diego, and Sacramento—all with at least 20,000 residents—to evaluate the relationship between density and land use. The study

finds that neighborhood density is negatively related to both automobile ownership rates and vehicle miles of travel, controlling for household income and size. When household densities double, vehicle miles of travel decline by 16 percent, controlling for such factors as transit service intensities and vehicle ownership. Better access to transit also reduces vehicle miles of travel. Shopping opportunities and the pedestrian environment, on the other hand, are not statistically significant in explaining travel behavior.

Although, income is controlled in this study, residents could still vary by number of children, number of workers, or other characteristics that influence travel behavior.

While, this cross-sectional analysis shows a relationship between density and automotive use in existing communities, it does not demonstrate that if low-density communities became denser fewer trips would be made by automobile.

Newman, Peter W. G., and Jeffrey R. Kenworthy. 1989a. *Cities and Automobile Dependence: An International Sourcebook.* Brookfield, VT: Gower Publishing.

Newman and Kenworthy assemble a set of data on the transportation and land-use characteristics of ten large U.S. cities, five Australian, twelve Western Europe, three Asian, one Canadian, and one Russian city for the period 1950 to 1980. Using gasoline consumption per capita as the primary measure of automobile dependence (other measures such as transit mode share are highly correlated with this measure), they identify the relationship between automobile dependence and urban density. Low densities are associated with high automobile dependence, and high densities with less dependence on the automobile. This relationship holds for regions as a whole, for inner areas (pre-World War II parts of the cities), and for outer areas. As a result, the authors conclude that more compact cities would reduce automobile use.

Reviewers, however, have questioned the validity of using gasoline consumption as the measure of automobile dependence, noting that many factors, such as gas prices and fleet characteristics, influence gasoline consumption. Newman and Kenworthy's analysis of automobile dependence also fails to make full use of the data collected, employing only a single variable—urban density—to explain automobile use, when other factors are clearly involved. As a result, the role of density may be overstated.

Parsons Brinckerhoff Quade and Douglas. 1996b. "Commuter and Light Rail Corridors: The Land Use Connection." In *Transit and Urban Form, Vol. 1*. Washington, DC: Transit Cooperative Research Program, Transportation Research Board. October.

This study updates the work of Pushkarev and Zupan (1982) by analyzing the effects of residential densities and CBD employment levels and densities on light rail and commuter rail boardings. The data are from eleven cities in the United States with a total of nineteen light rail lines and six cities with a total of forty-seven commuter rail lines. Boardings and transit service characteristic data were provided by transit agencies. Employment and population characteristics are from the *1990 Census*. The data are used to develop models of light rail and commuter rail boardings and costs. The empirical results are then used to estimate boardings and costs for

hypothetical light rail and commuter rail corridors.

The study finds that residential densities have a significant influence on light rail boardings. A 10 percent increase in residential density within two miles of stations increases station area boardings by 5.9 percent, holding constant other factors affecting ridership, such as income. Residential densities matter less for commuter rail boardings. Commuter rail is a high fare mode of travel, and many of the high-income riders come from low-density suburban areas some distance from the city center.

Both the size and density of the CBD influence light rail ridership. A 10 percent increase in CBD employment density raises light rail boardings per station by about 4.0 percent, holding constant the number of CBD employees, the residential density of stations, and other factors affecting ridership. For commuter rail, a 10 percent increase in CBD employment densities increases station boardings outside the CBD by 7.1 percent.

The study concludes that light rail is most cost-effective and efficient in the cities with larger CBDs and denser corridors. Commuter rail works best with dense CBDs. Other factors within the control of transit agencies, such as the availability of feeder bus service and park-and-ride lots, also influence ridership and costs.

Pushkarev, B., and J. M. Zupan. 1977. *Public Transportation and Land Use Policy*. Bloomington, IN: Indiana University Press.

The authors estimate the effects of population density on transit use by employing areawide population densities and transit use data from 105 urbanized areas. They show that population density explained 55 percent of the variation in transit use in 1960, and 66 percent in 1970.

The authors also estimate the effects of residential density, downtown floor space, and the presence or absence of rail transit for 27 urbanized areas. Using these factors increases the explanatory power of the equations, but the new variables are still less significant than residential density in explaining transit use. Pushkarev and Zupan attribute this result to greater variability in office floor space than in residential densities among the areas studied.

UNLIMITED OUTWARD EXTENSION

Davis, Judy. 1993. "The Commuting of Exurban Residents." *Urban Geography*, 14, 1: 7-29.

A comparison of the commuting times of workers who bought homes in the suburbs and those who bought homes in the exurbs of Portland, Oregon, shows that the average exurban home buyer has a commuting trip six to seven minutes longer than his counterpart in suburbia, controlling for occupation, income, and other household and job characteristics. The data is from a survey conducted by the author of about 750 households that bought and occupied homes in 1987.

Although some exurban households have commutes similar to those of suburban households, the average exurbanite appears to trade off longer travel times for more space, a rural environment, lower housing prices, a better place to raise children, or some combination of these factors. However, exurban residents seem to sort themselves out so that those who live close to the urban area have central city and suburban jobs, whereas those who live farthest out most likely work in exurban towns.

Parsons Brinckerhoff Quade & Douglas. 1997. "TCRP Project H-13A—Draft Report: Consequences of the Interstate Highway System for Transit." Washington, DC: Transit Cooperative Research Program, Transportation Research Board.

This report describes the intended and unintended consequences of the development of urban interstate highways for transit by examining four metropolitan areas in the United States, four selected cities in Germany, and one city in Canada. The report includes profiles of these communities, their transportation systems, and the positive and negative impacts of their transportation choices.

The authors gathered information from published articles, official plans, and interviews with officials and other knowledgeable people in each community. They also visited each site. Their goal was to understand the history of the development of the interstate highway system within the urbanized area and the interactions between high-speed limited-access roads and changes in the transit system and land-use patterns.

The case studies were selected to test two major hypotheses identified from the literature review: that the interstate highway program biased transportation investments in favor of high-speed limited-access highways that made automobile travel much more attractive than transit use; and that interstate highways facilitated the suburbanization of households and firms, producing a pattern of development that is difficult for public transit to serve.

The authors present evidence from these case studies that confirms that the development of the interstate highway system adversely affected public transit. The data show declines in transit ridership, increasing difficulty in maintaining transit service levels, and the decentralization and dispersion of households and jobs in case study regions with the highest use of interstate highways. Yet the authors correctly point out that transit was in decline well before the interstate system was operational, and other factors supported development in outlying areas, such as low property tax rates, inexpensive land, and the growth of competing local governments.

The authors couch their main findings within other significant influences in the decline of transit:

1) The magnitude and certainty of public funding has influenced modal investment choices. These choices, in turn, have affected regional travel.

2) Those cities whose citizens have shown a continuous commitment to, and investment in, high-quality transit service have strong urban centers and high transit use.

3) Strong, well-respected institutions build and operate transit systems in the regions where the impacts of highways on transit are low.

4) Active, well-organized citizen groups mitigated the impacts of highways by successfully opposing certain highway designs as well as highway construction itself.

5) The integration of transportation and land-use policies, plans, and projects has mitigated the impacts of automobile infrastructure.

6) In cities where highways' adverse impacts are fewest, public policies support the use of alternative modes of transportation.

7) In general, city centers with fewer freeways have experienced less adverse impacts from automobile travel.

SPATIAL SEGREGATION OF USES (LAND-USE MIX AND URBAN DESIGN)

Suburbs (Employment and Residential Areas)

1000 Friends of Oregon. 1996. *Making the Land Use, Transportation, Air Quality Connection (LUTRAQ): Analysis of Alternatives. Vol. 5.* Portland, OR. May.

This study compares auto-oriented versus transit-oriented alternatives of land use and transportation patterns in suburban Washington County, in the Portland, Oregon metropolitan area. Each alternative utilizes the same land area and has the same overall density.

In the auto-oriented alternatives, most new multifamily housing and jobs are at the urban fringe. The "no build" variation includes few transportation improvements, whereas the "highways" variation includes a bypass freeway and other highway improvements. With the transit-oriented alternatives, most new multifamily housing and jobs locate on vacant lands near transit routes. This alternative also takes into account transit investments, retrofitting of pedestrian improvements, selected highway improvements, and a demand management program that includes parking charges for work trips. The region's travel demand model, which was enhanced to increase its sensitivity to density and design, is used to simulate the transportation outcomes in 2010 of each of the alternatives.

The study finds that the package of transit-oriented development and transportation improvements that focus on non-automotive modes generates the following effects within the study area:

- Reduces auto ownership rates by 5 percent from auto-oriented levels
- Reduces single-occupant auto use for work trips to 58 percent compared to 76 percent in auto-oriented alternatives
- More than doubles the share of work trips made by transit over auto-oriented alternatives (18.2 percent versus 8.8 percent)
- Reduces daily vehicle trips per household from 7.5 to 7.2 trips
- Reduces the delay over "no build" levels by more vehicle hours than highway building alternative (53 percent reduction versus 43 percent reduction)
- Reduces peak period vehicle hours of travel at three times the rate that the "highway" building alternative does (15.7 percent reduction versus 5.6 percent)
- Reduces daily vehicle miles of travel by 6.4 percent, whereas the "highway" building alternative increases them by 1.6 percent.

One caveat, however, is important to note. The study area encompasses the fastest growing part of the Portland metropolitan area. The impacts would likely be less if transit-oriented land uses and transportation improvements were built throughout the metropolitan area, since the remainder of the region has less growth to focus toward transit-oriented developments.

Activity Centers

Cambridge Systematics. 1994. *The Effects of Land Use and Travel Demand Strategies on Commuting Behavior.* **Washington, DC: U.S. Department of Transportation, Federal Highway Administration.**

This study tests the influence of employment site design characteristics on commuting mode choice at suburban work sites in the Los Angeles area. The research involved on-site data collection of specific urban design and land-use attributes to ensure a careful calibration of the independent variables. The results indicate that the presence of land-use mix and certain urban design features, such as shade trees and sidewalks, in coordination with demand management programs, are responsible for increasing the percentage of work trips made by transit by three to four percentage points. An attractive urban environment proved to be the only factor that influenced mode choice in the absence of a travel demand program. In other words, mixed uses and access to services within the employment center were not strong enough incentives, by themselves, to generate more commuting by transit. This study did not control for factors such as the level of transit service to the site, however.

Cervero, Robert. 1989. *America's Suburban Activity Centers: The Land Use–Transportation Link.* **Boston: Unwin-Hyman.**

Cervero compares the commuting characteristics of workers in 57 suburban employment centers. These centers all have at least one million square feet of office space, 2,000 or more workers, and are at least five miles distant from the CBD. He uses cluster analysis to identify six types of centers—office park, office center, large mixed-use center, moderate mixed-use center, sub-city, and large corridor. Cervero then uses analysis of variance techniques to determine whether the center types differ in commuting characteristics. He concludes that locations of higher densities and greater land use mix do result in more commuting by transit, ridesharing, and walking. Ridesharing is greatest in the centers with higher densities, whereas walking is greatest in centers with significant retail activity and nearby multifamily housing. These denser, more mixed centers also have slower speeds of travel because of greater congestion within the centers. This study did not control for transit availability and the quality of the pedestrian environment, however.

Cervero, Robert. 1996. "Jobs-Housing Balance Revisited." *Journal of the American Planning Association* **62, 4: 492-511.**

Using data from the 1980 and 1990 Censuses, Cervero compares the jobs-housing balance of the 23 largest cities in the San Francisco Bay Area. His evidence shows that the jobs-housing balance generally improved during the decade, particularly as jobs increased in formerly housing-rich areas. However, housing did not grow significantly in job-rich areas, largely because zoning and growth controls prevented housing growth. Fifteen of the communities studied showed small increases in the ratio of internal commuting to external commuting. Nonetheless, about twice as many people commuted in and out of the average community as commuted within it. Thus, he concludes that despite less segregation of uses (measured at a gross city-wide scale), many people continue to commute considerable distances in part because of mismatches between the jobs

available in their community and the type of housing found there.

Among other things, this descriptive study demonstrates that the transportation consequences of spatial segregation of uses need more careful consideration than just a look at the numbers of residences and jobs. The mismatches between the incomes of employees and housing prices and between new jobs and housing availability also must be considered.

Neighborhoods

Cervero, Robert, and R. Gorham. 1995. "Commuting in Transit Versus Automobile Neighborhoods." *Journal of the American Planning Association* **61 2: 210-225.**

This study compares work trip mode shares and trip generation rates between matched pairs of transit-oriented and auto-oriented neighborhoods. Seven of the pairs are located in the San Francisco Bay Area, and six in the Los Angeles area. Transit-oriented neighborhoods are defined as those built around streetcars or rail stations prior to 1945, which have a grid street pattern. Auto-oriented neighborhoods are those built after 1945, with little orientation to transit, and with more curving streets and cul-de-sacs.

The neighborhood pairs in the study had similar incomes and, as far as possible, similar levels of transit service. Six of the seven San Francisco pairs showed the expected results of lower auto ownership and more use of transit and walking for work trips. (In one pair with a large university in the transit neighborhood, the transit neighborhood had less incidence of driving alone but walking often substituted for transit.) The difference in the share of drive-alone rates between neighborhood pairs ranged from 2.0 to

17.5 percent of trips. The results were more mixed in Los Angeles than in San Francisco, however.

The authors conclude that neighborhood design matters little in the Los Angeles area because of the overwhelming dominance of the automobile in this region. The results may also be muddled because transit service levels were less closely matched in the Los Angeles pairs than they were in the San Francisco pairs.

Ewing, Reid, P. Haliyur, and G. W. Page. 1994. "Getting Around a Traditional City, a Suburban PUD, and Everything In-Between." *Transportation Research Record* **1466: 53-62.**

In this study, the authors compare six communities in Palm Beach County, Florida, on the basis of work accessibility, neighborhood shopping opportunities, and pedestrian accessibility. They find little evidence that accessibility to retail affects mode choice or vehicle hours of travel per person. The shortest shopping and recreational trips occurred in a classic 1970s planned-unit development (i.e., a suburban auto-oriented community) because ample stores and recreational facilities could be found within the community. This result suggests that the mix of uses is as important as the layout of streets and other design features in determining travel behavior.

Handy, S. 1992. "Regional Versus Local Accessibility: Neo-Traditional Development and Its Implications for Non-Work Travel." *Built Environment* **18, 4: 253-267.**

Handy compares the shopping trip travel modes of residents of traditional and suburban neighborhoods in the San Francisco Bay Area. She finds that residents of traditional neighborhoods, where shopping opportunities are located nearby, make 2.75 to 5.5 times as many shopping trips by walking as residents of more auto-oriented neighborhoods. Residents of both types of neighborhoods make about the same number of auto trips to regional shopping malls, suggesting that neighborhood shopping trips may supplement rather than replace longer trips.

Handy, S. 1995. *Understanding the Link Between Urban Form and Travel Behavior.* **Paper presented at the 74th Annual Meeting of the Transportation Research Board, Washington, DC. January.**

In this study, Handy makes detailed comparisons of non-work trips in four suburban neighborhoods in the San Francisco Bay Area. A "traditional" and a "typical" suburban neighborhood are identified in Silicon Valley, where there are good transit connections to the rest of the region. Another pair is selected in Santa Rosa, on the fringe of the metropolitan area. The data used stem from original surveys. An analysis of variance shows that differences in travel behavior do occur because of urban form, controlling for household type (i.e., number of adults and number of workers). People make more shopping trips on foot in the "traditional" neighborhoods where the downtowns are connected to residential neighborhoods and offer services to those residents. It is not clear whether these trips replace auto trips, or merely supplement them, however. What is clear, is that people value choices and on average visit more than one grocery store and more than one regional mall in a month, if the choices are available. Having choice adds to travel since trips are made to places more distant from home.

Kitamura, R., P. L. Mokhtarian, and L. Laidet. 1994. *A Micro-Analysis of Land Use and Travel in Five Neighborhoods in the San Francisco Bay Area.* **Institute of Transportation Studies, University of California, Davis. November.**

The authors studied the travel behavior of several hundred families in five San Francisco Bay Area neighborhoods. The areas were selected because they had similar median incomes. But some had high density, some low, and they varied in mix of use and access to rail transit. Three-day travel diaries were collected, and site surveys were made to identify urban design characteristics. Models estimated individual travel behavior and, therefore, controlled for individual characteristics such as income, occupation, education, and vehicle ownership. Differences in travel were explained both by individual characteristics and by land-use measures, especially residential density, public transit accessibility, and the presence of sidewalks. Density was most important in explaining the share of non-motorized trips. Access to transit influenced the number of non-motorized trips and the share of transit trips. The mix of uses was not a very powerful indicator of travel behavior, but a dummy variable for place (combining all the land use attributes) was significant.

Overall, however, the models developed in this study had limited explanatory power; they were able to explain only about 15 percent of the variability in the number or share of trips by various modes.

Parsons Brinckerhoff Quade and Douglas. 1996c. "Influence of Land Use Mix and Neighborhood Design on Transit Demand." Unpublished report for TCRP H-1 Project. Washington, DC : Transit Cooperative Research Program, Transportation Research Board. March.

In this report, separate studies examine the effects of neighborhood land-use mix and urban design on the demand for transit and other alternatives to the automobile.

The first study uses *Annual Housing Survey* data for 1985 for 11 large metropolitan areas to compare mode choices for work trips of residents in areas with and without easy access to a "corner store" or other commercial activities. A second study of the greater Chicago area uses transit and land-use data to identify the factors that influence individual transit trips. The third study compares the mode choices for work and non-work trips in "traditional" and "suburban" neighborhoods in the San Francisco Bay Area, using original survey data. All of the studies use multi-linear regression techniques to control for income and other household characteristics.

Overall, the studies show that the types and mix of land uses do influence the demand for transit, as well as the use of non-motorized modes. People who live in mixed-used neighborhoods have a lower probability of commuting by car (3 to 4 percentage points), a slightly higher probability of using transit (1 to 2 percentage points), and a much higher probability of walking or bicycling (10 to 15 percentage points) for work trips. In the Chicago area, a 10 percent increase in residential density is associated with an 11 percent increase in the number of trips by transit. Residents of "traditional" neighborhoods in San Francisco are more likely to use non-automotive modes for non-work trips than residents of "suburban" neighborhoods. The neighborhood comparison study, however, did not find statistically significant differences in mode choice for work trips between the two types of neighborhoods.

Moreover, all these studies found it difficult to sort out the effects of land-use mix and urban design, because these characteristics are so strongly correlated with density. When density is included in an equation, mix and design variables generally explain little about mode choice. Each of the studies controlled for residential characteristics such as income and auto ownership. Because the studies are cross-sectional, however, they show only correlation between land-use characteristics and mode choice, not causality.

DISPERSED EMPLOYMENT

Cervero, Robert; Timothy Rood; and Bruce Appleyard. 1997. "Job Accessibility as a Performance Indicator: An Analysis of Trends and their Social Policy Implications in the San Francisco Bay Area." Institute for Urban Regional Development, University of California at Berkeley.

The authors claim that "accessibility," as an indicator of opportunities to reach destinations efficiently, has gained increasing attention as a complement to transportation planning's more traditional mobility-based measures of performance, like "average delays" and "levels of service." They maintain that evaluating transportation performance in terms of accessibility allows a more balanced approach to transportation analysis and problem-solving.

Increasing accessibility by bringing urban activities closer together through more compact development and the inter-mix of land uses, as well as by promoting tele-travel, can substitute for physical movements. Although not a replacement for mobility-based planning, accessibility measures help gauge progress toward meeting other regional objectives like sustainability and social equality.

The authors use census transportation planning data to study trends in job accessibility between 1980 and 1990, with the San Francisco Bay Area serving as a case context. The objectives of the analysis are multifold: 1) The work seeks to advance the use of accessibility indicators as inputs to long-range transportation planning and monitoring; 2) The work aims to enrich how job accessibility is measured by introducing an "occupational match" refinement; 3) The authors employ empirical measures of job accessibility to address the spatial mismatch question; and 4) The work calls for more formally institutionalizing and expanding the use of accessibility indicators for evaluating and monitoring long-term transportation system performance as well as progress toward achieving broader social welfare objectives.

The research showed that the Bay Area's largely market-driven patterns of regional employment growth failed to improve job accessibility among residents of the region's poorest inner-city neighborhoods. Minority neighborhoods in the inner East Bay and parts of downtown San Francisco averaged the worst occupational mismatches in terms of proximity to available jobs throughout the 1980s. Controlling for occupationally matched accessibility, educational levels, and vehicle availability, Bay Area neighborhoods with high shares of African Americans still had disproportionately high unemployment rates in 1990.

Cervero, Robert and Kang-Li Wu. 1996. "Subcentering and Commuting: Evidence from the San Francisco Bay Area, 1980-1990." Paper presented at the 1996 TRED Conference on Transportation and Land Use. Cambridge, MA: Lincoln Institute. October.

This paper examines the growth of dispersed subcenters in the San Francisco Bay Area and the effects of this growth on commuting. Cervero identifies 22 employment centers with 7 or more workers per gross acre and 9,500 or more employees in 1990. Downtown San Francisco is the largest and most densely populated subcenter. Other centers are in Silicon Valley and the East Bay core area (Oakland, Berkeley, and Emeryville); 16 more are located further out in suburbs. Two of the subcenters did not exist in 1980. Employment in these subcenters grew on average by 23.6 percent annually in the 1990s, increasing the regional share of employment in centers from 47.5 percent to 48.2 percent.

The growth of these subcenters has produced an increase in vehicle miles of travel (VMT) for commuting trips. On average, one-way VMT increased from 7.1 to 8.7 miles during the 1980s—a 23 percent increase, with the largest increases to be found in suburban centers. This increase in vehicle miles of travel is linked to both longer distances and to greater use of single-occupant vehicles. Of these, longer distances between home and work had more influence on VMT, since outside of downtown San Francisco and the eastern Bay Area, the vast majority of commuters used cars in both 1980 and 1990. Cervero estimates that more than four-fifths of the growth in VMT is due to

longer distances between home and work. Longer distances were especially important in increasing VMT in the more peripheral centers.

While at least one of their previous studies suggested that job decentralization shortened commutes, this result has been explained mainly in terms of recorded travel times, and typically measured at the aggregate, metropolitan-wide level. This study sought to refine the analysis of spatial implications on commuting by disaggregating data among employment centers, measuring highway and transit network distances, and examining commuting behavior during the 1980-1990 window of rapid suburban employment growth. When combining refined commute distance measures with data on shifts in modal distributions and occupancy levels, the finding is that employment decentralization is associated with substantial *increases* in commute VMT per employee. Cervero attributes these longer distances both to regional growth and to mismatches in the job and housing markets that necessitate long commutes.

THE COSTS OF TRAVEL

Apogee Research, Inc. 1994. *The Costs of Transportation: Final Report*. Conservation Law Foundation. March.

This report reviews the literature on the costs of transportation and estimates the per-mile costs of several modes for Boston, Massachusetts, and Portland, Maine. The study divides costs into three types: user costs, governmental costs, and societal costs. Extensive data were collected for the case study regions, in an effort to accurately reflect the cost of travel in these specific places. Some costs—land loss, water pollution, solid and hazardous waste pollution, and social isolation—could not be quantified and are not included in the analysis.

The report estimates costs for various modes, in different kinds of environments. For example, it estimates that a peak-period trip in a dense part of Boston using a single-occupant vehicle (SOV) on an expressway costs $1.05 per mile. Of the $1.05, $0.88 are user costs (including $0.24 for travel time), $0.05 are governmental costs not paid by the user, and $0.12 can be regarded as societal costs. In the off-peak period, the same trip costs $0.89 per mile, with $0.73 attributable to user costs ($0.10 for travel time), $0.05 to governmental costs, and $0.11 to societal costs. In a low-density setting the peak and off-peak SOV trips both cost $0.71. For the SOV mode, user costs, including travel time, vary the most among different settings.

By contrast, a high-occupancy vehicle (HOV) expressway trip in high-density Boston at peak hours costs $0.58 per mile, a commuter rail trip $0.58, a rail transit trip $1.04, a bus trip $1.09, a bicycle trip $0.73, and a walking trip $2.56. The relatively higher cost of rail transit, bus, and walking trips is primarily attributable to the added travel time. Costs in the smaller city of Portland are generally lower for all modes and densities.

The authors believe that transportation does influence sprawl, and this impact should be considered a societal cost of the transportation system. They do not, however, measure this cost, since studies have neither identified the full range of the costs of sprawl nor the proportion of these costs that are due to the transportation system.

This report documents the ways that travel costs differ with the physical environment and the modes available. As far as possible, costs are based on actual data for the locations studied, although measures of societal costs are generally taken from national studies.

DeCorla-Souza, Patrick; Rathi, Ajay K.; and Caldwell. 1992. "Nationwide Investment Requirements for New Urban Highway Capacity Under Alternative Scenarios," *Transportation Research Record 1359*: 57-67.

The paper provides cost estimates for maintaining the nation's urban highway capacity at 1985 levels of service through the year 2005. Besides providing the capital costs as a function of various levels of travel growth projections, the authors add a policy dimension to their estimates. Both land-use and transportation systems management policy constraints are included. While significant costs will be required despite policy levels, the paper demonstrates that appropriate policies could contain the capital investments required.

The cost models were run under the condition of no additional management imposed, then under moderate and high management conditions. The policy constraints incorporated were complex, containing several thrusts each in the land-use and traffic management areas.

Land use policies involved restricting development to where existing capacity was available, incentives for high density developments at commute trip terminus areas, mixed-use developments in the suburbs, and traditional neighborhood developments. On the transportation management side, policies included encouraging alternative commuting modes, work rescheduling programs, discouraging solo commuting, and increasing traffic control provisions.

The paper describes the process used in the analysis. There are two phases to the procedure: first to calculate the additional lane-miles required, then to calculate the equivalent dollars needed. The analysis yielded lane-mile increases ranging from 33 percent (low growth) to 49 percent (high growth) under baseline policy conditions. For the high management condition, the range was from 22 percent to 34 percent. At the low-growth condition which the authors thought was the more likely, policy management cut the required increase by a third. It should further be noted that with the elevated policy management, the high-growth condition almost equaled that of low growth and policy status quo condition. The capital investment needs varied from 1.2 trillion dollars under the high-growth, baseline management conditions down to 375 billion dollars under the low-growth, high management scenario.

The authors conclude that significant increases in highway funding (up to a possible 1.2 trillion dollars) will be required to maintain the 1985 levels of services. With the imposition of only a moderate increase in management policy and under the assumption of a low underlying travel growth rate, the required investment can be halved.

Delucchi, M. A. 1996. *The Annualized Social Cost of Motor-Vehicle Use in the U.S., 1990-1991: Summary of Theory, Data, Methods, and Results.* **Davis, CA: Institute of Transportation Studies. August.**

In this 20-volume study, Delucchi and his colleagues estimate the total social cost of automobile use in the United States for 1991. The study shows that many cost functions are non-linear and dependent upon location. Therefore, the study's estimates cannot be divided by total automobile mileage or some other measure of use to produce an accurate average price to use in other studies or analyses, although the methods may be applied in other studies.

Delucchi divides costs into six categories:

1) personal non-monetary costs, such as travel time;
2) motor vehicle goods and services priced in the private sector, such as vehicle ownership, maintenance, and use costs;
3) motor vehicle goods and services bundled with other goods and services in the private sector, such as employer- or business-provided parking;
4) publicly provided motor vehicle goods and services, such as roads;
5) monetary externalities of motor-vehicle use, such as accident costs not paid by the responsible party; and
6) nonmonetary externalities of motor vehicle use, such as air pollution and global warming.

This report estimates that the total social cost of motor vehicle use is between $1.88 trillion and $2.839 trillion per year. Of these costs, 38 to 50 percent of the costs are for private-sector goods and services; 21 to 22 percent of the costs are for personal non-monetary purposes; 13 to 21 percent are for non-monetary externalities; 4 to 5 percent are for monetary externalities; 4 to 8 percent are for bundled private-sector costs; and about 7 percent are for public infrastructure and services. Delucchi also estimates that payments by motor vehicle users total $109 billion to $173 billion dollars a year, which is less than the $125 to $207 billion estimate of the amount spent on public infrastructure and services. He argues, however, that it is not necessary for user payments to match government expenditures for efficient provision of resources. The difference between taxes paid by users and the provision of public goods and services related to motor-vehicle use must be judged on other grounds.

Delucchi does not include urban sprawl as a cost of automobile use. He argues that sprawl is a result of locational decisions, not motor vehicle use. Although transportation systems and costs may influence location decisions, he contends that the costs of different patterns of development are not directly a result of the use of motor vehicles. Furthermore, he claims the proper corrective action is to charge correctly for infrastructure provisions and other aspects of urban form, not to change automobile prices.

Ewing, Reid. 1997. "Is Los Angeles-Style Sprawl Desirable?" *and* **Gordon, Peter and Harry W. Richardson. 1997a. "Are Compact Cities a Desirable Planning Goal?"** *Journal of the American Planning Association* **63, 1 (winter): 107-126.**

These two articles published in the *American Planning Association Journal* debate the sprawl issue. The first article by Reid Ewing paints sprawl as undesirable. It defines sprawl not as suburbanization per se but rather as a wasteful form of outward development. Sprawl is characterized by: 1) leapfrog or scattered development; 2) commercial strip development; or 3) large expanses of low-density or single-use development. Ewing points out two indicators that typify sprawl—suburban environments that are *difficult to access* and those that *lack functional open space*. Locations that are difficult to access are those far from the core and from each other; locations that lack functional open space are defined as those where open space is

totally private and cannot be used to link neighborhoods, buffer incompatible uses, or provide space for social interaction, recreation or civic functions.

According to Ewing, sprawl is reinforced by consumer preference, technological innovation, public transportation subsidies, and the "more than shelter" concept of the housing market.

Costs of sprawl include increased: 1) vehicle miles traveled; 2) energy consumed; 3) public/private infrastructure; 4) depletion of developable and fragile lands; and 5) psychic and social stress. The cures for sprawl include more government oversight in the form of state and regional planning and more compact, mixed-use cluster development.

The second article by Peter Gordon and Harry W. Richardson attempts to attack "compact cities" as an alternative to spread-out metropolitan development—or sprawl. Gordon and Richardson define compact cities as those with 1) high densities at a macro or metropolitan level; 2) even higher densities at a micro or neighborhood/community level; or 3) even higher densities at a downtown or central city level. Gordon and Richardson reject compact cities because: 1) people like low, rather than high-density living; 2) there is no real chance that at either a national or global level there will be a shortage of land; 3) there is currently an energy glut, and therefore no need to alter residential preferences to conserve fuel; 4) the automobile is the most efficient and preferred way to access residential neighborhoods, and ideally suited to spread development; 5) suburbs are not congested and by their location have contributed to less inner-city and inner-suburb congestion; 6) inner city (compact) and suburban (spread) work and shopping trips are compatible; 7) agglomeration economies, once the province of cities, have now moved to suburbs; and 8) central locations have no market and continue to decline, and their rescue is a wasteful misallocation of public funds. Given these reasons, no case can be made for compactness as a description of desired urban form.

Which article is right? The answer is probably both. People appear to 1) prefer the accroutrements of suburban living but dislike strip commercial development; 2) want to distance themselves from urban problems, but worry about energy and land consumption; 3) like their automobiles but see merit in transit; 4) see a growing sophistication in suburbs but acknowledge a need for safe and functioning cities; and 5) travel and function in an environment that is less than efficient and less than beautiful, but very, very comfortable.

Hanson, M. E. 1992. "Automobile Subsidies and Land Use: Estimates and Policy Responses." *Journal of the American Planning Association* **58, 1: 60-71.**

This paper estimates the subsidies of automobile use in Madison, Wisconsin, a medium-sized city, in 1983. Hanson uses data on highway costs and taxes in the city and determines that direct subsidies for highway infrastructure, maintenance, and policing were equivalent to $0.024 per passenger-mile or $105 per person in 1983. Indirect subsidies for air and water pollution, petroleum prices, land-use opportunity costs, and personal injury were estimated from national data, and are, therefore, less precise than the highway data. Nonetheless, he calculates that indirect subsidies were equal to $0.034 per passenger-mile or $257 per person. In this estimation of costs, the largest subsidies were for personal injury

(36 percent), highways (23 percent), and air pollution (15 percent).

Hanson contends that subsidization of the automobile produces more dispersed patterns of development than would occur otherwise. Furthermore, he claims that sprawled development limits transportation options by making the automobile the only viable source of travel.

Litman, Todd. 1995. *Transportation Cost Analysis: Techniques, Estimates and Implications*. **Victoria, BC: Victoria Transport Policy Institute. February.**

Based on a review of existing studies, Litman estimates the cost per mile for a number of different modes of transportation: average car, fuel-efficient car, electric car, van, rideshare passenger, diesel bus, electric bus/trolley, motorcycle, bicycle, walking, and telecommuting. The report includes cost estimates for 20 different factors that affect travel choice, ranging from the costs of operating a vehicle to the cost of lack of transportation options.

Litman estimates that for urban travel during peak periods, a mile of travel by automobile costs $1.33. Of this amount, $0.16 is attributable to variable vehicle costs, $0.25 to fixed vehicle costs, $0.31 to user time and risk, and $0.61 to external or societal costs, such as pollution and land use impacts. The same mile of travel in an urban area during the off-peak hours costs $1.06, with $0.14 attributable to various vehicle costs, $0.25 to fixed vehicle costs, $0.33 to user time and risk, and $0.34 to external or social costs.

Litman does not separate out governmental costs of travel. Those costs paid by users, such as roads built with gasoline taxes, are considered user costs; those paid through general taxes, such as policing, are lumped in external costs. The largest external costs in Litman's scheme are for air pollution, accident costs not paid by the user, the opportunity costs of land currently used for roads, and external costs of energy consumption such as tax subsidies, energy security, and environmental damage.

Litman contends that land-use costs are a legitimate cost of automobile use because auto use encourages sprawl. It requires large amounts of land for transportation facilities and makes development of the urban fringe much easier. The effects include loss of prime farmland and wetlands, aesthetic degradation, loss of community, and higher transportation costs. Indeed, Litman estimates that land-use effects cost about 7 cents per mile, compared to 33 to 35 cents per mile for owning and operating the vehicle and 17 to 23 cents for travel time.

This study provides relative measures of the various costs of using the automobile versus other modes of travel; the calculations are based on estimates made by others. The data used rarely cover the full range of modes for which the author estimates costs. Thus, the figures in his tables are often simplified. The author attempts to monetize all costs despite the lack of hard data on many costs. The numbers are average estimates and do not consider location-specific factors such as differences in costs for urban and rural road building or congestion. The types of outcomes that the author counts as land-use impacts of transportation are generally counted elsewhere in an analysis of the costs of the sprawl and should not be counted again.

MacKenzie, J. J., R. C. Dower, and D. D. T. Chen. 1992. *The Going Rate: What It Really Costs to Drive*. Washington, DC: World Resources Institute.

This report estimates the amount spent on automobile subsidization in the United States; it defines subsidies as costs not paid directly by the user. According to the study, road users pay only about 60 percent of the $53.3 billion annual governmental costs of building and maintaining roads. They pay only 25 percent of the $91.0 billion police, fire, and other municipal costs associated with automobile use. Free employer-provided parking accounts for the largest portion of the subsidy. The authors estimate that 85 percent of the $100 billion cost of employee parking is not paid by the user. The report also estimates that users pay virtually none of the air pollution costs (estimated to be $37 billion), security costs for maintaining a reliable supply of oil ($25 billion), petroleum subsidy ($0.3 billion), or noise pollution costs ($9 billion). About 15 percent of accident costs, or $55 billion worth, are also estimated to be paid by someone other than the responsible party. The authors were unable to estimate some costs, however, such as the opportunity costs of land devoted to roads.

Estimates are based on data from previous studies. Estimates of externality costs are more speculative than other costs.

Parsons Brinckerhoff Quade and Douglas. 1996a. *Cost of Travel in Boulder*. City of Boulder, CO. July 15.

This study employs the methods of the Apogee study; local data for governmental costs; and national data for societal costs; and local and national data for user costs to estimate the total cost of typical trips by various modes within the built environment of Boulder. The study is based on actual travel times to and from specific locations.

The authors estimate that the cost of commuting to Denver (25.5 miles) is $24.61 by single-occupancy vehicle (SOV) and $15.79 by transit. The SOV trips breaks down as follow: $19.40 for user costs (mostly travel time); $1.16 for governmental costs; and $4.04 for societal costs. The transit trip includes $10.68 for user costs; $4.70 for governmental costs (mostly for transit provision), and $0.41 for societal costs. Although, in this case, transit is a cheaper trip, for a multi-purpose shopping trip of 9.75 miles within the city of Boulder, an SOV trip costs much less than a transit trip, $11.66 versus $29.17. Transit is more expensive because of the time involved and because of the relatively high governmental expenses for off-peak transit travel. For a short 2-mile trip to downtown Boulder, more options are considered. An SOV trip costs $4.02, a transit trip $3.43, a bike trip $1.74, and a pedestrian trip $5.59. The relatively high costs of pedestrian travel is due to the longer time needed to complete the trip.

This study shows that travel costs vary with the environment and by type of travel. Transit costs less for long commutes; walking and bicycling are viable alternatives for short trips in a compact city; the car is best for linked trips.

Voorhees, M. T. 1992. *The True Costs of the Automobile to Society*. City of Boulder, CO. January.

This study estimates the total annual cost of automobile use in the United States in 1990. The author divides costs into two main categories: 1) the direct expenses of automobile ownership and use, including the cost of highways; and 2) external costs, including direct monetary costs, for emergency medical care; lost economic gain due to air pollution and other externalities; and the opportunity costs of using land for roads and parking. Relying on data from other studies, he estimates that in 1990, the total cost of automobile use in the U.S. was $1.152 trillion. The largest costs were direct expenditures for automobile ownership and use ($440 billion, or 38 percent); land-use opportunity costs ($246 billion, or 21 percent); congestion costs ($146 billion, or 13 percent); air pollution costs ($100 billion, or 9 percent); and highway costs ($80 billion, or 7 percent). Voorhees also argues that the automobile has two major land-use impacts; it consumes large amounts of land for roads and parking and it encourages sprawl. He does not try to estimate the costs of sprawl, however, because he lacks data and because these costs are already calculated in the amount of fuel consumed and other costs of using the automobile that result from a more dispersed pattern of development.

His external cost estimates are quite subjective and would easily be changed by making different assumptions. The cost estimate for land opportunity costs is relatively large compared to estimates in other studies.

CHAPTER

Annotations of Studies

LAND/NATURAL HABITAT PRESERVATION

Land/natural habitat preservation seeks to protect unique lands and environments from development. Because it is assumed that this is the most logical and fertile area of potential improvement by anti-sprawl measures, this is often the component of the literature that receives the least empirical and analytical attention. The literature collected here for annotation contains discussions of the importance of natural environments to communities and the potential losses of natural environments to the development process. The annotated literature in this chapter is organized as follows:

Land Preservation and Community Cohesion

Land Preservation and Sprawl: Empirical Studies

The first category, *Land Preservation and Community Cohesion,* includes the works of Randall Arendt (1994b, 1996), Constance Beaumont (1994, 1996b, 1997), Reid Ewing (1995a), Moe and Wilkie (1997), and Arthur Nelson (1992b). The second category, *Land Preservation and Sprawl: Empirical Studies*, includes the works of Robert W.

Burchell (1995a) and John D. Landis (1995).

LAND PRESERVATION AND COMMUNITY COHESION

Arendt, Randall et al. 1994b. *Rural by Design*. Washington, DC: American Planning Association.

In this volume, Arendt and his fellow authors supply the reader with a great deal of material on a broad range of land design subjects, selected for their relevance to residents and local officials in rural and suburbanizing areas. The author's objective is to present pertinent information both to people working and living in small towns and to rural planners. The book's emphasis is on design issues, and it provides material that is not readily available outside of technical publications.

The authors work to provide answers to commonly asked questions, and supply readers with numerous examples of rural residential and commercial projects that have used creative design techniques.

Photographs and schematic site plans are used to show how these viable alternatives to conventional design approaches work.

One section of the book contains extensive information devoted to the "traditional town," in the belief that these rural communities will be able to conserve much of their remaining character and sense of place only if residents and local officials gain a fuller understanding of some of the basic principals underlying the form and the functioning of traditional towns. The authors see it as their role to encourage new development that complements, enhances, and builds upon historic town patterns.

Arendt, Randall. 1996. *Conservation Design for Subdivisions: A Practical Guide to Creating Open Space Networks.* **Washington, DC: Island Press.**

Arendt published this book in response to numerous inquiries concerning two earlier books on rural design principles. Readers wanted to know more about the techniques available to landowners, developers, local officials, and conservation organizations who were interested in conserving land in the development process. They were all looking for ways that land could be assembled and positioned so that communities could enjoy open space for years to come.

In this book, Arendt sets out principles that are far from novel, but presents them in a way that is easily understood by lay people. He addresses residential development around a central organizing principle—land conservation. He describes a way that open space can be arranged so that it will create an interconnected network of protected

lands. Arendt views the "conservation subdivision" as the key component of this community-wide system of open space.

Arendt's vision is for land-use planners to work much more closely with conservation professionals, and with developers and landscape architects, to help strengthen the "Greenspace Alliance." The author believes that this can be accomplished in a way that respects both the rights of landowners and the equity of developers. According to his view, developers can build at full density only when their design includes meadows, fields, and woodlands that would otherwise have been graded, and converted into house lots and overly wide streets.

Beaumont, Constance. 1996b. *Smart States, Better Communities: How State Governments Can Help Citizens Preserve Their Communities.* **Washington, DC: National Trust for Historic Preservation.**

In this book about restoring American communities, Beaumont examines the role of state governments in growth management, especially the way they deal with several primary aims of the historic preservation movement, such as protecting the economic viability of historic downtowns and neighborhoods; preserving the countryside and character of local communities; and maintaining a sense of community. These are often exactly the objectives that are thwarted by sprawl-type development, which results in older community disinvestment, a radical transformation of the countryside, and the creation of "centerless, featureless settlement patterns."

Beaumont begins her effort by first defining sprawl, and then she explains why sprawl creates problems for community livability and historic preservation. She also examines the economic assumptions underlying sprawl-type development, and looks at various state policies that aim to manage this type of growth.

Beaumont, Constance. 1994. *How Superstore Sprawl Can Harm Communities—And What Citizens Can Do About It.* **and 1997.** *Better Models for Superstores: Alternatives to Big-Box Sprawl.* **Washington, DC: National Trust for Historic Preservation.**

In *How Superstore Sprawl Can Harm Communities*, Constance Beaumont launches an attack on the increasing presence of big-box, generic superstore warehouses (such as those of Wal-Mart, Kmart, etc.), which locate at major interchanges at the outskirts of communities.

The author acknowledges that superstores have positive impacts. These include creating jobs, generating tax revenues, and providing affordable consumer goods. However, she believes that the hidden costs of these establishments are often overlooked. These hidden costs include:

- shifting retail activity out of downtowns and main streets to peripheral areas;
- taking retail spending money away from existing local businesses;
- increasing taxes by requiring infrastructure and services, such as new roads, water/sewer lines, and police protection, in formerly vacant areas;
- causing abandonment of previously developed areas;
- homogenizing America by building standardized structures that have no relation to their surroundings;

- increasing automobile dependence and its associated energy consumption and pollution effects.

In the second part of this work, Beaumont highlights several case studies in which local activists were successful in fending off superstore-type developments. From these experiences, Beaumont is able to provide a series of strategies and recommendations for other grassroots organizations. These include a review of relevant local, state, and federal laws that can be used against developers; tips for utilizing the media; a review of regulatory takings and property rights issues; and an action plan for concerned citizens.

In a companion piece, *Better Models for Superstores*, Beaumont reviews cases in which traditional big-box retailers chose nontraditional development in structures located in downtown.

According to Beaumont, retailers such as Target (Pasadena, CA), Toys R Us (Santa Monica, CA and Chicago, IL), Wal-Mart (Rutland, VT), Kmart (Manhattan, NY), and others are discovering that stores in downtowns can be profitable. Also, in some cases, the big-box stores are moving into historic structures that may have been abandoned for decades.

Beaumont concludes that to effectively prevent superstore sprawl, communities must have strong leadership, good design review mechanisms, defined land-use plans, and aggressive zoning policies. With these elements, communities can negotiate with retail chains and create alternative development patterns to revitalize the downtown, protect the environment, *and* generate profits for these national retailers.

Clearly, these writings advocate controlling the spread of these types of retail land uses. Notwithstanding the obvious point of view of the author, the two monographs present a significant amount of information on the land-use implications of superstore development.

Dahl, Thomas E. 1990. *Wetlands Losses in the United States: 1780s-1980s.* Washington, DC: U.S. Department of the Interior, Fish, and Wildlife Service.

Dahl points out that in colonial America, about 400 million acres of wetlands existed; by the 1980s, the wetlands inventory had dropped to 250 million acres.

Wetlands occur in every state in the nation in varying size, shape, and type. Variation occurs because of differences in climate, vegetation, soils, and hydrologic conditions.

Until recently, wetlands were generally considered a hindrance. Swamps, bogs, sloughs, and other wetland areas were regarded as wastelands, to be drained, filled, or manipulated to "produce" services and commodities. Recently, however, wetlands have come to be seen as vital areas that constitute a productive and invaluable public resource.

According to Dahl, in order to prevent continued wetlands losses, development must proceed in an environmentally responsible way. Development must respect the natural habitats of wetlands and other sensitive lands or these lands will be lost for all generations.

Ewing, Reid. 1995a. *Best Development Practices: Doing the Right Thing and Making Money at The Same Time.* Chicago: American Planning Association.

Ewing addresses the need for change in development policy and practice given Florida's expected rapid growth rates (approximately 5 million people during the next 20 years) and given Florida's dominant development pattern of urban sprawl. Ewing argues that increasing social and economic costs will occur due to the continuation of sprawl. In an attempt to minimize sprawl's costs, the author advocates a community development process in which public purposes are weighed against market considerations. He lists such public purposes as affordable housing, energy efficiency, and the preservation of natural land masses and resources.

Discouraging urban sprawl by creating vibrant more compact communities means placing an emphasis on population diversity (age and class), establishing street life, creating a sense of place, and establishing other features that contribute to "livability." Recommendations to realize these goals are presented in the form of "best development" practices, which are meant to be used as a basis for developing comprehensive plans for new communities and redevelopment projects, for structuring land development regulations, or for evaluating specific development proposals. Seven new communities (planned communities within the 300-500 acre range) are discussed in reference to his best development practices.

Lewis, Peirce F. 1995. "The Galactic Metropolis." In *The Changing American Countryside: Rural People and Places*, Emory N. Castle, ed. Lawrence, KS: University of Kansas Press.

The author believes the term "suburban sprawl" is a misnomer. Instead, he endorses a concept he terms "metropolitan dispersion." He utilizes this term to describe the disappearance of the boundary between the city and the country. Lewis provides two meanings for his use of "metropolitan." The first refers to the buildings, skyscrapers, parks, and other tangible aspects of the city. The second refers to intangible aspects, such as the people, institutions, ideas, and their interactions within the city's culture.

In the past, according to Lewis, the tangible and intangible aspects of a metropolitan city were intertwined. Lewis points to major old-world European cities which were centers of civil authority, military might, and religious focus. The architecture of these institutions was dominant and imposing on the city's landscape, including high defense walls, large palaces, and grandiose cathedrals. While these cities were also centers of commerce, this function played a secondary role to the others. Thus, markets flourished inside city walls for safety and security and in cathedral squares to attract customers.

In contrast, major American cities were exclusively centers of commerce. The central square was a market square, and the largest buildings were office buildings. Also in contrast to European cities, military, educational, and political institutions were dispersed into smaller communities outside the urban area instead of concentrated in the central city.

As a result, Lewis believes, major American cities were deprived of traditional metropolitan functions. Their single-minded economic focus alienated much of the regional population and generated anti-urban prejudices. Conversely, however, this dispersion of central metropolitan functions enriched non-urban and rural areas of America.

Over time, through the process of metropolitan dispersion, these urban and rural areas of America have begun to meld. The physical metropolis has followed the cultural metropolis into the countryside. Lewis names this new urban form the *galactic metropolis.*

How did this galactic metropolis arise? The primary factor, according to Lewis, was the widespread use of the automobile. The automobile allowed people to live outside the crowded cities. And although suburbs had previously existed, these new suburbanites discovered that they could also work and shop outside the city center. The interstate highway program further sealed the fate of central cities. High-speed highways made interchanges more accessible, more attractive, and less expensive than the downtown. In addition, the urban renewal programs of the 1950s and 1960s destroyed the infrastructure and architecture of many central cities. This combination of flexible transportation, rapid accessibility, and cheap land lured commercial and industrial enterprises out of the central city.

In conclusion, Lewis does not devise a plan to reform the new urban structure, realizing that it is not going away. Rather, he counsels that "we must *learn* to live with it." In particular, we must learn three things about the new metropolis: how it is arranged, why it is arranged that way, and how it works.

Michigan Society of Planning Officials (MSPO). 1995. *Patterns on the Land: Our Choices, Our Future.* **Rochester, MI: Michigan Society of Planning Officials.**

This report by the Michigan Society of Planning Officials (MSPO) reveals that, over the past three decades, Michigan has experienced a major population shift to suburban and rural areas. Sprawl is most apparent in Southeast Michigan, the Grand Rapids area, and Traverse City, but is also occurring in most of the lower half of the lower peninsula, and in a number of northern counties.

The study's authors claim that there is a growing sense of community degeneration, manifested by citizens at public hearings on land use. The authors warn that if this pattern of development continues, certain costs and problems will be created, including significant public capital and maintenance expenditures channeled to water, sewer, roads, and other infrastructure; the continued decline of urban areas; the loss of jobs in key resource-based industries such as agriculture, timber harvesting, and mining once open land is converted to residential and commercial uses; the loss of the aesthetic appeal of natural open spaces; and the loss of a distinct edge between city and country in the developing landscape.

The authors warn that, although the current pattern can be sustained for several decades, the impact on renewable resources and mineral deposits will be irreversible. On a more positive note, the study concludes that an informed public can achieve a different future through coordinated and integrated land use planning, creative use of new technology, and better information.

Moe, Richard, and Carter Wilkie. 1997. *Changing Places: Rebuilding Community in the Age of Sprawl.* **New York: Henry Holt.**

The authors begin with the premise that most of America's communities (new as well as old; suburban and rural as well as inner city) are not functioning as they should. There are a number of reasons for this, but Moe and Wilkie stress the fact that the leaders and residents of these communities have either made bad choices, allowed bad choices to be made for them, or made no choices at all. They claim that communities can be "shaped by choice" or they can be "shaped by chance." In other words, we can continue to accept the communities we get, or we can insist on getting the kind of communities we want.

Moe and Wilkie assert that the design of most contemporary American communities is largely determined by highway engineers and superstore developers. They have stepped into the void left by public officials (who are either resigned to, or eager for, this kind of development) and by citizens—who are either complacent or feel powerless. Communities are built in a series of steps, each one so apparently logical or innocuous that it goes unchallenged. The result, as the authors point out, is rampant sprawl, a phenomenon that has reduced the social and economic vitality of traditional communities and filled millions of acres of farmland and open space with "formless, soulless, structures unconnected to one another except by their inevitable dependence on the automobile."

Moe and Wilkie put forth two alternatives to sprawl: (1) better planning of how we use our land; and (2) the use (or reuse) of the capacity of older neighborhoods, towns, and downtowns to a greater extent than they are used currently. Both alternatives, claim the authors, are essential if we are to successfully manage growth and contain sprawl before it bankrupts society and local economies.

Nelson, Arthur C. 1992b. "Preserving Prime Farmland in the Face of Urbanization: Lessons from Oregon" *Journal of the American Planning Association* **58: 471-488.**

This article first reviews Oregon's effective combination of policies to preserve prime farmland despite intense urbanization pressures. It then proceeds to propose a scheme for comprehensive farmland preservation, building on Oregon's successes and mistakes.

Prime farmland near urban areas is required for three important reasons: the production of truck and specialty crops; the provision of key environmental functions such as flood water absorption, air cleansing, and water filtration; and for open space protection and the provision of spatial definition to urban areas.

Communities in every state have implemented farmland preservation techniques, with varying degrees of success. According to the author, for a policy to be successful, it must influence the land market in the several different ways. It must increase the productive value of farmland; it must stabilize, reduce, or eliminate the value of the farmland tract as a single-family homesite (the consumptive value); it must remove the speculative value of farmland; and it must eliminate the impermanence syndrome.

According to Nelson, *property tax relief* programs reduce the property tax farmers pay for urban and educational services which mostly benefit urban residents. As

a result, this policy subsidizes housing costs and turns farmers into speculators. *Right-to-farm laws* protect farmers from nuisance complaints from urban residents. However, although farmers usually win their legal battles, they often lose because of the heavy financial expense of the process. *Transfer of development rights (TDR)* and *purchase of development rights (PDR)* programs preserve farmland by compensating farm owners for maintaining their farmland. However, these programs often fail because the programs are randomly applied and usually result in isolated farmland tracts being surrounded by urban development. A final common strategy, *agricultural zoning*, restricts land uses to farming and other open space activities. *Non-exclusionary agricultural zoning* also restricts lot sizes to certain minimums. Smaller minimum lot sizes (higher densities) usually result in a form of development called rural sprawl. As a result, nonexclusive agricultural zoning is generally effective only when large lot size requirements (160-acre-minimum) are coupled with strict development review.

Exclusive agricultural zones, on the other hand, restrict all non-farm activities and require that farmland be used for commercial activities. This strategy can be effective only when all prime farmland is zoned for exclusive agricultural use and urban development pressures are diverted to other areas.

Oregon has implemented a statewide program to preserve farmland in the Willamette Valley. This 4,000-square-mile valley contains one-third of the state's prime farmland; produces 40 percent of the state's agricultural products; and houses more than two-thirds of the state's population.

Oregon's farmland preservation plan does not rely on a single strategy. Rather, it employs a multifaceted approach consisting of exclusive agricultural districts, urban growth boundaries, development restrictions in exurban areas, farm use tax deferrals, and right-to-farm provisions. Data from the 1987 Census of Agriculture suggest that Oregon's policies are working. They are preserving a viable agricultural economy while accommodating a craze for hobby farms.

The effectiveness of Oregon's efforts can be further analyzed by comparing developments in Oregon with those in nearby Washington, a state without a statewide farmland preservation plan. Oregon has lost more small farms than Washington, but it has gained more larger farms (over 500 acres), more commercial farms (over $10,000 in earnings), and more total farm acreage.

According to the author, a successful farmland preservation plan relies on multiple techniques and strategies that work together and reinforce each other.

LAND PRESERVATION AND SPRAWL: EMPIRICAL STUDIES

Burchell, Robert W., and David Listokin. 1995a. *Land, Infrastructure, Housing Costs, and Fiscal Impacts Associated with Growth: The Literature on the Impacts of Sprawl versus Managed Growth.* **Paper prepared for "Alternatives to Sprawl" Conference, Brookings Institution, Washington, DC. March.**

This short summary paper reviews the major studies on sprawl through 1995. It draws heavily upon the research done by the same authors for the State of New Jersey, as well as the work of James Duncan and James Frank in Florida. This paper, however, was prepared before Burchell's studies of Lexington

(Kentucky), the Delaware Estuary, Michigan, and South Carolina were released. The paper examines the implications of planned development versus more traditional decentralized development in the areas of land consumption, infrastructure costs, housing costs, and fiscal impacts.

Most of the studies reviewed in the paper contrast sprawl with at least one other development pattern. Sprawl is described as development that typically includes subdivision-style residential development and strip nonresidential development consisting of skipped-over, noncontiguous land development, including low-density residential and low floor-area ratio nonresidential developments. In contrast, planned development is described as seeking to contain new growth around existing centers and limiting development in rural and sensitive environmental areas, usually accomplished by increasing the share and density of development close in to existing development.

The growth analyzed in this paper is assumed to consist of household growth that in turn leads to job growth, which requires additional land. Ideally, this growth and the provision of facilities to accommodate it are handled in a timely, harmonious manner.

Traditional growth is shown to depart from the most harmonious possible path by locating residential and other development in "a new outer ring of the metropolitan area with access from this new outer ring oriented increasingly to a beltway or interstate [highway] rather than central core job locations." Increasing under-utilization of core land and infrastructures result. This process is associated with the development of "edge cities," which, in turn, generate a new farther-out ring of bedroom residential subdivisions. "The core of the metro-politan area, absent redevelopment, be-comes relatively abandoned by a variety of necessary and blue-chip economic activities and a home by default for poor residents who cannot follow . . . or are not allowed to follow upper-income residents to the suburbs (because of zoning). Even with redevelopment, the central core is a struggling entity with no soft-goods retail anchors, no quality supermarkets or movie theaters, a declining upwardly mobile population, public school systems being replaced by private, and increasingly higher property taxes to pay for rising public service costs" (3).

Traditional growth is costly because new infrastructure must be provided for those households and businesses located far out, and the old infrastructure must be maintained for those left behind. Yet in the short run, traditional growth is not bad for a region. It distributes firms and households to localities that minimize individual out-of-pocket costs. No consideration is given to the larger societal costs or impacts of these individual choices.

The alternative development pattern of planned growth channels the growth to more efficient locations over the long run. Most of the far-out growth which arises in traditional development is contained closer to existing infrastructure and built-up areas. Thus, "in the final equation . . . there is a more orderly and less wasteful relationship between old and new development" (5).

Another goal of planned development is the conservation of open space (i.e., agricultural land, forests, and environ-mentally sensitive areas). The New Jersey analysis compares the impacts of development in New Jersey for the period 1990 to 2010 under two development scenarios—TREND versus PLAN. The authors developed a series of models to examine the relative effects of each scenario.

They found that more than enough land existed statewide to accommodate the projected twenty-year development (1990-2010) of persons, households, and employees under both traditional (TREND) and managed (PLAN) growth. The authors estimated that development under TREND would consume 292,100 acres, whereas PLAN could accommodate the same level of growth but would consume only 117,600 acres—175,000 fewer acres than the alternative (Burchell et al. 1992b). PLAN's overall land drawdown was 60 percent less than TREND.

Managed growth would also offer the environmental advantage of preserving greater levels of frail and agricultural lands. If historical rates of loss are projected into the future, under TREND 36,500 acres of frail lands would be consumed for development during the 20-year period. By contrast, under PLAN, frail and agricultural consumption drops to 7,150 acres, only 20 percent of the TREND scenario. In other words, managed growth in New Jersey could accommodate future development and at the same time, save more than 30,000 acres of frail environmental lands. In a similar vein, although development under TREND would consume 108,000 agricultural acres between 1990 and 2010, under PLAN, only 66,000 agricultural acres would be drawn down, representing a savings of 42,000 acres, or 40 percent of prime agricultural land.

Diamond, Henry L., and Noonan, Patrick F. 1996. *Land Use in America.* **Washington, DC: Island Press.**

In this compilation of papers, essays, and vignettes, the authors and a dozen contributors argue that better land use is essential to the health and well-being of Americans and their communities. Using the nation's land well yields many benefits including cleaner air and water, and better towns and neighborhoods in which to live. The management of land, however, has been largely neglected in this country due to its highly politicized character and the confused nature of its regulatory structure. In an effort to rectify this wanting situation, the authors advocate a new political agenda:

1. Local communities must define a vision for the future by enlisting all sectors in devising land-use plans, and then executing those plans with greater efficiency and flexibility.
2. States must establish greater rules for land-use planning and provide leadership to encourage communities to deal with complex regional problems.
3. Rules governing the use of land must become more adaptable while ensuring predictability to developers.
4. The rights of landowners must be taken seriously.
5. Cooperation among agencies and coordination among policies are essential to achieving better land-use practices.
6. A federal trust fund for assisting acquisition is needed to provide states and local jurisdictions with funds and predictability so they can plan ahead.
7. To redevelop vacant and deteriorating areas, a clearing of the regulatory thicket is needed, especially those rules that unnecessarily encumber the reuse of land with a history of hazardous wastes.

8. Private initiatives for conservation and quality development require incentives; relief from regulations should be exchanged for efforts to enhance natural habitats.
9. Land trusts are an effective means of focusing upon geographic features of a landscape and must be encouraged as a means for citizen collaboration in the next century.
10. Land disputes should be resolved through negotiation or mediation, perhaps in conjunction with geographic information system tools.

This book is a self-described call for action. The authors intend it to be a rallying cry for land stewardship, quality development, and environmental progress. They call for the American public and its leaders to make a commitment to good land-use practices and to pursue an agenda for the next century that would improve land use, much as the environmental agenda of the past quarter century has largely accomplished its goals.

Landis, John D. 1995. "Imagining Land Use Futures: Applying the California Urban Futures Model." *Journal of the American Planning Association* **61, 4 (Autumn): 438-457.**

This article explains how the California Urban Futures (CUF) Model, a second generation metropolitan planning model, works to help planners and other individuals create and compare alternative land use policies. Landis demonstrates how the model simulates the impacts of regional and subregional growth policy and planning alternatives.

He expends much effort explaining the design principles and logic of the CUF model, and in presenting CUF model simulation results of three alternatives for growth policy and land-use planning for the San Francisco Bay and Sacramento areas. The three alternatives offered are a) "business-as-usual"; b) "maximum environmental protection"; and c) a "compact cities" scenario. Each alternative is evaluated for its impact on overall land consumption and the consumption of environmentally sensitive lands in particular, at the county level.

Alternatives (b) and (c) show considerable overall land savings and considerable savings in environmentally sensitive lands relative to the business-as-usual scenario. Total land saved in scenarios (b) and (c) were 15,000 and 46,000 acres, respectively. Redirected growth in scenario (b) saved nearly 60,000 acres of prime agricultural land, 10,500 acres of wetlands, and 3,000 acres of steep sloped land; scenario (c) saved 29,000 acres of prime agricultural

land, 10,500 acres of wetlands, and 8,000 acres of steep sloped lands.

Landis believes that the CUF model breaks new ground in that it incorporates GIS software to assemble, manage, display, and make available millions of pieces of information about land development potential. The CUF model also recognizes the role of land developers and home builders in determining the pattern, location, and density of new development. Finally, the CUF model is adept at incorporating realistic local development policies and options into the growth forecasting process. It serves a similar purpose as the Rutgers Land Consumption Model in that it specifies growth alternatives as a beginning point for all subsequent infrastructure analyses.

CHAPTER

12

Annotations of Studies

QUALITY OF LIFE

Quality of life reflects how we feel about our environments. Those who are concerned about living environments object to sprawl's loss of a sense of place and mourn the loss of unique environments. In this atmosphere, cities of scale are no longer viable, and replacement suburbs have no sense of identity. As "place" has become increasingly important to businesses and individuals, ratings of places have grown in the literature. Some of these are empirically based, whereas others merely reflect the opinions of raters. Place ratings and their limitations are a focus of this chapter.

Quality of life as a subject also has significant contributions from the fields of economics, sociology, and psychology. Attempting to catalog these contributions would dominate any compilation of annotations. These contributions are just briefly touched upon here.

The presentation of information in this chapter is as follows:

Popular Literature
Indicators, Reports Cards, and
  Benchmarks
Economics Literature

Sociology Literature
Psychology Literature

In the *Popular Literature* section, *Money Magazine's* "Best Places to Live in America," *Fortune Magazine's* "Best Cities: Where the Living is Easy," and the *Places Rated Almanac* are commented upon.

In the *Indicators, Report Cards, and Benchmarks* section, works by Dowell Myers (1987) and the Oregon Progress Board (1994) are included. In the *Economics Literature* section, works by N. E. Duffy (1994), Stuart Gabriel (1996), and Priscilla Salant et al. (1996) are included. In the *Sociology* and *Psychology* sections, works by David Popenoe (1979) and Oleg Zinam (1989) are found.

POPULAR LITERATURE

Fried, Carla, Leslie M. Marable, and Sheryl Nance-Nash. 1996. "Best Places to Live In America." *Money* (July): 66-95.

Money magazine publishes an annual ranking of "the Best Places to Live in America" that includes the country's 300 largest metropolitan areas. To determine the rankings, *Money* first surveys its subscribers and asks them to rate 41 quality-of-life factors. The magazine then collects data on specific measures for the 300 cities and assigns the data to nine broad categories: crime, economy, health, housing, education, weather, leisure, arts and culture, and transportation. The data are then weighted according to readers' preferences to produce the final ranking.

The top 10 quality-of-life characteristics, as rated by *Money* subscribers, are low crime rate, clean water, clear air, plentiful doctors, many hospitals, housing appreciation, good schools, low property taxes, low income taxes, and strong state government. *Money* points out, however, that the rating of quality-of-life characteristics differs by gender and by type of household.

Although informative, the *Money* ranking does have some drawbacks. Since the survey results are based on a poll of readers, the results are probably not representative of the U.S. population in general. Furthermore, *Money* does not reveal enough about its specific measures or scoring method to assess whether its rankings accurately reflect the survey results. In addition, because the survey asks *Money* subscribers to rate only 41 quality-of-life characteristics, it may not include every characteristic that readers think are important. Overall, however, this article provides insight into how the topic of quality of life is typically treated in the popular literature.

Hall, Bob, and Mary Lee Kerr. 1991. *1991-1992 Green Index: A State-By-State Guide to the Nation's Environmental Health.* **Washington, DC: Island Press.**

Drawing from a variety of private and public data sources, the *Green Index* uses 256 indicators to measure and rank each

state's environmental health. The indicators encompass a broad range of environmental conditions and are grouped into eight major categories: air sickness; water pollution; energy use and auto abuse; toxic, hazardous, and solid waste; community and workplace health; farms, forests, fish and fun; congressional leadership; and state policy initiatives. Based on these indicators, the authors identify the best and worst states overall.

Landis, John D. and David S. Sawicki. 1988. "A Planner's Guide to the *Places Rated Almanac." Journal of the American Planning Association* (Summer): 336-346.

In this 1988 critique of the *Places Rated Almanac* (1985 edition), the authors point out that the essential problem with the component measures used to rank places is that they have not been tested against the stated opinions of migrants or against observed migration behavior. The authors also cite an article that compared overall metropolitan scores (not rankings) in the *Places Rated Almanac* with a nonrandom sample of households and finds that only four of the nine categories included in the *Almanac* are actually statistically significant to migration decisions. These four categories are: housing costs, crime, education, and recreation. The authors also compare category rankings for 51 metropolitan areas in *Places Rated Almanac* with migration patterns between 1975 and 1980. This comparison finds that the rankings of housing cost and economic opportunity are significantly correlated with rates of in-migration.

Landis and Sawicki point out, however, that the *Places Rated Almanac* assumes that a person's quality of life is critically related to the qualities of the place where he or she lives or works. Research, however, indicates that most individuals rank personal causes of satisfaction and dissatisfaction as much more important determinants of their quality of life than geographical factors.

Precourt, Geoffrey and Anne Faircloth. 1996. "Best Cities: Where the Living is Easy." *Fortune* **(November 11): 126-136.**

This article identifies the 15 best U.S. cities and the five best international cities for work and family. Much of the article is devoted to qualitative descriptions of the best cities, with little explanation of the methods used for the rankings. Among the variables considered are the crime rate, quality of schools, availability of culture, traffic congestion, number of doctors, tax rates, price of real estate, and costs of a martini and a first-run movie. The article contains a table showing the attributes of the cities in the following six categories:

Demographics: Measured by 1996 population, projected percentage change in population 1996-2001, median household income, and percentage of population with bachelor's degree

Cost of living: Measured by the cost of living index, high-end housing price, low-end housing rent, and the cost of a loaf of French bread and a martini

Business: Measured by percentage employed in managerial positions, Class A office rental rate, best business hotel, recommended restaurant, and average commute time

Leisure: Measured by the number of art museums, public libraries, and 18-hole golf courses, as well as the most-visited attraction

Climate: Measured by the number of days below 32 degrees, above 90 degrees, and incidence of poor air quality

Quality of Life: Measured by violent crime rate and doctors per capita

Savageau, David, and Richard Boyer. 1993. *Places Rated Almanac.* **New York: Macmillan Travel.**

The authors use an extensive set of criteria to rank 343 U.S. and Canadian metropolitan areas by ten categories. These categories, with their specific component measures are:

Costs of Living: average house price, the cost of utilities, property taxes, college tuition, the cost of food at home, the cost of health care, and the cost of transportation, all indexed relative to the U.S. average

Jobs: the number and percent increase in new jobs

Housing: annual payment for average-priced home

Transportation: commute time, and the cost of mass transit, national highways, airline service, and passenger rail service

Education: number of students enrolled in community or two-year colleges and private and public four-year or graduate-level institutions

Health Care: number of general/family practitioners, specialists, short-term hospital beds, and hospitals

Crime: violent crime and property crime rates

The Arts: number of concert or classical-format radio stations, touring artists bookings (classical music, dance, professional theatre), resident arts companies (classical music, ballet, professional theatre), nonprofit art museums/galleries, and public library collections

Recreation: number of public golf courses, good restaurants, movie theatre screens, zoos, aquariums, and family theme parks; incidence of pari-mutual betting, professional and college sporting events, ocean or Great

Lakes coastlines, national forests, national parks, national wildlife refuges, and state parks

Climate: number of very hot and cold months, seasonal temperature variation, heating- and cooling-degree days, freezing days, zero-degree days, 90-degree days

Each of the measures is converted into a score. The scores are then summed to rank metropolitan areas in each category. The scoring method implicitly weighs the specific measures and describes the relationship between the measure and quality of life.

The ranks in each category are then summed for an overall score that is used to rank the metropolitan areas. Each category has equal weight in the overall ranking, however, the authors discuss how the reader can use his or her personal preferences to weight the categories to get a personalized overall ranking of metropolitan areas.

Although this book puts forth a common sense and anecdotal notion of quality of life, it provides no theoretical underpinning or review of relevant literature. The authors' scoring system implicitly weights the various measures with no apparent basis other than their own opinion. The book clearly acknowledges that individuals will have different preferences and unsuccessfully attempts to provide a method of weighting categories to reflect individual preferences.

INDICATORS, REPORT CARDS, AND BENCHMARKS

Andrews, James H. 1996. "Going by the Numbers." *Planning* **(September) 14-18.**

Many states, cities, and hamlets use indicators to measure their own economic and social health, and to set future goals. This article takes a look at these indicators which are often referred to as "benchmarks" or "vital signs." Local governments often create these measures, but they are sometimes developed by community groups. All indicator projects discussed in this article used some public process to identify specific measures. Certain indicator projects have a specific focus, such as government performance or the environment; others are more comprehensive. Three examples are listed below.

Jacksonville, Florida developed a Quality of Life index in 1985 and updates the index annually. A 1991 community review of the index revealed education as the community's top priority. The other categories in the index include the economy, public safety, natural environment, health, social environment, government and politics, culture and recreation, and mobility. Specific measures used in the index include the number of outdoor sign permits issued, the cost of 1,000 kwh of electricity, student fitness test scores in 50th percentile or better, and reports of commute times of less than 25 minutes. Jacksonville has recently developed an equity index that provides a neighborhood-level looks at measures from the Quality of Life index related to delivery of public services, such as police response times.

- "Sustainable Seattle" is an indicator project focused on the region's long-term cultural, economic, environmental, and social health and vitality. The project has developed a set of indicators with the headings "environment," "population and resources," "economy," "youth and education," and "health and community." Specific measures used to determine quality of life include the incidence of wild salmon, VMT and fuel consumption, amount of work required to pay for basic needs, ethnic diversity of teachers, and asthma hospitalization rate for children.

- The Upper Valley 2001 project in the upper Connecticut River valley has developed a list of indicators with 15 categories, including citizenship, community, communications, education, recreation, health care, personal and public safety, human services, the arts, transportation, businesses, farms and forests, resource use, and the natural environment.

The goal of all these indicators is to change policy and to move the measures in positive directions. Change, the author points out, does happen, but often on an ad hoc basis.

Myers, Dowell. 1987. "Internal Monitoring of Quality of Life for Economic Development." *Economic Development Quarterly* **1: 238-278.**

Quality of life is recognized as an important factor in economic development, but its exact role and the methods for measuring it are poorly understood. The author identifies four major limitations to developing quality of life measures to compare cities or regions: poor availability of comparable objective data; lack of subjective data necessary for addressing this inherently subjective topic; inability to address unique local

features; and the difficulties in choosing commonly valued weights for combining different components in overall indexes. This article argues for the monitoring of quality of life within a city or region as an important complement to external comparisons. Internal monitoring can measure changes in local quality of life over time to guard against deterioration of competitive advantages in the future.

Myers cites Austin, Texas as an example of a place where quality of life characteristics have played an important role in the city's development. Austin has relied on its quality of life to attract high-technology firms. Locals are now concerned that rapid development, particularly suburban "silicon strips," will cause the city's quality of life to decline, and with it, the city's attractiveness to those high-tech firms.

Austin's quality of life was a major factor in the location decision of one high-tech firm and an explicit element in the formal offer to the firm to locate in the city. Ten quality-of-life advantages were itemized: excellent schools, parks and playgrounds; ease of mobility around the city; close-by lakes for water recreation; other opportunities for hunting, fishing, and camping; access within two-hours flying to Colorado skiing and Mexican vacations; abundant cultural and entertainment possibilities; general cleanliness of the city; attractive topography and mild year-round climate; and an "open, receptive social structure, a population long noted for friendliness, and a reputation as a desirable place to live and raise children."

Accelerated growth triggered by the high-tech firm's move to Austin produced negative consequences for quality of life, including decreased housing affordability, traffic congestion, threats to the area's water quality and natural environment, and the perception that downtown office development threatened the city's music scene. These consequences were perceived locally to be caused by unmanaged development.

In reaction, the Austin Chamber of Commerce began a research program to measure trends in the area's quality of life. Leaders of interest groups were interviewed to identify significant aspects of Austin's quality of life; measures for these aspects were developed, and residents surveyed about the importance of these measures in their perceived quality of life. It was determined that residents placed more importance on concerns such as crime, cost of living, schools, traffic, and jobs, than they did on amenities such as shopping, restaurants, and entertainment. Sixty-two percent of recent migrants identified quality of life as an important factor in attracting them to Austin.

Oregon Progress Board. 1994. *Oregon Benchmarks: Standards for Measuring Statewide Progress and Institutional Performance.* **Report to the 1995 Legislature. Salem, OR: Oregon Progress Board. December.**

The Oregon Progress Board is a part of the State of Oregon's Economic Development Department. Oregon "Benchmarks for Quality of Life" are measurable indicators used at the statewide level to assess the state's progress toward broad strategic goals. The categories and subcategories of measures used for the benchmarks include:

Unspoiled Natural Environment: air, water, land, plants/fish/wildlife, and outdoor recreation

Developed Communities that are Convenient, Affordable, Accessible, and

Environmentally Sensitive: community design, transportation, housing, access for persons with disabilities, access between communities, and emergency preparedness

Communities that are Safe, Enriching, and Civic Minded, with Access to Essential Services: public safety, justice, access to cultural enrichment, sense of community, access to health care, and access to child care.

Other measure have been devised as "Benchmarks for People" and "Benchmarks for the Economy."

ECONOMICS LITERATURE

Duffy, N. E. 1994. "The Determinants of State Manufacturing Growth Rates: A Two-Digit-Level Analysis." *Journal of Regional Science* **34 (2): 137-162.**

This examination of the nation's manufacturing industries illustrates the potential importance of amenities and their impact on migration patterns. Duffy observes that, "One of the most noticeable economic phenomena of this century has been the change in the regional distribution of manufacturing." Duffy examines the factors related to interstate differences in the growth of employment in 19 manufacturing industries between 1954 and 1987. He finds that for four of the 19 industries, the pattern of employment growth was directly related to amenities. In the study, amenities are represented by two variables: one that distinguishes states with a warm climate from those with a cold climate; and another that identifies the states that exhibit both a high population of retirees and high in-migration rates. Duffy also finds that 18 of the industries studied had shifted closer to their product markets and 16 had shifted closer to workers.

Gabriel, Stuart A., Joe P. Mattey, and William L. Wascher. 1996. *Compensating Differentials and Evolution of the Quality-of-Life Among U.S. States.* **San Francisco: Federal Reserve Bank of San Francisco. 96-07. June.**

This article examines how changes in the quality and quantity of amenities can contribute to the evolution of quality of life over time and across places; in so doing it extends the existing "static" literature on regional differences in quality of life. The article provides estimates of quality of life rankings for U.S. states over the period 1981-1990.

Results indicate that sparsely populated mountainous western states such as Montana and Wyoming, rank highly in the estimated quality of life throughout the decade, whereas densely populated midwestern and eastern states consistently rank near the bottom in terms of quality of life. Reduced state and local government spending on highways, increased traffic congestion, and air pollution are found to be the most important contributors to the deterioration of quality of life. States that ascended in the quality of life rankings did so for a variety of reasons, including improved air quality, increased highway spending, reduced commuting times, and reduced state and local taxes.

Gottlieb, Paul D. 1995. "Residential Amenities, Firm Location and Economic Development." *Urban Studies* **32, 9: 1413-1436.**

In this article, Gottlieb investigates whether residential amenities can influence the locational decisions of high-tech firms in New Jersey. In order to determine whether firms evaluate amenities on behalf of potential employees, Gottlieb measures a variety of amenities at both the potential site of the firm and the residential area where potential employees are likely to live. Results of the study suggest that firms in the high-tech sector are repelled by disamenities like violent crime and high municipal expenditures at the work site. However, Gottlieb finds weak evidence to support his hypothesis that residential amenities, such as recreation, low traffic congestion, and strong public education, affect the locational decisions of high-tech firms.

Greenwood, Michael J., Gary L. Hunt, Dan S. Rickman, and George I. Treyz. 1991. "Migration, Regional Equilibrium, and the Estimation of Compensating Differentials." *American Economic Review* **81, 5: 1382-1390.**

This study examines the patterns of migration across the fifty states and attempts to determine the relative strengths of two primary motives that workers and households have for moving: (1) to earn a higher wage (adjusted for differences among the states in the costs of living); and (2) to have access to the particular amenities of the individual states. Based on migration patterns for 1971-87, the authors estimate the differential in wages for each state, relative to a national average, that is related to amenities.

Roback, Jennifer. 1982. "Wages, Rents, and the Quality of Life." *Journal of Political Economy* **90, 6: 1257-1278.**

Roback investigates the role of wages and rents in allocating workers to locations with varying quantities of amenities, both theoretically and empirically. Roback finds that regional differences in wages and land rents are largely explained by regional differences in amenities. The results of her empirical work indicate that crime, pollution, and cold weather are disamenities, while clear days and low population density are amenities. Amenities will decrease wages and increase land rents; disamenities will increase wages and decrease land rents.

Rosen, Sherwin. 1979. "Wage-Based Indexes of Urban Quality of Life." In Peter Mieszkowski and Mahlon Straszheim, eds., *Current Issues in Urban Economics*. Baltimore: Johns Hopkins University Press.

Rosen examines the determinants of inter-city wage differentials for 19 SMSAs. He finds that particulates, rain, crime, population growth, and unemployment are disamenities; whereas sunny days are amenities. Using regression estimates, he developed, Rosen computes an average quality-of-life ranking for the 19 SMSAs. Not surprisingly, he finds that the SMSAs with the highest average quality of life rankings in general exhibit less pollution, better climate, and lower crime rates than the SMSAs with the lowest rankings. He cautions the reader, however, that the rankings of the SMSAs may be altered depending on the weight given to the various city attributes, especially population density.

Salant, Priscilla, Lisa R. Carley, and Don A. Dillman. 1996. *Estimating the Contribution of Lone Eagles to Metro and Nonmetro In-Migration*. Pullman, WA: Social & Economic Sciences Research Center, Washington State University. 86-19. June.

The main objective of this study is to determine to what extent decisions to move to the state of Washington and subsequent employment are influenced by the availability and the use of information technology in the state. The study also investigates the push and pull factors that contribute to a migrant's decision to move.

The study estimates that 2,600 so-called lone eagles—individuals who are able to live anywhere and telecommute to work—moved to Washington in 1995 and that many of them did so for quality of life reasons. The most influential pull factors that lone eagles cited included the quality of the natural environment, outdoor recreational opportunities, a desirable climate, and a safe place to live. Influential push factors included urban congestion, undesirable climate, and fear of crime.

von Reichert, Christiane, and Gundars Rudzitis. 1992. "Multinomial Logistical Models Explaining Income Changes of Migrants to High-Amenity Counties." *Review of Regional Studies* 22, 1: 25-42.

This article uses a survey of migrants to, and residents of, 15 high-amenity wilderness counties to determine what factors can explain the migrants' willingness to accept declines in income after moving. Survey respondents were asked about their dissatisfaction/ satisfaction with their previous location (push factors) and the importance of certain attributes in their destination county in their migration decision (pull factors).

On the push side, such factors as environmental quality, pace of life, crime, scenery, and the lack of outdoor recreation in their previous locations produced higher levels of dissatisfaction than did the employment opportunities and cost of living there. In a similar manner, survey respondents placed more importance on such pull factors as environmental quality, scenery, outdoor recreation, and other natural resource amenities in their new locations than they did on employment opportunities and cost of living.

The study finds that approximately half of the surveyed migrants received lower incomes and that quality of life and amenities were more important factors in attracting migrants to the counties than employment opportunities.

SOCIOLOGY LITERATURE

Popenoe, David. 1979. "Urban Sprawl: Some Neglected Sociological Considerations." *Sociology and Social Research* **63, 2: 255-68.**

Urban sprawl is defined by the author as very low-density urban development, oriented to the automobile, with detached single-family houses on relatively large lots. For Popenoe, urban sprawl implies a scatteration of jobs, shops, and services, often in the form of strip commercial development; a scarcity of large open or green spaces; and a lack of community focus in both the physical and social sense. Despite its negative image, however, he points out that most Americans live in environments characterized by urban sprawl.

Many Americans, including some sociologists, see urban sprawl as desirable when compared to crowded, noisy, violent, and corrupt cities. Urban sprawl gives the individual more space, increased safety, more privacy, and a piece of land to call one's own. Urban sprawl, however, has been attacked as expensive and a significant user of natural resources, especially land and gasoline. This article examines the effects on residents of living in low-density, suburban residential environments. Since the positive consequences of suburban living are reasonably well known, this

article is devoted instead to the negative consequences.

Four negative consequences have been fairly well-documented by sociologists:

1. Low-density suburban development has led to an intensification of residential segregation by race and social class.

2. The benefits of urban sprawl are distributed regressively with respect to wealth.

3. Of all the alternative forms of urban expansion, urban sprawl is the one that is most destructive to the center city.

4. Although not an inherent consequence of low-density development, urban sprawl, when linked up with America's small scale, semi-autonomous local governments, has led to the proliferation of fragmented and overlapping governmental units.

The negative consequences of urban sprawl appear most tangible when considering the situations of five groups: women, teenagers, the poor, the elderly, and the handicapped. The author states that "it is hard to escape the conclusion that urban sprawl is an urban development form designed by and for men, especially middle-class men." Urban sprawl functions best when a resident has regular and direct access to an automobile, and middle-class men have more access to an automobile than the people in the five groups listed above. Furthermore, a major negative consequence of urban sprawl is deprivation of access. Even where community facilities and services are present and people can afford to use them, a large percentage of the population is disenfranchised from their use, due to inadequate transportation.

A closely related negative consequence is environmental deprivation from a deficiency of local elements that provide activity, stimulation, and well-being. This consequence applies particularly to teenagers. The walking environment of the low-density American suburb is virtually the sole environment for the teenage resident. Yet in this environment homes are often placed so far apart that access to local friends is difficult. Moreover, there is little diversity or variety of activities. The best amenity that usually is offered is a shopping center, or perhaps a fast-food restaurant, where teenagers are often made to feel unwelcome if they just hang out.

Popenoe mentions other potential negative consequences, including "sensory underload" and the "fall of public man." He also points out that the suburban trend of differentiation of residential areas by stages in the life cycle—with families, single adults, and the elderly inhabiting entirely separate neighborhoods—breaks up the "round of life" and may have negative consequences for young people.

PSYCHOLOGY LITERATURE

Zinam, Oleg. 1989. "Quality of Life, Quality of the Individual, Technology and Economic Development." *American Journal of Economics and Sociology* **48, 1: 55-68.**

This article relates Maslow's (1970) "hierarchy of needs" to components of quality of life. These needs and the corresponding components are:

1. Physical—safety of natural habitat
2. Peace—security
3. Physiological—material well-being
4. Reputation, Love, Belongingness—social harmony and justice
5. Independence—freedom, human rights, and dignity
6. Collective Self-actualization—cultural heritage and consensus on values
7. Personal Self-actualization—moral perfection

It is now generally accepted that there is a direct positive relationship between quality of life and quality of the person; that a higher quality of life improves the quality of the person in a self-reinforcing manner. But there is also ample evidence of the possibility of an inverse relationship—i.e., a higher quality of life may reduce the quality of the person (moral decay) and that a lower quality of life may increase the quality of the person ("adversity builds character").

CHAPTER

13

Annotations of Studies

SOCIAL ISSUES

Sprawl is the movement of residential and nonresidential land uses to the outer reaches of the metropolitan area. As land uses move increasingly outward, the tax bases of the areas left behind are weakened. Unless there is a way to compensate for peripheral growth, the urban center will almost always suffer. The literature of sprawl and social issues is concerned with both the aftereffects of, and curative measures for, outward growth. The literature concentrates on why outward growth takes place, alternatives to outward growth, the costs and benefits of outward growth, and ways to counter outward growth. These substantive declensions form the basis for the organization of this chapter.

The chapter is composed as follows:

The Growth of Cities and Metropolitan Areas
Urban Decline
Urban Renewal

In the section on *The Growth of Cities and Metropolitan Areas,* the works of Jonathan Barnett (1995), Robert Fishman (1987), Gordon and Richardson (1997, 1997b), Arthur Nelson et al. (1997), and David Rusk (1993) are annotated. The section on *Urban Decline* includes the

works of Marcellus Andrews (1994), Katharine Bradbury (1982), Anthony Downs (1994), Keith Ihlanfeldt (1995), James Kunstler (1993), Myron Orfield (1997), and Henry Richmond (1995). The section on *Urban Renewal* examines the works of Peter Calthorpe (1993) and Peter Katz (1994).

THE GROWTH OF CITIES AND METROPOLITAN AREAS

Barnett, Jonathan. 1995. *The Fractured Metropolis: Improving the New City, Restoring the Old City, Reshaping the Region.* **New York: Harper Collins.**

This strictly narrative analysis of metropolitan area trends advances the thesis that U.S. metropolitan settlements are splitting apart into "old cities" and "new cities." It covers much of the same ground as Anthony Downs's *New Visions for Metropolitan America* but in a much less systematized, non-quantitative way. The author proposes redirecting a share of future growth into older cities where they have been "emptied out," and integrating new and old cities with strong public transit networks.

Barnett's analysis is heavily skewed toward physical design, since he is an architect and urban planner. He attacks strip commercial development in suburbs and advances many of the ideas of the "new urbanism." He favors compact development over continued sprawl. He supports strong tree preservation ordinances and other environmentally sensitive regulations.

Barnett traces the historic development of older core areas and shows why the desire of the rich to live away from the poor, combined with transportation improvements, caused a withdrawal of resources from the center of our metropolitan areas.

> Attracting new investment to the bypassed areas of the older city is also the other side of the coin of policies to restrict growth at the urban fringe. One will not work without the other. (118)

He argues that some urban central business districts (CBDs) have been growing, but the remaining portions of older cities have been shrinking.

> The current market for a new suburb in derelict parts of an old city is likely to consist of people from nearby areas who have started to make a little money, plus people whose other housing choice is a small house or a mobile-home way out on the urban fringe. (146)

> The minimum requirements [of successful inner-city revival] are to foster a community [with] affordable housing, public safety, and effective schools. (163)

> The future of older cities depends ultimately on public policy initiatives that cannot be controlled directly. Older centers and neighborhoods need rapid-transit links to the new centers in formerly suburban areas so that the metropolitan area can function as one economy. Metropolitan services have to

be supported by an equalized tax base; there needs to be limits to growth at the metropolitan fringe accompanied by major new investment in bypassed residential neighborhoods and derelict industrial districts. Reintegrating the metropolitan area is necessary for the survival of cities, suburbs, and the regional eco-system. (175)

The book's weakness is that Barnett does not indicate how to implement his recommendations or how to grapple with the political forces involved.

He claims there have been major changes in the environment for metropolitan development, including the following:

- The addition of design methods to the practice of planning.
- Community participation in planning.
- The rise of the conservation ethic and the concept of sustainability.
- Environmental conservatism.

He points out that we need positive planning about how to grow in the future. But, he says:

> [L]ocal governments are not accustomed to making affirmative decisions about which areas of the natural landscape ought to be preserved and which areas should be built up. (191)

> The basic components of any city design are the organization of public open space—including streets, plazas, and parks or gardens—the architectural relationships among buildings, and the composition of building mass in relation to the landscape or the skyline. (193)

> The most difficult and central problems of urban design today [are] reconciling tall buildings with lower structures, or the need to incorporate parking and highway

viaducts within a physical fabric defined by streets and buildings. (196)

Experience has led city designers to seek to reestablish the primacy of the street in urban settings and go back to a mix of uses in central areas, rather than create the separate tower zones for office buildings that characterized many urban renewal plans." (196)

His national action agenda includes the following:

- Creating urban growth boundaries around all metropolitan areas.
- Adopting state planning laws in all 50 states.
- Creating regional revenue sharing based upon state-mandated revenue equalization formulas.
- Restoring natural ecosystems in urban areas.
- Having local plans that encourage compact neighborhoods with a mix of housing types and dense commercial centers.
- Expanding public transit systems, beginning with more buses.
- Renovating public housing.
- Helping some low-income households move out of areas of concentrated poverty.
- Spending more on inner-city schools, rather than industrial subsidies.

  The environmental movement could be a strong political constituency for the maintenance and restoration of the old city. (236)

Although this book contains an accurate analysis of basic trends, it lacks quantified analysis and political savvy about how its broad recommendations might be accomplished in real-world settings.

Drucker, Peter F. 1992. "People, Work, and the Future of the City." *Managing the Future.* **New York: Dutton. 125-129.**

In this short essay, Drucker explains how the growth of cities in the nineteenth century was due to advances in transportation that enabled people to move to centralized locations to work together. But now the author points out, it is cheaper and more convenient to move information to where the people are. Nevertheless, big corporations will still want their top people together; and many people will still want to work in groups. But, in the future, these groups will no longer need to be gathered in downtown office clusters. Work will be out-sourced to specialized firms that are not necessarily located downtown. We are probably at the end of the big boom in office construction in major city downtowns, Drucker concludes.

This essay covers no more than a fragment of the overall subject, without much depth of analysis and with very little supporting data.

Fishman, Robert. 1987. *Bourgeois Utopias: The Rise and Fall of Suburbia.* **New York: Basic Books.**

This book discusses the role of suburbs in the historic development of modern urban life. It looks at the two phases of suburbia—the "original" suburb, and the post-industrial "technoburb."

The original suburb, as defined by Fishman, was a retreat from the tumult of industry and commerce and high-density residences that characterized the early industrial city into an exclusively residential community. It first appeared in the London area in the late eighteenth century, and became more prominent in the nineteenth and twentieth centuries, both in England and in America.

The original suburbs were almost exclusively residential areas, occupied almost entirely by the middle-class elite; they excluded all industry and commerce, and all lower-income households. They were a retreat from the ills of city life into a more utopian scene linked to nature through the prevalence of single-family homes with private yards. Suburban life was family-oriented and separated middle-class women from the world of work; it placed them in a world exclusively focused on the family. In Fishman's view, the suburb was a specialized bedroom community, the employed residents of which commuted into either the central city downtown or its industrial areas; the employed residents never worked in suburbs themselves. *Exclusion was at the heart of the suburbs as thus conceived.* Industry, commerce, diversity, jobs for women, and low-income households were all perceived as potential threats to the primacy of the family-centered, lot-linked single-family home.

Over time, however, the suburbs have gradually evolved into a completely different urban arrangement, structured around what Fishman calls the "technoburb." It can also be called *the urban network form.* What most people conceive of as the suburbanization of America, Fishman considers a shift to a development pattern that radically undermines the original suburbs—and the old central city. Although suburbs maintained their specialized roles as bedroom communities into the 1950s, the migration of so many other types of activities into suburban areas since then has changed the basic nature of these communities. As they acquired first shopping facilities, then warehouses, then industrial firms, and finally offices,

they lost their exclusively residential character. They have been transformed into fully urban communities, but with no single center, and with very low densities. This transformation was made possible by innovations in automobiles, roadways, and communications.

Today, the metropolitan area is a non-centered amorphous growth, resembling an amoeba without a nucleus. Although regional downtowns still exist, and central cities still specialize in housing the poor and some central facilities and amenities, the vast majority of both residences and workplaces are scattered throughout the area in no particular pattern. They are linked by a huge network of roads and electronic communications. The center of each person's life is his or her own home, and the universe of each consists of the territory he or she can reach within one hour's drive from home. There is no single centralized urban form because each household essentially has its own unique network. The overall form is an undefined massive overlapping of all these individual networks. The exclusivity of the old suburb has been destroyed, although poor people still seem concentrated in older core areas. But all types of activities are now found at all distances from any one spot; there is no single center that everyone relates to. This uncentered network has replaced the monocentric city of old, and even the polycentric city of the 1960s and 1970s. What most people perceive of as suburbanization today involves the destruction of the former suburbs and their full urbanization in a totally decentralized form.

A key question concerning the future of this trend is: "Is the low density of the new city destructive to all cultural diversity?" (200) Since this new network contains very few public spaces and no set of places in which a large fraction of the community habitually gathers or interacts physically, there is no sense of community. Television greatly aggravates this outcome because it fosters passive, home-centered separation of each household from all others, although it does provide some commonality of experience across the multitudes (which may be undermined by the multiplication of channels). Fishman believes we are still working out the cultural implications of this new form:

> The new city will probably never be able to compete culturally with the old centers. There will be for the foreseeable future a division founded on choice between those who seek out even at great cost the kind of cultural excitement that can only be found in the center, and those who choose the family-centered life of the outer city. (202)

Fishman, however, underestimates the degree to which cultural activities can take place in the outer regions of such networks, because people with common cultural interests can still gather together in outlying locations in sufficient numbers to support cultural activities like symphonies, theaters, etc.

> Seen in historical perspective, suburbia now appears as the point of transition between two decentralized eras: the preindustrial rural area and the postindustrial information society. . . Suburbia kept alive the ideal of a balance between man and nature in a society that seemed dedicated to destroying it. That is its legacy. (206-207)

Glaeser, Edward L. 1994. "Cities, Information, and Economic Growth." *Citiscape* 1, 1 (August): 9-47.

This article explores recent contributions to the theory of cities concerning how information flow and usage contribute to city growth or decline. Glaeser argues that simple capital and labor accumulation models fail to explain city growth. A variable relating to human capital and one relating to abstract intellectual capital should be included in any analysis to explain certain failings in simpler models.

One aspect of cities that is not often discussed is that of informational externalities. These help explain why people and firms locate in cities, and why cities grow. They also have negative impacts, they allow rioting to spread rapidly, and increases in crime to be communicated quickly.

Growth theory regards increases in the stock of human knowledge as a central aspect of economic progress over time. Because knowledge is more easily accessed by people living close together, "closeness contributes to the degree of appropriability." (11)

Growth theory based upon capital and labor accumulation had an inconsistency: it could not explain why countries and cities did not converge on a steady state. Only an exogenous technological change variable could explain that. But increasing returns to scale from intellectual knowledge also made it possible to explain continuous growth. However, increasing returns to scale are not compatible with an economy based upon perfect competition, because the former leads to monopolistic results. Also, marginal prices lie under average prices, which means firms would be losing money.

Romer solved this problem by indicating that private profits did not have increasing returns to scale, but social benefits produced by general increases in knowledge did. His argument made perfect competition among private firms possible in theory, but also allowed growth to continue over time due to the social benefits of accumulated knowledge. Lucas focused this idea on returns to human (private) capital, but the truth must be that both private capital and general social knowledge gain from innovations in the long run.

These ideas are related to cities because people living and working close together can more easily tap into the store of accumulated knowledge and exchange ideas with each other. The externalities of knowledge exchange are clearly facilitated by urban proximity, as opposed to its alternatives.

Barro regressed growth in per capita GDP against several other variables across countries, and discovered that poor governmental qualities are negatively correlated with rapid growth. His basic findings were that education and absence of regulation were positively correlated with rapid growth.

Rauch found that SMSA cities with high levels of human capital had both higher property costs and higher wages than other cities, holding individual traits constant.

Glaeser and others arrived at the following findings: (1) initial concentration in an industry does NOT seem to foster subsequent creativity, therefore scale economies in a local industry do not really create growth; (2) urban diversity is positively related to later growth; and (3) more competitive industries grow more quickly.

In general equilibrium theory, real differences in incomes among cities should be quickly eliminated by migration of workers and capital. Any remaining differences should reflect negative amenities in the higher-income cities that must be offset by higher incomes.

A strong finding from U.S. census data is that the cities that grew quickly between 1950 and 1970 also grew quickly between 1970 and 1990. Growth in the first period was established as the best single predictor of city growth in the second period. Thus, growth begets further growth in spite of congestion problems. At least, that is one interpretation of the data.

Another finding is that areas with highly educated work forces at the outset of a period tend to have higher levels of education at the end. The well-educated are either born or move to areas where other well-educated people are already located.

High—and low—unemployment rates among cities also tend to persist over time. No convergence occurs, such as what might be predicted by general equilibrium theory. This lack of convergence may reflect permanent maladies in the structure of those cities with high unemployment rates. Similarly, high crime rates are persistent over time among cities.

Rioting is a phenomenon found mainly in cities, because of contagion and other effects. Almost every city has a potential for rioting if some spark ignites a crowd.

Neighborhoods play key roles in the accumulation of human capital. Both skills and behavioral habits are learned from peers and neighbors and mentors. Stability of occupancy in neighborhoods may be important, because, according to game theory the length of relationships influences the types of behavior one is willing to carry out. If you have a long-term relationship with other players (neighbors), for example, you are more likely to take the impacts of your actions upon them into account, because they can retaliate against you in the future, and you must live with them for a long time. Thus, residents in stable neighborhoods can more strongly reinforce good behavior than residents in unstable areas—a finding that presents an argument for subsidizing homeownership, which creates greater residential stability.

Cities also foster proximity to political power, which is concentrated there. This proximity may influence people to undertake actions to change the behavior of key authorities located in cities. Political agitation is much more likely to work in cities than in rural areas for that reason. There are also more people to get agitated per unit of effort in cities than in rural areas.

One of the most critical challenges in the future is reducing informational barriers between ghettos and downtown power centers.

Suburbanization provides many of the benefits of urban agglomeration while avoiding many of its negative impacts, such as high rates of crime, greater probability of rioting and less residential stability in local neighborhoods to inhibit negative behaviors.

Gordon, Peter, and Harry W. Richardson. 1997b. "The Destiny of Downtowns: Doom or Dazzle?" *Lusk Review* (Fall): 63-76.

The authors remark that the prospect of successful downtowns is often promised

as a source of metropolitan economic strength and prestige—but offer evidence that suggests this is rhetoric at best, and profit-seeking at worst. Gordon and Richardson assert that the futility of large-scale downtown-focused projects is easy to understand—the push-pull factors of spatial decentralization constantly reinforce each other. Improved mobility has given people more and better choices at lower cost, as witnessed by continually increasing automobile use. Furthermore, the telecommunications revolution has irreversibly changed our concept of distance, making the concentrated, vertical city a transient phenomenon.

The authors explain how these transitions will continue to accelerate as new technology makes it possible for work, shopping, learning, entertainment, and socializing to be at-home activities. These anti-urban trends are further reinforced by "push" factors like crime, panhandlers, and "dysfunctional public agencies" that are found in downtown locations. People continue to leave these ills for better amenities and more pleasant shopping opportunities in America's suburbs.

It is the authors' contention that these push-and-pull forces explain more than just the continuing demise of downtowns; they also explain the outward expansion of cities into suburbs and exurbs. Although the current political debate is about the contest between cities and suburbs, it is becoming less relevant. The more important question hinges on how much future development will occur in suburbs, exurbs, and rural areas. Gordon and Richardson point out that most U.S. job growth since the late 1980s has occurred outside of large Metropolitan Statistical Areas (MSAs). This silent migration, the authors conclude, has had little impact on public policy because it does not match the conventional, but hopelessly outdated, paradigm of how cities evolve.

Gordon, Peter; Harry W. Richardson; and Gang Yu. 1997. "Metropolitan and Non-Metropolitan Employment Trends in the U.S.: Recent Evidence and Implications." Los Angeles, CA: School of Urban Planning and Development and Department of Economics, University of Southern California.

This study looks at employment change in seven major industrial sectors over a twenty-six-year time span (1969-1994), using the Bureau of Economic Analysis Regional Economic Information System (REIS) file that reports one-digit SIC employment and income data at the county level.

The authors observe a steady decentralization, often beyond the suburbs into both exurban and rural areas. They see new and mobile firms choosing locations according to their demand for agglomeration benefits. These are now available throughout suburban and parts of exurban America, obviating the advantages of traditional centers and of central counties as a whole. Exurban and rural settings are increasingly attractive to firms because of breakthroughs in goods handling and in the transmission of information. The authors' work shows a negative and sometimes absolute decline in CBD employment over the period of study.

The study suggests that the locational decisions of households are influenced more by workplace accessibility than by the availability of amenities, recreational opportunities, and public safety. In addition, the locations of firms are less tied to place because of access to information technologies, just as core diseconomies have displaced the original

agglomeration economies that pulled people and economic activities together. The authors therefore conclude that central cities are not coming back any time soon.

Nelson, Arthur C., and Thomas W. Sanchez. 1997. "Exurban and Suburban Households: A Departure From Traditional Location Theory." *Journal of Housing Research* 8, 2.

In this article, Nelson and Sanchez describe how modern social, cultural, economic, and technological changes have permitted households to settle farther from urban centers than in the past. They then test the proposition that exurbanites are different from suburbanites in household characteristics, occupation of household heads, accessibility to employment, and residence characteristics.

Nelson and Sanchez use a variety of nonparametric and cluster analysis techniques, and find that exurbanites and suburbanites are more similar than previously thought. They conclude that the rise of polycentric urban areas seems to have pushed the suburban fringe further out.

The results of this analysis suggest that the primary differences between exurbanites and suburbanites is that the former have a greater desire to locate away from urban-related problems and disamenities, especially households with middle incomes and families with small children. In contrast, smaller families or families at the early or late stages of life are more likely to choose suburban locations.

In conclusion, the authors speculate that the continued outward expansion may be attributable to the inability of urban and suburban governments to provide suitable public facilities and services at prices affordable to residents, and to suburban policies that constrain the supply of housing relative to demand through opposition to affordable housing or innovative housing configurations, and through otherwise exclusionary zoning practices.

Rusk, David. 1993. *Cities Without Suburbs*. Washington, DC: Woodrow Wilson Center Press.

This book is a detailed and comprehensive look at sprawl and at least one of its alternatives, written by the former mayor of Albuquerque, New Mexico. Its basic thesis is that cities which have elastic boundaries—i.e., those that can annex surrounding territories—are much healthier than cities which have inelastic boundaries—i.e., those where boundaries are frozen because they are surrounded by incorporated suburban municipalities. The elastic cities can expand outward as their metropolitan areas grow, enabling them to retain access to the new taxable bases created outside the original boundaries of these cities as they grew. In contrast, inelastic cities cannot reach out to new taxable resources as growth expands beyond their borders. Both elastic and inelastic cities have disproportionate shares of poor people within their original boundaries, but the former can counteract the negative effects by expanding their boundaries. Inelastic cities are stuck with rising percentages of poor residents and falling tax bases, causing them to have falling taxable resources per capita at the very time that they need more such resources to cope with the rising percentages of poor residents.

Rusk presents a great deal of statistical information to support his claim that elastic cities are healthier economically and socially than inelastic ones. He does not use regression analysis, but rather presents paired city comparisons and compares averages of groups of cities with different degrees of elasticity.

This book is one of the most comprehensive and intelligent analyses of sprawl and other urban problems yet written. However, it has one serious flaw. The author believes that unified metropolitan government is the best solution for inelasticity, but there appears to be no political support for this arrangement whatever. Even so, Rusk's analysis is definitely one of the best studies of urban problems.

Where Rusk particularly excels is in analysis of three aspects of the urban problem. First, he fearlessly confronts the racial aspects of urban problems. Second, he offers concrete recommendations for solving the problems that he describes. His recommendations include: regional governance of land-use planning; regional tax-base sharing; a regional program of creating desegregated affordable housing for the poor; and promotion of region-wide economic development. Third, Rusk presents a cogent analysis of the "point of no return" for central cities. He identifies three benchmarks: a low ratio of per capita income in a city relative to that of its suburbs (70 percent or less); a high fraction of minority-groups (30 percent or more of the total population); and substantial and sustained population loss (20 percent or more). He claims that no city that has crossed all three of these thresholds has ever even begun to recover.

Sclar, Elliot, and Walter Hook. 1993. "The Importance of Cities to the National Economy." In Henry G. Cisneros, ed., *Interwoven Destinies: Cities and the Nation*. New York: American Assembly of Columbia University. 1-26.

This is the lead article in a volume of essays presented at the 82nd American Assembly held in Harriman, New York in April 1993. The authors argue that central cities are the vital centers of production in the American economy. They complain that most policy analysts in recent decades have viewed cities mainly as homes for the poor. They cite the following facts in support of their view on central cities:

- In most metro areas, the higher paying jobs are located in the central city. Such jobs constitute 32.2 percent of all jobs nationally, but garner 37.7 percent of nationwide earnings (no source for this data is cited). Wages of central city jobs are 20 percent higher on average than those of suburban jobs, and this gap has been widening.

- Many suburban residents have jobs in central cities. A survey by Arthur Goldberg of the suburban areas of the nation's 100 largest cities showed that half of suburban families had at least one worker in the central city.

- The same survey showed heavy suburban dependence on central city services. Approximately 67 percent of suburban residents depend on the city for major medical care; 43 percent have family members attending or planning to attend an institution of higher learning in the city; 46 percent believe their property values would be hurt by a serious decline in their central city.

- The top 24 counties accounted for 39 percent of all jobs in information-intensive industries but had only 27 percent of total jobs. Wages for jobs in

downtown Boston were 3.55 times higher than wages for jobs in the same categories in the suburbs, and 2.37 times higher in New York City than in its suburbs.

- The production advantages of central cities include: (1) minimized transportation and communications costs for both workers and customers; (2) easy face-to-face contact among experts, which facilitates analysis; (3) superior telecommunications infrastructures which facilitates international transactions; and (4) more specialized producer services, which tend to be located where the size of the market is greatest.

One reason suburban locations continue to grow faster than central cities is that the costs of moving are not fully borne by the businesses that move. Some of the cost is borne by their employees and public taxpayers. If suburbanization were so efficient, one would see more of it in international competitor nations. Instead, the growth of the suburbs in the United States indicates that U.S. urban policy is more concerned with stimulating demands for consumer products—such as housing and autos—than it is with productive efficiency.

Suburbanization has also been encouraged by biased public policies, such as home tax deductions and federal highway finance—a subsidy that was not reflected in public transit aid until very recently. The nature of pricing of telephone and other services has allowed higher-cost suburban services to be priced at the same rate as lower-cost city services.

The authors argue that continued dispersal poses major costs to society, especially concerning the inputs of private firms. The need for virtually all employees to own automobiles, for example, increases wage demands. Auto dependence also increases our trade deficit because we must import so much oil. We already spend far more on travel and telecommunications than rival nations. The Japanese spend 9.4 percent of GNP on transportation, while we spend 15-22 percent. Traffic congestion imposes high costs on production. The authors claim that most metropolitan areas devote over half of their available land to road infrastructure. By undermining the tax base of central cities, society has been unable to invest properly in the education and training of the labor force, or in the infrastructure outside the downtown that is critical to productive efficiency. U.S. investment in education through the high school level is the lowest among the seven most industrialized nations—4.1 percent of GNP, compared to 4.6 percent in West Germany and 4.7 percent in Japan. We need much more investment in the labor force and infrastructure in central cities to remain competitive.

URBAN DECLINE

Andrews, Marcellus. 1994. "On the Dynamics of Growth and Poverty in Cities." *Citiscape* **1, 1 (August): 53-73.**

This article presents a model of how poverty concentrations within cities are related to city growth rates. "The central theme of this article holds that the logic of meritocracy creates class divisions in the urban labor market which may undermine the very conditions that make rapid economic growth possible" (53). The need for high-skilled workers in a modern high-tech economy creates two classes of workers: those with the requisite skills, and other unskilled workers. But schools in many large cities are failing to provide their students with the skills needed to be in the first class. This failure creates a caste-like result,

since the primary determinant of the school performance of children is the educational level of their parents.

The basic dynamic, Andrews points out, is as follows:

- Members of the "underclass" within cities strive to attain a higher standard of living and jobs suitable for high-skilled workers, but are frustrated by their inability to do so because of the poor quality of city schools. The lifestyles of the middle class have a demonstrable effect upon the underclass, encouraging them to want to consume more.

- The resulting frustration leads to criminal behavior and violence on the part of the underclass. Members of this class perceive that they have only two sources of income—transfer payments and crime.

- The behavior of the underclass drives middle-class (upper-tier) workers and households out of the city into the suburbs where they can escape from crime and violence.

- The departure of the middle class weakens the fiscal position of the city government, thereby reducing its ability to provide good quality schooling to the underclass. This creates a negative downward spiral—a "vicious circle."

A key variable in this dynamic system is the "middle-class ratio"—that is, the percentage of the total population consisting of middle-class residents.

Another key variable is the attitude of students towards academic achievement. The author argues that membership in the underclass causes anti-academic attitudes among students.

Andrews also argues that there is a "critical failure ratio" among city students which determines whether the middle class will grow or decline within the city. If the actual failure rate among students (which determines whether they will become middle-class or under-class members) rises above this critical rate, the middle-class ratio will decline because the behavior of the underclass, then larger, will drive middle-class residents out. If the actual failure rate is below the critical level, then more students will graduate into the middle-class, and the incentives for middle-class residents to leave is reduced—even though greater competition in the labor market among the larger numbers of middle-class workers may cause the unemployment rate to rise.

The author regards this entire situation as a negative externality—an unintended consequence of technological change that has raised the skill requirements for high-wage workers. But it is society that has provided unequal access to learning among its young people. Thus, "the increasing importance of knowledge capital in economic growth contributes to the problem of urban poverty." (63)

The future of the city, and particularly its ability to change the way it grows, may ultimately depend upon the willingness of the middle class to remain in the city despite the difficulties of caste division and crime that are the underside of the role of knowledge capital in economic life. In turn, a national government policy that encourages the exodus of middle-class citizens from the city may make significant urban reform and reconstruction impossible. (63)

The federal government must recognize the role of knowledge capital in unwittingly exacerbating the urban crisis. In particular any urban policy that intends to make cities into virtuous circles must recognize the folly of forcing local governments to deal with the negative

aspects of knowledge capital with diminishing economic resources. Further, a macroeconomic growth strategy that emphasizes human capital must carefully address the inequality, poverty, violence, and crime that result from educational failure. (63)

Bradbury, Katharine L., Anthony Downs, and Kenneth Small. 1982. *Urban Decline and the Future of American Cities.* Washington, DC: Brookings Institution.

A central component of this book is the idea that every city has certain specific social functions, and therefore changes in its ability to perform those functions constitutes *urban decline*. In contrast, a low level of ability to perform those functions—a static concept—constitutes *urban distress*. The authors point out that not all cities with high urban distress are declining. Some may even be growing rapidly—cities with high poverty rates and high immigration, for example.

The specific index of *urban decline* used in this study is based upon change over time of four variables: the unemployment rate, per capita income, the violent crime rate, and the government debt burden. The *index of urban decline* was calculated by ranking all cities for each of these variables, and assigning points to each based on its *relative position* in the ranking on each variable. Cities in the lowest third (in terms of desirability) received a -1 for that specific variable; cities in the highest third, a +1, and cities in the middle third, zero. The scores of each city on all four variables were then summed. The highest possible index score was +4 and the lowest was -4. A similar index was computed for *city urban distress*. This index was based on five variables, each at a single point in time: the unemployment rate, the incidence of poverty, the violent crime rate, the percent of housing considered old, and the city's tax revenue relative to that of its metropolitan area.

It is notable that neither city population change nor city employment change was used as part of the decline measure. The reason is that not all population declines are bad (if the city is overcrowded to start). Moreover, the authors used declining population as a separate measure that they related to the index of decline. They reasoned that the unemployment rate captured some aspect of employment change.

Two other measures were computed in this study: *city disparity*, a measure of the difference between each central city's scores for these variables and the score of its suburban areas; and *city divergence*, a measure of the rate of change in city disparity over time.

This book contains a relevant discussion of the future of large cities. It points out that although both self-reinforcing and self-limiting factors are involved in urban decline, the former seem to be much more powerful than the latter. Hence the concept of a *self-reinforcing downward spiral* of decline is validated by the book's analysis.

Downs, Anthony. 1994. *New Visions for Metropolitan America.* **Washington, DC. The Brookings Institution.**

The most dangerous result of growth management policies, claims Downs, is that they help perpetuate the concentration of very poor households in depressed neighborhoods in big cities and older suburbs. These neighborhoods, containing a small percentage of the nation's population, are riddled with four problems that are undermining social

cohesion and economic efficiency: crime and violence, poor families, poor public education, and the lack of labor integration. Downs makes the argument that these problems are aggravated by low-density growth, which most people favor, so they don't seem to threaten the status quo. But if they are allowed to fester, says Downs, they will gravely impair the political unity, productivity, and economic efficiency of American society and the personal security of everyone.

The situation is not clear-cut, and it is difficult for communities to decide how best to respond to rapid growth. Downs seeks to clarify this situation by answering the following series of questions: Are the undesirable conditions really caused primarily by growth? Which policies might succeed in ameliorating them? Which might have severe side effects or make conditions worse? Is limiting local growth desirable at all for either a given locality or society as a whole? If so, what should the goals of such limitations be? To what extent do communities need to coordinate growth management policies with other communities to achieve effective results? Can the multiplicity of governments in metropolitan areas manage growth effectively, or does that arrangement need to be modified? If so, how?

In addition to attempting to answer these questions, Downs considers the problems associated with rapid metropolitan growth from a perspective that encompasses inner-city problems as well as examines the effects of growth management in communities that have tried to alter the course of urban growth. Downs also analyzes three other ways growth could occur—alternatives that might reduce the problems that have arisen from the pattern of unlimited low-density development—focusing on the relationships between central cities and their suburbs. Finally, Downs attempts to identify the policies likely to be most effective in helping to resolve growth-related problems.

Downs concludes with a call for America to strengthen the bases for its continued unity by placing more emphasis on social solidarity and less on individualistic values, beginning in early school years, and by engaging the news media and advertising industry in the discussion. He proposes that we begin by persuading residents of suburbs across the country that their concerns in many ways are similar to those of central city residents. This would lay a political foundation for major federal funding of nationwide programs that disproportionally aid central cities and their residents, both of which are vital to the long-run prospects of the entire U.S. economy.

Ihlanfeldt, Keith R. 1995. "The Importance of the Central City to the Regional and National Economy: A Review of the Arguments and Empirical Evidence." *Citiscape* **1, 2 (June): 125-150.**

This article reviews most of the literature on the linkages between central cities and suburbs. According to the author, there are five basic linkages: (1) Outsiders' perceptions of the appeal of an entire metropolitan area are influenced by conditions prevailing within its central city; (2) Cities contain many amenities valued throughout their regions; (3) Individual cities may provide a "sense of place" valued by both their residents and outsiders; (4) Fiscal problems in central cities may eventually raise taxes on suburbanites and thereby reduce suburban economic development; and (5) Agglomeration economies create special roles for central cities in their regional economies.

The author does not cite two other linkages that are believed to be important: (1) Cities provide low-cost housing for low-wage workers employed in—and necessary for—activities in suburbs where those workers cannot afford to live; and (2) Cities provide many jobs for suburban residents that increase suburban incomes.

The author claims that there is no empirical evidence either supporting or denying the first four factors he cites; therefore he dispenses with them in two pages. He does not deny that these linkages exist, but says that no one knows how strong or important they are because no studies have measured them. He devotes most of his article to agglomeration economies, which have been studied at length and by many people.

Agglomeration economies are, essentially, increasing returns to scale in processing activities. Ihlanfeldt refers to them as "the economies of large-scale production, commonly considered, [and] the cumulative advantages accruing from the growth of industry itself—the development of skill and know-how; the opportunities for easy communication of ideas and experience; the opportunity of ever-increasing differentiation of processes and of specialization in human activities." (128, quoted from Nicholas Kaldor—1970)

Agglomeration economies are divided into two types: *localization economies* that arise from the concentration of similar activities (such as a single industry) either in one place or very near each other; and *urbanization economies* that arise from the location of an activity in an area that has a wide diversity of activities—so production costs decline as the size of the area concerned rises. Urbanization economies generate benefits for all types of firms located in an area; whereas localization economies generate benefits only for those firms in industries that are highly concentrated in an area. Central cities are considered to have advantages over their suburbs for both types of economies.

Both types of agglomeration economies have three major causes: (1) labor market economies; (2) scale economies in the production of intermediate inputs; and (3) communication economies. Labor market economies cause localization economies because the concentration of many similar firms together creates a large pool of workers skilled in that industry, and reduces search and training costs for the firms. Urbanization economies also arise from large diversified labor pools. However, these labor pool economies do not favor central cities much over suburbs in large metropolitan areas.

The other two causes of agglomeration economies, however, clearly favor central cities. Both types involve face-to-face contacts, which occur most efficiently in or around downtown areas. The importance of communications economies has also been increased by the shift from goods-producing to information-producing activities. Innovations in communications technology, however, have made face-to-face contacts less necessary for the sharing of information.

The author reviews numerous empirical studies of these economies. One of the more interesting shows that both suburban firms and central city firms rely heavily on central-city suppliers for certain corporate services, such as investment banking, commercial banking, and legal, auditing, and actuarial services. The study, authored by Stanbeck in 1991, dealt with 14 large metro areas, and also demonstrated that suburban companies tend to be smaller and more

likely to be in manufacturing than central city companies.

Several other studies have correlated conditions, such as levels of per capita income in cities and their suburbs. These studies all show positive linkages between cities and suburbs. Voith (1994), for example, shows that positive city income growth is highly correlated with positive suburban income growth.

The author's conclusions are:

- Significant linkages clearly exist.
- The maturation of the suburbs has weakened these linkages over time.
- Telecommunications changes will NOT greatly weaken the importance of central cities.
- "The hypothesis that cities make an important contribution to regional and national economic growth is attractive," though not fully proven (139).

Kunstler, James. 1993. *The Geography of Nowhere: The Rise and Decline of America's Man-Made Landscape.* New York: Simon & Schuster.

Kunstler has written a polemic—a true "exagger-book"—about the aesthetic and other qualities of metropolitan development in the United States, especially during the post World War II era. The tone of this book is conveyed in the following quotations from the first chapter:

> More and more we appear to be a nation of overfed clowns living in a hostile cartoon environment.

> Eighty percent of everything ever built in America has been built in the last fifty years, and most of it is depressing, brutal,

ugly, unhealthy, and spiritually degrading.

> To me, it is a landscape of scary places, the geography of nowhere, that has simply ceased to be a credible human habitat.

These statements convey the spirit in which Kunstler denounces everything American. There seems to be nothing about American life that appeals to him. He attacks individualism, low-density development, business, you name it:

> Riverside seems a template for all the ghastly automobile suburbs of the postwar era—individual houses on big blobs of land along curvy streets. (49)

> Yet, for all their artificiality and impermanence, the early railroad suburbs were lovely places to live.

He decries architectural modernism and the art-deco style, and high-rise office buildings generally. But his greatest enemy is the automobile and highways. Still, he admits that:

> The suburban subdivision was unquestionably a successful product. For many, it was a vast improvement over what they were used to. . . . The main problem with it was that it dispensed with all the traditional connections and continuities of community life, and replaced them with little more than cars and television. (105)

The development of suburbs drained activity out of cities: "The cities, of course, went completely to hell. The new superhighways . . . drained them of their few remaining taxpaying residents." (107)

The separation of households and activities inherent in low-density suburbs has also ruined any sense of community

life, according to Kunstler. And because of the spending of all public money on highways, all other aspects of public life have become impoverished.

> The motive force behind suburbia has been the exaltation of privacy and the elimination of the public realm. (189)

This book contains no statistics, no quantitative analyses, and no databases. It is an endless diatribe expressing the author's contempt for modern suburban, auto-oriented life. He claims we can no longer live this type of life because it has become too costly, both in economic and social terms. The social costs include the destruction of community and family life. In the last chapter, Kunstler puts forth policy suggestions including the following:

- We must rebuild our cities and towns.
- We shall have to give up mass automobile use. (248)
- We should adopt the approach of the new urbanism in designing small towns. (He specifically discusses Seaside and Peter Calthorpe's pedestrian pockets as cures for all the ills he has been blasting. Mandatory open space zoning is also praised.)
- Until we do these things, "the standard of living in the United States is apt to decline sharply, and as it does the probability of political trouble will rise." (274)
- We will have to give up our fetish for extreme individualism and rediscover public life. . . . We will have to downscale our gigantic enterprises and institutions—corporations, governments, banks, schools, hospitals, markets, farms—and learn to live locally, hence responsibly.

He offers no guidance about how to achieve these ends, however.

Ledebur, Larry C., and William R. Barnes. 1992. *Metropolitan Disparities and Economic Growth: City Distress and the Need for a Federal Local Growth Package.* **Washington, DC: National League of Cities. March.**

This is a statistical study of the relationship between income disparities in central cities and their suburbs on the one hand, and metropolitan area growth rates on the other. The basic conclusion is that: "During the period 1988-1991, metropolitan areas with greater internal disparities tended to perform less well economically than metropolitan areas with lesser disparities" (1).

Overall, central city per capita income as a percentage of suburban per capita income has declined from 105 percent in 1960 to 96 percent in 1973, to 89 percent in 1980, and to 59 percent in 1987. Much of this article aims at justifying a substantial federal aid package to cities, especially cities in distress. Data on children being raised in poverty, by race, are presented. In 1990, 45 percent of all black children under the age of four were being raised in poverty, compared to 38 percent of Hispanics and 20.6 percent of all children. These proportions were higher in central cities, and lower in suburbs.

Orfield, Myron. 1997. *Metropolitics: A Regional Agenda for Community and Stability.* **Washington, DC: Brookings Institution Press and Lincoln Institute of Land Policy.**

In this study published jointly by the Brookings Institution and the Lincoln Institute of Land Policy, Orfield asserts that the way to restrain suburban sprawl is for central cities and rural and environmental interests to ally themselves with older and inner-ring suburban communities.

Until this occurs, Orfield maintains new suburbs will continue to siphon off the tax base from older cities and suburbs. Further, unrestrained growth will continue to consume farmland and forests, threatening regional ecosystems.

These problems call for a sweeping realignment of traditional political divisions. According to Orfield, reformers must: unite voters in central cities and declining suburbs; demonstrate to these voters that tax-base sharing lowers their taxes and improves local services; and convince them that fair housing will stabilize residential change in their communities.

Orfield's ultimate strategy is the creation of a regional authority in each metropolitan area, whose mission would be to encourage new suburbs to permit the development of affordable housing according to a fair-share formula. Other goals for this regional authority would be to help bring about tax-base sharing, limits on outward expansion of the metropolitan boundary, and efficient use of new and existing infrastructure.

Richmond, Henry R. 1995. *Regionalism: Chicago as an American Region.* **Chicago: John D. And Catherine T. MacArthur Foundation. December 6.**

This is the most comprehensive attack on sprawl yet launched. Henry Richmond, one of the architects of the Oregon state planning system, has collected every known argument against sprawl and woven them into one long polemic—but a relatively sensible one. Among the arguments he marshals against sprawl:

• Sprawl concentrates poverty in inner-city areas, undermining their fiscal viability. This concentration also produces a host of other negative conditions.

- Sprawl undermines the transition of the inner-city unskilled workforce to a high-tech workforce.
- Sprawl thereby weakens the international competitive positions of U.S. metropolitan areas.
- Sprawl reduces the efficiency of businesses and the productivity of agricultural land.
- Sprawl undermines equality of opportunity within metropolitan areas, thereby raising inner-city unemployment with all the resulting pernicious effects.
- Sprawl destroys the viability of inner-city schools and contributes to students' failure to make the proper labor-force transition.
- Sprawl breeds crime that drives viable firms and households out of cities, and weakens the ability of young people raised there to sustain themselves economically.
- Sprawl undermines middle-class security, especially the security of working-class households whose investments in home equities are jeopardized by racial transition.
- Sprawl damages the environment in terms of air pollution, and water pollution; it ruins historic buildings and wrecks environmentally sensitive sites.
- Sprawl undermines the sense of community in suburban areas, and the solidarity of our entire society by separating suburban residents from city ones.
- Sprawl makes urban development inefficient by generating indecisive governments, disputes, and delays that add to costs.

Richmond believes that a significant number of public policies at all levels have generated sprawl, and perpetuate it.

He catalogs these at length. He then presents a political analysis of why these forces are not likely to change.

After having set forth all these points in general, he applies the argument to the Chicago region in detail. He then sets forth his recommendations on how to attack sprawl and the many institutional supports underlying it. In this regard, he comes up with a more comprehensive set of ideas than anyone else. As a result, this document is an invaluable reference for both arguments against sprawl and possible tactics to remedy it. It has not been given widespread publicity, but it is a very solid linkage of causes and remedies.

Thompson, J. Phillip. 1996. "Urban Poverty and Race." In Julia Vitullo-Martin, ed., *Breaking Away: The Future of Cities*. New York: Twentieth Century Fund: 13-32.

This author discusses the status of poverty and its relationship to race in inner-city areas, primarily in reference to New York City. He points out that the middle-class is still dominant in most large American cities, but it has become a minority-group middle class as whites continue to leave the city. In six of the nation's eight largest cities, a majority of the population in 1990 consisted of minority-group members—only Philadelphia (48 percent minority) and San Diego (42 percent) were exceptions. In New York, the number of persons with incomes above the median remained about the same in the 1980s, but the ethnic composition changed to become minority-dominated, as the white population fell by 432,000.

Thompson reviews various theories of why poverty persists in inner-city neigh-borhoods.

- The *cultural deprivation theory* stresses that some families are less intelligent than others, and a deprived culture is partly a genetic phenomenon. A newer view is that poor families are stuck in poor communities, where conditions are ripe for a negative subculture to develop around excessive teenage sexual promiscuity, a separate street language, and a depreciation of academic achievement. Both views stress deviancy and immorality of behavior among many poor people, with the newer theory attributing the behavior to the spatial isolation of the poor and especially of the poor blacks from white culture. Christopher Jencks claims that centuries of racial subordination and prejudice have created an unwillingness among blacks to do certain types of work or to work in white cultural environments. Black alienation from certain types of jobs is rarely discussed in analyses of poverty.

- The *racial discrimination theory* says that black poverty in particular is caused primarily by continued racial discrimination and the resulting spatial segregation. Massey and Denton, advocates of this view, argue that housing discrimination isolates poor blacks in poverty-concentrated neighborhoods with other poor blacks as their only neighbors. But discrimination itself is not new; so how can it explain rising crime rates or family instability, which are recent developments? Massey and Denton claim that white prejudice and discrimination cause spatial isolation, which in turn results in cultural deprivation.

- The *structural transformation theory* claims that black unemployment results from a change in labor markets and industry that has shifted more jobs to the higher-skill category and moved industrial jobs out of big cities where

racial minorities live. William Julius Wilson is a leading proponent of this view. But unemployment does not explain many of the other pathologies of inner-city poverty areas. Wilson also claims the departure of middle-class blacks from poverty areas has removed good role models, and the resulting negative culture is the result of economic deprivation and lack of jobs. But is it not clear whether cultural traits of blacks, rather than discrimination by whites, causes whites not to hire black workers.

- The *social breakdown theory* claims that poverty itself does not cause a cultural shift to negative values. Many poor neighborhoods do not exhibit such traits—especially poor areas occupied by immigrants. There are a variety of cultures in poor neighborhoods, and only in those where family networks break down does the culture of poverty arise.

What remedies to alleviate poverty might be used? Cultural deprivation theorists stress the personal responsibility of the poor themselves, and claim they need to change their behavior. Their remedies involve orphanages for children of misbehaving mothers; forcing all poor people to work—including mothers; forcing fathers to pay for support for children; and making all government benefits temporary. (It appears that these arguments were embodied in the recent welfare "reform" bill.)

A major problem with this approach is that it assumes job opportunities exist for the poor with wages high enough to support decent living standards. This is not the case; public jobs programs would be necessary if all poor people were forced to work. Also, making all mothers work would reduce supervision over children and might worsen the children's behavior. Cultural deprivation theorists do not study or seem to care about the internal dynamics of poor communities, and pay too little attention to what might result if their remedies are tried.

Racial discrimination theorists want strong anti-discrimination measures, and a big effort to spatially integrate society racially. This would require immense movements of people, a scheme that is politically opposed by the vast majority of Americans, including Congress.

Structuralist theorists want labor market changes, such as the introduction of a public jobs Marshall Plan for inner cities, job travel and information center programs to link inner-city workers to suburban jobs, and provision of day care, job training and drug treatment programs for inner-city residents. These remedies are quite expensive.

Local-oriented strategies include enterprise and empowerment zones to improve conditions where the poor live now. The purpose is to create "vibrant" businesses where poor unemployed people are located. Community-based efforts fit into this view, and many such efforts are now underway across the nation. Building local housing is one of their major activities. A whole host of questions is raised by the author that might be answered by more careful study of community activities currently underway.

Thompson explores why the election of black mayors and city officials has not improved conditions in inner-city neighborhoods very much, if at all. And he asks why black leadership has not increased black participation in politics. Among the reasons he cites are: (1) Black mayors have no control over national trends toward decentralization of jobs; (2) The shift of population to the suburbs has reduced the national political power of big-city mayors of all types in Congress

and in the state legislature, reducing the willingness of these bodies to aid cities; (3) The need of individual cities to maintain favorable tax rates and bond ratings prevents mayors from engaging in redistributive activities—as observed by Paul Peterson in *City Limits*; (4) The fear of being charged with racism has prevented criticism of black local leadership by either whites or blacks; and (5) The civil rights movement has become conservative and has not shifted from national issues to local ones to support black local leaders.

HUD's rules against building public housing in poor communities have blocked the efforts of many black mayors to put new low-rise public housing units in inner-city poverty areas, thereby upgrading those areas. In New York City, court actions have prevented giving preference in public housing projects to persons living in nearby communities. Voting district formation has reduced representation by minorities on city councils and in Congress. Struggles over crime rates have pitted civil rights advocates—who want less incarceration of blacks—against local residents who want more secure neighborhoods. Similar struggles have occurred over schools. Those who want better schools have tried to shift disruptive students into separate "academies"—a move that is opposed by traditional civil rights advocates.

The problems of inner-city poverty demanded an agenda from black mayors dealing with neighborhood economic development, reform of education, police, human services, public housing bureaucracies, and relations with Latinos and Asians. Such an agenda might have required alteration of traditional liberal coalitions that elect black mayors, with possible fallout from municipal and teachers' unions, civil rights organizations, and fellow black politicians. Few black mayors have pursued such a politically risky and administratively arduous course. (31)

Thompson recommends supporting community-building strategies, because little help will come from the federal government. These strategies cannot end poverty, but they may improve the quality of life in inner-city areas.

URBAN RENEWAL

Calthorpe, Peter. G. 1993. *The Next American Metropolis: Ecology, Community, and the American Dream.* Princeton: Princeton University Press.

This book, written by an architect and urban planner, looks at the spirit of American communities and the "new urbanism" approach to altering that spirit. He primarily discusses changes in urban design, and presents relatively little quantified analysis. As the author says, "Social integration, economic efficiency, political equity, and environmental sustainability are the imperatives which order my thinking about the form of community" (11). He contrasts those themes to the excessive privatization and individualism he believes have been embodied in the suburban development process in the post-1945 period.

The scale of our environment is now set in proportion to large institutions and bureaucracies rather than community and neighborhood (11).

The suburb was the . . . physical expression of the privatization of life and specialization of place which marks our time (9).

The alternative to sprawl is simple and timely: neighborhoods of housing, parks, and schools placed within walking distance of shops, civic services, jobs, and transit—a modern version of the traditional town (16).

As is the case for most planners, Calthorpe dislikes the automobile and the scaling of the urban landscape to accommodate it. He wants to change the scale to allow walking to suburban transit and linkages among outlying areas and the downtown area by transit. Caltorpe wants to make both housing units and lots smaller, link neighborhoods by walking paths, and encourage accessory housing. He strongly supports regional growth management, channeling growth inward to in-fill sites and limiting outward extension.

At the core of this alternative, philosophically and practically, is the pedestrian. . . . Pedestrians are the lost measure of a community, they set the scale for both center and edge of our neighborhoods. . . . Two complementary strategies are needed. A tough regional plan which limits sprawl and channels development back to the city or around suburban transit stations; and a matching greenbelt strategy to preserve open space at the edge of the region. We cannot revitalize inner cities without changing the patterns of growth at the periphery of metropolitan regions; it is a simple matter of the finite distribution of resources. (20)

This calls for regional policies and governance which can both educate and guide the complex interaction of economics, ecology, jurisdiction, and social equity. . . . Adding transit oriented new towns and new growth areas can reinforce the city's role as the region's cultural and economic center (32).

Three constituencies—environmentalists, enlightened developers, and inner-city advocates—can find common purpose in regional planning goals. They can form a powerful coalition (36).

Identifying rational infill and revitalization districts, New Growth Areas and potential New Town sites should be the work of an agency which spans the numerous cities and counties within a metropolitan area. Lacking such entities, counties, air quality boards, and regional transportation agencies often take on the tasks without legal power to fully implement the results. Regional governments are needed if growth is to be managed and directed in a sustainable manner (51).

Suburbs are built upon a fundamentally wrong spirit and orientation:

The rise of the modern suburb is in part a manifestation of a deep cultural and political shift away from public life. . . . Socially, the house fortress represents a self-fulfilling prophecy. The more isolated people become and the less they share with others unlike themselves, the more they *do* have to fear. . . . The private domain, whether in a car, a home, or a subdivision, sets the direction of the modern suburb. . . In fact, one of the primary obstacles to innovations in community planning remains the impulse toward a more gated and private world (37).

Calthorpe's design strategy is based upon three major principles:

First . . . the regional structure of growth should be guided by the expansion of transit and a more compact urban form; second, . . . our ubiquitous single-use zoning should be replaced with standards for mixed-use, walkable neighborhoods; and third, . . our urban design policies should create

an architecture oriented toward the public domain and human dimension rather than the private domain and auto scale (41).

He advances the concept of the TOD, or Transit Oriented Development—a basic building block in his regional development scheme. It features "pedestrian pockets" within one-quarter of a mile of transit stops—an easy walking distance. These pockets contain mixed-use development including commercial centers and public services. Farther out from the stations are secondary areas containing primarily housing. He believes automobile usage in such communities would be much lower than it is now, because more people would walk to activities. There would be both urban TODs and neighborhood TODs (for lower-density areas). Average residential densities of 10 units per acre would be maintained to support bus service, with higher densities to support rail transit. In other areas, he recommends net densities of 18 units per acre. Calthorpe would also like a 40-60 percent split between transit and auto usage, even though that split still implies a majority of travel by autos.

His larger regional scheme shows transit stops one mile apart. Each TOD around such a stop contains 288.5 acres—a circle of 2,500 feet in radius. A key element in the planning process is what fraction of the land should be used for housing. At 40 percent, housing would consume 115.4 acres; at 65 percent, it would consume 187.5 acres. Next, he asks what average density of housing would prevail? Calthorpe suggests a range from 10 to 25 units per acre, but in another section, he indicates that neighborhood TODs should have minimum densities of 7 units per acre (5,600 persons per square mile) and a minimum average of 10 units per acre (8,000 persons per square mile—just a bit higher than the city of Los Angeles). In urban TODs, the minimum density should be 12 units per acre, with an average of 15 units, and with maximums set by local plans. At 15 units per net acre, the gross density would be 15,600 persons per square mile if the residential land coverage was 65 percent. Gross density would be 12,000 persons per square mile if residential coverage was 50 percent—the coverage used to calculate other statistics in this paragraph.

According to Calthorpe, secondary areas should have a minimum average density of 6 units per net acre, or 4,800 persons per square mile with 50 percent residential land coverage. This, he says, should be the minimum permissible density anywhere in the developed region.

Much of the book sets forth design guidelines for parks, commercial areas, transit stops, and a set of specific projects developed by Calthorpe embodying his ideas.

Clark, Charles S. 1995. "Revitalizing the Cities: Is Regional Planning the Answer?" *CQ Researcher*, 5, 38 (October 13): 897-920.

This article is an analysis of whether regional planning and other arrangements are necessary ingredients in any effective strategy to halt the decline of so many large cities. It is a broad overview of the issues involved condensed into a few pages. The analysis begins with a description of how out-migration to the suburbs is still occurring in large cities, partly in response to the much higher crime rates in the cities. Clark presents a potpourri of quotations on all sides of the issue, rather than a clear or straightforward analysis leading in a

single direction. As a result, the article presents few conclusive results. Studies showing linkages between suburban and city prosperity are cited. Proponents of regionalism, including David Rusk and Anthony Downs are quoted; and cities such as Portland and the Twin Cities are cited as models. Yet, "in all of U.S. history, voters have approved only 20 city-county consolidations while a hundred have been voted down, according to . . . HUD." (904) Selling regionalism as a way to help the poor is considered "the kiss of death" politically. The best way to proceed, says Clark, is to develop practical approaches to regional relationships and try to sell them in individual areas.

Katz, Peter. 1994. *The New Urbanism: Towards an Architecture of Community.* New York: McGraw Hill.

This book contains five very short essays on "the new urbanism," plus copious illustrated examples of projects carried out under that rubric. The authors include the primary players in this field: e.g., Peter Calthorpe, Andres Duany, and Elizabeth Plater-Zyberk. Calthorpe's essay is a very condensed version of his book (discussed earlier).

Andres Duany and Elizabeth Plater-Zyberk have written an essay about the neighborhood, the district, and the corridor. It is only a few pages long and has little or nothing to do with sprawl.

Elizabeth Moule and Stefanos Polyzoides provide an essay about the street, the block and the building. However, the scale of this article is too "micro" to be applicable to sprawl.

Todd W. Bressi's essay, entitled *Planning the American Dream* discusses the overall approach of the "new urbanists," repeating much of what is in Calthorpe's book. He claims that the suburban explosion after World Wars I and II achieved certain desirable outcomes, but at heavy costs. The suburban explosion "reinforced the Victorian notion that a neighborhood was a protective enclave requiring insulation from commerce, work, and traffic, and held that the functional and literal center of a neighborhood should be an elementary school." The suburbanization movement also "liberated significant numbers of people from crowded, unhealthy living conditions." But it created the following problems: (1) It raised the cost of homeownership and acceptable housing too high for many households; (2) It forced people to spend more and more time commuting [this point is debatable]; (3) It undermined the mobility of people who cannot afford cars or cannot drive them; (4) It created air pollution; (5) It absorbed attractive rural landscape into urban uses, and (6) Most important of all but most problematic—it undermined civic life.

The main principles of the new urbanism, as he describes them, are as follows:

- The center of each neighborhood should be defined by a public space and activated by locally oriented civic and commercial facilities.
- Each neighborhood should accommodate a range of household types and land uses.
- Cars should be kept in perspective.
- Architecture should respond to the surrounding fabric of buildings and spaces and to local traditions.

New urbanists draw upon several past traditions, including the City Beautiful and Town Planning movements.

> Calthorpe has written that in theory 2,000 homes, a million square feet of commercial space, parks, schools and day care could fit within a quarter-mile walk of a station, or about 120 acres.

The strategy of the new urbanists is to change local zoning regulations to force the adoption of their principles, or at least to permit them to be followed.

In fact, it has been difficult to implement TOD schemes, since most areas do not have rail transit systems. Some critics claim that the new urbanists emphasize visual style over planning substance. They claim that the large-scale proposals seem to continue sprawl, rather than change it. Moreover, the critics argue that the impact of the new urbanists' approach will be minimal unless some type of regional governance is more widely adopted. Finally, the new urbanists have largely ignored the growing divisions of wealth and power among households. As Katz notes: "New Urbanism is a welcome step forward, but it is only a step."

The remainder of the book is a series of illustrated case studies that detail the new urbanism approach to designing residential and nonresidential neighborhoods.

Ravitch, Diane. 1996. "The Problem of the Schools: A Proposal for Renewal." In Julia Vitullo-Martin, ed., *Breaking Away: The Future of Cities*. New York: Twentieth Century Fund 77-87.

The author criticizes New York's schools because they are run by a top-heavy bureaucracy that makes all decisions centrally and leaves almost no authority for decision making within individual schools themselves. The results are terrible—only about 50 percent of all students who enter high school graduate, even after 5 years of classes. According to Ravitch, we now demand that our schools educate all young people, something that was never done in the past. We must educate them, she says in order to prepare them for life in a high-tech world. To do this, we must abandon centralized control and change to a system in which "each school must be managed by a group of adults who have direct, personal, and professional responsibility—and accountability—for the success of their students." (81)

It may be that the best direction for reforming the schools is to seek a diversity of providers that are publicly monitored, rather than a bureaucratic system controlled by the mandates of a single government agency. What would a system look like in which a government did the steering and let many others do the rowing (82)?

She advocates three major principles for radical reform:

Autonomy—Each school should control its own budget and hire (and fire) its own teachers and other personnel. Each should be told how much money it has (based upon enrollments, plus allowances for disadvantaged students) and allowed to allocate that money as it sees fit—knowing that it would be rigorously audited by public officials.

Choice—Teachers should be able to freely decide where they will work, and students and parents should be able to decide where they want to send their children to school.

Quality—The centralized authorities should set standards for performance, periodically assess performances of every school, and constantly inform parents and the public of the results. Central authorities would also oversee large capital improvements, negotiate union contracts (without inhibiting schools from hiring whomever they wish), approve the creation of new schools, and audit performance and finances.

Schools that want to manage their own affairs should be allowed to conduct elections among staff and parents to become chartered schools, and immediately be given autonomy. This would permit successful schools to become self-governing right away. A second element of the strategy would include contracting out the management of several or many schools to specific organizations. A basic idea is to encourage as many new schools to be formed as possible. A third element in the strategy is to provide means-tested scholarships to poor students who could choose to use them in whatever schools they wanted. These would essentially be vouchers paid to the students or their parents, not to the institutions themselves—thereby finessing the religious school issue. This procedure has been successfully adopted in some other programs around the country.

REFERENCES

This chapter presents the bibliography of sprawl. Of the approximately 500 citations that follow, almost all (475) deal directly with sprawl, whether or not it is specifically identified by that term. Approximately five percent of the citations comprise general references and data sources. A number and letter appear after each citation and are found in the key below. The numbers serve to sort the literature into five impact categories— *Public/Private Capital and Operating Costs, Transportation and Travel Costs, Land/Natural Habitat Preservation, Quality of Life, and Social Issues*—plus a sixth category termed *Related Materials*. The letters sort the literature by the type of analysis used in the study. These are *descriptive, secondary, case study, engineering/per capita, retrospective, prospective, and econometric/regression analyses*. The summation of numbers and letters for the entire bibliography serves as the basis for statements made concerning both the literature and analysis concentrations of Chapter 8.

KEY

NUMBER (SUBSTANTIVE CONCERN)		LETTER (TYPE OF ANALYSIS)	
1	Public/Private Capital and Operating Costs	A	Descriptive/Conceptual Analysis
2	Transportation and Travel Costs	B	Secondary/Survey Analysis (Government Data or Other Sources)
3	Land/Natural Habitat Preservation	C	Case Study (Single or Multiple Locations)
4	Quality of Life	D	Engineering/Per Capita Analysis
5	Social Issues	E	Retrospective Analysis
6	Related Material	F	Prospective Analysis
		G	Econometric/Regression Analysis

Aberger, Will, and Luther Propst. 1992. *Successful Communities: Managing Growth to Protect Distinctive Local Resources.* Washington, DC: Conservation Foundation. **[3C]**

Abrams, Charles. 1971. *The Language of Cities.* New York: Viking Press. **[6A]**

Adams, Thomas, Edward M. Bassett, and Robert Whitten. 1929. *Neighborhood and Community Planning: Regional Survey,* Vol. VII. Committee on Regional Plan of New York and Its Environs. **[3B]**

Adelaja, A. O.; D. Kerr; and K. Rose-Tank. 1989. "Economic and Equity Implications of Land Use Zoning in Suburban Agriculture." *Journal of Agricultural Ethics* 2: 97-112. **[3G]**

Al-Mosaind, M. A.; K. J. Dueker; and J. G. Strathman. 1993. "Light Rail Transit Stations and Property Values: A Hedonic Price Approach." *Transportation Research Record* 1400: 90–4. **[2G]**

Altshuler, Alan A. 1977. "Review of *The Costs of Sprawl.*" *Journal of the American Planning Association* 43, 2: 207-9. **[1B]**

Altshuler, Alan A., and Jose A. Gomez-Ibanez. 1993. *Regulation for Revenue: The Political Economy of Land Use Exactions.* Washington, DC: Brookings Institution. **[1A]**

American Farmland Trust (AFT). 1986. *Density-Related Public Costs.* Washington, DC: AFT. **[1D]**

American Farmland Trust. 1992a. *Does Farmland Protection Pay? The Cost of Community Services in Three Massachusetts Towns.* Washington, DC: AFT. **[1C]**

American Farmland Trust. 1992b. *The Cost of Community Services in Three Pioneer Valley, Connecticut, Towns: Agawam, Deerfield, and Gill.* Washington, DC: AFT. **[1C]**

American Farmland Trust. 1994. *Farming on the Edge: A New Look at the Importance and Vulnerability of Agriculture Near American Cities.* Washington, DC: AFT. **[3B]**

American Farmland Trust. 1997. *Farming on the Edge II.* DeKalb, IL: Northern Illinois University. **[3B]**

American Planning Association (APA). 1997. *Growing Smart Legislative Guidebook (Phase I - Interim Edition).* Chicago, IL: APA. **[4A]**

Anderson, William P.; Pavlos S. Kanaroglou; and Eric J. Miller. 1996. "Urban Form. Energy and the Environment: A Review of Issues, Evidence and Policy." *Urban Studies* 33, 1: 7-35. **[4B]**

Andrews, James H. 1996. "Going by the Numbers." *Planning* (September): 14-18. **[1D]**

Andrews, Marcellus. 1994. "On the Dynamics of Growth and Poverty in Cities." *Citiscape* 1, 1 (August): 53-73. **[5B]**

Apogee Research, Inc. 1994. *The Costs of Transportation: Final Report.* Conservation Law Foundation. March. **[2D]**

Archer, R. W. 1973. "Land Speculation and Scattered Development: Failures in the Urban-Fringe Market. *Urban Studies* 10, 3: 367-72. **[3G]**

Archimore, A. 1993. "Pulling the Community Back into Community Retail." *Urban Land* 52, 8: 33-8. **[5A]**

Arendt, Randall. 1994a. *Designing Open Space Subdivisions: A Practical Step-by-Step Approach.* Natural Lands Trust, Inc. **[3A]**

Arendt, Randall. 1994b. *Rural by Design.* Washington, DC: American Planning Association. **[3C]**

Arendt, Randall. 1996. *Conservation Design for Subdivisions: A Practical Guide to Creating Open Space Networks.* Washington DC: Island Press. **[3A]**

Arendt, Randall. 1997. *Growing Greener.* Washington, DC: Island Press. **[3A]**

Armstrong, R. J., Jr. 1994. *Impacts of Commuter Rail Service as Reflected in Single-Family Residential Property Values.* Paper presented at the 73rd Annual Meeting of the Transportation Research Board, Washington, DC. **[2G]**

Arrington, G. B., Jr. 1995. *Beyond the Field of Dreams: Light Rail and Growth Management in Portland.* Portland, OR: Tri-Met. **[2C]**

Audirac, Ivonne; A. H. Shermyen; and M. T. Smith. 1990. "Ideal Urban Form and Visions of the Good Life: Florida's Growth Management Dilemma." *Journal of the American Planning Association* 56 (Autumn): 470-482. **[4C]**

Audirac, Ivonne, and Maria Zifou. 1989. *Urban Development Issues: What is Controversial in Urban Sprawl? An Annotated Bibliography of Often-Overlooked Sources.* Council of Planning Librarians. CPL Bibliography 247. **[6A]**

Avin, Uri P. 1993. *A Review of the Cost of Providing Government Services to Alternative Residential Patterns.* Columbia, MD: LDR International. **[1B]**

Babcock, Richard F. 1966. *The Zoning Game.* Madison, WI: University of Wisconsin Press. **[6A]**

Bahl, Roy M. 1968. "A Land Speculation Model: The Role of the Property Tax as a Constraint to Urban Sprawl." *Journal of Regional Science* 8, 2: 199-208. **[1G]**

Baldassare, Mark. 1986. *Trouble in Paradise: The Suburban Transformation of America.* New York: Columbia University Press. **[5B]**

Baltimore County. 1978. *Growth Management Program Technical Memorandum No. 11, Environmental Assessment.* Towson, Baltimore County, MD. **[3A]**

Bank of America, California Resources Agency, Greenbelt Alliance, Low-Income Housing Fund. 1995. *Beyond Sprawl: New Patterns of Growth to Fit the New California.* San Francisco: Bank of America et al. **[1B]**

Barnett, Jonathan. 1995. *The Fractured Metropolis: Improving the New City, Restoring the Old City, Reshaping the Region.* New York: HarperCollins. **[5B]**

Baumann D., and B. Dziegielewski. 1990. "Urban Water Demand Forecasting and Analysis of Conservation." London: Planning and Management Consultants Ltd. **[1G]**

Beatley, Timothy, and David Brower. 1993. "Sustainability Comes to Main Street." *Journal of the American Planning Association* 59, 5. **[4A]**

Beaumont, Constance. 1994. *How Superstore Sprawl Can Harm Communities—And What Citizens Can Do About It.* Washington, DC: National Trust for Historic Preservation. **[4A]**

Beaumont, Constance. 1996a. *Historic Preservation.* Washington, DC: National Trust for Historic Preservation. **[4A]**

Beaumont, Constance. 1996b. *Smart States, Better Communities: How State Governments Can Help Citizens Preserve Their Communities.* Washington, DC: National Trust for Historic Preservation. **[4A]**

Beaumont, Constance. 1997. *Better Models for Superstores: Alternatives to Big-Box Sprawl.* Washington, DC: National Trust for Historic Preservation. **[4A]**

Bernick, M., and Robert Cervero. 1994. *Transit-based Residential Development in the United States: A Review of Recent Experiences.* Working Paper 611. Institute of Urban and Regional Development, University of California at Berkeley. March. **[2B]**

Berry, David, and Thomas Plaut. 1978. "Effects of Urbanization on Agricultural Activities." *Growth and Change* 9, 3: 2-8. **[3C]**

Black, J. Thomas. 1996. "The Economics of Sprawl." *Urban Land* 55, 3: 6–52. **[1A]**

Blair, John P.; Staley, Samuel R.; and Zhang Zhongcai. 1996. "The Central City Elastic Hypothesis: A Critical Appraisal of Rusk's Theory of Urban Development." *Journal of the American Planning Association* 63, 2 (Summer): 345. **[5G]**

Blomquist, Glenn C.; Mark C. Berger; and John P Hoehn. 1988. "New Estimates of Quality of Life in Urban Areas." *American Economic Review* 78, 1: 89-107. **[4G]**

Bohi, Douglas R., and Joel Darmstadter. 1994. "Twenty Years after the Energy Crisis: What Lessons Were Learned?" *Resources* 116: 16-20. **[4A]**

Bookout, L. 1992. "Neotraditional Town Planning: The Test of the Marketplace." *Urban Land* 51, 6: 12-17. **[3C]**

Bookout, L., and J. Wentling. 1988. "Density by Design." *Urban Land* 47: 10-15. [3C]

Bourne, Larry S. 1992. "Self-Fulfilling Prophecies? Decentralization, Inner City Decline, and the Quality of Urban Life." *Journal of the American Planning Association* 58: 509-513. [5B]

Bradbury, Katharine L.; Anthony Downs; and Kenneth Small. 1982. *Urban Decline and the Future of American Cities*. Washington, DC: Brookings Institution. [5B]

Bradford, Susan. 1996. "The New Hometowns; Planned Unit Developments." *Builder* 19, 7: 96. [5A]

Brindle, Ray. 1994. "Lies, Damned Lies and 'Automobile Dependence.'" *Australian Transport Research Forum* 19. [2B]

Brower, David, David Dodschalk, and Douglas R. Porter. 1989. *Understanding Growth Management: Critical Issues and a Research Agenda*. Washington, DC: Urban Land Institute. [3A]

Brueckner, J. K. 1990. "Growth Controls and Land Values in an Open City." *Land Economics* 66: 237-248. [1G]

Bruegmann, Robert. 1998. "Blight, Then Sprawl: Is the American City Ready for Reform?" Paper prepared for Drachman Institute Conference, "Urban Growth: Addressing the Reality of Suburbia," Phoenix, Arizona. May. [4A]

Buchanan, Shepard C., and Bruce A. Weber. 1982. "Growth and Residential Property Taxes: A Model for Estimating Direct and Indirect Population Impacts." *Land Economics* 58, 3 (August): 325-37. [1G]

Burchell, Robert W. 1990. "Fiscal Impact Analysis: State of the Art and State of the Practice," in Susan G. Robinson, ed., *Financing Growth: Who Benefits? Who Pays? and How Much?* Government Finance Officers Association. [1A]

Burchell, Robert W. 1992a. *Impact Assessment of the New Jersey Interim State Development and Redevelopment Plan, Report II: Research Findings*. Trenton: New Jersey Office of State Planning. [1F]

Burchell, Robert W. 1992b. *Impact Assessment of the New Jersey Interim State Development and Redevelopment Plan, Report III: Supplemental AIPLAN Assessment*. Trenton: New Jersey Office of State Planning. [1F]

Burchell, Robert W. 1997a. *Fiscal Impacts of Alternative Land Development Patterns in Michigan: The Costs of Current Development Versus Compact Growth*. Southeast Michigan Regional Council of Governments. [1F]

Burchell, Robert W. 1997b. *South Carolina Infrastructure Study: Projection of Statewide Infrastructure Costs 1995-2015*. New Brunswick, NJ: Center for Urban Policy Research, Rutgers University. [1F]

Burchell, Robert W., and David Listokin. 1978. *The Fiscal Impact Handbook: Estimating Local Costs and Revenues of Land Development*. New Brunswick, NJ: Center for Urban Policy Research, Rutgers University. [1D]

Burchell, Robert W., and David Listokin. 1982. *Energy and Land Use*. New Brunswick, NJ: Center for Urban Policy Research, Rutgers University. [4A]

Burchell, Robert W., and David Listokin. 1990. *Fiscal Studies*. Report to the Governor's Commission on Growth in the Chesapeake Bay Region. Annapolis, MD: 2020 Commission. [1B]

Burchell, Robert W., and David Listokin. 1991. *Fiscal Impact Analysis: A Manual and Software for Builders and Developers*. Washington, DC: National Association of Home Builders. [1D]

Burchell, Robert W., and David Listokin. 1994a. *Fiscal Impact Procedures and the Fiscal Impact Hierarchy*. Paper prepared for the Association for Budgeting and Financial Management, Annual Conference on Public Budgeting and Finance, Washington, DC. October. [1A]

Burchell, Robert W., and David Listokin. 1994b. *The Economic Effects of Trend versus Vision Growth in the Lexington Metropolitan Area*. Report prepared for Bluegrass Tomorrow, Lexington, KY. November. **[1F]**

Burchell, Robert W., and David Listokin. 1995a. *Land, Infrastructure, Housing Costs, and Fiscal Impacts Associated with Growth: The Literature on the Impacts of Traditional versus Managed Growth*. Paper prepared for "Alternatives to Sprawl" Conference, Brookings Institution, Washington, DC. March. **[1B]**

Burchell, Robert W., and David Listokin. 1995b. *The Economic Impacts of Trend versus Vision Development in the Lexington (Kentucky) Metropolitan Area*. Report prepared for Blue Grass Tomorrow. January. **[1F]**

Burchell, Robert W., and David Listokin. 1996. *Determinants of Municipal and School District Costs*. Report prepared for Sterling Forest Corporation, Tuxedo, New York. **[1G]**

Burchell, Robert W., David Listokin, and William R. Dolphin. 1980. *Practitioner's Guide to Fiscal Impact Assessment*. New Brunswick, NJ: Center for Urban Policy Research. **[1D]**

Burchell, Robert W., David Listokin, and William R. Dolphin. 1985. *The New Practitioner's Guide to Fiscal Impact Assessment*. New Brunswick, NJ: Center for Urban Policy Research. **[1D]**

Burchell, Robert W., David Listokin, and William R. Dolphin. 1994. *The Development Impact Assessment Handbook*. Washington, DC: Urban Land Institute. **[1G]**

Burchell, Robert W., and Harvey S. Moskowitz. 1995. *Impact Assessment of DELEP CCMP versus STATUS QUO on Twelve Municipalities in the DELEP Region*. Report prepared for the Local Governments Committee of the Delaware Estuary Program. Philadelphia, PA. August 15. **[1F]**

Burchell, Robert W., and Emilie Schmeidler. 1993. *The Demographic and Social Difference Between Central Cities and Suburbs as They Relate to the Job Fulfillment of Urban Residents*. Paper presented at the National Conference on Metropolitan America in Transition: Implications for Land Use and Transportation Planning. Cambridge, MA: Lincoln Institute of Land Policy. **[5C]**

Burchell, Robert W., and Naveed A. Shad. 1998. "The Incidence of Sprawl in the United States." Washington, DC: Transportation Cooperative Research Program (TCRP H-10) (forthcoming). **[4F]**

Burnell, James, and George Galster. 1992. "Quality of Life Measurement and Urban Size." *Urban Studies* 29, 5: 727-35. **[4B]**

"Bye-bye Suburban Dream: Fifteen Ways to Fix the Suburbs." 1995. *Newsweek* CXXV, 20 (April). **[5A]**

California Department of Treasury, Office of Planning and Research (OP&R). 1982. *Paying the Piper: New Ways to Pay for Public Infrastructure in California*. Sacramento, CA: California Department of Treasury. December. **[1C]**

Calthorpe, Peter G. 1993. *The Next American Metropolis: Ecology, Community, and the American Dream*. Princeton: Princeton University Press. **[4A]**

Cambridge Systematics. 1994. *The Effects of Land Use and Travel Demand Strategies on Commuting Behavior*. Washington, DC: U.S. Department of Transportation, Federal Highway Administration. **[2C]**

Cameron, Michael W. 1994. *Efficiency and Fairness on the Road: Strategies for Unsnarling Traffic in Southern California*. New York: Environmental Defense Fund. **[2A]**

Carlson, Allan. 1996. "Two Cheers for the Suburbs." *American Enterprise* 7, 6. **[5A]**

Carson, Richard H. 1998. *Paying for Our Growth in Oregon* (the POGO Report). Portland, OR: New Oregon Meridian Press. **[1B]**

Cervero, Robert. 1986. *Suburban Gridlock*. New Brunswick, NJ: Center for Urban Policy Research, Rutgers University. **[2C]**

Cervero, Robert. 1989. *America's Suburban Activity Centers: The Land Use–Transportation Link.* Boston, MA: Unwin-Hyman. **[2B]**

Cervero, Robert. 1991a. "Congestion Relief: The Land-Use Alternative." *Journal of Planning Education and Research* 10: 119-29. **[2G]**

Cervero, Robert. 1991b. "Land Use and Travel at Suburban Activity Centers." *Transportation Quarterly* 45, 4: 479-491. **[2G]**

Cervero, Robert. 1994a. "Transit-Focused Development: Does It Draw People into Transit and Buses?" *IURD Universe* 4: 3-5. **[2G]**

Cervero, Robert. 1994b. "Transit Villages: from Idea to Implementation." *Access* 5: 8-13. **[2G]**

Cervero, Robert. 1996. "Jobs-Housing Balance Revisited." *Journal of the American Planning Association* 62, 4: 492-511. **[4B]**

Cervero, Robert. Forthcoming 1998. *The Transit Metropolis.* New York, NY: Island Press. **[2B]**

Cervero, Robert, and Kang-Li Wu. 1996. "Subcentering and Commuting: Evidence from the San Francisco Bay Area, 1980-1990." Paper presented at the 1996 TRED Conference on Transportation and Land Use. Cambridge, MA: Lincoln Institute. October. **[2G]**

Cervero, Robert; M. Bernick; and J. Gilbert. 1994. *Market Opportunities and Barriers to Transit-Based Development in California.* Working Paper 621. Institute of Urban and Regional Development, University of California at Berkeley. **[2C]**

Cervero, Robert, and R. Gorham. 1995. "Commuting in Transit Versus Automobile Neighborhoods." *Journal of the American Planning Association* 61, 2: 210-225. **[2C]**

Cervero, Robert, and Kara Kockelman. 1996. "Travel Demand and the 3Ds: Density, Diversity, and Design." *Transportation Research Digest* 2, 3: 199-219. **[2G]**

Cervero, Robert; Timothy Rood; and Bruce Appleyard. 1997. "Job Accessibility as a Performance Indicator: An Analysis of Trends and Their Social Policy Implications in the San Francisco Bay Area." Institute for Urban Regional Development. University of California at Berkeley. **[2G]**

CH2M Hill. 1993. *Cost of Providing Government Services to Alternative Residential Patterns: Literature Review.* Maryland•Pennsylvania•Virginia: Chesapeake Bay Program. **[1A]**

Chesapeake Bay Executive Council. 1988. *Population Growth and Development in the Chesapeake Bay Watershed to the Year 2020: The Report of the Year 2020 Panel of Experts.* Annapolis, MD: Chesapeake Bay Executive Council. **[3B]**

City of San Diego. 1984. *A Review and Evaluation of Progress in Achieving the Goals and Objectives of the City's Residential Growth Management Strategy.* San Diego, CA. **[3E]**

Clark, Charles S. 1995. "Revitalizing the Cities: Is Regional Planning the Answer?" *CQ Researcher* 5, 38 (October 13): 897-920. **[5B]**

Clavell, Pierre. 1986. *The Progressive City.* New Brunswick, NJ: Rutgers University Press. **[5A]**

Clawson, Marion. 1962. "Urban Sprawl and Speculation in Suburban Land." *Land Economics* 38, 2: 99-111. **[3G]**

Cochrun, Stephen E. 1994. "Understanding and Enhancing Neighborhood Sense of Community." *Journal of Planning Literature* 9, 1: 92-99. **[4B]**

Consultants. 1980. "Source Material Task II—Needs Assessment for the New Jersey Statewide Water Supply Plan." New Jersey Department of Environmental Protection, Division of Water Resources. **[1G]**

Cook, Christine C. 1988. "Components of Neighborhood Satisfaction: Responses from Urban and Suburban Single-Parent Women." *Environment and Behavior* 20, 2: 115-149. **[4B]**

Coughlin, Robert E., and John C. Keene. 1981. *The Protection of Farmland: A Reference Guidebook for State and Local Governments.* Report prepared for the National Agricultural Lands Study. Amherst, MA: Regional Science Research Institute. **[3A]**

Crane, R. 1996. "Cars and Drivers in the New Suburbs: Linking Access to Travel in Neo-traditional Planning." *Journal of the American Planning Association* 62, 1: 51-65. **[2B]**

Cushing, Brian J. 1987. "Location Specific Amenities, Topography, and Population Migration." *Annals of Regional Science* 21, 2: 74-85. **[4B]**

Dahl, Thomas E. 1990. *Wetlands Losses in the United States: 1780s-1980s.* Washington, DC: U.S. Department of the Interior, Fish and Wildlife Service. **[3B]**

Daniels, P. W. 1972. "Transport Changes Generated by Decentralized Offices." *Regional Studies* 6: 273-89. **[2C]**

Daniels, T. L., and J. W. Keller. 1991. "What Do You Do When Wal-Mart Comes to Town?" *Small Town* (September-October): 14-18. **[5B]**

Davis, Judy. 1993. "The Commuting Patterns of Exurban Residents." *Urban Geography* 14, 1: 7-29. **[2G]**

Davis, Judy, and Samuel Seskin. 1997. "Impacts of Urban Form on Travel Behavior." *The Urban Lawyer* 29, 2 (Spring). **[2B]**

Davis, Mary. 1993. "The Gautreaux Assisted Housing Program." In Thomas C. Kingsley and Margery A. Turner, eds., *Housing Markets and Residential Mobility.* Washington, DC: Urban Institute Press: 243–252. **[5C]**

DeChiara, Joseph, and Lee E. Koppelman. 1975. *Manual of Housing/Planning and Design Criteria.* Englewood Cliffs, NJ: Prentice-Hall. **[6A]**

DeCorla-Souza, P. 1992. *The Impacts of Alternative Urban Development Patterns on Highway System Performance.* Paper presented at Institute of Transportation Engineers International Conference, Washington, DC. **[2B]**

DeCorla-Souza P., Rathi, Ajay K., and Caldwell. 1992. "Nationwide Investment Requirements for New Urban Highway Capacity Under Alternative Scenarios." *Transportation Research Record* 1359:57-67. **[2B]**

DeGrove, John M. 1989. "Growth Management and Governance." In D. Brown et al., *Understanding Growth Management.* Washington, DC: Urban Land Institute. **[3A]**

DeGrove, John M. 1990. "The Pay As You Go Challenge: Financial Management in a Growth Environment." In Susan G. Robinson, ed. *Financing Growth: Who Benefits? Who Pays? How Much?* Washington, DC: Government Finance Officers Association. **[1B]**

Delafons, John. 1962. *Land Use Controls in the United States.* Cambridge, MA: Harvard-MIT Joint Center for Urban Studies. **[6A]**

Delucchi, M. A. 1996. *The Annualized Social Cost of Motor-Vehicle Use in the U.S., 1990-1991: Summary of Theory, Data, Methods, and Results.* Davis, CA: Institute of Transportation Studies. August. **[2B]**

Devaney, F. 1992. *Housing in America: 1989/90.* Washington, DC: Bureau of the Census. **[5F]**

Diamond, Henry L., and Noonan, Patrick F. 1996. *Land Use in America.* Washington, DC: Island Press. **[3A]**

Dougharty, Laurence; Sandra Tapella; and Gerald Sumner. 1975. *Municipal Service Pricing Impacts on Fiscal Position.* Santa Monica, CA: RAND. **[2G]**

Dowall, David E. 1984. *The Suburban Squeeze.* Berkeley, CA: University of California Press. **[5B]**

Dowall, David E., and John Landis. 1982. "Land Use Controls and Housing Costs: An Examination of San Francisco Bay Area Communities." *American Real Estate and Urban Economics Association Journal* 10 (Spring): 67-93. **[1C]**

Downing, Paul B., ed. 1977. *Local Services Pricing and Their Effect on Urban Spatial Structure.* Vancouver: University of British Columbia Press. **[1G]**

Downing, P. B., and R. D. Gustely. 1977. "The Public Service Costs of Alternative Development Patterns: A Review of the Evidence." In P. B. Downing, ed., *Local Service Pricing Policies and Their Effect on Urban Spatial Structure.* Vancouver: University of British Columbia Press. **[1G]**

Downs, Anthony. 1970. "Uncompensated Nonconstructive Costs Which Urban Highways and Urban Renewal Impose Upon Residential Households." In Julius Margolis, ed., *The Analysis of Public Output.* New York, NY: National Bureau of Economic Research, Inc. **[2D]**

Downs, Anthony. 1973. *Opening Up the Suburbs: An Urban Strategy for America.* New Haven, CT: Yale University Press. **[5A]**

Downs, Anthony. 1981. *Neighborhoods and Urban Development.* Washington, DC: Brookings Institution. **[5A]**

Downs, Anthony. 1985 *The Revolution in Real Estate Finance.* Washington, DC: Brookings Institution. **[6A]**

Downs, Anthony. 1992. *Stuck in Traffic: Coping with Peak Hour Traffic Congestion.* Washington, DC: Brookings Institution; and Cambridge, MA: Lincoln Institute of Land Policy. **[2B]**

Downs, Anthony. 1994. *New Visions for Metropolitan America.* Washington, DC: Brookings Institution; and Cambridge, MA: Lincoln Institute of Land Policy. **[5A]**

Drucker, Peter F. 1989. "Information and the Future of the City." *Urban Land* 48: 38-9. **[5A]**

Drucker, Peter F. 1992. "People, Work, and the Future of the City." In *Managing the Future.* New York, NY: Dutton: 125-129. **[5B]**

Duany, Andres, and Elizabeth Plater-Zyberk. 1995. "Neighborhoods and Suburbs." *Design Quarterly* (March): 10. **[5A]**

Dubin, R. 1991. "Commuting Patterns and Firm Decentralization." *Land Economics* 67: 121-129. **[2G]**

Dueker, K. J.; J. G. Strathman; I. P. Levin; and A. G. Phipps. 1983. "Rural Residential Development Within Metropolitan Areas." *Computers, Environment and Urban Systems* 8: 121-129. **[5B]**

Duensing, Edward. 1977. *Suburban Shopping Centers versus the Central Business District: A Bibliography.* Monticello, IL: Vance Bibliographies. **[6A]**

Duffy, N. E. 1994. "The Determinants of State Manufacturing Growth Rates: A Two-Digit-Level Analysis." *Journal of Regional Science* 34 (2): 137-162. **[5G]**

Duncan, James E. et al. 1989. *The Search for Efficient Urban Growth Patterns.* Tallahassee: Florida Department of Community Affairs. **[1D]**

Dunphy, R. T., and K. M. Fisher. 1994. *Transportation, Congestion, and Density: New Insights.* Paper presented at the 73rd Annual Meeting of the Transportation Research Board, Washington, DC. January. **[2B]**

Dunphy, R. T.; D. L. Brett; S. Rosen-bloom; and A. Bald. 1997. *Moving Beyond Gridlock: Traffic and Development.* Washington, DC: ULI-Urban Land Institute. **[2B]**

DuPage County Development Department. 1989, 1991. *Impacts of Development on DuPage County Property Taxes.* DuPage County, IL: DuPage County Regional Planning Commission. **[1G]**

Durand, Roger; Kim Hill; and Laura Roy. 1986. "Citizen Reactions to Urban Growth: Attitudes Toward Quality of Life and Local Public Services in an Expanding Sunbelt Community." *Journal of Urban Affairs* 8 (Fall): 15-26. **[4B]**

Dyckman, John W. 1976. *Speculations on Future Urban Form.* Working Paper, Johns Hopkins University, Center for Metropolitan Planning and Research. **[5A]**

Dziegielewski, B., and J. J. Boland. 1989. "Forecasting Water Use: The IWR—MAIN Model." *Water Resources Bulletin* 25, 1 (February). **[1G]**

Dzurik, Andrew. 1993. "Transportation Costs of Urban Sprawl: A Review of the Literature." *State Transportation Policy Initiative.* Center for Urban Transportation Research. November. **[5A]**

ECONorthwest. 1994. *Evaluation of No Growth and Slow Growth Policies for the Portland Region.* Portland, OR: Metropolitan Portland Government. **[1B]**

ECONorthwest. 1996. *Summary: Technical Reports for 2040 Means Business.* ECONorthwest. November. **[6A]**

ECONorthwest, Parsons Brinckerhoff Quade and Douglas, and COMSIS Corporation. 1995. *Least-Cost Planning: Principles, Applications, and Issues.* Washington, DC: U.S. Department of Transportation, Federal Highway Administration. **[2D]**

Ehrenberg, R. G., and R. S. Smith. 1994. *Modern Labor Economics: Theory and Public Policy.* 5th ed. HarperCollins. **[6A]**

Ellwood, David T. 1986. "The Spatial Mismatch Hypothesis: Are There Teen-age Jobs Missing in the Ghetto?" In Richard B. Freeman and Harry J. Holzer, eds., *The Black Youth Employment Crisis.* Chicago, IL: University of Chicago Press. **[5B]**

Environmental Protection Agency (EPA). 1971. *Community Noise.* Washington, DC: U.S. Government Printing Office. **[4D]**

Environmental Protection Agency (EPA). 1973. *The Quality of Life Concept: A Potential New Tool for Decision Makers.* Washington, DC: EPA, Office of Research and Monitoring, Environmental Studies Division. **[4B]**

Etzioni, Amitai. 1993. *The Spirit of Community: Rights, Responsibilities, and the Communitarian Agenda.* New York: Crown Publishers. **[4A]**

European Conference of Ministers of Transport. 1994. *Short-Distance Passenger Travel.* Report of 96th Round Table on Transport Economics, Paris, France. **[2B]**

Evaluation of City of San Diego Growth Management Program. 1978. San Diego, CA: San Diego Area Governments (SANDAG). **[3E]**

Ewing, Reid. 1991. *Developing Successful New Communities.* Washington, DC: Urban Land Institute. **[4A]**

Ewing, Reid. 1994. "Characteristics, Causes, and Effects of Sprawl: A Literature Review." *Environmental and Urban Issues* (Winter): 1-15. **[2A]**

Ewing, Reid. 1995a. *Best Development Practices: Doing the Right Thing and Making Money at the Same Time.* Chicago: American Planning Association. **[3A]**

Ewing, Reid, 1995b. "Beyond Density, Mode Choice, and Single-Purpose Trips." *Transportation Quarterly* 49, 4:15-24. **[2G]**

Ewing, Reid, 1995c. "Measuring Transportation Performance." *Transportation Quarterly* 49, 1:91-104. **[2G]**

Ewing, Reid. 1997. "Is Los Angeles-Style Sprawl Desirable?" *Journal of the American Planning Association* 63, 1 (Winter): 107-126. **[4A]**

Ewing, Reid. 1997b. *Transportation and Land Use Innovations.* Chicago, IL: Planners Press, American Planning Association. **[4A]**

Ewing, Reid; P. Haliyur; and G. W. Page. 1994. "Getting Around a Traditional City, a Suburban PUD, and Everything In-Between." *Transportation Research Record* 1466: 53-62. **[2C]**

Ewing, Reid; MaryBeth DeAnna; and Shi-Chiang Li. 1996. "Land-Use Impacts on Trip Generation Rates." *Transportation Research Record* 1518: 1-7. **[2C]**

Fannie Mae. 1985, 1989, 1992, 1994, 1996. *Survey of Residential Satisfaction of Housing Occupants.* Washington, DC: Federal National Mortgage Association (Fannie Mae). **[4B]**

Feagin, Joe R., and Robert Parker. 1990. *Building American Cities: The Urban Real Estate Game.* 2d ed. Englewood Cliffs, NJ: Prentice Hall. **[5A]**

Federal Bureau of Investigation (FBI). 1996. *Crime in the United States.* Press Release. U.S. Department of Justice, Federal Bureau of Investigation. October 13. **[4B]**

Federal Highway Administration. 1997. *Our Nation's Travel: 1995 NPTS Early Results Report.* Lanham, MD: Nationwide Personal Transportation Survey (NTPS). **[2B]**

Fischel, William A. 1985. *The Economics of Zoning Laws: A Property Rights Approach to American Land Use Controls.* Baltimore: Johns Hopkins University Press. **[1G]**

Fischel, William A. 1990. *Do Growth Controls Matter?* Cambridge, MA: Lincoln Institute of Land Policy. May. **[1C]**

Fischel, William A. 1997. Comment on Carl Abbott's "The Portland Region: Where City and Suburbs Talk to Each Other—and Often Agree." *Housing Policy Debate* 8, 1: 65-73. **[5A]**

Fischer, Paul B. 1991. *Is Housing Mobility an Effective Anti-Poverty Strategy? An Examination of the Cincinnati Experience.* Cincinnati, OH: Stephen H. Wilder Foundation. **[5C]**

Fishman, Robert. 1987. *Bourgeois Utopia: The Rise and Fall of Suburbia.* New York: Basic Books. **[5B]**

Florida Advisory Council on Intergovernmental Relations (FACIR). 1986. *Impact Fees in Florida.* Tallahassee, FL: FACIR. November. **[1D]**

Florida Growth Management Act. 1985. *Local Government and Comprehensive Planning and Land Development Regulation Act of 1985.* **[6A]**

Fodor, Eben V. 1997. "The Real Cost of Growth in Oregon." *Population and Environment* 18, 4. **[1D]**

Foster, Kathryn A. 1996. "Specialization in Government: The Uneven Use of Special Service Districts in Metropolitan Areas." *Urban Affairs Review* 31, 3: 283-313. **[1B]**

Frank, James E. 1989. *The Costs of Alternative Development Patterns: A Review of the Literature.* Washington, DC: Urban Land Institute. **[1B]**

Frank, L. D., and Gary Pivo. 1994. *The Relationship Between Land Use and Travel Behavior in the Puget Sound Region.* WA-RD 351.1. Olympia, WA: Washington State Department of Transportation. **[2C]**

Freilich, Robert H. 1980. *Saving the Land: The Utilization of Modern Techniques of Growth Management to Preserve Rural and Agricultural America.* Illinois Farmers Home Administration. **[3A]**

Freilich, Robert H., Elizabeth A. Garvin, and S. Mark White. 1993. "Economic Development and Public Transit: Making the Most of the Washington Growth Management Act." *University of Puget Sound Law Review* 16 (Spring): 949. **[2C]**

Freilich, Robert H., and Bruce G. Peshoff. 1997. "The Social Costs of Sprawl." *The Urban Lawyer* 29, 2: 183-198. **[5B]**

Freilich, Robert H., and S. Mark White. 1991. "Transportation Congestion and Growth Management: Comprehensive Approaches to Resolving America's Major Quality of Life Crisis." *Loyola University of Los Angeles Law Review* 24: 915. **[4A]**

Fried, Carla, Leslie M. Marable, and Sheryl Nance-Nash. 1996. "Best Places to Live In America." *Money* (July): 66-95. **[4B]**

Gabriel, Stuart A.; Joe P. Mattey; and William L. Wascher. 1996. *Compensating Differentials and Evolution of the Quality-of-Life Among U.S. States.* San Francisco: Federal Reserve Bank of San Francisco. 96-07. June. **[4B]**

Gaffuri, E., and G. Costa. 1986. "Applied Aspects of Chronoergohygiene." *Chronobiologia* 13: 39-51. **[4A]**

Gans, Herbert J. 1967. *The Levittowners: Ways of Life and Politics in a New Suburban Community.* New York, NY: Pantheon Books. **[5B]**

Gans, Herbert; J. Kasarda; and H. Molotch. 1982. "Symposium: The State of the Nation's Cities." *Urban Affairs Quarterly* 18, 2: 163-86. **[5B]**

Garreau, Joel. 1991. *Edge City: Life on the New Frontier.* New York: Doubleday. **[5B]**

Georgia Conservancy. 1997. *Blueprints for Successful Communities: A Guide for Shaping Livable Places.* Atlanta, GA: The Georgia Conservancy. **[4A]**

Giuliano, Genevieve. 1995a. "Land Use Impacts of Transportation Investments: Highways and Transit," in Susan Hanson, ed., *The Geography of Urban Transportation.* 2nd ed. New York, NY: The Guilford Press. **[2B]**

Giuliano, Genevieve. 1995b. "The Weakening Transportation–Land-Use Connection. *Access* 6 (Spring): 3-11. **[2B]**

Glaeser, Edward L. 1994. "Cities, Information, and Economic Growth." *Citiscape* 1, 1 (August): 9-47. **[5B]**

Glickman, Norman J., Michael L. Lahr, and Elvin K. Wyly. 1996. *State of the Nation's Cities.* Report and database prepared for U.S. Department of Housing and Urban Development, Washington, DC. **[5B]**

Glynn, Thomas J. 1981. "Psychological Sense of Community Measurement and Application." *Human Relations* 34, 7: 789-818. **[4B]**

Goldberg, Michael A., and John Mercer. 1986. *The Myth of the North American City.* Vancouver: University of British Columbia Press. **[5B]**

Gomez-Ibanez, Jose A. 1991. "A Global View of Automobile Dependence." *Journal of the American Planning Association* 57. **[2A]**

Gordon, Peter; A. Kumar; and Harry W. Richardson. 1989. "The Influence of Metropolitan Spatial Structure on Commuting Time." *Journal of Urban Economics* 26: 138-151. **[2B]**

Gordon, Peter, and Harry W. Richardson. 1989a. "Gasoline Consumption and Cities: A Reply." *Journal of the American Planning Association* 55: 342-46. **[2B]**

Gordon, Peter, and Harry W. Richardson. 1989b. "Notes from the Underground: The Failure of Urban Mass Transit." *Public Interest* 94: 77-86. **[2C]**

Gordon, Peter, and Harry W. Richardson. 1994a. "Sustainable Congestion." In J. Brotchie, ed., *Cities in Competition: The Emergence of Productive and Sustainable Cities for the 21st Century.* **[2B]**

Gordon, Peter, and Harry W. Richardson. 1994b. *Geographic Factors Explaining Worktrip Length Changes.* Prepared for the U.S. Department of Transportation, Federal Highway Administration. **[2B]**

Gordon, Peter, and Harry W. Richardson. 1994c. "Congestion Trends in Metropolitan Areas." In National Research Council, *Curbing Gridlock: Peaking Period Fees to Relieve Traffic Congestion.* Washington, DC: National Academy Press. 1-31. **[2B]**

Gordon, Peter, and Harry W. Richardson. 1995. "Beyond Polycentricity: The Dispersed Metropolis, Los Angeles, 1970-90." *Journal of the American Planning Association* 61. **[5C]**

Gordon, Peter, and Harry W. Richardson. 1996. "Los Angeles Among Other CMSAs: Outlier or the Norm?" *Environment and Planning A.* **[2B]**

Gordon, Peter, and Harry W. Richardson. 1997a. "Are Compact Cities a Desirable Planning Goal?" *Journal of the American Planning Association* 63, 1 (Winter). **[5B]**

Gordon, Peter, and Harry W. Richardson. 1997b. "The Destiny of Downtowns: Doom or Dazzle*?" Lusk Review* (Fall): 63–76. **[5B]**

Gordon, Peter; Harry W. Richardson; and Y. Choi. 1992. "Tests of the Standard Urban Model: A Micro (Trade-off) Alternative." *Review of Urban and Regional Development Studies* 4, 1: 50-66. **[5B]**

Gordon, Peter; Harry W. Richardson; and Myung-Jin Jun. 1991. "The Commuting Paradox: Evidence from the Top Twenty." *Journal of the American Planning Association* 57, 4: 416-420. **[2B]**

Gordon, Peter; Harry W. Richardson; and Gang Yu. 1997. "Metropolitan and Non-Metropolitan Employment Trends in the U.S.: Recent Evidence and Implications." Los Angeles, CA: School of Urban Planning and Development and Department of Economics. University of Southern California. **[5B]**

Gordon, Peter, and H. L. Wong. 1985. "The Cost of Urban Sprawl: Some New Evidence." *Environment and Planning A* 17: 661-66. **[2B]**

Gore, Al. 1998. "Building Livable Communities." Remarks delivered at The Brookings Institution, Washington, DC. **[4A]**

Gottdiener, Mark. 1977. *Planned Sprawl: Private and Public Interests in Suburbia.* Beverly Hills, CA: Sage. **[5A]**

Gottlieb, Paul D. 1995. "Residential Amenities, Firm Location and Economic Development." *Urban Studies* 32, 9: 1413-1436. **[4B]**

Governor's Commission on Growth in the Chesapeake Bay Region. 1991. *Fiscal Studies.* Baltimore, MD: Maryland Office of Planning. **[1F]**

Green, K. 1995. *Defending Automobility: A Critical Examination of the Environmental and Social Costs of Auto Use.* Policy Study No. 198. Los Angeles, CA: Reason Foundation. December. **[2B]**

Greene, David L., and Donald N. Jones. 1995. *The Full Costs and Benefits of Transportation: Conceptual and Theoretical Issues.* Paper presented at the Conference on the Full Social Costs and Benefits of Transportation. **[2G]**

Greenwood, Michael J.; Gary L. Hunt; Dan S. Rickman; and George I. Treyz. 1991. "Migration, Regional Equilibrium, and the Estimation of Compensating Differentials." *American Economic Review* 81, 5: 1382-1390. **[4G]**

Growth Management Planning and Research Clearinghouse, University of Washington. 1993. *Literature Review of Community Impacts and Costs of Urban Sprawl.* Washington, DC: National Trust for Historic Preservation. **[1A]**

Hagevik, George. 1972. *The Relationship of Land Use and Transportation Planning to Air Quality Management.* New Brunswick, NJ: Center for Urban Policy Research, Rutgers University. **[3G]**

Haines, V. 1986. "Energy and Urban Form: A Human Ecological Critique." *Urban Affairs Quarterly* 21, 3: 337-53. **[4B]**

Hall, Bob, and Mary Lee Kerr. 1991. *1991–1992 Green Index: A State-By-State Guide to the Nation's Environmental Health.* Washington, DC: Island Press. **[4B]**

Handy, S. 1992. "Regional Versus Local Accessibility: Neo-Traditional Development and Its Implications for Non-Work Travel." *Built Environment* 18, 4: 253-267. **[2C]**

Handy, S. 1994. "Highway Blues: Nothing a Little Accessibility Can't Cure." *Access* 5: 3-7. **[2A]**

Handy, S. 1995. *Understanding the Link Between Urban Form and Travel Behavior.* Paper presented at the 74th Annual Meeting of the Transportation Research Board, Washington, DC. January. **[2B]**

Hanson, M. E. 1992. "Automobile Subsidies and Land Use: Estimates and Policy Responses." *Journal of the American Planning Association* 58, 1: 60-71. **[2B]**

Harris, C. 1992. "Bringing Land Use Ratios into the '90s." Planning Advisory Service Report. Chicago: American Planning Association. **[3D]**

Harrison, Bennett. 1974. "Discrimination in Space: Suburbanization and Black Unemployment in Cities." In George M. von Furstenburg, Bennett Harrison, and Ann Horowitz, eds., *Patterns of Racial Discrimination, Vol. I: Housing.* Lexington, MA: Lexington Books. **[5G]**

Hartshorn, Truman A. 1980. *Interpreting the City: An Urban Geography.* New York, NY: Wiley. **[5B]**

Hartshorn, Truman A., and Peter O. Muller. 1989. "Suburban Downtowns and the Transformation of Metropolitan Atlanta's Business Landscape." *Urban Geography* 10: 375-395. **[5C]**

Hartshorn, Truman A., and Peter O. Muller. 1992. "The Suburban Downtown and Urban Economic Development Today." In Edwin S. Mills and John F. McDonald, eds., *Sources of Metropolitan Growth.* New Brunswick, NJ: Center for Urban Policy Research, Rutgers University. **[5C]**

Harvey, G. 1990. *Relation of Residential Density to VMT per Resident: Oakland.* Metropolitan Transportation Commission. **[2C]**

Harvey, Robert Q., and W.A.V. Clark. 1965. "The Nature and Economics of Urban Sprawl." *Land Economics* 41, 1: 1-9. **[5G]**

Healy, Robert G. 1998. Op-Ed Memo on the Currency of Sprawl. Durham, NC: Duke University, Nicholas School of the Environment. (unpublished). **[6A]**

Heikkila, E. et al. "What Happened to the CBD-Distance Gradient? Land Values in a Polycentric City." *Environment and Planning A* 21: 221–32. **[1C]**

Heimlich, Ralph E. 1989. "Metropolitan Agriculture—Farming in the City's Shadow." *Journal of the American Planning Association* 55, 4: 457-66. **[3B]**

Herbers, J. 1982. *The New Heartland: America's Flight Beyond the Suburbs and How It Is Changing our Future.* Herbers Publishers. **[5B]**

Herson, Lawrence J. R. 1992. "The New Suburbanization: Challenge to the Central City." *Annals of the American Academy of Political and Social Science* 522: 184. **[5B]**

Hidlebaugh, Allen R. 1981. *Agricultural Land Data Sheet: America's Agricultural Land Base.* National Agricultural Lands Study, Washington, DC. **[3B]**

Hiss, Tony. 1990. *The Experience of Place.* New York: Vintage Books. **[4A]**

Hodge, G. 1981. "The Citification of Small Towns: A Challenge to Planning." *Plan Canada* 21: 43-7. **[5B]**

Holtzclaw, J. 1990. *Explaining Urban Density and Transit Impacts on Auto Use.* Paper presented to the State of California Energy Resources Conservation and Development Commission by Natural Resources Defense Council and the Sierra Club. April 19. **[2B]**

Holtzclaw, J. 1994. *Using Residential Patterns and Transit to Decrease Auto Dependence and Costs.* San Francisco, CA: Natural Resources Defense Council. **[2B]**

Howard County (Maryland) Planning Commission. 1967. *Howard County: 1985.* Howard County, MD: Howard County Planning Commission. April. **[6A]**

Hughes, Mark A. 1991. "Employment Decentralization and Accessibility—A Strategy for Stimulating Regional Mobility." *Journal of the American Planning Association* 57, 3: 288-98. **[2B]**

Hummon, D. 1990. *Commonplaces: Community Ideology and Identity in American Culture.* Binghamton, NY: SUNY Press. **[4A]**

Ihlanfeldt, Keith R. 1995. "The Importance of the Central City to the Regional and National Economy: A Review of the Arguments and Empirical Evidence." *Citiscape* 1, 2 (June): 125-150. **[5B]**

Ihlanfeldt, Keith R., and David L. Sjoquist. 1990. "Job Accessibility and Racial Differences in Youth Employment Rates." *American Economic Review* 80: 267-76. **[5G]**

Institute of Transportation Engineers. 1984. *Recommended Guidelines for Subdivision Streets*. Washington, DC: Institute of Transportation Engineers. **[6A]**

Isard, Walter, and Robert E. Coughlin. 1957. *Municipal Costs and Revenues Resulting from Growth*. Wellesley, MA: Chandler-Davis. **[1C]**

Jackson, Kenneth T. 1976. "The Effect of Suburbanization on the Cities." In P. Dolce, ed., *Suburbia: The American Dream and Dilemma*. Garden City, NY: Doubleday. **[5C]**

Jackson, Kenneth T. 1985. *Crabgrass Frontier: The Suburbanization of the United States*. New York: Oxford University Press. **[5B]**

Jacobs, Jane. 1961. *The Death and Life of Great American Cities*. New York: Vintage Books. **[5A]**

Jarrell, Stephen, and Roy M. Howsen. 1990. "Transient Crowding and Crime." *American Journal of Economics and Sociology* 49, 4: 483-494. **[4B]**

Johnson, Jerald W. 1998. "Portland's Urban Growth Boundary: Density and Housing Costs." Paper prepared for Drachman Institute Conference, "Urban Growth: Addressing the Reality of Suburbia," Phoenix, Arizona. May. **[5C]**

Johnson, Thomas G. 1987. "Fiscal Impacts of Economic Development." In *Responding to the Crisis in the Rural South: Selected Public- and Private-Sector Initiatives*. Southern Rural Development Center, Mississippi State University. **[1C]**

Jones, L., and M. D. Woods. 1985. "Determining the Impacts of New Industry on Small Towns in Texas." *Small Town* (September-October): 22-5. **[1C]**

Jones, P. 1989. "Regional Shopping Centers—Planning Issues." *Town and Country Planning* 58, 10: 280-2. **[5A]**

Joseph, Nadine. 1992. "Mommy Myths; Attitudes Toward Working Mothers." *Redbook* (October): 130. **[4B]**

Kain, John. 1967. *Urban Form and the Costs of Urban Services*. Cambridge, MA: Harvard University. **[1C]**

Kain, John. 1988. "Choosing the Wrong Technology: Or How to Spend Billions and Reduce Transit Use." *Journal of Advanced Transportation* 21. **[2B]**

Kain, John. 1991. "Trends in Urban Spatial Structure, Demographic Change, Auto and Transit Use, and the Role of Pricing." Statement prepared for the United States Senate, Committee on Environment and Public Works. **[2B]**

Kain, John. 1992. "The Spatial Mismatch Hypothesis: Three Decades Later." *Housing Policy Debate* 3, 2: 371-459. **[5B]**

Kaman Sciences Corporation. 1972. *Land Use Planning for Air Quality in the Pikes Peak Area*. Colorado Springs, CO: Kaman Sciences Corporation. August. **[3C]**

Kasarda, John D. 1990. "City Jobs and Residents on a Collision Course: The Urban Underclass Dilemma." *Economic Development Quarterly* 4, 4: 313-19. **[5B]**

Katz, Lawrence, and Kenneth Rosen. 1987. "The Interjurisdictional Effects of Growth Controls on Housing Prices." *Journal of Law and Economics* 30 (April): 149-60. **[1C]**

Katz, Peter. 1994. *The New Urbanism: Towards an Architecture of Community*. New York: McGraw Hill. **[5A]**

Kelbaugh, Douglas. 1993. "The Costs of Sprawl." *Cascadia Forum* 1: 20-26. **[1A]**

Kenworthy, J. and P. Newman. 1993. *Automobile Dependence: The Irresistible Force?* Murdoch University, Institute for Science and Technology Policy. **[2B]**

Kingsley, G. Thomas, and Margery Austin Turner, eds. 1993. *Housing Markets and Residential Mobility*. Washington, DC: Urban Institute Press. **[5B]**

Kitamura, R., L. Laidet, P. Mokhtarian, C. Buckinger, and F. Gianelli. 1994. *Mobility and Livable Communities*. State of California Air Resources Board. **[2C]**

Kitamura, R., P. L. Mokhtarian and L. Laidet. 1994. *A Micro-Analysis of Land Use and Travel in Five Neighborhoods in the San Francisco Bay Area.* Institute of Transportation Studies, University of California, Davis. November. **[2C]**

Knapp, Gerrit, and A. C. Nelson. 1992. *The Regulated Landscape: Lessons on State Land Use Planning from Oregon.* Washington, DC: Lincoln Institute of Land Policy. **[3C]**

Knapp, Thomas A., and Philip E. Graves. 1989. "On the Role of Amenities in Models of Migration and Regional Development." *Journal of Regional Science* 29 (1): 71-87. **[4G]**

Koslowsky, Meni, and Moshe Krausz. 1994. "On the Relationship Between Commuting, Stress Symptoms, and Attitudinal Measures: A LISREL Application." *Journal of Applied Behavioral Science* 29, 4: 485-492. **[4G]**

Kotkin, Joel. 1996. "Make Way for the Urban Confederates." *American Enterprise* 7, 6. **[5B]**

Kotval, Zenia, and John R. Mullin. 1992. *A Fiscal Impact Analysis Technique: The Pawling Model.* Hadley, MA. **[1D]**

Krieger, Alex, ed. 1991. *Towns and Town-making Principles: The Work of Andres Duany and Elizabeth Plater-Zyberk.* New York: Rizzoli International Publishers. **[4A]**

Krizek, Kevin J., and Joe Power. *A Planner's Guide to Sustainable Development.* Chicago, IL: Planning Advisory Service, American Planning Association. **[4A]**

Krote, James J. 1992. "Is Downtown Worth Saving?" *Planning* 58, 8: 148-62. **[5B]**

Kunstler, James. 1993. *The Geography of Nowhere: The Rise and Decline of America's Man-Made Landscape.* New York: Simon & Schuster. **[4A]**

Kunstler, James. 1996a. "Home From Nowhere: Zoning Laws' Effects on Quality of Life." *Atlantic Monthly* 278, 3: 43. **[4A]**

Kunstler, James. 1996b. Statement made at Michigan Society of Planning Officials Annual Conference, Lansing, Michigan. Spring. **[4A]**

Ladd, Helen F. 1992. "Population Growth, Density, and the Costs of Providing Public Services." *Urban Studies* 29, 2: 273-96. **[1G]**

Ladd, Helen F., and William Wheaton. 1991. "Causes and Consequences of the Changing Urban Form." *Regional Science and Urban Economics* 21 (July): 157-162. **[5G]**

Ladd, Helen F., and J. Yinger. 1989. *America's Ailing Cities: Fiscal Health and the Design of Urban Policy.* Baltimore, MD: Johns Hopkins University Press. **[5G]**

Lafferty, R. N., and H. E. Frech. 1978. "Community Environment and the Market Value of Single-Family Homes: The Effect of the Dispersion of Land Uses." *Journal of Law and Economics* 21: 380-393. **[4G]**

Lake, Robert W. 1997. "Research Workshop: Toward a Comprehensive Geographical Perspective on Urban Sustainability." Proposal to National Science Foundation. Rutgers University, Center for Urban Policy Research, New Brunswick, New Jersey. **[5A]**

Landis, John D. 1994. "The California Urban Futures Model: A New Generation of Metropolitan Simulation Models." *Environment and Planning* 21: 399-421. **[3G]**

Landis, John D. 1995. "Imagining Land Use Futures: Applying the California Urban Futures Model." *Journal of the American Planning Association* 61, 4 (Autumn): 438–457. **[3F]**

Landis, John D., and David S. Sawicki. 1988. "A Planner's Guide to the *Places Rated Almanac.*" *Journal of the American Planning Association* (Summer): 336-346. **[4B]**

Lang, Robert E., and Steven P. Hornburg. 1997. "Planning Portland Style: Pitfalls and Possibilities." *Housing Policy Debate* 8, 1 (April): 1-16. **[5B]**

Langdon, Philip. *A Better Place to Live: Re-shaping the American Suburb.* 1994. Amherst: University of Massachusetts Press. [4B]

Lansing, John B. et al. 1970. *Planned Residential Environments.* Ann Arbor, MI: Institute for Social Research, University of Michigan. [5B]

Ledebur, Larry C., and William R. Barnes. 1992. *Metropolitan Disparities and Economic Growth: City Distress and the Need for a Federal Local Growth Package.* Washington, DC: National League of Cities. March. [5B]

Lee, Douglas B. 1995. *Full-Cost Pricing of Highways.* Washington, DC: U.S. Department of Transportation. [2B]

Leithe, J. L., T. Muller, J. E. Petersen, and S. Robinson. 1991. *The Economic Benefits of Preserving Community Character: Case Studies.* Chicago, IL: Government Finance Research Center. [4C]

Lemann, Nicholas. 1989. "Stressed Out in Suburbia." *Atlantic Monthly* (November): 34-48. [4A]

Leonard, Jonathan S. 1987. "The Interaction of Residential Segregation and Employment Discrimination." *Journal of Urban Economics* 21: 323-46. [5G]

Lessinger, J. 1962. "The Case for Scatteration." *Journal of the American Institute of Planners* 28, 3: 159-69. [5A]

Levinson, D. M., and A. Kumar. 1994. "The Rational Locator: Why Travel Times Have Remained Stable." *Journal of the American Planning Association* 60: 319-332. [2B]

Lewis, Peirce F. 1995. "The Galactic Metropolis." In *The Changing American Countryside: Rural People and Places,* by Emory N. Castle, ed. Lawrence, KS: University of Kansas Press. [3C]

Linneman, Peter. 1995. Speech at Brookings Institution/Lincoln Institute/National Trust Conference (Spring). [5B]

Lisansky, J. 1986. "Farming in an Urban Environment: Agriculture Land Use Conflicts and Right to Farm." *Human Organization* 45: 363-371. [3B]

Listokin, David, and Carole Walker. 1990. *The Subdivision and Site Plan Handbook.* New Brunswick, NJ: Center for Urban Policy Research, Rutgers University. [6A]

Litman, Todd. 1995. *Transportation Cost Analysis: Techniques, Estimates and Implications.* Victoria, BC: Victoria Transport Policy Institute. February. [2D]

Logan, John, and H. Molotch. 1987. *Urban Fortunes: The Political Economy of Place.* Berkeley, CA: University of California Press. [4A]

Logan, John, and Mark Schneider. 1981. "Suburban Municipal Expenditures: The Effects of Business Activity, Functional Responsibility, and Regional Context." *Policy Studies Journal* 9: 1039-50. [1C]

Lopez, Rigoberto A., Adesoji O. Adelaja, and Margaret S. Andrews. 1988. "The Effects of Suburbanization on Agriculture." *American Journal of Agriculture Economics* 70, 2: 346-58. [3B]

Lower Mainland Regional Planning Board. 1956. *Urban Sprawl.* Lower Mainland, New Westminster, B.C. April. [4A]

Lowry, I. 1988. "Planning for Urban Sprawl." In *Transportation Research Board Special Report 221: Looking Ahead, the Year 2000.* Washington, DC: Transportation Research Board. [2A]

MacKenzie, J.; R. C. Dower; and D. D. T. Chen. 1992. *The Going Rate: What It Really Costs to Drive.* Washington, DC: World Resources Institute. [2B]

Maher, Ian. 1992. "Commuting Calculations." *Journal of the American Planning Association* 58: 386-87. [2B]

Maine (State of). 1988. *Comprehensive Growth Management Act.* Augusta, ME. [6A]

Mandelker, Daniel R. 1962. *Green Belts and Urban Growth.* Madison, WI: University of Wisconsin Press. [3A]

Marcuse, Peter. 1998. "Sustainability Is Not Enough," *Planners Network,* vol. 129. May. **[5A]**

Maryland Office of Planning (MOP). 1989. *Environmental and Economic Impacts of Lot Size and Other Development Standards.* Baltimore, MD: Office of State Planning. **[1B]**

Maryland Office of Planning (MOP). 1997. *What You Need to Know About Smart Growth and Neighborhood Conservation.* Baltimore, MD. **[4A]**

Maryland-National Capital Park and Planning Commission and Montgomery County Planning Department. 1989. *Comprehensive Growth Policy Study. A Policy Vision: Centers and Trails.* Silver Spring, MD. **[3A]**

Maslow, Abraham Harold. 1970. *Motivation and Personality.* 2d ed. New York: Harper & Row. **[4A]**

McDonald, John, Charles Orlebeke, Ashish Sen, and Wim Wiewel. 1992. *Real Estate Development and Property Taxes in DuPage County: Final Report.* Project #342. Chicago, IL: University of Illinois, School of Urban Planning and Policy, Center for Urban Economic Development. February. **[1G]**

McHarg, Ian. 1969. *Design With Nature.* Garden City, NY: The Natural History Press. **[3A]**

McHarg, Ian. 1996. *A Quest For Life.* New York, NY: John Wiley and Sons. **[3A]**

McKee, David L., and Gerald H. Smith. 1972. "Environmental Diseconomies in Suburban Expansion." *The American Journal of Economics and Sociology* 31, 2: 181-88. **[5G]**

McMillan, David W., and David M. Chavis. 1986. "Sense of Community: A Definition and Theory." *Journal of Community Psychology* 14, 1: 6-23. **[4A]**

Meck, Stuart. 1996. "Planning Practice." *Planning.* November. **[4A]**

Metro. 1994. *Region 2040 Recommended Alternative Decision Kit.* Portland, OR. **[4A]**

Meyer, J., and J. A. Gomez-Ibanez. 1981. *Autos, Transit, and Cities.* Cambridge, MA: Harvard University Press. **[2B]**

Meyer, S. M. 1992. *Environmentalism and Economic Prosperity: Testing the Environmental Impact Hypothesis.* Cambridge, MA: MIT Press. **[4G]**

Michigan Society of Planning Officials (MSPO). 1995. *Patterns on the Land: Our Choices, Our Future.* Rochester, MI: Michigan Society of Planning Officials. **[4A]**

Middlesex•Somerset•Mercer Regional Council. 1989. *The Growth Management Handbook.* Princeton, NJ. **[4A]**

Middlesex•Somerset•Mercer Regional Council. 1990. *Mixed-Use Development: Traffic and Other Impacts.* Princeton, NJ. **[2C]**

Middlesex•Somerset•Mercer Regional Council and The Regional Plan Association. 1994. *Redesigning the Suburbs: Turning Sprawl into Centers.* Princeton, NJ. **[5A]**

Mieszkowski, Peter, and Edwin S. Mills. 1993. "The Causes of Metropolitan Suburbanization." *Journal of Economic Perspectives* 7, 3: 135-47. **[5G]**

Mills, David E. 1981. "Growth, Speculation, and Sprawl in a Monocentric City." *Journal of Urban Economics* 10: 201-226. **[3C]**

Mills, Edwin S. 1991. *Critique of "Impacts of Development on DuPage County Property Taxes."* Kellogg Graduate School of Management, Northwestern University. June. **[1G]**

Mills, Edwin S., and Bruce W. Hamilton. 1994. *Urban Economics.* New York: HarperCollins. **[6A]**

Mills, Edwin S., and John F. McDonald. 1992. *Sources of Metropolitan Growth.* New Brunswick, NJ: Center for Urban Policy Research, Rutgers University. **[5A]**

Miness, D., and R. C. Einsweiler. 1992. *Managing Community Growth and Change.* Cambridge, MA: Lincoln Institute of Land Policy. **[4A]**

Mobility for the 21st Century Task Force. 1996a. *Mobility for the 21st Century: A Blueprint for the Future.* Washington, DC: American Public Transit Association. October. **[2A]**

Mobility for the 21st Century Task Force. 1996b. *Strategic Goals for the 21st Century.* Washington, DC: American Public Transit Association. **[2A]**

Moe, Richard. 1995. In Dwight Young, *Alternatives to Sprawl.* Cambridge, MA: Lincoln Institute of Land Policy; Washington, DC: Brookings Institution and National Trust for Historic Preservation. **[3A]**

Moe, Richard. 1996. *Growing Smarter: Fighting Sprawl and Restoring Community in America.* Washington, DC: National Trust for Historic Preservation. **[4A]**

Moe, Richard, and Carter Wilkie. 1997. *Changing Places: Rebuilding Community in the Age of Sprawl.* New York: Henry Holt. **[4A]**

Mofson, Phyliss. 1997. Interview by Robert W. Burchell. Tallahassee, FL: Florida Department of Community Affairs. November 5. **[6A]**

Montgomery County, Maryland. 1989. *Alternative Scenarios: Analysis and Evaluation.* **[1F]**

Moore, Terry, and Paul Thorsnes. 1994. *The Transportation–Land-Use Connection: A Framework for Practical Policy.* Planning Advisory Service Report 448/449. Chicago: American Planning Association. **[2B]**

Muller, Peter. 1986. "Transportation and Urban Form: Stages in the Spatial Evolution of the American Metropolis." In Susan Hanson, ed., *Geography of Urban Transportation.* New York: Guilford Press. **[2B]**

Myers, Dowell. 1987. "Internal Monitoring of Quality of Life for Economic Development." *Economic Development Quarterly* 1: 238-278. **[4B]**

Myers, Dowell. 1989. "The Ecology of 'Quality of Life' and Urban Growth." In *Understanding Growth Management: Critical Issues and a Research Agenda.* Washington, DC: Urban Land Institute. **[4B]**

Nasar, Jack L., and David A. Julian. 1995. "The Psychological Sense of Community in the Neighborhood." *Journal of the American Planning Association* 61, 2: 178-184. **[4A]**

Nathan, Richard P., and Charles Adams. 1976. "Understanding Central City Hardship." *Political Science Quarterly* 91, 1. **[5B]**

National Agricultural Lands Study. 1981. *America's Agricultural Land Base.* Washington, DC. **[3B]**

National Trust for Historic Preservation. 1993. "Potential Effects of a Mega-Store in Kent County." Report prepared by James Hendry. Washington, DC: National Trust for Historic Preservation. **[5C]**

Natural Resources Defense Council (NRDC) and Surface Transportation Policy Project (STPP). 1997. *The Toolkit for Smart Growth.* Washington, DC. **[4A]**

Nelessen, Anton C. 1994. *Visions for a New American Dream: Process, Principles, and an Ordinance to Plan and Design Small Urban Communities.* Chicago: American Planning Association. **[4B]**

Nelson, Arthur C. 1988. "Development Impact Fees." *Journal of the American Planning Association* 54, 1 (Winter): 3-6. **[1D]**

Nelson, Arthur C. 1992a. "Economic Critique of Prime Farmland Preservation Policies in the United States." *Journal of Rural Studies* 6, 2: 119-42. **[3B]**

Nelson, Arthur C. 1992b. "Preserving Prime Farmland in the Face of Urbanization: Lessons from Oregon." *Journal of the American Planning Association* 58: 471-88. **[3C]**

Nelson, Arthur C., and James Duncan. 1995. *Growth Management Principles and Practice.* Chicago, IL: Planners Press, American Planning Association. **[3C]**

Nelson, Arthur C.; William J. Drummond; and David S. Sarvider. 1995. "Exurban Industrialization: Implications for Economic Development Policy." *Economic Development Quarterly* 9, 12. **[5B]**

Nelson, Arthur C., and Thomas W. Sanchez. 1997. "Exurban and Suburban Households: A Departure from Traditional Location Theory." *Journal of Housing Research* 8, 2. **[5B]**

Nelson, Robert H. 1977. *Zoning and Property Rights: An Analysis of the American System of Land-Use Regulation.* Cambridge, MA: MIT Press. **[6A]**

Neuman, Michael. 1991. "Utopia, Dystopia, Diaspora." *Journal of the American Planning Association* 57, 3: 344-347. **[4A]**

New Jersey (State of). 1995. *Statement of Financial Condition of Counties and Municipalities.* Trenton, NJ: Department of Community Affairs. **[6A]**

New Jersey Institute of Technology (NJIT) and Rutgers University. 1997. *TELUS: Transportation Economic and Land Use System—State-of-the-Art Information System for the 21st Century.* Newark, NJ: NJIT and New Brunswick, NJ: Rutgers University. **[2G]**

New Jersey State Planning Commission (NJSPC). 1992. *Communities of Place: The New Jersey State Development and Redevelopment Plan.* Trenton, NJ: NJSPC. June. **[4A]**

New Jersey State Planning Commission (NJSPC). 1997. *Communities of Place: The New Jersey State Development and Redevelopment Plan.* Trenton, NJ: NJSPC. June. **[4A]**

New Jersey Transit. 1994. *Planning for Transit-Friendly Land Use: A Handbook for New Jersey Communities.* Newark, NJ: New Jersey Transit. **[2A]**

Newman, Peter W. G., and Jeffrey R. Kenworthy. 1989a. *Cities and Automobile Dependence: An International Sourcebook.* Brookfield, VT: Gower Publishing. **[2B]**

Newman, Peter W. G., and Jeffrey R. Kenworthy. 1989b. "Gasoline Consumption and Cities: A Comparison of U.S. Cities with a Global Survey." *Journal of the American Planning Association* 55: 24-37. **[2B]**

Newman, Peter W. G., and Jeffrey R. Kenworthy. 1991. "Transportation and Urban Form in Thirty-Two of the World's Principal Cities." *Transport Reviews* 11, 3. **[2B]**

Nicholas, James C. 1989. "The Costs of Growth: A Public vs. Private Sector Conflict or a Public/Private Responsibility." In David Brower, David R. Godschalk, and Douglas R. Porter, eds., *Understanding Growth Management.* Washington, DC: Urban Land Institute. **[1C]**

Nicholas, James C., Arthur C. Nelson, and Julian C. Juergensmeyer. 1991. *A Practitioner's Guide to Development Impact Fees.* Chicago, IL: Planners Press (APA). **[1A]**

Novaco, Raymond W.; Daniel Stokols; J. Campbell; and J. Stokols. 1979. "Transportation, Stress, and Community Psychology." *American Journal of Community Psychology* 7: 361-380. **[4C]**

Novaco, Raymond W.; Daniel Stokols; and Louis Milanesi. 1990. "Objective and Subjective Dimensions of Travel Impedance as Determinants of Commuting Stress." *American Journal of Community Psychology* 18, 2: 231-257. **[4C]**

Nowlan, David, and Greg Stewart. 1991. "Downtown Population Growth and Commuting Trips: Recent Experience in Toronto." *Journal of the American Planning Association* 57: 165-82. **[2C]**

O'Connor, Kevin. 1988. *Suburbia Makes the Central City: A New Interpretation of the City–Suburb Relationship.* Berkeley, CA: Institute of Urban and Regional Development, University of California at Berkeley. **[5A]**

Ohls, James C., and David Pines. 1975. "Discontinuous Urban Development and Economic Efficiency." *Land Economics* 3 (August): 224-234. **[3G]**

1000 Friends of Oregon. 1995. *Making the Land Use, Transportation, Air Quality Connection (LUTRAQ): Projections.* Vol. 5. Portland, OR. **[2C]**

1000 Friends of Oregon. 1996. *Making the Land Use, Transportation, Air Quality Connection (LUTRAQ): Analysis of Alternatives.* Vol. 6. Portland, OR. May. **[2C]**

Oregon Progress Board. 1994. *Oregon Benchmarks: Standards for Measuring Statewide Progress and Institutional Performance.* Report to the 1995 Legislature. Salem, OR: Oregon Progress Board. December. **[6A]**

Orfield, Myron. 1997. *Metropolitics: A Regional Agenda for Community and Stability.* Washington, DC: Brookings Institution Press and Cambridge, MA: Lincoln Institute of Land Policy. **[5A]**

Orlando, Florida. 1981. *Urban Area Growth Management Plan.* **[3A]**

Orski, C. Kenneth. 1992. "Congestion Pricing: Promise and Limitations." *Transportation Quarterly* 46, 2: 157-67. **[2G]**

O'Sullivan, Arthur M. 1993. *Urban Economics.* 2d ed. Homewood, IL: Irwin. **[6A]**

Parsons Brinckerhoff Quade and Douglas. 1993. *The Pedestrian Environment.* Portland, OR: 1000 Friends of Oregon. **[2C]**

Parsons Brinckerhoff Quade and Douglas. 1996a. *Cost of Travel in Boulder.* City of Boulder, CO: July 15. **[2C]**

Parsons Brinckerhoff Quade and Douglas. 1996b. "Commuter and Light Rail Corridors: The Land Use Connection." In *Transit and Urban Form*, Vol. 1. Washington DC: Transit Cooperative Research Program, Transportation Research Board. October. **[2D]**

Parsons Brinckerhoff Quade and Douglas. 1996c. "Influence of Land Use Mix and Neighborhood Design on Transit Demand." Unpublished report for TCRP H-1 project. Washington DC: Transit Cooperative Research Program, Transportation Research Board. March. **[2D]**

Parsons Brinckerhoff Quade and Douglas. 1996d. "Transit, Urban Form, and the Built Environment: A Summary of Knowledge." In *Transit and Urban Form*, Vol. 1. Washington DC: Transit Cooperative Research Program, Transportation Research Board. October. **[2D]**

Parsons Brinckerhoff Quade & Douglas, Inc. 1997. "TCRP Project H-13A—Draft Report: Consequences of the Interstate Highway System for Transit." Washington, DC: Transit Cooperative Research Program,. Transportation Research Board. **[2C]**

Parsons Brinckerhoff Quade and Douglas, and ECONorthwest. 1996. *A Framework for Evaluating the Impacts of Alternative Urban Forms.* Washington, DC. **[2A]**

Parsons, George R. 1992. "The Effect of Coastal Land Use Restrictions on Housing Prices." *Journal of Environmental Economics and Management* (February): 25-27. **[1G]**

Pastore, Ann L., and Kathleen Maguire, eds. 1996. *Sourcebook of Criminal Justice Statistics 1995.* Albany, NY: Hindelang Criminal Justice Research Center, University of Albany. **[4B]**

Peiser, Richard B. 1984. "Does It Pay to Plan Suburban Growth?" *Journal of the American Planning Association* 50: 419-33. **[1D]**

Peiser, Richard B. 1989. "Density and Urban Sprawl." *Land Economics* 65, 3 (August): 193-204. **[3G]**

Petersen, John. 1996. Statement made at Lincoln Institute for Land Policy Conference, April 1992. Reaffirmed Summer 1996. **[5B]**

Pickrell, Donald H. 1989. "Urban Rail Transit Projects: Forecast vs. Actual Ridership and Costs." *Urban Mass Transportation Administration Report.* United States Department of Transportation. Washington, DC: United States Government Printing Office. **[2E]**

Pigou, A. C. 1920. *The Economics of Welfare.* Macmillan. **[6A]**

Pisarski, Alan E. 1987. *Commuting in America: A National Report on Commuting Patterns and Trends.* Westport, CT: Eno Foundation. **[2B]**

Pisarski, Alan E. 1992a. *New Perspectives in Commuting.* Washington, DC: U.S. Department of Transportation. July. **[2B]**

Pisarski, Alan E. 1992b. *Travel Behavior Issues in the 90s*. Office of Highway Information Management, Federal Highway Administration. **[2B]**

Pivo, G. 1990. "The Net of Beads: Suburban Office Development in Six Metropolitan Areas." *Journal of the American Planning Association* 56, 4: 457-69. **[5B]**

Plotkin, Sidney. 1987. *Keep Out: The Struggle for Land Use Control*. Berkeley, CA: University of California Press. **[1C]**

Popenoe, David. 1979. "Urban Sprawl: Some Neglected Sociological Considerations." *Sociology and Social Research* 63, 2: 255-68. **[4B]**

Popper, Frank J. 1981. *The Politics of Land-Use Reform*. Madison, WI: University of Wisconsin Press. **[6A]**

Porter, Douglas R. 1989. "The States Are Coming, the States Are Coming." *Urban Land* (September): 16-20. **[3A]**

Porter, Douglas R., ed. 1992. *State and Regional Initiatives for Managing Development: Policy Issues and Practical Concerns*. Washington, DC: Urban Land Institute. **[3A]**

Porter, Douglas R. 1996. *Profiles in Growth Management*. Washington, DC: Urban Land Institute. **[3C]**

Porter, Douglas R. 1997. *Managing Growth in America's Communities*. New York, NY: Island Press. **[3A]**

Power, T. M. 1980. *The Economic Value of the Quality of Life*. Boulder, CO: Westview Press. **[4A]**

Precourt, Geoffrey, and Anne Faircloth. 1996. "Best Cities: Where the Living is Easy." *Fortune* (November 11): 126-136. **[4B]**

Propst, Luther, and Mary Schmid. 1993. *The Fiscal and Economic Impacts of Local Conservation and Community Development Measures: A Review of Literature*. Tucson, AZ: Sonoran Institute. **[1A]**

Pucher, John. 1995a. "Budget Cutters—Looking at Wrong Subsidies." *Passenger Transport* 3 (March). **[2B]**

Pucher, John. 1995b. *The Costs of Transit versus the Automobile*. Paper presented at National Trust for Historic Preservation "Costs of Sprawl" Conference. Spring. **[2B]**

Pucher, John. 1995c. "Urban Passenger Transport in the United States and Europe: A Comparative Analysis of Public Policies, Part I. Travel Behavior, Urban Development, and Automobile Use." *Transport Reviews* 15, 2: 99-117. **[2B]**

Pugh, Margaret. 1998. *Barriers to Work: The Spatial Divide between Jobs and Welfare Recipients in Metropolitan Washington, DC*. Washington, DC: The Brookings Institution, Center on Urban and Metropolitan Policy. **[5A]**

Purvis, C. L. 1994. *Changes in Regional Travel Characteristics and Travel Time Budgets in the San Francisco Bay Area: 1960-1990*. Paper presented at the Transportation Research Board 73rd Annual Meeting, Washington, DC. January 9-13. **[2B]**

Pushkarev, B., and J. M. Zupan. 1977. *Public Transportation and Land Use Policy*. Bloomington, IN: Indiana University Press. **[6A]**

Pushkarev, B., and J. M. Zupan. 1982. "Where Transit Works: Urban Densities for Public Transportation." In H. S. Levinson and R. A. Weant, eds., *Urban Transportation: Perspectives and Prospects*. Westport, CT: Eno Foundation. **[2D]**

Ravitch, Diane. 1996. "The Problem of the Schools: A Proposal for Renewal." In Julia Vitullo-Martin, ed., *Breaking Away: The Future of Cities*. New York: Twentieth Century Fund: 77-87. **[5A]**

Ray, J. R.; S. E. Polzen; and S. E. Bricka. 1994. *An Assessment of the Potential Saturation in Men's Travel. NPTS Demographic Special Report*. Washington, DC: Office of Highway Information Management, Federal Highway Administration. **[2B]**

Real Estate Research Corporation (RERC). 1974. *The Costs of Sprawl: Environmental and Economic Costs of Alternative Residential Development Patterns at the Urban Fringe: (Volume I: Detailed Cost Analysis; Volume II: Literature Review and Bibliography)*. Washington, DC: U.S. Government Printing Office. **[1D]**

Regional Plan Association. 1929. *Neighborhood and Community Planning*. New York, NY: Committee on Regional Plan of New York and Its Environs. **[5A]**

Reilly, William K. 1973. *The Use of the Land: A Citizen's Policy Guide to Urban Growth*. Crowell, NY: Rockefeller Brothers Fund. **[3A]**

Resource Management Consultants, Inc. 1989. *Development in Wright County, Minnesota: Cost-Revenue Relationship*. Minneapolis: Resource Management Consultants. **[1C]**

Rice Center for Urban Mobility Research. 1987. *Houston's Major Activity Centers and Worker Travel Behavior*. Houston: Joint Center for Urban Mobility Research. **[2C]**

Richardson, Harry W., and Peter Gordon. 1989. "Counting Nonwork Trips: The Missing Link in Transportation, Land Use, and Urban Policy." *Urban Land* (September): 6-12. **[2B]**

Richardson, Harry W., and Peter Gordon. 1993. "Market Planning: Oxymoron or Common Sense?" *Journal of the American Planning Association* 59: 347-52. **[5A]**

Richmond, Henry R. 1995. *Regionalism: Chicago as an American Region*. Chicago: John D. and Catherine T. MacArthur Foundation. December 6. **[5A]**

Roback, Jennifer. 1982. "Wages, Rents, and the Quality of Life." *Journal of Political Economy* 90, 6: 1257-1278. **[4B]**

Roback, Jennifer. 1988. "Wages, Rents, and Amenities: Differences Among Workers and Regions." *Economic Inquiry* 26: 23-41. **[4B]**

Robinson, Susan K., ed. 1990. *Financing Growth: Who Benefits? Who Pays? And How Much?* Chicago: Government Finance Officers Association, Government Finance Research Center. **[1A]**

Roisman, Florence, and Hilary Botein. 1993. "Housing Mobility and Life Opportunities." *Clearinghouse Review* 27, 4 (August). **[4A]**

Rosen, Sherwin. 1979. "Wage-Based Indexes of Urban Quality of Life." In Peter Mieszkowski and Mahlon Straszheim, eds., *Current Issues in Urban Economics*. Baltimore: Johns Hopkins University Press. **[4B]**

Rossetti, M. A. and B. S. Eversole. 1993. *Journey to Work Trends in the United States and Its Major Metropolitan Areas, 1960-1990*. Washington, DC: U.S. Department of Transportation. **[2B]**

Rudel, Thomas K. 1989. *Situations and Strategies in American Land-Use Planning*. New York: Cambridge University Press. **[3A]**

Rusk, David. 1993. *Cities without Suburbs*. Washington, DC: Woodrow Wilson Center Press. **[5B]**

Salant, Priscilla; Lisa R. Carley; and Don A. Dillman. 1996. *Estimating the Contribution of Lone Eagles to Metro and Nonmetro In-Migration*. Pullman, WA: Social and Economic Sciences Research Center, Washington State University. 86-19. June. **[4B]**

Savageau, David, and Richard Boyer. 1993. *Places Rated Almanac*. New York: Macmillan Travel. **[4B]**

Savitch, H. V., et al. 1993. "Ties That Bind: Central Cities, Suburbs, and the New Metropolitan Region." *Economic Development Quarterly* 7, 4: 341-57. **[5B]**

Schaeffer, M. H.; S. W. Street; J. E. Singer; and S. Baum. 1988. "Effects of Control on Stress Reactions of Commuters." *Journal of Applied Social Psychology* 18: 944-957. **[4B]**

Schafer, Robert. 1975. *Exclusionary Land Use Controls: Conceptual and Empirical Problems in Measuring the Invisible Wall.* Cambridge, MA: Harvard University Press. **[5B]**

Schneider, Mark. 1989. *The Competitive City: The Political Economy of Suburbia.* Pittsburgh: University of Pittsburgh Press. **[5B]**

Schultz, Marilyn S., and Vivian L. Kasen. 1984. *Encyclopedia of Community Planning and Environmental Management.* New York, NY: Facts on File, Inc. **[6A]**

Schwartz, Seymour I.; David E. Hansen; and Richard Green. 1981. "Suburban Growth Controls and the Price of New Housing." *Journal of Environmental Economics and Management* 8 (December): 303-320. **[1E]**

Schwartz, Seymour I.; Peter M. Zorn; and David E. Hansen. 1989. "Research Design Issues and Pitfalls in Growth Control Studies." *Land Economics* 62 (August): 223-33. **[1E]**

Sclar, Elliot, and Walter Hook. 1993. "The Importance of Cities to the National Economy." In Henry G. Cisneros, ed., *Interwoven Destinies: Cities and the Nation.* New York: American Assembly of Columbia University: 1-26. **[5B]**

Seidel, Stephen. 1978. *Housing Costs and Government Regulations.* New Brunswick, NJ: Center for Urban Policy Research, Rutgers University. **[1C]**

Seyfarth, J. T., and W. A. Bost. 1986. "Teacher Turnover and the Quality of Worklife in Schools: An Empirical Study." *Journal of Research and Development in Education* 20, 1: 1-6. **[4B]**

Sheppard, Stephen. 1988. "The Qualitative Economics of Development Controls." *Journal of Urban Economics* 24, 3: 310-330. **[1G]**

Sherrod, D., and S. Cohen. 1979. "Density, Personal Control, and Design." In J. Aiello and A. Baum, eds., *Residential Crowding and Design.* New York: Plenum Press. **[4C]**

Sherwood-Call, Carolyn. 1994. *The 1980s Divergence in Per Capita Personal Incomes: What Does It Tell Us?* San Francisco: Federal Reserve Bank of San Francisco. August. **[4B]**

Shilling, James D., C. F. Sirmans, and Krisandra A. Guidry. 1991. "The Impact of State Land-Use Controls on Residential Land Values." *Journal of Regional Science* 31, 1: 83-92. **[1G]**

Shore, William B. 1995. "Recentralization: The Single Answer to More than a Dozen United States Problems and a Major Answer to Poverty." *Journal of the American Planning Association* 61, 4: 496-503. **[5B]**

Siemon, Charles L. 1997. "Successful Growth Management Techniques." *The Urban Lawyer* 29, 2: 233-250. **[3A]**

Siemon, Larsen and Purdy. 1990. *Crossroads: Two Growth Alternatives for Virginia Beach. Virginia Beach (VA) Growth Management Study.* Chicago, Illinois. **[3A]**

Sierra Club. 1998. *The Dark Side of the American Dream: The Costs and Consequences of Suburban Sprawl.* College Park, MD: Sierra Club. **[3B]**

Simonds, John. 1978. *Earthscape: A Manual of Environmental Planning and Design.* New York, NY: Von Nostrand Reinhold. **[3A]**

Skogan, W. 1986. "Fear of Crime and Neighborhood Change." In A. Reiss and M. Torny, eds., *Communities and Crime.* Chicago, IL: University of Chicago Press. **[4A]**

Small, K. 1980. "Energy Scarcity and Urban Development Patterns." *International Regional Science Review* 5, 2: 97-117. **[4B]**

Soll, Michael, and Fritz Wagner. 1991. "Coping with Growth in a Suburban Town: The Case of Mandeville, Louisiana." *Small Town* (July-August): 18-24. **[3C]**

Solomon, Arthur P., ed. 1981. *The Prospective City.* Cambridge, MA: MIT Press. **[5A]**

Souza, Paul. 1995. *New Capital Costs of Sprawl, Martin County, Florida.* Gainesville, FL: University of Florida. **[1C]**

Spain, Daphne. 1988. "An Examination of Residential Preferences in the Suburban Era." *Sociological Focus* 21, 1: 1-8. **[4B]**

Sperling, Daniel. 1995. *Future Drive: Electric Vehicles and Sustainable Transportation.* Washington, DC: Island Press. **[2D]**

Steiner, Bill. 1992. "The Future of Downtowns: Issues to Consider As We Approach 2001." *Small Town* (November-December). **[5A]**

Steiner, R. L. 1994. *Residential Density and Travel Patterns: A Review of the Literature and Methodological Approach.* Paper presented at 73rd Annual Meeting, Transportation Research Board, Washington, DC. **[2A]**

Sterling Forest Corporation (SFC). 1995. *Draft Generic Environmental Impact Statement for the Sterling Forest Community: Overview.* Volume 1 of 6. Tuxedo, NY: SFC. **[3A]**

Sternlieb, George. 1966. *The Tenement Landlord.* New Brunswick, NJ: Center for Urban Policy Research, Rutgers University. **[5C]**

Sternlieb, George. 1975. *Housing Development and Municipal Costs.* New Brunswick, NJ: Center for Urban Policy Research, Rutgers University. **[1B]**

Sternlieb, George, and W. Patrick Beaton. 1972. *The Zone of Emergence: A Case Study of Plainfield, New Jersey.* New Brunswick, NJ: Transaction Books. **[5C]**

Sternlieb, George, and Robert W. Burchell. 1977. *Residential Abandonment: The Tenement Landlord Revisited.* New Brunswick, NJ: Center for Urban Policy Research, Rutgers University. **[5C]**

Sternlieb, George, and James W. Hughes. eds. 1975. *Post-Industrial America: Metropolitan Decline and Interregional Job Shifts.* New Brunswick, NJ: Center for Urban Policy Research, Rutgers University. **[5B]**

Stokols, D., and R. W. Novaco, eds. 1981. *Transportation and Well-Being.* New York: Plenum Press. **[4B]**

Stokols, D.; R. W. Novaco; J. Campbell; and J. Stokols. 1978. "Traffic Congestion, Type-A Behavior, and Stress." *Journal of Applied Psychology* 63: 467-480. **[4B]**

Stone, Kenneth E. 1993. *The Impact of Wal-Mart Stores on Other Businesses and Strategies for Coexisting.* Ames, IA: Iowa State University. **[5C]**

Strategic Goals for the 21st Century. 1996. American Public Transit Association's Mobility for the 21st Century Task Force, and Robert L. Olson, Institute for Alternative Futures. October. **[2A]**

Taylor, P., and C. Pocock. 1972. "Commuter Travel and Sickness: Absence of London Office Workers." *British Journal of Preventive and Social Medicine* 26: 165-172. **[4C]**

Taylor, Ruth. 1992. "The Economics of Open Space As If People and Wildlife Matter." *Mountain Country.* Fall. **[3A]**

Taylor, Ruth, and S. Gottfredson. 1986. "Environmental Design, Crime, and Prevention: An Examination of Community Dynamics." In A. Reiss and M. Torny, eds., *Communities and Crime.* Chicago, IL: University of Chicago Press. **[4C]**

Thompson, J. Phillip. 1996. "Urban Poverty and Race." In Julia Vitullo-Martin, ed., *Breaking Away: The Future of Cities.* New York: Twentieth Century Fund:13-32. **[5B]**

Tiebout, Charles M. 1956. "A Pure Theory of Local Expenditures." *Journal of Political Economy* 64, 1: 416-424. **[1A]**

Tischler & Associates, Inc. 1989. "Analyzing the Fiscal Impact of Development." *MIS Report* 20, 7. Washington, DC: International City Management Association. **[1A]**

Tischler & Associates, Inc. 1990. *Service Level, Cost and Revenue Assumptions: Evaluation of Development Concepts— Howard County, Maryland.* Bethesda, MD: Tischler & Associates. **[1C]**

Tischler & Associates, Inc. 1994. *Marginal Cost Analysis of Growth Alternatives— King County, Washington.* Bethesda, MD: Tischler & Associates. **[1C]**

Tischler, Paul S. 1992. "DuPage County & Economic Development: Good or Bad?" *Journal of the American Planning Association.* July. **[1A]**

Transit Cooperative Research Program. 1995. "An Evaluation of the Relationship between Transit and Urban Form." *Research Results Digest* 7 (June). **[2A]**

Turque, Bill, and Frank Washington. 1991. "Are Cities Obsolete?" *Newsweek* (September 9): 42-45. **[5A]**

Ulrich, R. S.; R.F. Simons; B. D. Losito; E. Florito; M. A. Miles; and M. Zelson. 1991. "Stress Recovery During Exposure to Natural and Urban Environments." *Journal of Environmental Psychology* II: 201-230. **[4C]**

U.S. Department of Commerce. Bureau of the Census. 1980. 1990. *U.S. Census of Population and Housing.* Washington, DC. **[6A]**

U.S. Department of Commerce. Bureau of the Census. 1982, 1987, 1992. *U.S. Census of Governments.* Washington, DC. **[6A]**

U.S. Department of Housing and Urban Development. 1972. *Total Energy and Pneumatic Waste Collection Demonstrations.* Ref. No. 07-028. **[4C]**

U.S. Department of Housing and Urban Development. 1980. *Metropolitan Development Patterns: What Difference Do They Make?* Washington, DC: U.S. Department of Housing and Urban Development, Office of Policy Development and Research. **[5B]**

U.S. Department of Housing and Urban Development. 1995. *Cityscape: A Journal of Policy Development and Research.* 1, 2. Washington, DC. U.S. Department of Housing and Urban Development, Office of Policy Development and Research. **[5A]**

U.S. Department of Transportation, Bureau of Transportation Statistics. 1994. *Transportation Statistics Annual Report 1994.* Washington, DC: U.S. Department of Transportation. **[2B]**

U.S. Department of Transportation, Federal Highway Administration. 1997. *Our Nation's Travel: 1995 NPTS Early Results Report.* Washington, DC: U.S. Department of Transportation. **[2B]**

Urban Land Institute (ULI). 1963. *Innovations vs. Traditions in Community Development.* Technical Bulletin No. 47. Washington, DC: ULI. **[3A]**

Urban Land Institute (ULI). 1980. *The Affordable Community.* Washington, DC: ULI. **[3A]**

Urban Land Institute (ULI). 1998. *Smart Growth: Economy, Community, Environment.* Washington, DC: ULI. **[5A]**

Urban Land Institute, National Association of Home Builders, and American Society of Civil Engineers. 1976. *Residential Streets: Objectives, Principles, and Design Considerations.* Washington, DC: Urban Land Institute. **[6A]**

Van der Ryn, S., and P. Calthorpe. 1993. *Sustainable Communities.* San Francisco, CA: Sierra Club Books. **[4A]**

Vermont League of Cities and Towns and Vermont Natural Resources Council. 1988. "The Tax Base and The Tax Bill." Montpelier, VT: Vermont League of Cities and Towns. September. **[1C]**

Vincent, Mary Jayne, et al. 1994. *NPTS Urban Travel Patterns: 1990 NPTS.* Washington, DC: Office of Highway Information Management, Federal Highway Administration. **[2B]**

VNI Rainbow Appraisal Service. 1992. *Analysis of the Impact of Light Rail Transit on Real Estate Values.* San Diego, CA: MTDB. **[2G]**

Voith, Richard. 1992. "Cities and Suburban Growth: Substitutes or Complements?" *Federal Reserve Bank of Philadelphia Business Review:* (September-October) 21-33. **[5B]**

Voith, Richard. 1993. "Changing Capitalization of CBD-Oriented Transportation Systems: Evidence from Philadelphia, 1970-1988." *Journal of Urban Economics* 33: 361-76. **[2C]**

Voith, Richard. 1996. "Central City Decline: Regional or Neighborhood Solutions?" *Federal Reserve Bank of Philadelphia Business Review* (March-April): 3-16. **[5B]**

von Reichert, Christiane, and Gundars Rudzitis. 1992. "Multinomial Logistical Models Explaining Income Changes of Migrants to High-Amenity Counties." *Review of Regional Studies* 22, 1: 25-42. **[4G]**

Voorhees, M. T. 1992. *The True Costs of the Automobile to Society.* City of Boulder, CO. January. **[2D]**

Wachs, Martin. 1989. "United States Transit Subsidy Policy: In Need of Reform." *Science:* 244. **[2B]**

Webber, Melvin M. 1976. "The BART Experience—What Have We Learned?" *Public Interest* 45. **[2C]**

Webber, Melvin M. 1993. *The Marriage of Autos and Transit: How to Make Transit Popular Again.* Presented to the Fourth International Research Conference, Center for Transportation Studies, University of Minnesota. **[2A]**

Wendell Cox Consultancy. 1996. *Population and Land Area for Urbanized Areas with More Than 1 Million Population in 1990.* www.publicpurpose.com/inf-usua.htm **[3B]**

Wheaton, William L., and Morton J. Schussheim. 1955. *The Cost of Municipal Services in Residential Areas.* Washington, DC: U.S. Department of Commerce. **[1C]**

Whyte, William H. Jr. 1957. "Urban Sprawl." In *The Exploding Metropolis.* Garden City, NY: Doubleday. **[5A]**

Wiewel, Wim. 1993. "The Fiscal Impact of Commercial Development." *Land Development* (Spring-Summer). **[1B]**

Wilson, William Julius. 1987. *The Truly Disadvantaged: The Inner City, the Underclass, and Public Policy.* Chicago, IL: University of Chicago Press. **[5B]**

Wilson, William Julius. 1996. *When Work Disappears: The World of the New Urban Poor.* New York, NY: Knopf. **[5B]**

Windsor, Duane. 1979. "A Critique of *The Costs of Sprawl.*" *Journal of the American Planning Association* 45, 2 (July): 279-92. **[1A]**

Wish, Naomi, and Stephen Eisdorfer. 1996. *The Impact of the Mount Laurel Initiatives: An Analysis of the Characteristics of Applicants and Occupants.* South Orange, NJ: Seton Hall University. **[5B]**

Wohl, Martin. 1976. "The Case for Rapid Transit: Before and After the Fact." *Transportation Alternatives in Southern California.* Los Angeles: University of Southern California, Institute for Public Policy Research, Center for Public Affairs. **[2B]**

York, Marie L. 1989. *Encouraging Compact Development in Florida.* Fort Lauderdale, FL: Florida Atlantic University–Florida International University Joint Center for Environmental and Urban Problems. **[3A]**

Young, Dwight. 1995. *Alternatives to Sprawl.* Cambridge, MA: Lincoln Institute of Land Policy. **[3A]**

Zimmer, B. G. 1985. "Metropolitan Development and the Changing Journey to Work." *Social Science Quarterly* 66: 519-532. **[2B]**

Zinam, Oleg. 1989. "Quality of Life, Quality of the Individual, Technology and Economic Development." *American Journal of Economics and Sociology* 48, 1: 55-68. **[4B]**

Zorn, M.; D. E. Hansen; and S. I. Schwartz. 1986. "Mitigating the Price Effects of Growth Control: A Case Study of Davis, California." *Land Economics* 62 (February): 47-57. **[1E]**

LIST OF
ANNOTATED STUDIES BY AUTHOR

Author	Year	Page	Title
Altshuler, Alan A.	1977	144	"Review of *The Costs of Sprawl*"
Altshuler, Alan A., and Jose A. Gomez-Ibanez	1993	145	*Regulation for Revenue: The Political Economy of Land Use Exactions*
American Farmland Trust	1986	146	*Density-Related Public Costs*
American Farmland Trust	1992a	146	*Does Farmland Protection Pay? The Cost of Community Services in Three Massachusetts Towns*
Andrews, James H.	1996	198	"Going by the Numbers"
Andrews, Marcellus	1994	215	"On the Dynamics of Growth and Poverty in Cities"
Apogee Research, Inc.	1994	175	*The Costs of Transportation: Final Report*
Arendt, Randall, et al.	1994b	183	*Rural by Design*
Arendt, Randall	1996	184	*Conservation Design for Subdivisions: A Practical Guide to Creating Open Space Networks*
Barnett, Jonathan	1995	205	*The Fractured Metropolis: Improving the New City, Restoring the Old City, Reshaping the Region*
Beaumont, Constance	1994 1997	185	*How Superstore Sprawl Can Harm Communities— And What Citizens Can Do About It* and *Better Models for Superstores: Alternatives to Big-Box Sprawl*
Beaumont, Constance	1996b	184	*Smart States, Better Communities*
Black, Thomas J.	1996	153	"The Economics of Sprawl"

Author	*Year*	*Page*	*Title*
Bradbury, Katherine L., et al.	1982	216	*Urban Decline and the Future of American Cities*
Buchanan, Shepard C., and Bruce A. Weber	1982	147	"Growth and Residential Property Taxes: A Model for Estimating Direct and Indirect Population Impacts"
Burchell, Robert W., et al.	1992a	136	*Impact Assessment of the New Jersey Interim State Development and Redevelopment Plan, Report II: Research Findings*
Burchell, Robert W., et al.	1997a	137	*Fiscal Impacts of Alternative Land Development Patterns in Michigan: The Costs of Current Development Versus Compact Growth*
Burchell, Robert W., et al.	1997b	135	*South Carolina Infrastructure Study: Projections of Statewide Infrastructure Costs 1995-2015*
Burchell, Robert W., and David Listokin	1995a	190	*Land, Infrastructure, Housing Costs, and Fiscal Impacts Associated with Growth: The Literature on the Impacts of Traditional versus Managed Growth*
Burchell, Robert W., and David Listokin	1995b	137	*The Economic Impacts of Trend Versus Vision Growth in the Lexington Metropolitan Area*
Burchell, Robert W., and Harvey Moskowitz	1995	137	*Impact Assessment of DELEP CCMP versus STATUS QUO on Twelve Municipalities in the DELEP Region*
Calthorpe, Peter	1993	225	*The Next American Metropolis: Ecology, Community, and the American Dream*
Cambridge Systematics	1994	170	*The Effects of Land Use and Travel Demand Strategies on Commuting Behavior*
Cervero, Robert	1989	170	*America's Suburban Activity Centers: The Land Use–Transportation Link*
Cervero, Robert	1991b	161	"Land Use and Travel at Suburban Activity Centers"
Cervero, Robert	1996	171	"Jobs-Housing Balance Revisited"
Cervero, Robert, et al.	1997	174	"Job Accessibility as a Performance Indicator: An Analysis of Trends and Their Social Policy Implications in the San Francisco Bay Area"
Cervero, Robert, and R. Gorham	1995	171	"Commuting in Transit Versus Automobile Neighborhoods"
Cervero, Robert, and K. Kockelman	1996	162	"Travel Demand and the 3Ds: Density, Diversity, and Design"
Cervero, Robert, and Kang-Li Wu	1996	175	"Subcentering and Commuting: Evidence from the San Francisco Bay Area, 1980-1990"
Clark, Charles S.	1995	227	"Revitalizing the Cities: Is Regional Planning the Answer?"
Dahl, Thomas E.	1990	186	*Wetlands Losses in the United States: 1780s-1980s*

Author	*Year*	*Page*	*Title*
Davis, Judy	1993	168	"The Commuting of Exurban Residents"
DeCorla-Souza, Patrick, et al.	1992	176	"Nationwide Investment Requirements for New Urban Highway Capacity Under Alternative Scenarios"
Delucchi, M. A.	1996	177	*The Annualized Social Cost of Motor-Vehicle Use in the U.S., 1990-1991: Summary of Theory, Data, Methods, and Results*
Diamond, Henry L., and P. Noonan	1996	192	*Land Use in America*
Dougharty, Laurence, et al.	1975	148	*Municipal Service Pricing Impacts on Fiscal Position*
Downing, Paul	1977	148	*Local Services Pricing and Their Effects on Urban Spatial Structure*
Downs, Anthony	1992	159	*Stuck in Traffic: Coping with Peak Hour Traffic Congestion*
Downs, Anthony	1994	217	*New Visions for Metropolitan America*
Drucker, Peter F.	1992	207	"People, Work, and the Future of the City"
Duffy, N. E.	1994	200	"The Determinants of State Manufacturing Growth Rates: A Two-Digit-Level Analysis"
Duncan, James E., et al.	1989	137	*The Search for Efficient Urban Growth Patterns*
Dunphy, R. T., and K. M. Fisher	1994	163	*Transportation, Congestion and Density: New Insights*
DuPage County Development Department	1989 1991	149	*Impacts of Development on DuPage County Property Taxes*
Dzurik, Andrew	1993	163	"Transportation Costs of Urban Sprawl: A Review of the Literature"
ECONorthwest	1994	138	*Evaluation of No Growth and Slow Growth Policies for the Portland Region*
Ewing, Reid	1995a	186	*Best Development Practices: Doing the Right Thing and Making Money at the Same Time*
Ewing, Reid, et al.	1994	172	"Getting Around a Traditional City, a Suburban PUD, and Everything In-Between"
Ewing, Reid	1997b	159	*Transportation and Land Use Innovations*
Ewing, Reid *and* Gordon, Peter, et al.	1997 1997a	178	"Is Los Angeles-Style Sprawl Desirable?" *and* "Are Compact Cities a Desirable Planning Goal?"
Fishman, Robert	1987	207	*Bourgeois Utopias: The Rise and Fall of Suburbia*
Fodor, Eben V.	1997	138	"The Real Cost of Growth in Oregon"
Frank, James E.	1989	139	*The Costs of Alternative Development Patterns: A Review of the Literature*

Author	*Year*	*Page*	*Title*
Frank, L. D., and Gary Pivo	1994	165	*The Relationship Between Land Use and Travel Behavior in the Puget Sound Region*
Fried, Carla, et al.	1996	195	"Best Places to Live In America"
Gabriel, Stuart A., et al.	1996	201	*Compensating Differentials and Evolution of the Quality-of-Life Among U.S. States*
Glaeser, Edward L.	1994	209	"Cities, Information, and Economic Growth"
Gordon, Peter, et al.	1989	165	"The Influence of Metropolitan Spatial Structure on Commuting Times"
Gordon, Peter, et al.	1991	157	"The Commuting Paradox: Evidence From the Top Twenty"
Gordon, Peter, et al.	1997	212	"Metropolitan and Non-Metropolitan Employment Trends in the U.S.: Recent Evidence and Implications"
Gordon, Peter, and H. W. Richardson	1997b	211	"The Destiny of Downtowns: Doom or Dazzle?"
Gottlieb, Paul D.	1995	201	"Residential Amenities, Firm Location and Economic Development"
Greenwood, Michael J., et al.	1991	201	"Migration, Regional Equilibrium, and the Estimation of Compensating Differentials"
Hall, Bob, and Mary Lee Kerr	1991	196	*1991-1992 Green Index: A State-By-State Guide to the Nation's Environmental Health*
Handy, S.	1992	172	"Regional Versus Local Accessibility: Neo-Traditional Development and Its Implications for Non-Work Travel"
Handy, S.	1995	172	*Understanding the Link Between Urban Form and Travel Behavior*
Hanson, M. E.	1992	179	"Automobile Subsidies and Land Use: Estimates and Policy Responses"
Holtzclaw, J.	1990	166	*Explaining Urban Density and Transit Impacts on Auto Use*
Holtzclaw, J.	1994	166	*Using Residential Patterns and Transit to Decrease Auto Dependence and Costs*
Ihlanfeldt, Keith R.	1995	218	"The Importance of the Central City to the Regional and National Economy: A Review of the Arguments and Empirical Evidence"
Katz, Lawrence, and Kenneth Rosen	1987	150	"Interjurisdictional Effects of Growth Controls on Housing Prices"
Katz, Peter	1994	227	*The New Urbanism: Towards an Architecture of Community*
Kitamura, R., et al.	1994	173	*A Micro-Analysis of Land Use and Travel in Five Neighborhoods in the San Francisco Bay Area*

Author	*Year*	*Page*	*Title*
Kunstler, James	1993	219	*The Geography of Nowhere: The Rise and Decline of America's Man-Made Landscape*
Ladd, Helen F., and William Wheaton	1991	153	"Causes and Consequences of the Changing Urban Form"
Landis, John D.	1995	192	"Imagining Land Use Futures: Applying the California Urban Futures Model"
Landis, John D., and David S. Sawicki	1988	196	"A Planner's Guide to the *Places Rated Almanac*"
Ledebur, Larry C., and William R. Barnes	1992	221	*Metropolitan Disparities and Economic Growth: City Distress and the Need for a Federal Local Growth Package*
Levinson, D. M., and A. Kumar	1994	158	"The Rational Locator: Why Travel Times Have Remained Stable"
Lewis, Peirce F.	1995	187	"The Galactic Metropolis"
Litman, Todd	1995	179	*Transportation Cost Analysis: Techniques, Estimates and Implications*
Logan, John, and M. Schneider	1981	150	"Suburban Municipal Expenditures: The Effects of Business Activity, Functional Responsibility, and Regional Context"
MacKenzie, J. J., et al.	1992	180	*The Going Rate: What It Really Costs to Drive*
McKee, David L., and G. Smith	1972	154	"Environmental Diseconomies in Suburban Expansion"
Metro	1994	160	*Region 2040: Recommended Alternative Decision Kit*
Michigan Society of Planning Officials	1995	188	*Patterns on the Land: Our Choices, Our Future*
Mills, David E.	1981	154	"Growth, Speculation, and Sprawl in a Monocentric City"
Mobility for the 21st Century Task Force	1996b	160	*Strategic Goals for the 21st Century*
Moe, Richard, and Carter Wilkie	1997	188	*Changing Places: Rebuilding Community in the Age of Sprawl*
Myers, Dowell	1987	199	"Internal Monitoring of Quality of Life for Economic Development"
Nelson, Arthur C.	1992b	189	"Preserving Prime Farmland in the Face of Urbanization: Lessons from Oregon"
Nelson, Arthur C., and T. W. Sanchez	1997	212	"Exurban and Suburban Households: A Departure From Traditional Location Theory"
Newman, Peter W.G., and Jeffrey R. Kenworthy	1989a	166	*Cities and Automobile Dependence: An International Sourcebook*

Author	_Year_	_Page_	_Title_
Ohls, James C., and David Pines	1975	155	"Discontinuous Urban Development and Economic Efficiency"
1000 Friends of Oregon	1996	169	_Making the Land Use Transportation Air Quality Connection: Analysis of Alternative_
Oregon Progress Board	1994	200	_Oregon Benchmarks: Standards for Measuring Statewide Progress and Institutional Performance_
Orfield, Myron	1997	221	_Metropolitics: A Regional Agenda for Community and Stability_
Parsons Brinckerhoff Quade and Douglas	1996a	180	_Cost of Travel in Boulder_
Parsons Brinckerhoff Quade and Douglas	1996b	167	"Commuter and Light Rail Transit Corridors: The Land Use Connection"
Parsons Brinckerhoff Quade and Douglas	1996c	173	"Influence of Land Use Mix and Neighborhood Design on Transit Demand"
Parsons Brinckerhoff Quade and Douglas	1997	168	"TCRP Project H-13A—Draft Report: Consequences of the Interstate Highway System for Transit"
Parsons, George	1992	151	"The Effects of Coastal Land Use Restrictions on Housing Prices"
Peiser, Richard B.	1984	139	"Does It Pay to Plan Suburban Growth?"
Peiser, Richard B.	1989	155	"Density and Urban Sprawl"
Pisarski, Alan E.	1992	158	_New Perspectives in Commuting_
Popenoe, David	1979	203	"Urban Sprawl: Some Neglected Sociological Considerations"
Precourt, Geoffrey, and Anne Faircloth	1996	197	"Best Cities: Where the Living is Easy"
Propst, Luther, and Mary Schmid	1993	151	_The Fiscal and Economic Impacts of Local Conservation and Community Development Measures: A Review of Literature_
Pushkarev, B., and J. M. Zupan	1977	167	_Public Transportation and Land Use Policy_
Ravitch, Diane	1996	228	"The Problem of the Schools: A Proposal for Renewal"
Real Estate Research Corporation (RERC)	1974	140	_The Costs of Sprawl: Environmental and Economic Costs of Alternative Residential Development Patterns at the Urban Fringe_
Richardson, Harry W., and Peter Gordon	1989	158	"Counting Nonwork Trips: The Missing Link in Transportation, Land Use, and Urban Policy"
Richmond, Henry R.	1995	221	_Regionalism: Chicago as an American Region_
Roback, Jennifer	1982	201	"Wages, Rents, and the Quality of Life"

Author	_Year_	_Page_	_Title_
Rosen, Sherwin	1979	202	"Wage-Based Indexes of Urban Quality of Life"
Rossetti, M. A., and B. S. Eversole	1993	159	_Journey to Work Trends in the United States and Its Major Metropolitan Areas, 1960-1990_
Rusk, David	1993	213	_Cities Without Suburbs_
Salant, Priscilla, et al.	1996	202	_Estimating the Contribution of Lone Eagles to Metro and Nonmetro In-Migration_
Savageau, David, and Richard Boyer	1993	197	_Places Rated Almanac_
Schwartz, Seymour I., et al.	1981	152	"Suburban Growth Controls and the Price of New Housing"
Schwartz, Seymour I., et al.	1989	152	"Research Design Issues and Pitfalls in Growth Control Studies"
Sclar, Elliot, and Walter Hook	1993	214	"The Importance of Cities to the National Economy"
Souza, Paul	1995	141	_New Capital Costs of Sprawl, Martin County, Florida_
Thompson, J. Phillip	1996	222	"Urban Poverty and Race"
Tischler & Associates	1994	142	_Marginal Cost Analysis of Growth Alternatives— King County, Washington_
von Reichert, Christiane, and Gundars Rudzitis	1992	202	"Mutinomial Logistical Models Explaining Income Changes of Migrants to High-Amenity Counties"
Voorhees, M.T.	1992	181	_The True Costs of the Automobile to Society_
Windsor, Duane	1979	142	"A Critique of _The Costs of Sprawl_"
York, Marie L.	1989	143	_Encouraging Compact Development in Florida_
Zinam, Oleg	1989	204	"Quality of Life, Quality of the Individual, Technology and Economic Development"

INDEX